MAKING BREAD:

The Ultimate Financial Guide for Women Who Need Dough

by GAIL HARLOW

Founding Editor of MAKING BREAD *:
The Magazine for Women Who Need Dough*

with ELIZABETH LEWIN

MAKING BREAD *Contributing Editor
and Financial Planner*

RUNNING PRESS
PHILADELPHIA · LONDON

Library of Congress Control Number: 2004097405

ISBN 0-7624-2201-7

Cover and interior illustrations by Mona Daly.

Interior design by Amanda Richmond
Edited by Jennifer Kasius
Typography: Futura and Bembo

This book may be ordered by mail from the publisher.
Please include $2.50 for postage and handling.
But try your bookstore first!

Running Press Book Publishers
125 South Twenty-second Street
Philadelphia, Pennsylvania 19103-4399

Visit us on the web!
www.runningpress.com

MAKING BREAD

*For my mother, Nina Newhart, who embodied
the indomitable power of the female spirit*
—Gail Harlow

*To the memory of my mother,
Edith Hecht Samelson*
—Elizabeth Lewin

TABLE OF CONTENTS

Part Two: Success & Savings Strategies

INTRODUCTION:
WHY **MAKING BREAD** IS "THE ULTIMATE CHICK LIT"

I've always had a love-hate relationship with money. Loved spending it; hated not having enough to spend. My mother, a stay-at-home mom all her life, was the same way. My father brought home a respectable salary, but it wasn't nearly enough to keep her in the style to which she wanted to become accustomed. My mother's financial advice to me: Marry a wealthy man.

It never occurred to her that I could become my own breadwinner. I married for love not money, pursued a career as an editor, and though I made a decent salary working for first one, then another of the largest magazine companies in the country, too often an unexpected emergency would crop up (cars and water heaters aren't supposed to break down—ever!) and I'd be juggling bills, trying to come up with the money to cover the hole in our household budget. I could never seem to get ahead. Because the amount I could afford to save from every paycheck (after paying off the cards on which I'd charged designer suits and other luxuries) was so small, saving seemed pointless. Big mistake No. 1.

I know that now: every penny counts. With that kind of spending history, it might seem odd that I should end up starting a digital women's finance magazine called MAKING BREAD: *The Magazine for Women Who Need Dough*. When it came to

writing this book based on the magazine, even my husband asked, "Is it a comedy?" (You've got to love a man with a sense of humor!) But it was precisely because of the unenviable financial position I found myself in when I reached my forties that I began to realize that my education in all things monetary left something to be desired. And, speaking with other women, I realized that I wasn't alone. Far from it! What my friends and I all needed was what I like to think of as "the ultimate chick lit."

Forget *Bridget Jones' Diary* and all those other bestsellers whose heroines mope and fret till they find a man. What we really need is something that speaks to us about money: making it, keeping it, spending it, saving it, investing it—using it to gain independence and take control of our lives.

What I realize now is that while money can buy you many things, the most important thing it can purchase is freedom of choice and freedom from worry. If you marry the wrong man, when you have money saved up, you can afford to leave him. If you hate your job, when you have money in the bank, you can "fire" the boss and find another one—or become the boss in a company of your own making. Money gives you choices. The best gift you can give yourself is money in the bank. It gives me a warmer, fuzzier feeling than any cashmere sweater I've ever bought.

But the true impetus for my financial conversion and the genesis for MAKING BREAD was watching my spendthrift mother become thrifty, virtually overnight, when she had to take over the finances after my father's death. Her transformation was an inspiration for me, as was so much that she did. Her situation, left alone to cope on a widow's military pension at 78, is typical (stereotypical you might even say).

I know that now, too. As a group, women live longer, earn less, and save half as much as men do for their retirement. Often focusing on family at the expense of their careers, they end up playing a million-dollar game of catch-up, without even realizing it: The average college-educated woman who takes five years off from the workforce to stay at home with her children ends up earning a million dollars less than the man in the cubicle or corner office next to hers, over the course of her working lifetime. Yet that same woman could go a long way towards making up the difference with one simple act: asking for an increase of $5,000 on the first job offer she gets. Boosting her first salary by that seemingly insignificant amount could increase her lifetime earnings by more than half a million dollars. And, guess what? Men are four times more likely than women to make that request, according to Linda Babcock, co-author of *Women Don't Ask*.

I learned that and other eye-opening statistics in researching stories first for the magazine and later for this book. Statistics like:

>> **FIFTY-THREE PERCENT** of single women say they live from paycheck to paycheck, and 54 percent say they are more likely to accumulate 30 pairs of shoes than $30,000 in retirement savings.

>> **DEBT AMONG** college students is at an all-time high, and female students tend to carry higher credit-card balances, on top of their college loans, entering the work force with large bills to pay off before they can start saving.

>> **NINE OUT OF 10** working women earn less than $50,000 a year, and—42 years after the Equal Pay Act was passed in 1963—women still earn 76 cents for every dollar men make on the job. When you break out the statistics for African American and Hispanic women, the wage gap grows even wider, with African American women earning 67 cents and Hispanic women earning 55 cents for every dollar (white) men earn. The wage gap is costing American families $200 billion a year, according to the American Association of University Women.

>> **ONE-THIRD** of working women don't have health insurance as a job benefit, either on their own or through a husband's coverage, and those who are covered under a husband's plan are more vulnerable to losing it as a result of divorce or widowhood.

>> **TWENTY-EIGHT PERCENT** don't have pension or retirement benefits on the job, and those who do receive roughly half the amount that men receive.

>> **ON AVERAGE**, one year after divorcing, a woman's income decreases by 30 to 45 percent, whereas a man's income increases by at least 10 percent.

Is it any wonder that 75 percent of the elderly poor in the United States are women? In time, wage disparity between men and women doing the same work—outlawed by the Equal Pay Act of 1963—should disappear, say the experts. But women aren't waiting politely for companies to wise up. Major discrimination suits have been brought to the courts in the last five years, denouncing corporations that have unfair pay and promotion practices. These suits will have a sensitizing ripple effect, as other companies begin to examine their employment practices. In the meantime, it's important for all of us to close the information gap. By educating ourselves about our options and the consequences of every financial move we make, we can compensate for our lost earning power and save for a secure retirement. And speak up—ask for that raise when you feel you deserve it! Lobby for paid family leave, government-sponsored or on-site corporate day care benefits, Social Security credits for stay-at-home moms—all things that would help women manage their work/family responsibilities without being penalized financially.

While many of the specifics of financial advice offered in this book reflect U.S. economic realities, this is a global economy, and the basic principles of money management that we urge women to practice pertain everywhere: be a breadwinner, save as much as you can, and buy real estate.

These days, most women grow up prepared to earn their own bread or to contribute to a dual-income household. (Single women are the fastest-growing demographic group, and 56 percent of all married couples are dual-income couples.) But, for a number of reasons, women don't always know what to do with the bread they earn. We're too busy, for one thing, working and raising our families, to take the time to learn about the bulls and the bears. Some of us still prefer to leave financial decisions to our spouses; others of us believe, mistakenly, that we don't have enough money to manage. Or we've been made to feel uncomfortable in previous close encounters with condescending financial advisers. Few of us fully understand the price we pay for not paying more attention to our finances.

Whatever the reason, the bottom line is that what we don't know about money can hurt us. Take, for instance, the woman who divorced her husband after nine and a half years of marriage. If she had only been able to stick it out for six more months, until she'd reached her tenth anniversary, she would have been eligible to claim her husband's Social Security benefits when she reached retirement age. Since her husband's salary was considerably higher than her own, not knowing about the ten-year "marriage-vesting" rule cost her a lot of dough.

Through the stories women have shared with me in the course of editing MAKING BREAD magazine and writing this book, I am more convinced than ever that learning how to manage the resources we have—taking control of our lives by taking control of our finances—is crucial to our well-being and our financial security. We're not talking hedge funds and arbitrage secrets here; we're talking bread-and-butter financial basics. Understanding your options and

> The bottom line is that what we don't know about money can hurt us.

teaching yourself to consider the consequences of every financial move you make will keep you from becoming a statistic—one of those "75 percent of the elderly poor" who are women.

And the sooner you begin the better off you'll be. Did you know that if you start saving $2,000 a year (approximately $40 a week or $6 a day) in your twenties and put away just that amount every year for 5 years, saving not a dime after that, through the magic of compound interest you could have almost half a million dollars by the time you're in your sixties? I wish I'd known that when I was 21.

What if you're coming to the subject late in life, as I did? Don't worry—just hurry. We'll show you how to make the most of what you have. Organized by life stages, this book will walk you through the smart financial moves to make at every age. As in the magazine, each chapter will be a mix of expert advice, quick "One Thing You Can Do Right Now" tips, and real women's stories. Every chapter will frame money issues in the context of real women's lives—women like you; women you can relate to. While poking fun at lingering stereotypes about purse strings and apron strings, in this book and in our magazine, we aim to inform, explore, challenge, and change your attitudes about money. And entertain you in the bargain.

Who are "we"? Well, besides me, it's the very knowledgeable Elizabeth Lewin, who is a financial planner and contributing editor to MAKING BREAD, as well as the author and co-author of many other finance-related books. But it's also so many other women. Something wonderful happened when I began to talk about launching a women's finance magazine three years ago. Friends, former colleagues, and strangers started

sharing their money stories, submitting articles, tips, and strategies, because they believe so strongly that women need a financial wake-up call. The magazine, its companion Web site, www.makingbread.com and this book are a collaborative effort of an amazing group of women who have come together to get the word out about financial independence and its importance for women. Carole Wible, Victoria Secunda, Elizabeth Kaminsky, Sharon Sorokin James, Marcia Eckerd, Allison Acken, Nissa Simon, Patricia Schiff Estess, Rosemary Rys, JoAnn Hines, Laurie Lesser, Jane Resnick, Vivian Shic, Clio Mallin . . . and so many more shared their experiences, good and bad, with that man on the face of the dollar bill—George Washington—for this ultimate example of chick lit.

The journey that led to the writing of this book has been an incredible one, rewarding in so many ways, the least of which, it turns out, is monetary. One of the most important lessons I've learned from the many women who have become involved in this project is that—as important as money is—it *isn't* everything.

Speeding to work, in a rush to catch my train one recent morning, I glimpsed a street sign out of the corner of my eye: "Birchrunville 2 miles," it said, and an arrow pointed down a narrow country lane. It was a road I'd noticed before, its off-the-beaten-track quality whispering to me to slow down, make a left turn, take a detour, and explore new territory. The moment was fleeting—as dreamlike as any roadside distraction seems to a driver behind the wheel of her car, as she pushes the speed limit, thinking about the challenges and annoyances that await when she arrives at the office.

But for me on that morning, that sign started

me thinking about roads less traveled, journeys not taken and destinations deferred. It brought to mind some of the brave women I know who refused to settle for the ruts they'd found themselves in, who listened to the whispers—those inner voices urging them to try something new. Just the day before, I'd heard from Dawn, who had been unhappy in a job that didn't challenge her or utilize her talents well. After a year of looking for something else, she finally found a position that thrills her. It's "the start of a creative career and is much more aligned to 'feeding me' because it gives me the opportunity to 'feed others' in a way that is much more important than pushing papers around," she wrote to me.

I've heard friends speak about that hunger before. Another wonderful woman, Susan, who'd been a talented and respected editor for various national magazines in New York for years, decided her life would be more meaningful as a reading teacher, so she went back to school to realize that dream. Sharon, a lawyer friend of mine, recently decided to cut back from five to four days on the job, so that she would have time to devote to her family and to herself and *her* dream of writing a novel. Sande walked away from a lucrative corporate career to open a ground-breaking art gallery, and Mary Ellen left the art department of a national magazine to create and license her own designs.

Many of these women took pay cuts to follow their passions. Some of them later became wealthier than they had ever hoped. But even when there was a huge financial payoff, money wasn't the driving force for change. They were hungry for an inner satisfaction and creative challenges that their old jobs simply didn't offer them.

I admire these women enormously for the courage they have to go after what makes them happy. They were my guides as I began my own scary journey as editor of a digital magazine about women and money. I don't really know where the road will lead. I don't have all the answers about how women can use their money to their best advantage, but I do have a lot of questions. In this book, you'll find many of the answers my writers and I have gathered.

All of us at MAKING BREAD invite you to come along for the ride. After you've read the book, visit the Web site (www.makingbreadmagazine.com), download a free trial issue, and, if you like what you see, subscribe to the magazine for a regular fix of financial information and inspiration. (Whether through our magazine or some other source, it's important to keep up to date on changes in Federal laws that may impact your options, your tax liability, and the way you manage your money.) And if you're feeling unfulfilled in the job you find yourself in today, like Dawn, Susan, Sharon, Sande and Mary Ellen, I hope you'll begin searching for another road to your occupational Shangri-La.

I can hear it now: the chatty drive-time reporter on AM radio announcing a traffic jam on the road less traveled. That would be all of us women finally deciding to go after what we really want!

PART ONE:

Female Finance Time Line

One thing *you can do right now*: Keep a favorite photograph of yourself as a young girl in your bedroom and focus on it every morning as you do your exercises, get dressed, or meditate to clear your mind for the day. Ask yourself: *Are you fulfilling that little girl's dreams?* If not, ask yourself: *Why not?* And start looking for ways to make those dreams come true! That's an exercise I follow every morning, and, as an adult, it's kept me on course when I've lost my way or my belief in myself has faltered. Whether you're 18 or 55, the young girl that you once were still lives deep inside your psyche—and so do her dreams. Looking her in the face every morning, how can you let her down?

Getting back in touch with that girl can help jumpstart dreams deferred along the way. But the best way to make your dream *du jour* (your dreams will change over time) a reality is to create a financial plan and start saving the minute you begin earning money. That means saving a dime here, a dollar there from your allowance or babysitting money in high school, and at least 20 percent of every after-school or summer paycheck you earn. Making saving a habit isn't easy; it's not fun. And it can be particularly hard when you're faced with peer pressure to buy the latest clothes, high-tech gadgets or thigh-high boots.

But, before you plop $300 of your hard-earned money down on an iPod or a Dooney & Bourke

WHAT EVERY GIRL NEEDS TO KNOW:
The Real Difference Between Men and Women

>> Women live an average of seven years longer than men. You're going to need a bigger nest egg to cover those extra years.

>> Women are more likely than men to work part-time, and part-time jobs provide neither pension benefits nor enough discretionary income to invest for retirement.

>> Women tend to leave the workforce to raise a family or take care of a sick husband or elderly parent. As a result, they spend an average of 17 years in the workforce, compared with 38 years for men. These "missing years" represent more than $1.5 million in lost wages, retirement savings, and Social Security benefits for them.

>> Thirteen percent of women over 65 receive a private pension versus 33 percent of men, and those who have pensions receive half as much as men do: Private pensions average $3,940 annually for women and $7,468 for men.

>> Women earn about 25 percent less than men. For every dollar a man earns, a women earns 76 cents. But the wage gap doesn't just affect immediate earnings; there is a ripple effect: Pension benefits, retirement savings, and Social Security benefits (based on number of years worked, age at retirement, and total lifetime earnings) will also be less.

bag, consider the facts, and you'll understand why it's so important for women to make saving a priority.

Given these statistics, it's clear that women need to devise strategies for "getting even" with men in the money department. And the earlier you start the better off you'll be. By taking these facts to heart and letting them inform every financial move you make from the time you are a teen-ager to the time you retire, you can compensate for their negative effects. If retirement seems like it's a lifetime away when you're a teen or just out of high school, you'd be right—but that's the good news. All those years are pure gold to you: Start saving in your teens and twenties, and you will be able to make up the difference caused by the social and economic factors cited here. Start saving with your first paycheck, and you could be a multimillionaire by the time you retire.

STRATEGIES FOR 'GETTING EVEN' WITH THE BOYS IN THE MONEY DEPARTMENT

Some women know the importance of money almost instinctively from the time they are very young. "I was always a self-sufficient child," says successful businesswoman and author of *Sister CEO* Cheryl Broussard. "Even when I was a little girl, I was industrious in terms of making things, baking. I used to make headbands and sell them in the schoolyard for a dollar. I was a big Barbie Doll fan. When I would get an allowance, I would save my money, so that I could buy Barbie Doll clothes. I was probably 7, maybe 8 years old. I knew from then on that all I had to do was save my money, and I could buy whatever I wanted to buy."

Broussard, who was raised by a single mom,

One thing you can do right now ...

TALK TO YOUR MOM ABOUT MONEY

Ask her why she made the choices she did: career, marriage, staying at home, or continuing to work after having children. Talk to her about what she gets out of work, and what her goals and dreams are. Does she seem happy? What qualities do you most admire in her? Then think about what your strengths are and what you want in life. Set your goals; save for them; learn that money can empower you and protect you.

made two very important discoveries at an early age: Saving money would give her the power to get what she wanted, and she alone was responsible for her own welfare. She knew that she couldn't and shouldn't depend on anyone else.

"Money in the bank is the best gift you can give yourself" and "be your own breadwinner" are the most important financial lessons that any young girl, or woman, can learn. Add to them "get real (estate)," and you have MAKING BREAD's recipe for female financial security. Living by these three principles will help you to counter the effects of the financial triple whammy that women as a group tend to face: we live longer, earn less, and consequently save half as much as men do for retirement.

The following suggestions will help you earn (and keep) the bread to put those principles into practice as you move from your teen years into womanhood.

Dare to dream. Then plan to make it reality. Decide what you want to do with this incredible gift of time stretching before you. Ask yourself: What do you care about? What do you enjoy? How are you going to use your talents to make your mark in this world? Then figure out how you can make money doing it and what sort of education or training you will need to prepare yourself.

"The advice I'd give young girls is not to worry about what you want to be; figure out what you like to do first," says Angela Nissel—author of *The Broke Diaries*—in an interview with MAKING BREAD. "Poor kids; we start asking them: 'What do you want to be when you grow up?' way too early," she continues. "We should ask: 'What makes you happy?' As a matter of fact, maybe we should stop asking adults, 'What do you do for a living?' and ask them what they do for fun. Jobs take up large parts of our days, but they are small parts of who we are as people."

Nissel had one more important piece of advice for girls, when we talked with her: "Instead of working as a group, girls tend to see one another as enemies. I tutored a group of girls, and it saddened me how many of them claimed they hated other women and only hung out with guys." The message: start early to form a network of female support that could last you a lifetime.

Nissel's gift of gab, her love of communicating, inspired her to create a Web diary; the Web diary attracted enough of a following that she was offered a book contract; and the success of the book led to an opportunity to develop a TV series. Be like Nissel: Do what you love; follow your heart to your destiny. But be smart about it.

Maximize your lifetime earnings by getting a college degree. Nissel told us the best advice her mother ever gave her was: "Invest in your education. They can steal your wallet, but they can't steal your diploma. I disliked high school so much, there was a time I was thinking about dropping out. I'm so glad I didn't, and even more glad that I went forward to get my college degree. Whenever I start a new venture that I'm not sure will fly, I always know the temp agencies pay a little more to people with college degrees," she says.

Nissel is an entrepreneur at heart, and her college degree gives her insurance; it's something to fall back on. For those pursuing professional careers, a four-year degree can increase lifetime earnings by more than $600,000, compared with earnings of the average high-school educated worker, according to an American Council on Education study. Even if you don't have any money saved after high school, there are ways to get that degree. Later in this chapter, we'll share some strategies and the stories of women who have put themselves through college on their own dime.

Even if Prince Charming does show up, he may not stick around. All women need a career of their own. At 17.3 million strong, single women (those never married, divorced, or widowed) are the fastest-growing demographic group, according to the U.S. Census Bureau. And dual-career married couples with children outnumber married couples with children who manage on one income by more than two to one. Even if your dream is to be a wife and a stay-at-home mom, you must have a career to fall back on, a way to make your own living, should you become a divorcee or a widow—or your spouse is laid off.

And here's another important reason to work: Unless you accumulate a record of 10 years of earnings (or are married for at least 10 years to someone who has), you won't be eligible for Medicare when you retire.

Credit cards are not an extension of your salary. It's tempting to see them as such when you're struggling to make ends meet. But if you don't pay off your balances immediately, you can easily end up tripling the amount of money you pay for each item. So the next time you're confronted with an object of overwhelming desire, before you reach for your wallet, take a deep breath and ask yourself: "Will I still enjoy this when the credit card bill comes?" Unless you pay off your credit card balances immediately, that 100 bucks is likely to stick to your credit card's interest-collecting bottom line like the effects of an ice cream binge stick to your hips.

Your credit report is as important as your report card in school. More and more, your credit score is being used as a measure of your reliability and credit risk. Landlords, utility companies, insurance firms, even prospective employers consult it to learn more about you, and you may be denied loans, charged higher interest rates or premiums, even lose a job offer, if yours is in bad shape.

You aren't depriving yourself—you're giving yourself a gift—when you save money. That's an important distinction. Once you understand it, you'll be stashing away money every chance you get. The best way is to establish an automatic deposit from your paycheck into a savings account every pay period. That way you won't even miss the money. Start small—$5 a pay period—and add to it every year or every time you get a raise.

SAVINGS HAVENS FOR TEENS

What should you do with the dollars you earn from your babysitting, after-school or summer-job? Exactly what adults do (or should do). Look for the highest interest rate you can find and stash as much money away as you can afford to. Options (which we'll discuss in more detail in Chapter Two) include statement savings accounts, certificates of deposit, bank money-market accounts, mutual fund money-market accounts, and yes, even IRAs.

"Any child with earned income can have an IRA. If your kids baby sit, or flip burgers, or have paper routes, work as tutors or camp counselors, or shovel snowy driveways in the winter, they can and should have IRAs," says Wall Street reporter Ingrid DuBois, in an article for www.making-breadmagazine.com. Dubois's son opened a Roth IRA at age 10 after earning money for a TV commercial. At age 18, his account was worth $22,000, and she predicts that, if he continues to make the maximum contribution each year, it could be worth $2.8 million when he's ready to retire.

The downside: because not all financial institutions offer "kid IRAs," or "IRAs for minors," you'll have to do some legwork. (Another form of custodial IRA, in which boomer adults manage the finances of their aging parents, is more common). Start by checking for more information with the Vanguard Group (www.vanguard.com) and TD Waterhouse (www. tdwaterhouse.com), both of which do offer them. Other factors to consider: One of your parents must assume legal responsibility for the account until you are 18, and if you're college-bound, the money held in such an account may count as an asset and disqualify you from college aid. Still, the interest rates your money will earn, compared with other options, make such an account worth considering, as long as you don't need to take money out for emergencies.

Be sure to select a Roth rather than a traditional IRA for such an account. What's the difference? The money you invest in a Roth IRA is not tax-deductible, as it is with a traditional IRA, but all withdrawals are. As a minor, you're bound to be in a low tax bracket (if you owe tax on earnings at all), so you won't need the tax advantage that you'd get with a traditional IRA. By choosing a Roth, you'll be able to avoid a big tax hit later, when you do withdraw the money on retirement and you are in a higher tax bracket.

If you're eager to dip your toes into the stock market, look into Direct Reinvestment Plans, or DRIPS, which, depending on the company whose shares you purchase, may allow you to get started with as little as $10. Your dividends are automatically invested in the purchase of more stock, and you can generally also set up monthly purchases of more stock. There are many advantages to DRIPS, and some disadvantages. (Be sure to check for fees, as with any service, and be careful that you don't put all your financial eggs in one basket, by buying just one company's stock.) To learn more about DRIPs and how to get started, visit www.dripcentral.com or www.sharebuilder.com.

For more information about your options and to learn about how to invest your spare change, check the Web sites listed in the "Best Net Bets for Kids" box on page 26.

ESTABLISHING YOUR CREDIT CREDENTIALS

Think of credit as a tool: Use it to your advantage and don't abuse it. Credit card issuers are targeting high school and college students, so if you are a student, there may be no shortage of opportunities to get a card. Applications for credit cards are usually available on campus, but they come with a high price. If you go for one of these cards, be very sure to read the fine print carefully. According to Nancy Deevers, director of education and community relations at the Consumer Credit Counseling Service of Northeastern Ohio, "Cards for students often have extra-high finance charges." This makes it all the more important for you to use the card wisely and to pay off balances on time. It wouldn't hurt to stay a "credit virgin" for as long as possible.

But sometime before you leave school you should accept at least one offer, in order to start building your credit history. It will be difficult to get a car loan or a mortgage without a credit history later, and if you do get a loan, the interest rate you're charged is likely to be higher, because you're considered a bigger risk. Similarly, if you want to rent an apartment, your security deposit will likely be higher. Car insurance rates could be higher; utility companies may require a deposit. Without a good credit history, life is much more complicated and expensive. The operative term there is "good." Don't think of your credit balance as an extension of your salary, or something to bank on. It's to be used for emergencies and paid off as quickly as possible. Cardinal rule No. 1 when it comes to credit cards: NEVER pay just the minimum. The system is rigged to keep you paying that bill

PLUS INTEREST for as long as possible, if you pay only the minimum required.

If you are not being swamped with credit card offers, but you are working, try a local bank with which you or your parents have a relationship. Ask the banker about your chances of acquiring the card before you actually apply. You don't want to establish a history of rejections. Also check www.bankrate.com for a list of banks and the rates and fees that they offer.

If you run into a problem getting a card on your own, you can always ask your parents to co-sign on a credit card. They may be reluctant to do so, because—let's face it—they will be liable for unpaid balances on the card, and that will affect *their* credit history. For starters, agree to a card with a low credit line, let's say $250. Your parents might go along, if the bill is sent to them and they can monitor your spending. Charge a few small items, and pay the balance off at the end of the month. That way you'll start to build your own good credit history.

One other option to consider is signing up for a prepaid card. These secured cards are like telephone calling cards. You deposit money (generally $300 to $500) in a savings account as collateral or security, and that dollar value is tapped whenever you charge against the card. You're really borrowing from yourself, but you have the convenience of using a card, and you show creditors that you can manage credit. Eventually, if you pay back on time, the institution that has given you the prepaid card will increase the credit line beyond the balance that you have in the account.

The downside: Fees and rates for these cards tend to be higher than with unsecured cards. Check www.bankrate.com for best offers. And be sure that the card you apply for reports to the three credit bureaus; some smaller institutions that issue cards don't. Always read the fine print; beware of secured cards with built-in application and set-up fees that eat up your entire deposit up front, leaving you with nothing but a large bill to pay off.

The advantage: You can limit your spending by keeping the amount you borrow against manageable. It can also help you budget. The companies offering these cards provide educational material for you. Log onto www.prepaids.net/creditcards for more information.

However you acquire your first card, use it wisely; don't abuse it. Pay on time (late fees are getting higher and higher), and don't carry a balance from month to month. If you can't pay off the entire balance, always—I repeat—make more than the minimum payment. Balances have a way of creeping up with scary speed, and if you make only the minimum payment, you end up paying just a dollar or two more than the interest due. You won't live long enough to pay the balance off that way. Remember, the purpose of getting a card is to build a good credit history, not bad debt. For more information on managing your credit, read Chapter Nine.

TUITION INTUITION: BECAUSE WOMEN CAN'T AFFORD NOT TO GET A DEGREE

College costs are rising, and those of us who have to figure out how to pay for them are beginning to feel more and more like we're going to the School of Hard Knocks. According to the latest figures issued by the College Board, public college tuition rose 14 percent in 2003 (largely as a result of State budget cuts), and private college tuition rose 6 percent. Over the last decade, average tuition and fees rose 47 percent ($1,506) at four-year public colleges and universities and 42 percent ($5,866) at private colleges. That's before all the other expenses, like room, board, books— the national average for books at a four-year private college is more than $800 a year—and personal expenses, all of which also continue to rise dramatically.

Still, when you weigh those rising costs against the difference of more than $600,000 a college degree can make over a lifetime in earnings, you don't have to do advanced math to see the upside. Getting a college degree is one of the best ways a woman can compensate for the financial triple whammy we all face. So, don't give up. Whether you're saving for your own degree or putting your kids through school, here are some strategies to help you pay the piper.

The Good News. Only 8 percent of students enrolled in four-year institutions pay tuition and fees of $24,000 or more, with almost 70 percent spending less than $8,000 per year and about 29 percent spending less than $4,000.

Moreover, while the cost of college is rising, so is the amount of financial aid for which students can apply. In 2004, the College Board reported that there is more than $105 billion in grants, loans, work-study opportunities and federal education tax credits available to today's students. That's an increase of more than 15 percent from the previous year, and some of it is earmarked just for women. If you want to tap into this money, then you need to educate yourself about financial aid.

Show Me the Money! Best Sources of Financial Aid. Financial aid is any type of assistance used to pay college costs based on financial need. It's meant to make up the difference between what your family can afford to pay and what college costs. The amount your family is able to contribute is referred to as the Expected Family Contribution (EFC). Your EFC is determined by whomever is awarding the aid—usually the federal government or individual colleges and universities. The formulas for aid assume that your EFC will be paid through a combination of savings (your assets, as well as your parents'), current income, and borrowing.

The Federal Student Aid Form: You will need to fill out a financial-aid application, if you are applying for grants, loans, or work-study. It can be lengthy and complex, but there are many resources, both on- and off-line, to help you. Start by visiting www.collegeboard.com. The College Board recommends that your parents complete their income tax returns before filling out the form, because much of the information is the same. January 1 is the first day you are eligible to file the aid application—and it is recommended that you file as close to that date as possible, since school, state, and private-aid deadlines may be much earlier than federal deadlines.

Grants and Scholarships: Grants come from federal and state governments and from individual colleges. They are the closest thing to heaven

Tip: For each qualifying student, you must choose to claim either the Hope Scholarship Credit or the Lifetime Learning Credit. You don't qualify in a year in which you take money out of an education IRA. If your parents do expect to qualify for these tax credits, they should skip the education IRA in favor of the tax benefits. They can still invest in a state plan without jeopardizing the credits. More information is available in IRS publication 8863.

for a financially strapped student, because they represent "free" money, or money that doesn't have to be repaid. Scholarships are available from thousands of private organizations, as well as directly from colleges and universities. These are usually based on merit and need—and they're not all athletic scholarships, either, though you might think so from all the press college athletes get. You'll find scholarships for kids who show an interest and aptitude in music, art, or in the tsetse flies of a specific region of Africa, and any number of other areas of study.

Loans: This source of funding provides the most

Tip: Don't wait until you are a senior in high school to learn about the financial aid form. Check your local library and consult your guidance counselor. Call the Federal Student Aid Information Center at 1-800-433-3243 with any questions. Online, surf on over to www.ed.gov.

money, but it must be repaid—though not until after graduation. Most loans are awarded on financial need. Most are low-interest loans, subsidized by the government.

Perkins loans are available to those who have exceptional financial need. You can't apply for them on your own. They are awarded by a college as part of a financial aid package. The government pays the interest on the loan, while you are in school and for the following nine months. These loans are for low-income students.

If a college says you do not qualify for need-based grants and loans, never fear—you can borrow money from other sources, provided that

you pass a credit check. Among the possibilities:

Stafford loans are offered by the U.S. Depart-

Tip: Check with your guidance counselor about local associations that give out scholarships. Online, check out: www.ed.gov, www.salliemae.com, www.college-scholarships.com, www.guaranteed-scholarships.com, www.wiredscholar.com, www.scholarships.com, and www.fastweb.com. And don't forget to look into any scholarship funds that might be available through your parents' employers, or through trade organizations or unions you or your parents might belong to.

ment of Education and are either subsidized or unsubsidized, depending on income. First-year students may receive up to $2,625 annually; second-year students, $3,500; third- and fourth-year students, $5,500, if the loan is subsidized by the government. The interest rate equals the 91-day Treasury bill plus 1.7 percentage points, adjusted annually with a cap of 8.25 percent. Repayment begins six months after the student leaves school, with the government covering the interest in the interim. The unsubsidized version of the Stafford loan is available to all families, whether or not they meet the government's qualifications for aid. The terms are similar, except that borrowers may choose to either begin interest payments immediately or defer them until after graduation.

PLUS (Parent Loan for Undergraduate Students) permits your parents to borrow the cost of tuition less the amount of financial aid you will receive from the school. They are not allowed to defer the interest payments until a later date. You don't have to demonstrate financial need, but you do need to have a good credit history. You begin to repay 60 days after the final loan is made.

Work-Study Aid: These programs, which are subsidized by the federal government, require

Tip: Interest on student loans that is repaid during the first 60 months after payments begin is partially tax-deductible.

part-time employment. Pay is based on federal minimum wage standards, but varies with job requirements, skill, and experience levels. When you apply for federal financial aid, indicate on your application that you want work-study assistance. Check www.mapping-your-future.org for more information, ask your guidance counselor, or call 1-800-4-FED-AID.

Federal Tax Credits: Several years ago, two federal tax credits were created to provide some relief for the high cost of education: the Hope Scholarship and Lifetime Learning credits. The credits apply to each student in the household (you, your siblings, and even your parents). Your parents will only get a partial credit, if their income is between $80,000 and $100,000, filling jointly ($40,000 to $50,000, if single). Parents who earn more than $100,000, filing jointly ($50,000, if single) are *not* eligible for these credits. The amount of the credit is subtracted from the tax they owe in any given year.

The Hope Scholarship Credit applies to qualified educational expenses incurred during the first two years of college. The credit totals $1,500 per year— 100 percent of the first $1,000 and 50 percent of the next $1,000. This allows a qualifying student to attend a community college for almost nothing.

The Lifetime Learning Credit applies to the next two years of college. It allows a maximum credit per taxpayer (not per student) of 20 percent of the first $10,000 in expenses, or $2,000. This credit can be used by adults returning to school to upgrade their job skills, as well as by college students.

Grow Me the Money! Here are some smart ways you or your parents can start saving for your college tuition. *Education IRAs* (also known as a Coverdell Education Savings Accounts) have been available since 1997. The annual contribution is $2,000 per beneficiary. However, there is an income limit: an adjusted gross income (AGI) of $220,000 for married couples and $110,000 for singles. Earnings accumulate tax-free and withdrawals are tax-free, provided that the funds are used to pay for tuition, fees, books, supplies, and room and board. Any funds that remain in the Education IRA after they've financed their firstborn's education, or when their firstborn turns 30, can be rolled over to another child in the family. The account is in the parent's name and won't be factored into financial aid calculations down the road—so it won't make it more difficult for you to obtain loans or grants.

STATE 529 COLLEGE SAVINGS PLANS

Section 529 plans are state-sponsored savings plans and can be set up for the benefit of any child or adult. These plans are established by individual states, which hire money managers to invest the funds. Most states allow non-residents to invest in their plans and the future student is not restricted to colleges in a specific state.

The disadvantages: You can't control the investment of your contributions. The money manager, hired by that state, makes the investment decisions. They will be more aggressive in investing your money if your child is young. And fees can be high.

You are now allowed to contribute to both a

THE ADVANTAGES OF 529 PLANS

1. The maximum contributions vary from state to state but can be as much as $250,000.

2. Earnings grow tax-free, and withdrawals to pay for tuition or college expenses are also *tax-free*. In some states, residents can get tax breaks on their state income tax, if they use the state's 529 plan.

3. Currently, assets in these savings plans will not have a major impact on financial aid. The money in these plans is treated as a "parental" asset. However, Congress might make changes. If the assets in these plans are considered the child's, eligibility for financial aid will be reduced.

4. Wealthy parents, godparents, or grandparents can reduce their taxable estate by gifting to a 529 plan. The annual gift tax exclusion is $11,000; the recipient does not treat this as taxable income. Individuals can take five annual gift tax exclusions, or $55,000, in one year (up to $110,000 from married couples), without incurring federal gift taxes, as long as no further gifts to or for that beneficiary are made during the next five years. This is a great way to get an account started.

5. Funds not used by the beneficiary by age 30 can be transferred to benefit another family member—even a niece, nephew, or cousin.

529 plan and an education IRA in the same year. Make sure you understand how these plans work before you set one or both up. There are numerous Web sites to consult for further information, including www.collegesavings.org, www.salliemae.com, and www.sensible-investor.com. You can also call the Department of Education (or Department of Higher Education) in the state where you live. You would also benefit by meeting with a financial adviser before you open one of these accounts.

529 Prepaid Plans. Because, with these plans, you're purchasing future tuition at local public colleges at today's prices, these act as a hedge against rising costs. They're great if you expect to attend one of your state's colleges or universities. However, budget cutbacks have increased tuition costs at state schools, and assets in the plans have been reduced because of the declining stock market. Therefore, many plans have been forced to impose fees, restrict enrollment, or increase prices. Currently, prepaid plans reduce eligibility for financial aid.

Independent 529 Plans. With these plans, you can lock in tuition at more than 220 private colleges at a slightly discounted rate. You'll get your money back (adjusted for fund performance), if your child decides not to go to one of these schools. You can roll over the funds without a penalty to another beneficiary or to a state 529 plan or prepaid plan. Distributions reduce eligibility for financial aid. For a list of participating schools, check out www. independent529plan.org, or call 1-888-718-7878.

U.S. Savings Bonds. Don't write off savings bonds as a way to save for college. The government guarantees the bonds, and some or all of the income they generate is tax-free, if it is used for tuition and fees. If you earn less than $87,750, the income earned is tax-free. (The tax bite is reduced, if you earn $87,500 to $117,750.) If you're single, the income is tax-free, as long as you make less than $58,500, and reduced if you earn between $58,500 and $73,500. If you earn more than the upper limits, then none of the income is tax-free. Savings bonds usually have little or no effect on financial aid, because they are usually purchased by adults (parents or grandparents). Learn more about government savings bonds at www.savingsbonds.gov.

Remember, when starting any of these savings funds, that assets held in a child's name will be considered funds available for college expenses and will be factored into any financial aid package; the child gets control of the money at majority, usually 18 years of age.

Accounts held in the parents' name have greater flexibility and investment options. These accounts have little effect on how much aid your child will get. Make a point of keeping on top of financial aid and other tax changes that might affect your college fund. Stay on top of these changes as they occur, so that you can readjust your financial game accordingly.

Divorce & College Savings. If your mom is divorced or about to be divorced and expects to seek financial aid for you, remember it is in your best interest to live with the parent who has the lesser income. Some private schools will ask for a financial statement of the non-custodial parent.

If the divorce agreement specifies that Dad is

WOMAN TO WOMAN:
PUTTING YOURSELF THROUGH COLLEGE
IF I CAN DO IT, SO CAN YOU!

Dear MAKING BREAD

I'm an 18-year-old New Jersey high-school student with a part-time job that doesn't pay much, and I have no money saved for college. What can I do?
—Future Student

Dear Future Student,

Congratulations! You have just taken the first step toward your college education by saying that you want to go! College may be expensive, but there are many ways to limit those expenses while getting a great education. How do I know? I did it. I was the first person in my family to go to college. We lived in a rental-assistance apartment, and my mom was a single working parent who never finished high school. It was her dream for me to go to college, but most important, it was my dream, too. Here's how we did it:

1. **I went to my guidance counselor at school.** Thankfully, he was a pretty good guy, and he helped me fill out the financial-aid paperwork. Once I filled all that out, I found out that I could qualify for some grants for low-income families, and I could also qualify for student loans.

2. **I worked hard to keep my grades up.** That helped me apply for scholarships from my old elementary school and my church. I went to both of them in my senior year of high school and asked if they gave scholarships. I filled out some papers, gave them a copy of my report card, and on graduation day, I got $500 from each of them. That paid for books and some fees. Many community organizations give scholarships to kids from the neighborhood. Kiwanis, Rotary, Optimists, Elks,

churches, synagogues, clubs, and businesses often have scholarships that go unclaimed, because no one applies for them. Your school should know about them, but if not, start asking the adults in your community. Tell everybody you know that you want to go to college and are looking for help. That's how I found out about the one from my church.

3. **Taking core courses at the local community college is a great way to save money.** In New Jersey, most community college courses are about $70 per credit, or $210 per three-credit class, not including the fees. Many successful students take their required math, science, history, and English classes at the community college, and then transfer to a four-year school to complete their degree. Rutgers, our state university, has agreements with many of the community colleges in New Jersey, so transferring credits is pretty easy. Most other schools do, too. Community colleges have great libraries and technology centers, and most even have athletic facilities and child-care. These schools are a great value and a great way to ease into college life.

4. **If you want to start right up with a four-year school, your best bet is to stay in state and commute to school.** That way, you don't have to pay for room, board, and food on campus. Most state colleges give a great tuition break for in-state residents.

5. **Work-study programs or internships are great ways to get free education and even earn a little extra money, too.** Some programs offer credit for working at an on-campus job—for instance, in the library or the admissions office. Other programs offer pay and could give you a break on other things like student fees. Work-study programs easily fit into the student's schedule. I did work-study during the school year and then worked at other jobs during holiday and summer breaks to earn even more money for

school. The best part is, these jobs count as work experience and will help you build your resume for when you graduate.

6. **Give it some hustle! I never stopped looking for ways to make extra money.** And I kept re-applying for grants and scholarships every year, even if I got turned down. It paid off in my senior year, when I finally qualified for a small scholarship ($250) that paid for my books. It doesn't sound like a lot, but it was a great help, and it meant that I didn't have to find that money someplace else.

7. **If you are a very motivated person and you have access to a computer, you could take some courses on-line.** These courses cost money—some of them are very expensive—and the amount of financial aid may not be as much as you would find for a community college or four-year school. But, if the credits are transferable and you are the type of person who works well alone, this option might be for you.

Whatever you decide, know that there are ways to get a college education without going broke. And don't believe all the hype about "name" schools. State and community colleges provide high-quality educations that stack up with the best of them. I have also learned that once you graduate, that's really all that matters to employers. Where you went to school is never as important as the fact that you finished and got your degree.

Hang in there. You can do it!

Sincerely,
Elizabeth Kaminsky

Elizabeth Kaminsky has extensive experience in personal finance and investor relations. She frequently writes about financial matters as they relate to women and is a contributing editor to MAKING BREAD.

to contribute $5,000 toward education, that fig-ure will be considered part of the family contribution, whether he pays it or not.

Finally, if your mother remarries, your stepfa-ther's income will be included as money available for the family contribution. That's why, in some situations, it's wise for Mom not to remarry until the kids are educated.

THREE WAYS TO WATCH YOUR FINANCIAL FIGURE(S)

>> **Get a college degree**. A four-year degree can increase lifetime earnings by more than $600,000, compared with earn-ings of the average high-school educated worker, according to an American Council on Education study. Even if you don't have any money saved after high school, there are ways to get that degree. Go for it!

>> **Start saving with your first pay-check**. If you save just $2,000 a year for five years in an IRA in your twenties, and don't save a dime more, by the time you retire, you could have almost half a million dollars.

>> **Ask for a $5,000 increase on your first job offer.** Men are eight times more likely than women to do this, and doing so could add nearly half a million dollars to your lifetime earnings, according to Carnegie Mellon University economics pro-fessor Linda Babcock, co-author of *Women Don't Ask: Negotiation and the Gender Divide.*

Best Net Bets for Kids

www.aba.com, the Web site of the American Bankers Association, has a comprehensive "Get Smart about Credit" department aimed at young adults, plus a "KidStuff!" section, suggesting free activities parents can do with their younger kids to help educate them about money matters.

www.independentmeans.com promotes financial independence for girls, offering board games, seminars, and books to help them learn the financial ropes. The site also sponsors a Business Plan competition, with a $10,000 scholarship prize going to the winner.

www.kidsbank.com, brought to you by Sovereign Bank, aims to explain the "fundamentals of money and banking" and the importance of sav-ing to children. It includes a "Millionaire Calculator" that you can use to figure out how long it will take you to save a million dollars, based on principal, interest, and weekly savings.

www.orangekids.com, sponsored by ING Direct, allows you to choose one of two cartoon kids, Amy or Cedric, as your guide through "Planet Orange" to explore "Moneyland," "Investor Islands," "The Republic of Savings," and "South Spending."

www.teenvestor.com is geared for teens "who are interested in investing, starting their own businesses, and improving their lives in other positive ways."

Female Finance Checklist: The Teen Years

☐ **Goals:** Decide what you want to do with your life, and figure out how you can make money doing it. Make financial independence throughout your life your uppermost priority. Begin your financial education by studying your financial options, and figure out how to use what you have to get what you want. Start a mock investment club with your girlfriends. Talk about money with your parents. Learn everything you can about how to make and save dough.

☐ **Career:** Invest in yourself by getting a college degree to maximize your lifetime earnings. Explore the costs of community colleges and four-year public and private educational institutions. Then begin to investigate scholarships, grants, and other financial aid options.

☐ **Investments:** Save as much as you can from baby sitting, after-school and summer jobs to help cover tuition costs. Open a "Kid IRA," start a money-market mutual-fund account, or purchase CDs (no, not the kind you play… certificates of deposit).

☐ **Real Estate:** After you leave home, it's rentals and roommates, until you save up enough to buy your first home. Make purchasing real estate your next big investment goal.

☐ **Insurance:** At this stage, you should still be covered under your parents' health plans (if they are covered). As soon as you leave home, look for a job that includes health coverage as a benefit.

☐ **Wills:** Unless you have major assets, none is needed at this time. Your biggest asset is probably your health right now; so take care of yourself. Consider preparing a living will and signing organ-donation consent forms.

When *Sex and the City* ended in the spring of 2004, there was much watercooler talk about the mixed messages sent by the show's final episode. Many women felt the show placed too much emphasis on hooking up with a man, any man, even if it meant settling for less than one's "soul mate."

"Do women need a marriage license and a man to be happy and secure?" was the question on many lipsticked lips. After all, millions of women never marry (married-couple households, now at 51 percent, are on the decline, according to census figures), and millions more women end up divorced or widowed and alone again when they least expect it.

At 17.3 million strong, single women are America's fastest-growing population segment, with 42 percent of women 18 and older never married, divorced, or widowed. And their financial picture is dismal: A 2003 report by the Federal Reserve Board states that the median net worth of households headed by single women in 2001 was $27,850, compared with $140,000 for married couples and $46,990 for single men. According to the study, only 35 percent of single women had 401(k)s, IRAs, or other retirement accounts, compared with 63 percent of married couples and 42 percent of single men, and only 8 percent of unmarried women have traditional pensions.

We don't need men, but we do need to take better care of our money, saving and investing it for a secure future, whether a soul mate comes along or not.

Below, we outline seven financial moves that every single woman should consider.

BE SINGLE-MINDED ABOUT YOUR MONEY

1. Learn the basics of sound money management. Whether you've never been married or are newly divorced or widowed, you are solely responsible for financial decision-making. Your financial future is in your hands. One of the first things to do is to create a spending plan. Singles tend to spend more on clothing, entertainment, and credit-card purchases than each member of a dual-income family. Spending more means saving less toward buying a house or investing for your own retirement. Start taking an active role in managing your money: Talk to your friends about money, attend financial seminars, read financial books, read the financial section of a major newspaper.

2. Establish an emergency fund. Who would support you during a layoff? You should have six months' salary saved up, just in case. Barbara knew she would be laid off about five months in advance. "I stopped spending on all extras—dining out, theater, etc. As far as my clothes, I made do with what I had," she says, "I was amazed with what I could do without."

3. Become a homeowner. Once you have an emergency fund established, your next goal should be becoming a homeowner; it's the best long-term investment any woman can make. So start saving for the down payment and other associated costs of home-ownership as soon as you can. Home ownership can give singles, who tend to have fewer tax advantages than couples with children, a sizable break: mortgage interest and real-estate taxes are deductible.

4. Nurture your career. Keep up to date in your field, do good work, seek promotions, and ask for raises when you deserve them. If you need a dual income to meet your goals, take a second job on the side.

5. Save for retirement. When do you start saving for retirement? With your first pay check. If you don't think about retirement right from the start of your career, you may have a tough time getting there. There is something called the time value of money: if you invest the same amount annually from age 20 to 30 then stop and just let the money grow, you'll have as much or maybe even more than someone who invests the same amount from age 30 to 60, because the money invested has a longer time to accumulate interest.

If you work for a company with a 401(k) plan, take advantage of it, even if you just start by having 1 percent of your pay taken out each pay period. With each raise, increase the amount you have taken out. If your company doesn't have a 401(k), open an IRA, and invest in CDs and mutual funds. Stash as much of your cash away as you can. Even if you're a single mom and would like to save for your children's college tuition, make your own long-term security a top priority. Your kids can always get scholarships. Three-quarters of the elderly poor are women; you don't want to be one of them.

6. Purchase the right kind of insurance. Do you need life insurance? To answer that question, women have to ask themselves another one: "Is *anyone* dependent on my income?" Single women who have no children have little need for life insurance, unless elderly parents are dependent on their income, or they own a business.

The business might be the largest asset that you have. Life insurance will ensure that the business can continue in the event of your death. By insuring yourself and naming your partners as beneficiaries, the proceeds provide the surviving members with the money to purchase your share in the company.

How much insurance is needed? Enough to equal your interest in the business. This should be formalized in a buy-sell agreement between (or among) the partners. In the case of a business owned by a single individual, life insurance can provide a beneficiary with money to live on while the business is liquidated; it can save the beneficiary from the complications of taking over a business that he or she may not understand or want to run.

Disability insurance is generally more important for a single woman than life insurance. Ask yourself some more questions: What is your most valuable asset? Your house? Your stock portfolio? Your pension? Think again. For singles just starting out, the most valuable asset is your earning power. What happens if you are unable to work because of an accident or an illness?

The odds of being disabled before you reach 65 are greater than the odds of dying before then. And for anyone disabled at least 90 days, the average length of disability is two and a half years. Scary? You bet. If you are disabled, the chances are high that your income will drop and your medical bills will soar. This could be fatal to your finances. If you depend on your own salary to survive, you must have disability insurance that insures a monthly income. Even a partial disability can pose a threat to your flow of income, if you are forced to change the work you do or the hours you spend on the job. Since Social Security and group plans do not usually pay as much as you really need if you are disabled, a supplementary disability policy is important for single women. Carrying your own disability policy has several advantages: The coverage is portable and goes with you if you change jobs; benefits are generally tax-free, if you pay the premiums with after-tax dollars; and you can purchase coverage that protects you from partial as well as total disability. Premiums will be based on your age, condition of health, occupation, and income. (See "Don't Make a 'Grave' Mistake: What You Need to Know About Insurance," in Chapter Four for more details on purchasing disability and life insurance.)

Next, ask yourself: Who will be there to care for you, if you're sick and need assistance? This is an important question, especially for women, who outlive men as a group by about seven years. That means that even if you're not single now, you may well be some day. How can women protect themselves against the significant financial risk posed by the potential need for long-term care services, either in a nursing home or in their own homes? Long-term care insurance might be the answer. Long-term care goes beyond medical care and nursing care to include all the assistance you could need if you ever have a chronic illness or disability that leaves you unable to care for yourself for an extended period of time.

One year in a nursing home can average more than $60,000, according to the Met Life Mature Market Institute. In some areas, it can cost twice that amount, and, as with everything else, costs are rising. About one-third of all nursing-home costs are paid out-of-pocket by the individual or their families. Generally, long-term care is not covered by health insurance.

Home care is less expensive, but adds up. Bringing an aide into your home three times a week (two to three hours per visit) can easily cost you $1,000 per month. If you can afford long- term care insurance, it will give you added peace of mind. For more information, visit the American Association for Long Term Care Insurance Web site (www.aaltci.org) or www.aarp.org.

7. **Leave instructions.** Being single, you need to authorize someone to make medical and financial decisions on your behalf, should you become physically or mentally incapacitated. This could be a sibling, close friend, lover, live-in, niece, or nephew.

A durable power of attorney allows one or more persons to take over your financial affairs. You can specify which accounts and matters each designated person can handle.

A living will or durable health-care power of attorney allows you to designate what medical services you want, in the event you become too ill to make appropriate medical decisions.

Write a will. Having one is the only way you can be sure that your assets will end up where you want them to go. Without a will, the state will appoint someone to make decisions about disposition of your property and charge the estate for its services. Your assets will then be distributed according to state law. With a will *you decide* how to distribute your property, and you name the executor, which can save undue expenses. You might want to set up a trust, providing assets to a charity or organization you want to support. Preparing a will can be done for as little as $59 on www.legalzoom.com, or you can hire a local attorney to draft your will and other directives. Then let a close friend or relative know where your important papers are located.

One isn't "the loneliest number," as the song goes— unless it's a single dollar bill longing for companionship in your bank account. So get busy giving those little bills lots of company.

Bread-and-Butter Basics

Now that we've outlined in broad strokes MAKING BREAD's seven smart money moves for single women, we'll get down to the "bread-and-butter" basics in more detail—the financial facts that every young woman starting out after high school or college should learn.

Here are some financial baby steps to take, before you learn to run with the bulls on the stock market.

Shop for a bank. The first step in establishing your financial identity is opening a checking account. Your day-to-day personal banking can be handled by a commercial bank, a savings and loan bank, an online bank, or a credit union. Anyone can use a commercial, online or savings bank, but credit unions, like clubs, are associations of people united by a "common bond," often, for instance, a place of employment.

Does it really matter which bank you choose? Consider this example: One bank has a $3 monthly service fee. There is no fee for the first eight checks written and a 50 cent charge thereafter. It doesn't charge to use the bank's ATM, but a $1 charge is levied when you access your money at a non-bank ATM. Another bank has a $6 monthly fee and charges 30 cents for every check written. You'd have to write more than ten checks every month to make the second bank worth considering.

In many banks, you can avoid monthly charges altogether by keeping a minimum balance in the checking account or in a savings account. Check how large the minimum to qualify for a no-fee checking account is. Some banks require that you keep as much as $750 to $800 in a checking account or $1,500 in a savings account. And you must meet these minimums every day during your statement cycle. Will you be able to leave that money where it is?

Look for a bank that will "pay you" for keeping your money. With interest-paying checking, you earn a small amount of interest on the balance in your account. The catch, as with many no-fee accounts, is that you have to keep a minimum balance, generally ranging from $1,000 to $5,000. Fees are charged if you fall below the minimum any time during the statement period. Banks will waive the fees if you are 65 or older—or younger and already receiving Social Security payments, which you have automatically deposited to your account. Sometimes this fee is waived if you arrange for your employer to electronically deposit your net pay into your checking account.

Hidden fees to watch out for. Some banks charge a teller transaction fee for in-branch banking—banking that could have been done through an ATM machine, by telephone, or by your computer. Believe it or not, some banks even have penalties for depositors with inactive accounts or for those who make too many withdrawals or deposits.

Do you need overdraft protection? This service covers you in the event that you write a check for more than the amount you have in your account. (Read "Be a Calculating Woman: Conquer Your Fear of Numbers—and Balance Your Checkbook!" in this chapter to learn how to avoid doing that.) Basically, overdraft protection is a line of credit, used to avoid the "nonsufficient funds" fee and the embarrassment associated with bouncing checks. But it is expensive, with annual percentage rates of 18 percent or more. Do not even think of it as a form of credit, and try not to activate it. Many banks will link your checking to your savings to give you overdraft protection, and we recommend that you look for a bank that offers such a plan. Just be sure to keep a sufficient amount in your linked savings account to cover emergencies and mistakes. Even with such over-draft protection, the bank may charge you a transaction fee.

The automatic teller machine, or ATM, is here to stay. No doubt about it, ATMs make life easier for those of us who are on the run. But along with the convenience comes temptation. The money you get from an ATM may seem like "easy money," but in actuality you're robbing yourself of hard-earned dough every time you make a withdrawal to help get you through the week. And if you use an ATM that charges a fee, you're adding insult to injury to your budget.

Here's an ATM Survival Guide:

>> Enter *all* ATM deposits and withdrawals in your checkbook right away. Get receipts from each transaction to remind you.

>> When choosing a Personal Identification Number (PIN), don't use your birthday, Social Security number, street address, or telephone number—all passwords that someone might be able to guess.

>> Use the ATM at your own bank, so you're less likely to be charged a fee when you withdraw

Tip:

Credit unions often offer lower penalty and service fees, and, particularly now when banking fees are on the rise, they are definitely worth considering; if your own company doesn't have a credit union, check whether your parents' place of employment has one that you might be eligible to join.

Evaluate service, convenience, fees, and interest rates when shopping for a financial institution you can bank on. You want your savings to earn the highest interest rate possible and your loans or credit cards to carry the lowest rate possible. You also want no-fee checking, if you can get it. Remember the triple whammy women face? As a group, we tend to live longer, earn less, and save half as much as men do. Every penny you save will help you beat those odds and achieve a secure retirement. Your saving starts here, with the first financial decision you make: which financial institution you choose.

Before you open an account, find out about min-imum balance requirements and service charges. Look at the full schedule of fees: monthly fees, fees for each check written, ATM fees, monthly mainte-nance fee, fee for exceeding the number of monthly transactions, fee for below-minimum balance, bounced-check fees, stop-payment fees. Then con-sider how you will use the checking account. What is your money style? Do you write a lot of checks every month? Find an account that doesn't have a per-check charge. Find out whether the institution offers online bill payment, and if so, what it charges for the service. Can you save money by paying your bills online and cutting back on the number of checks that you write? If you're a student, look for a bank that offers free student checking.

money. Another popular strategy for avoiding ATM fees: when you use your ATM card to pay for groceries at the supermarket or to buy stamps at the post office, ask for money back if you need cash.

>> Keep alert—some banks are beginning to charge their own customers for ATM withdrawals at their own machines, and an even higher fee if you use the ATM at another bank.

>> Don't overdo it. ATMs make spending far too easy. Try this exercise: Add up all those $20 and $40 withdrawals you make in an average week. That's the amount you've gone over your budget. Instead, figure out how much cash you'll need for the week, make one withdrawal on Friday night or Saturday morning, and stick to it. Keep track of how you spend the cash. The next time you find yourself in front of an ATM, ask yourself: Would I walk into a bank and cash a check for the amount I'm about to withdraw?

>> Always be aware of your physical safety when using an ATM. Protect your PIN number, and remember to take your card with you before you leave.

Use the Web to narrow your choices. Thanks to the Web, it's easier than ever to compare services, interest rates, and penalty fees for all types of financial institutions. Start by visiting www.

Tip: Before you sign up for overdraft protection in the form of a line of credit, ask the bank how you will be expected pay off the amount you borrow. Some banks treat the overdraft as a cash advance, and you get a monthly statement (like a credit-card statement), which requires only a minimum payment. There can be a time lapse between the advance and the arrival of the statement, meaning that you might end up paying 18 percent on a $500 advance for two to three weeks. This can only get you deeper in debt. Find a bank that will deduct the full amount you owe from the first bank deposit you make after the advance, to pay off the entire amount (including the interest) that you

bankrate.com. Though they might not seem as convenient as your local branch bank, credit unions and online banks are definitely worth considering in the mix. Both generally are able to offer lower banking fees and higher interest rates on savings accounts.

Cut the cost of bill-paying. This is increasingly becoming a paperless society. Get used to it. If you become accustomed to paying your bills online, you'll save money on the cost of re-ordering checks. You'll also escape the fees that some companies are beginning to charge for mailing and bill-payment processing. When you do order checks, save money by buying them from private companies, instead of directly from your bank. Don't worry, they will meet all national standards. Be sure to double-check your account number, name, and address when you receive them, just as you would if your own bank produced them for you. Even Wal-Mart (www.walmartchecks.com) sells checks now. You can find companies that sell checks by doing an "order checks" search online.

Ways to Pay the Piper. Cash is nice but it moves fast. Always remember to record your

ATM withdrawals immediately. As a backup, establish online access to your checking account and double check your written record against the online record on a nightly or weekly basis.

Writing checks creates a paper trail of where your money was spent. Make sure you write this information on the check stub or check register before you sign the check: what the check was for and to whom it was made out.

You can use your credit cards to give yourself a free 30-day loan, as long as you pay off the balance before the "grace period" is over and interest is charged. Be aware that grace periods have dropped considerably from 30 days to as low as 15 in some cases. Collect your credit-card receipts and use them to verify your monthly charges; mistakes (and identity theft) can occur.

Using a debit card to pay for goods or services is just like writing a check: the amount is

> **Tip:** An ATM can be very useful if you are taking a trip, especially overseas. Use your ATM card, and you'll get a better exchange rate and avoid the fees associated with traveler's checks. Ask your bank for a list of banks that are compatible with your ATM card in the country you will be visiting before you leave.

deducted from your checking account. As with your ATM withdrawals, be sure to record your purchases immediately in your checkbook. You don't want to bounce any checks.

And then there are online bill-paying services—not your grandmother's payment method (though she might love this new wrinkle). These services are a terrific money-management and time-saving tool and well worth the minimal fee that you may have to pay for them.

Check to see if your bank offers one and whether you are eligible to have the fee waived. (Some banks offer the service for free to customers who keep a certain amount in their accounts.) Yahoo, MSN, and Quicken also offer bill-payment services.

Use online bill-paying to schedule automatic payments of fixed expenses such as rent, mortgage payments, utility bills, insurance premiums, loan installments, etc. You control the timing of the payments, you always know when the money is going out of your account, and you can change payment dates when you have to. Online bill payment is a foolproof way to make sure that your bills are paid on time, thereby avoiding late payment fees, which have risen dramatically in the last few years, and protecting your credit rating. Again, once you've set a payment schedule, be sure to keep track of those withdrawals by recording them in your checkbook. That part is not automatic. Though there will always be an online record as a backup, you need to know how much is in your account before you write a paper check.

Cash flow a fizzle? Is there more month than money? Then you have two choices: increase your income (ask for a raise, take a second job, create income through a hobby) or reduce your spending. Look carefully at your expenses. Do you need that $3.50 latte every day? Could you survive without cable TV? Think about it: Aren't most of your favorite shows available for rent on DVD? How much could you reduce spending by taking lunch to work several times a week?

Get Back in Touch With Your Girlhood Dreams

Okay. You've opened a bank account—a place to stash your cash and make it work for you. Have you thought about what you're working toward? Goals are just another word for dreams. Remember the little girl inside you? It's up to you to find a way to make her dreams—or your new ones—come true. Realistic financial goals do several things: They establish a framework for financial stability. They help you to utilize your income to its best advantage. They act as a brake on excessive spending, or any other behavior that might put your goals in jeopardy.

Goals aren't something you pick up at the supermarket. You have to look deep inside yourself to figure out what you value, what you want to get from life, and what you want to contribute in

ATM Doesn't Stand For "At Their Mercy"

Doesn't it always seem like there's an ATM within reach whenever you're thinking about spending money? There's no doubt that the ubiquitous nature of these money machines has made it harder for us to stick to our budgets. But ATM doesn't stand for "At Their Mercy"!

When the automated teller machine most convenient for me to use during the workweek upped its transaction fee from $1.50 to $1.75 (I've heard that some charge as much as $2.50), I said, "That's it!" Now I make it my policy to walk the extra block to one that charges no fee. I know someone else who always asks for cash back when she uses her debit card at the supermarket so she doesn't find herself at the mercy of an exorbitant fee-charging ATM later in the week. And, remember, just because you have money in your checking account doesn't mean you have to spend it!

What's the Rush?

Now there's a card to help those whose credit history makes it difficult for them to open a bank account or get a credit card. The brainchild of def poetry/hip hop mogul Russell Simmons, this card, called the Rush Prepaid Visa Card, is "just like a credit card—without the debt." It offers an alternative to expensive check-cashing agencies, which often charge as much as 20 percent per check for their services.

Rush cardholders can have their employer deposit paychecks directly into their account, or add funds through a money order or wire transfer, then use the card to pay bills, charge items, or withdraw cash at more than 780,000 ATMs worldwide. Detailed statements of all activity are provided. You can only spend what you have, and the only fees are an initial $19.95 activation fee, plus a $1 fee per Visa transaction. There are no minimum income requirements, and no credit check or security deposit is required; you must be a U.S. resident.

To find out more about it, visit www.rush card.com.

Be a Calculating Woman:

Conquer Your Fear of Numbers—And Balance Your Checkbook!

By Elizabeth Kaminsky

Your palms are sweating. Your pulse races. You squirm. You fidget. You feel sickly. Where are you, exactly? Next in line for an upside-down mega-coaster ride? At the opening of a new Stephen King movie? Or, are you perched at your kitchen table, calculator in hand, with your tax forms and your checkbook set out in front of you?

It may seem ridiculous to think math phobia is an issue for today's woman, but, for many women, it still is. How can otherwise strong, competent women be paralyzed by a column of (gasp) numbers? Perhaps the fear is fueled by the myths of childhood. When we were girls, the fairy tale never mentioned Cinderella comparison-shopping for the castle's toilet paper. We didn't play with stockbroker dolls, who came with a portfolio of financial assets and a killer retirement plan, instead of 40 pairs of tiny shoes and a pink convertible. And the talks some of us had with our parents were more about finding Prince Charming than becoming Princess in Charge.

Early on in school, we might have been math whiz kids. But as we grew, we were discouraged by teachers or parents from furthering our mathematical competency. I met recently with a woman I'll call Jane who was working to get her GED. She's 53, with grown children and grandchildren. She has studied and struggled twice before and has not passed the test. Jane shared with me that her father discouraged her from learning algebra, geometry or any other higher math, because she "was going to get married anyway and all that stuff would be her husband's job." Did I mention that she's divorced now and raising those grandchildren herself? For her, math is a very real demon blocking the door to earning her diploma and getting a better job.

GO FIGURE!

M-A-T-H was always a four-letter word to me. In fact, my fear of math is the reason I became a writer. Imagine my dismay when I was offered a very lucrative job as a technical writer in the finance department of a large company. My first project was preparing the company's annual report to shareholders. It was full of dastardly little devils all lined up, digits stretching into the millions in front of my dyslexic eyes. Was I intimidated? You bet. I mustered up the courage to come clean with my boss. After reminding me that she'd hired me for my writing skills, she gleefully told me that "numbers were my friends." What I found even more valuable is that she showed me—a skeptical, math-phobic writer—how to "make friends" with these foreigners.

Here are three of her tips, which still help to get me through the maze:

1. **Learn the Language of Numbers**. The "math" I was learning about on the job dealt with money. After all, isn't that the most important math any of us will need to know about? I was eager to learn all I could about money, especially since I had grown up without any. My boss began by using my strengths and encouraging me to learn the language of numbers. Every profession has its lingo, and finance or money management are no exception. Get yourself a good reference book that explains things in plain English, like Jean Chatzky's *Talking Money* or Jane Quinn's *Making the Most of Your Money*.

   When you learn the language, you will start to see some key concepts that make sense elsewhere in life. I figured out that the company's net profit numbers were somewhat like the balance in my checking account (except that, in my case, it was sometimes a "net loss"). Learning the language is critical to slaying the dragons of numerical nervousness. Think about it—

learned to cook, you learned a language that included new terminology. When you learned to drive, the same thing happened. Any specialized activity in life has its vernacular, and you can become fluent in it. Every profession has its lingo, and finance or money management are no exception.

2. **Understand That It's All About Relationships.** We all know the saying, "It's all relative." That's certainly true when dealing with numbers. We may not think about numbers as having anything to do with relationships or trends, but they do. Since most women have keen abilities to manage relationships and spot trends, we are naturals for mastering these little monsters. Some tricks my boss taught me may be helpful to you. For example, looking at the big picture, then describing it in words, helped to lift my fog. I could pick out the amount of dividends paid from one quarter to the next and see where the numbers were headed. Were they going up or down? Did they stay the same? Using my newly acquired finance-language

skills, I began to unravel what these trends were telling me. How the numbers related to one another told a story, and that was something I could understand.

3. **Take a Chance on Yourself.** That boss of mine did a wonderful thing—she took a chance on me. I say take a chance on yourself when it comes to conquering your fear of numbers. The biggest fear for most of us is fear of the unknown. Learn the language of numbers. Read, watch, or listen to the financial news. Ask questions. Be a sponge. Invest in yourself. Take charge of your financial education. When you do, you'll find there's nothing to be afraid of. Numbers truly are your friends; they are tools you can use to help you manage your money better.

Remember that even if our jobs don't call directly for math skills, we use those skills expertly every day when we figure out a markdown price, leave a tip at a restaurant, or double a recipe. We pay bills, we budget, we comparison shop for the best deal. When you put numbers in the context of your life, you'll find that you really are good at math, after all.

life. One of my biggest mistakes was not setting any financial goals. Because I wasn't saving for anything in particular, I ended up spending almost every penny I made.

Start by asking yourself, "What is important to me?" Make a list of everything that matters to you, and organize the items in order of priority: getting an education, owning a home, having a family, taking a trip around the world, establishing a foundation to aid the homeless. Unless you're Oprah Winfrey—whose $1 billion net worth qualified her to become the first African American woman to appear on *Forbes'* list of billionaires in 2003—you're going to have to make some hard choices about how you spend your money. Establishing goals and priorities will help make those choices easier; once you've committed to going for one of your goals, your spending and saving choices will become automatic.

There are three types of goals:

A *short-term goal* is something you want to do within the next year: It might be paying off a credit card balance, or saving up money so you can pay cash for your holiday gifts this year,

WOMAN TO WOMAN:
THREE TIPS FOR KEEPING TRACK OF YOUR MONEY

Write it Down: Most of us get into checkbook trouble for the things we forget to record in our register. If you don't carry a checkbook, but use your ATM card instead, keep an index card to write down what you have deposited and what you've spent. Say you can't find the time to do this little chore? How about doing it when you are waiting in line, commuting to work, sitting in the doctor's office? Or make a date with yourself every night in front of the computer, and record the day's transactions listed online in your check recorder.

Round It Off: Accountants everywhere are cringing right now, but don't drive yourself nuts over a few cents. If you spent $23.56 at the drugstore, write down that you spent $24. Yes, you'll be off when you try to reconcile with your bank statement. But what you are really doing is building a little cushion for yourself to help cover those items that may have slipped your mind, like a bank account fee or a small purchase. Some women I know deliberately "short" themselves for emergencies. For example: Bea deposits $750 at the beginning of the month, but only records $650 in her checkbook. She pays her bills and lives her life based on the $650 figure. She says this method of hiding it from herself has saved her countless times. Once a year, she treats herself to something with part of her built-in emergency fund.

Use What Works for You: There are many methods for keeping track of your monthly finances, with or without a checkbook. Decide what's best for your skills and interests. Some people do quite well using cash and envelopes for all of the expenses they have identified, i.e. an envelope for food, one for utilities, one for rent, one for transportation, etc. When they cash their paycheck, they put amounts of cash in each of the envelopes to cover those expenses, and then pay the bills with money orders. Others prefer the more traditional checkbook approach, which looks something like this:

BALANCE FROM LAST MONTH: $130.00

	DEPOSITS	WITHDRAWALS	BALANCE
Deposit pay	$800		$930
Check 252		$350.00	$580
ATM withdrawal		$100.00	$480
Check 253		$290.00	$190
Monthly account fee		$3.00	$187

With this method, the last number in the "Balance" column is what you have left after bills are paid and deposits are made. Most preprinted registers that come with checkbooks are set up to work this way.

—*Elizabeth Kaminsky*

instead of charging everything. Maybe you want to splurge on a state-of-the-art music system or a digital camera. A *mid-term goal* is something with a three-to-five-year time horizon: renting a larger apartment, perhaps, or buying a new car; paying off your college debts or saving for a trip down the Nile. *Long-term goals* cover major expenses, such as buying a home, education for the kids or yourself, and your own financial security in retirement. And buying a home should be at the top on your list right now.

Your first and most important short-term goal should be establishing an emergency fund— enough money to pay for auto repairs, unreimbursed medical costs, and your living expenses for six months, in the event that you're laid off or become ill. Such emergencies, without the reserves ready to pay for them, could force you to increase your credit obligations. That, in turn, would add to your fixed obligations each month, giving you more to pay, more to worry about, and less for savings and discretionary spending. Your goals and needs will, no doubt, change as you grow and change, and the size of your emergency fund will increase as you add more financial responsibilities. You're not locked into a specific goal. But, by the same token, you should never use the money set aside for a mid- or long-term goal to pay for something you want now.

Plan to Spend— Create a Spending Plan

That's just another, nicer, term for budget. Your spending plan defines your lifestyle and reflects your goals and values. Think of it as your roadmap to achieving your dreams, your plan for paying for what you need now and saving for what you want in the future.

Before you prepare a spending plan, you need to measure your current cash flow: How much money you have coming in and going out. Money comes into your household in two ways: You earn it by working, and you put your money to work for you, earning interest and dividends. It goes out of your household like water leaving a sieve, unless you plug some holes. Track your income and expenses for two or three months. Play detective and learn where your money is going, so that you can start making conscious choices about how to best use what you earn to your advantage.

Here's how to start: First, figure out what income you can expect to receive every month: If you are just starting out, on your own for the first time, your income will probably come primarily from wages; interest and dividends from investments, if any; and family contributions, if any. Check your pay-stub and look at the take-home, or net, amount, after taxes, Social Security, and other deductions have been taken out. That's what you have to work with. Then, divide your expenses into two categories: fixed and flexible expenses.

Fixed expenses include rent or mortgage, utilities, transportation costs, insurance premiums, and loan repayments. Reviewing your checkbook can help you pinpoint your fixed expenses. Flexible expenses might include food (at-home and restaurant) clothing, dry cleaning, entertainment, recreation (dues to a gym), etc. Did you take $100 from the ATM on Friday and catch yourself wondering where the money went, when you can't afford a bagel on Monday morning? To find out where it all went, get in the habit of keeping a notebook or PDA in your car or pocketbook and immediately record whatever you spend. It's your flexible expenses that you'll have to eyeball to find ways to cut back so that you can fund a

WOMAN TO WOMAN:
QUICK TIP FOR
CALCULATING TIPS

Use this handy rule of thumb when figuring out how much to tip in a restaurant. Since I used to be a waitress, I usually tip 20 percent. If the bill is $32.40, I move the decimal point one space to the left, then double the number: $3.24 + $3.24 = $6.48. For simplicity's sake, I'd probably round that up to $6.50.

—*Elizabeth Kaminsky*

savings account. Your credit-card bills will help identify flexible expenses.

Some other tips for making this process easier: When you're tracking your expenses, round figures up or down to keep your accounting simple. *Don't* nickel and dime it. If you let yourself get caught up in the small change, you'll go crazy. Here's another tip: Try using a personal-finance software program like Quicken (www.quicken. com) to help you keep track of your expenses.

During the two or three months that you're tracking your expenses, also take time to think about where you want to be in six months, three years, and ten years. Write down specific short-, mid-, and long-term goals, and decide how much you will need to save to make them a reality. Calculators are available online (visit www. bankrate.com or www.finaid.com) to help you figure out how much you need to save each month to hit a target in a certain amount of time.

When it's time to sit down and create your new spending plan or budget, *don't* go by what others spend. Establish your own priorities. They might be very different from your roommate's or the person at the next desk. Don't expect miracles. A spending plan is a tool to help you manage your money more efficiently. It will not give you more money or cut your expenses by itself. The choices you make determine that. Finally, *don't* be inflexible. Circumstances change. Be ready and willing to evaluate, revise, and adjust your spending plan to meet your needs.

Sherry found that she had to move back home for two years after college, when she couldn't find a full-time position. "It wasn't easy moving back in with my parents." But she got a part-time job, lived frugally, and was able to save enough money to put a down payment on a new car and fund an emergency account. "I didn't pay rent, but I paid for my own phone line and some of the groceries. When I finally got a full-time position, I was thrilled to get out and into my own apartment." Now that she has a full-time job, she has 8 percent automatically deducted from each paycheck and invested in a retirement fund. She did all of this by realizing the value of saving.

Become a "Bill" Collector

Collect dollar bills, 20s, 50s and 100s, with the same passion that you might once have collected cashmere sweaters, Barbie dolls, or stamps. Money is what will buy you both your short- and long-term security. Once you understand that and the reasons why women must save early and often, saving will become a habit. You'll actually start to crave savings.

Now that you know how much you need to save to reach your goals—short-, mid-, and long-term—it's time to put your spending plan into

---

THE TWO MOST EXPENSIVE WORDS IN THE ENGLISH LANGUAGE: "IT'S ONLY"...

As in "It's only $20" or "It's ONLY $99.95." Used by consumers to justify purchases they want but don't really need and often can't really afford, and by advertisers to entice consumers into buying their products. True, it's ONLY money, but we ONLY have so many years to save for our kids' college and our own retirement!

action. Don't fall for the trap of opening a different account for each goal (vacation, holiday, mortgage downpayment, etc.); you'll earn more interest in one large account than you will from three smaller ones.

Most important, learn to pay yourself first. In other words, treat your savings as a bill from your future self to your current self and pay that bill before you pay any others.

To find the money to save, look at your flexible expenses and finds ways to cut back. "How do I do that?" I can hear you asking. You have to start somewhere. Maybe you'll have to delay buying a new computer, or drive your current car for another few years. And you'll be surprised how small changes to your daily spending habits can make a big difference. If you are not in the habit of saving, make it easy on yourself by having a set amount withheld from your paycheck every month and direct-deposited into a savings account or transferred from checking to savings. Find an amount you are comfortable with, and then slowly increase it. Save part of your bonus and all of your tax refund. When you get your next raise, put the difference in savings.

No matter how tight your budget is, saving is possible. The secret is simple: you've got to sweat the small stuff. As James McWhinney, who became a homeowner at 17, said in an article for MAKING BREAD, "Major expenses aren't what keep people living paycheck to paycheck. It's the small stuff. That 99 cents per day spent on coffee, the $5.50 for lunch, and the $3.95 for a magazine quickly add up to hundreds of dollars a month and thousands of dollars a year. Just $2 a day adds up to $62 a month, $744 a year. Add that to the daily cost of a fast-food lunch, and you've got several thousand dollars that can go

into your 401(k) or other savings account."

It's not how much you make, but how much you spend that counts. "Spend less than you earn," says McWhinney. "That's it. No magic tricks, no get-rich-quick schemes. Just live within your means." Doesn't that sound just like a guy? No nonsense, no sympathy, just cut to the chase. He's right that there aren't any magic tricks—unless you count the mind games you can play with yourself. Keep that image of the young girl you once were in your head. Are you taking care of her? Are you working toward fulfilling her dreams and creating a safe retirement for her? We know how hard saving can be, but it's even harder getting out of debt once you've amassed a fortune in debt. Throughout this book, you'll find the stories of women who found ways to change their spending habits. We hope they serve as inspiration for you.

Where do you put your savings? For your short-term savings—money that you might need to tap into for emergencies—you have several account options, outlined below. Each offers easy liquidity, or the ability to withdraw your money when you need to use it. When selecting a savings account, follow the same process you used in choosing a bank: look for the highest interest paid and the lowest service fees charged. As you did in your search for a bank, you may find the best savings deals online or at a credit union.

SAFE KEEPING FOR YOUR SAVINGS
Because it's important to know your savings will be accessible when and if you need it, you'll want to put your just-in-case money into low-risk accounts that don't penalize you for withdrawals. Your best options include:

Savings and Money-Market Accounts. The interest offered on these accounts is very low today, but they provide quick access to your money. Don't keep your emergency savings in your checking account. Even if it pays you interest, you'll be tempted to spend it. And in most cases, the interest you'll earn in a savings account will be higher than that paid on funds kept in a checking account.

Rates on passbook savings accounts (think of them as your grandmother's savings account) are extremely low. The only advantages they offer are ease of withdrawal and, in most cases, very low minimum deposits (sometimes as low as $5). You're better off keeping your savings in a money-market account, which you can access by writing checks (the number you can write per month could be limited) and, in some cases, even by ATM withdrawals.

Money-market accounts offered by banks and mutual-fund companies have slightly higher rates than savings accounts. Bank money-market accounts are almost always federally insured by the Federal Deposit Insurance Corporation, or FDIC. (This federal agency was established after the Great Depression, when many banks closed their doors, and it protects up to $100,000 of savers' investments.) Mutual-fund money market accounts are insured by the Securities Investors Protection Corporation (SIPC) up to $500,000 in securities and $100,000 in cash, but only against theft or unauthorized trading and only in the event the brokerage firm that manages the account goes under. You'll usually need a minimum dollar amount of $500 to $2,500 to open up a money-market account.

If you decide to open a savings account or money-market account at your bank, make sure that the minimum balance requirements are reasonable. If you can't manage them, any interest could be offset by service charges. Another factor to consider when selecting an account is how interest is calculated. Find out whether it's compounded daily, weekly, quarterly, or annually. The more often interest is compounded, the higher the rate of return.

If you decide to open a money-market account with a mutual-fund company rather than a bank (not a bad idea, frankly, because they tend to be more generous when it comes to interest), make sure you read all the fine print. Check the minimum required to open the account and the number of withdrawals you are allowed to make over a given period of time, as well as the maximum amounts of such withdrawals. Comparison shop for lowest rates and fees before making your selection. You can do this easily at www.bankrate.com. Vanguard (www.vanguard.com) and Fidelity (www.

One thing you can do right now ...

PAY YOURSELF FIRST

Treat the amount you put in your savings every week as a bill from your future self to your current self, and pay that bill before you pay any others. The most painless way to do that is to make it automatic: set up a direct deposit from your paycheck to your savings account, and you won't even see the money you're putting away. Out of sight, out of mind. It works!

fidelity.com) are examples of mutual-fund companies that offer money markets.

Certificates of Deposit. CDs pay a higher rate of interest than money markets, but they don't allow you quick access to your money. Banks offer CDs for a specific time period: 90 days, six months, a year, all the way up to five years. If you need the money before the CD matures, your bank will penalize you for taking an early withdrawal. If you have several thousand dollars saved for emergencies, you could "ladder" your money, or invest it in CDs of varying maturities. That way, you'll earn higher interest and still have a shot at having some money available when you need it.

Check out www.bankrate.com for an up-to-date list of CD interest rates around the country. You'll find that some local banks offer better rates than the larger national banks. If you're considering one that's out of state, make sure that it accepts out-of-state deposits.

Online banks, such as E-Trade (www.etrade.com) and ING DIRECT (www.ingdirect.com), also tend to offer very competitive rates. If you belong to a credit union where you work, that's a likely source for an attractive rate.

Short-Term Treasury Securities. The U.S. government offers Treasury bills for the short-term saver. They are backed by the full faith and credit of the U.S. government. Bills come in minimum denominations of $1,000. They can be purchased from any commercial bank, on-line broker, or directly from the Treasury. To open an account through the Treasury Direct program, look in your local phone book under federal government for the nearest Federal Reserve Bank. Maturity for Treasury bills is less than a year. You can purchase them for 13 weeks or 26 weeks.

Treasury bills are offered at a discount from face value. A $1,000 Treasury bill is purchased for less than $1,000, but the Treasury pays the full $1,000 at maturity. The difference between what you pay and what the U.S. Treasury pays back at maturity is the interest earned. The interest is taxed by the federal government but not by the states. For more information on T-bills, check out www.publicdebt.treas. gov and www.investinginbonds.com.

Short-Term Bond Mutual Funds. Mutual funds that invest in bonds have greater earning potential than CDs, but also more risk. Still, they are less risky than stock funds. When interest rates go up, bond rates go down and vice versa. A bond fund might be a good place to stash cash for a longer-term emergency account, if you're comfortable with the possibility that your funds may fluctuate in value.

Spread the Wealth. Once you've built up your emergency account, you don't have to put it all in one place. Using the laddering technique described above, you might deposit one or two months' savings in a money-market account and the balance in a short-term CD or Treasury bill, with each of them maturing at a different time. Having a rainy-day fund is especially important in today's uncertain economic climate. Start by depositing small amounts every payday and just keep adding to it, increasing the amount whenever you can. You'll be thankful when the rainy days come. As sure as April showers bring spring flowers, they will.

Wherever you stash your cash, arrange to have a certain amount withdrawn from each paycheck to go into the account. What you don't see, you don't spend.

For mid- and long-term goals, you'll want to put your money in high interest-bearing accounts that offer some tax advantages. These will most likely include stock and bond mutual funds, IRAs, 401(k) plans and, if you have children, 529 college savings plans.

Secure your future

It's difficult (Ok, it's virtually impossible) to envision yourself as a retiree when you're starting out in your first job. But the earlier you plan for a secure retirement, the better off you'll be. If you start early, you can amass a small fortune by saving relatively small amounts. It's your choice: Invest $500 a year (that's less than $10 a week) for 10 years, starting at age 20, in a stock mutual fund earning an annual return of 10 percent. Even if you don't put a penny more in after age 30, at age 65 your investment of $5,000 will have grown to nearly $250,000. Double your annual investment to $1,000 (or $20 a week—that's a cappuccino a day) and you'll have nearly half a million dollars at retirement. *Or* wait until you're 40 to begin saving $500 a year. If you stop after 10 years, you'll end up with a measly $37,000 when you're 65. To make up for the lost years of compound interest, you'd have to invest $6,000 a year, or more than $115 a week to come up with $250,000 at retirement.

Start with your 401(k). The best place to start is by participating in your employer's retirement plan, if there is one. In the typical 401(k) plan, a percentage of your pay is deducted from your paycheck before taxes, immediately reducing your taxable income. While the money is in the plan, it grows without being taxed. Only when

you begin to make withdrawals (after age $59\frac{1}{2}$) will it be taxed. Many employers match your contributions with as much as 50 cents on the dollar, up to six percent of your pretax salary. If you don't take advantage of those matching contributions, you're passing up free money. Women cannot afford to pass up *any* money!

Let's say your salary is $35,000. Assuming

HOW DOES THAT GREEN STUFF GROW?

Thanks to the power of compound interest, every dollar you save becomes a dollar *plus* the percent interest your savings earns. Compound interest is paid on the original amount you put in (called the "principal") and on the accumulated past interest, and every month, when the interest is calculated and added to the pot, the pot grows bigger. This allows your nest egg to keep on growing, even if you don't keep putting money in. And it's why you should try to avoid taking money out of a savings account, because the more money you have in it, the more interest you will earn. Below, see how your money can grow over 30 years, assuming an 8 percent interest rate, compounded monthly. (Tax consequences aren't reflected.)

MONTHLY SAVINGS	5 YEARS	10 YEARS	20 YEARS	30 YEARS
$50	$3,698	$9,208	$29,647	$75,015
$200	$14,793	$36,833	$118,589	$300,059
$500	$36,983	$92,008	$296,474	$750,148

annual 5 percent raises, contributions of 6 percent, an employer match of 3 percent, and an interest rate of 8 percent, you could have $370,677 in 25 years. Just be sure to heed the lessons of Enron, and select a diversified fund; never invest it all in company stock. (Do some fortune telling by trying www.bankrate.com's 401(k) calculator to see how much you'll have at retirement, given your current contributions.) See "Best Places to 'Retire' Your Money" in Chapter Six for more detailed information on 401(k) accounts. If your employer doesn't offer a retirement plan, then you've got to create your own. Think IRA.

Open an IRA. How much do you have to stash at 8 percent to have $100,000 in your IRA by the time you're 50? Let's assume that you have 30 years to save: you'll need to put away $835 annually. That's nothing! Wait 10 years to begin your retirement savings plan and you'll have to save $2,110 each year. Big difference, so don't delay.

Should you put your money in a Roth or a traditional IRA? In general, if you anticipate being in a high tax bracket at retirement (and if you start saving for retirement early, you will be), a Roth, in which withdrawals are not taxed but contributions (made when you are earning less) are, makes the most sense. (Read Chapter Ten for more information on investing for your retirement.)

Retire those college loans

Thousands of students graduate from college every May, degrees in hand and debts on their mind. Studies show that 65 percent of new graduates are up to their eyeballs in debt. Most will face their financial obligations with little if any financial

management skills or training. (According to a Jump$tart Coalition for Financial Literacy survey, 60 percent of high-school seniorss failed a financial-literacy exam last year.) Add to these worries the tight labor market and, instead of elation, there is frustration. It's a quick course in growing up. And women are among the most affected.

Owe, what a bill! Now that you've got your spending plan in place and have started to think about retirement, it's time to concentrate on retiring your student loan. The bill comes due six months after graduation, unless you've dropped out, in which case you start paying back the loan immediately.

According to Nellie Mae, a New England educational foundation that administers grant programs, the average education debt is $18,900—up 16 percent from 1997. The average monthly undergraduate debt payment is $182. When you factor in graduate-school loans, the number rises to a monthly average of $261. Graduates who pay 7 percent of their gross monthly income toward paying off their student loans feel their debt is manageable. However, the debt-to-income ratio of one-third of graduates is a whopping 12 percent. Obviously, those with higher rates of debt are feeling the pinch.

If you're having difficulty paying your student loans, contact the loan agency immediately. Most providers are willing to work out a mutually beneficial repayment schedule. If you're a teacher serving in a low-income or subject-matter short-

> Tip: If you marry right after graduation and are thinking about consolidating your loans with your spouse's, don't. If the marriage dissolves, you'll both still be liable for this joint loan—and if your spouse defaults, you alone will carry the full burden.

age area, it may even be possible for you to cancel or defer your student loans. Stafford loans are forgiven and paid off if a graduate agrees to work as an educator in a teacher-shortage area for five consecutive years. For further information on loan forgiveness, repayment of loans and loan management, check out the Student Guide at www.ed.gov.

There are several ways to structure your repayment:

Under the **Standard Repayment**, you make principal and interest payments each month throughout your loan term. Your payment never changes (unless you have a variable-rate loan). This plan lets you pay the least total amount of interest.

Graduated Repayment. The Graduated Repayment lets you make smaller payments in the early years, when you might be earning less money, but still requires repayment within the

Standard Repayment period, usually ten years. Initial interest-only monthly payments can be more than 40 percent lower than payments made with the Standard Repayment plan. But later payments balloon to make up the difference.

Hardship Repayment Plans. For those who are experiencing serious financial hardship, Income Sensitive Repayment and Income Contingent Repayment Plans are available. These two plans deal exclusively with the Federal Direct Loan Program. Payments are a fixed percentage of your income and the loan repayment is 15 years with the Sensitive Repayment Plan, and 25 years for the Income Contingent Plan. You must reapply annually to qualify.

Loan Consolidation. Something every graduate should consider, depending on prevailing interest rates, is loan consolidation. Under this strategy, all eligible (and most are) federal loans are combined into a single loan with a single monthly payment, under a new fixed rate, based on the average of all the loans being consolidated. This rate can't exceed 8.25 percent. Consolidate before your six-month grace period is up, and you'll be eligible for the much lower in-school interest rate set by the government every July, but you must begin repaying right away, so it's probably a good idea to postpone your application until a month or so before your grace period is up. Once approved, your old loans are paid off by the issuer of the new loan, and you begin making one payment to that lender. This type of loan usually offers the lowest monthly payments for the longest period of time.

Take the tax break. You can deduct all the interest you pay on your college loans, up to

$2,500. You are not eligible for this deduction if you are claimed as a dependent on your parent's return. The maximum allowable deduction is gradually reduced for single taxpayers whose incomes exceed $50,000 ($100,000 for married, filing jointly) and is not available for singles with incomes over $65,000 ($130,000 for married, filing jointly). In January of each year, you will receive a 1098-E form from the lending institution, indicating how much interest was paid during the year. You can claim the deduction even if you don't itemize.

EXTRA (COLLEGE) CREDIT

Dear MAKING BREAD,

I'm graduating in May. With my commencement comes the hard realization that I will finally have to pay off all my loans. Yikes! I once heard that if graduates take government jobs, the government will pay off their Stafford loans. Is this true?
—Loan-some in Philadelphia

Dear Loan-some,
Sorry to have to debunk that rumor: According to Jane Glickman from the National Department of Education (www.nea.org), it's not true. "There are simply too many people who work for the government," says Glickman. Think what our deficit would be, if we paid off all those loans!

What the Department of Education does offer is something called "loan forgiveness." Stafford loans are forgiven and paid off if a graduate agrees to work as an educator in a teacher-shortage area—for instance, at an inner-city school—for five consecutive years. "We need good teachers in high poverty areas," Glickman says. "If you want to make a difference, there are provisions for that."

For further information on loan forgiveness, repayment of loans and loan management, check out the Student Guide at www.ed.gov.

Finance questions got you stumped on campus? Submit your EXTRA (COLLEGE) CREDIT questions to editor@makingbreadmagazine. com, and one of our interns will track down the answer.

Get your credit under control

The average debt among the 78 percent of college students who carry credit cards is $2,748—and 13 percent owe up to $7,000. Women tend to leave college carrying more credit-card debt than men do, according to Consolidated Credit Counseling Services, a non-profit group based in Fort Lauderdale, Florida. If you're carrying a lot of cards with high balances, make a concerted effort to pay off the ones that have the highest interest rates, first. Systematically up the amount you pay down on the balance each month.

Always pay more than the minimum, and *always* pay on time to avoid late fees. If you have a hard time paying more than the minimum, it's time to cut up your credit cards. Once they're paid off, cancel all but one of your cards, which you can use for emergencies. Remember this rule: "If you can't pay cash, then you can't buy it." Not convinced? Here's a hair-raising example: If you pay $50 on a credit-card balance of $2,500 the first month (2 percent of the bill), then continue to make your 2 percent minimum monthly payment each month after that, it will take you 28 years to pay off the balance, and you'll end up paying $5,896 in interest. It doesn't take a Rhodes Scholar to figure out that's not a good deal.

Know your score. It's crucial to have a good credit score. This "report card" will impact everything from your ability to rent an apartment and purchase utilities to getting a good mortgage interest rate. These days, even your insurance rates are affected by your credit score. Your credit rating is established the moment your first credit-card application is approved. The three major credit bureaus collect data on all of your credit accounts: The types of loans that are outstanding, how many cards you have (the more you have the more of a credit risk you are considered to be), how long you've had them, your balance, whether or not you pay on time, whether you've missed payments. This information is recorded in your credit file and made available to prospective creditors—and even prospective employers, who may use it to determine whether you would be a reliable employee. Not only credit-card companies report on your creditworthiness; utilities, hospitals, landlords, and banks all give you "grades."

Every woman should have credit in her own name. If you're married, then divorce, you don't want to have to play catch up, establishing a credit history at a time when you may need credit more than you ever have before. The way to establish a good credit history is to borrow money and pay it back. Negative entries in your credit report stick around for a long time. If you miss a payment or are late with a payment, the fact will remain on your credit history for the next seven years.

To check your credit score—something you should do at least once a year to ensure its accuracy—contact any of the three credit bureaus: Equifax (1-800-685-1111; www.equifax.com); Experian (1-800-397-3742; www.experian.com) or TransUnion (1-800916-8800; www.tuc.com). The Fair and Accurate Credit Transactions Act, signed in December 2003, mandates one free credit report a year from each of the three major credit bureaus. To get it, go to www.annualcreditreport.com. We are also eligible to receive a free report whenever we are denied credit, insurance, or a job as a result of a poor score; when we are on welfare or unemployed and looking for work; and whenever there is an inaccuracy as a result of fraudulent activity, such as ID theft, on our report.

Limit your tax hit

Your employer will give you a W-4 form to fill out, listing the number of "personal allowances" you want to claim. This figure is used to determine the amount of taxes that will be withheld from your paycheck each pay period—something called "payroll withholding." Taxes are taken out before you receive your wages, deposited in an IRS account, and credited to you when you file your return. If you figure your allowances correctly, you should neither owe a great deal nor receive a big refund. You want to avoid sending excess money to the IRS. Even though you get it back in the form of a refund later, it's more valuable to you, earning interest in your savings account now, than earning interest for Uncle Sam.

Generally, you claim one allowance for yourself, one for your spouse, and one for each of your dependents, if you have any. However, this number can be adjusted, up or down, depending on the amount of money you earn and the number of tax deductions you claim. You can even claim zero and ask that extra be taken out, if you find that you owe too much come April. If you end up with a big refund, increase your allowances, so that less is taken out.

If you're starting out, you'll probably have just yourself as a dependent and will claim one allowance. If you're working two jobs, you'll need to update your W-4 to avoid owing more at tax time. You should usually increase the amount withheld from your primary paycheck. You can ask your payroll office to change the amount deducted at any time. Check the withholding calculator at www.irs.gov to figure out how much to have your payroll department deduct.

The withholding doesn't stop there, of course. You'll also see Social Security (listed as FICA, which stands for Federal Insurance Contributions Act) withheld from your paycheck and your share of any medical benefits received through your employer. The amount deducted for Social Security is 6.1 percent of your salary, up to the base maximum earnings of $90,000. This will go to the government for future retirement benefits. Meanwhile, you are building a Social Security record of earnings. An additional 1.45 percent is deducted on all wages (no cap) to go into the Medicare Trust fund. Your employer will also deduct state taxes and 401(k) contributions, if any, from your gross income.

April 15 doesn't have to be a hassle. Figuring your income tax is made easy by software programs, such as Quicken and Turbo Tax. But you can also do it the old-fashioned way. Add up your total income. This includes your wages, interest, and dividends. Subtract your deductions. This might include a contribution to an Individual Retirement Account, a student loan interest deduction, as well as any eligible itemized deductions (medical expenses, state and local taxes, mortgage interest, charitable contributions). Then take the standard deduction of $4,750, or if your itemized deductions exceed the standard deduction, claim them, instead. As your income increases and you own a home, you will most likely use the itemized deduction. You are also allowed a personal exemption of $3,200, which is adjusted each year. Apply the tax rates on your 1040EZ form to find your tax. Subtract what has already been paid (your employer will give you a W-2 form, listing your wage and withholding) to determine the amount you owe or the amount of the refund.

If you're a procrastinator, you can request a filing extension until August 15. But that doesn't get you off the hook from paying by April 15. You are expected to estimate your tax owed and pay it anyway.

Keep alert for deductible job-related expenses. You might have to spend money on work-related items throughout the year. Keep good records, because you can claim some of these expenses as a deduction. In general, to be allowed as deductions, job-related expenses must be required by your employer, be a condition of employment, or be necessary to perform assigned responsibilities. Examples of expenses required by your employer but paid out of pocket by you might include: a physical examination, union dues, office supplies not provided on the job, professional and trade association dues, safety clothes and equipment, and any special uniforms. You will need tax form 2106 to claim these deductions.

Insure yourself

Unless you have a child or other dependent, life insurance still isn't a necessity. But health insur-

CREDIT & THE SELF-EMPLOYED SINGLE WOMAN: TRYING TO FIND MONEY IN A MAN'S WORLD

BY SABINA LOUISE PIERCE

Credit isn't something you get automatically. You have to earn it by proving you can pay it back. Sounds like a Catch-22, doesn't it? When you're young, single, and self-employed, it can feel like you've got three strikes against you, even if you think you've been a responsible, bill-paying citizen. That's the way I felt when I was establishing myself as a freelance photographer after college, and I applied for a car loan.

Most of us get our first credit card in college. Mine was from Citibank. I kept up with the payments and slowly increased my available line of credit. After I graduated, I started freelancing as a photographer. My income and clients were pretty steady, and I thought I had good enough credit to buy a car. Well, I did have good credit—and I didn't. I had no "work history," no employer, and no assets. I had only been working for myself, and I couldn't show a "salary." I was 26, a female, single, and doomed, even though my credit rating was a "10."

The bank rejected me, saying I had no large investments, and no spouse's salary, let alone a spouse to rely on. I was told that if my grandmother would agree to co-sign, they would give me the loan, but not otherwise. I took it out on the poor car salesman. I argued with him; he said I should produce receipts, bank statements, anything that showed that I made money—that would prove that I could afford a $258 monthly payment. *So I did.* I pulled out all my bank statements for the four years I had been working, and I printed out several bills and my tax statements. It was tough, but, in the end, they approved the loan.

I learned a valuable lesson from that experience: I needed assets! I needed real estate! It didn't take long to find a house that I really adored. It had been on the market for more than three months. I had driven past it a million times—it was a beautiful pre-Civil War corner row home, tucked away in an up-and-coming neighborhood in Philadelphia. It had a bakery on the first floor and was considered R-9 mixed (commercial and residential) use. With a beautiful apartment above (that needed lots of work) and commercial rental below to help me pay most of the mortgage, it was perfect for me. But when I met the realtor, he looked me over and asked whether I had a husband or parents. I laughed this off and told him that I was there alone . . . and that I was 28—not 12.

I decided to make an offer. They highballed me; I lowballed, pointing out that the place had been on the market for months, that the neighborhood could go either way. I was sorry if the previous owner had paid too much, but I wasn't going to. In the end, the realtor became my ally. He said he admired my spunk. He had a daughter my age and told me that he wished that she were more like me. Even though he represented the owner and not me, he went to bat for me, and I got the house for 30 percent less than the asking price. But I still had to get a mortgage.

Because the building was mixed use, I needed a commercial loan. Few banks do commercial loans, because they are considered risky. Complicating things even further, I was a single, self-employed woman. A mortgage broker eventually found me a 30-year mortgage with a 10 percent interest rate for the first two years, floating with the LIBOR (London Interbank Offering Rate) after that. It wasn't a great deal, but it was the only one I could afford.

I went through the process of having my financial life scrutinized, but I had done that before, so I was prepared. I signed the mortgage, and proceeded to clean out my bank accounts of the $28,000 I'd managed to save in the previous three years to cover the 30 percent down payment. And that's how I became a homeowner.

I stayed in that mortgage for the 2 years that it was fixed at 10 percent. Then I found a better loan with a small savings and loan. This time, it wasn't as much of a hassle. I had history—I had two years of paying off my house. I got a 12-year loan at 8.5 percent. My monthly payments were $20 dollars more, but I'd be paying off my loan 18 years earlier.

With seven years left on the loan, I'm now paying more principal than interest, and I think I made the right choice. Not only do I have history; I have an asset that grows in value every year. And no lender can ever prejudge me because I'm (still) single and self-employed!

SABINA'S SEVEN TIPS FOR SINGLE WOMEN
Psst ... They Work for the Rest of Us, Too!

Here are a few things I did that really helped make the difference when I applied for credit as a self-employed, single woman:

1. I made sure that every bill was paid on time.

2. I paid all my credit cards in full each month. Sometimes I even paid more than I owed.

3. I kept only a few credit cards. This shows that you are less likely to run up huge bills.

4. If I was hit with a late-payment fee, because I was a day or two late or the mail happened to be slow that week, I called up the credit-card company to remind them that I was a good customer and ask that the fee be removed. Because I never made a habit of it, they usually did it for me.

5. I checked my credit rating every year. (Visit www.annualcreditreport.com to check yours.)

6. I put all my business expenses on one credit card to prove that I could handle a large payment.

7. I saved every penny I could so that, when I bought my house, I could put 30 percent down, which helped to lower my mortgage payments.

Sabina Louise Pierce is a freelance photographer whose work has appeared in The New York Times, Vanity Fair, People, *and many other publications.*

ance is. Many of you were covered under your parents' medical plan until you were 19 or 22, if you were a full-time student. The biggest shift for the woman striking out on her own is the sudden lapse in health coverage.

Nearly 3 in 10 women are uninsured annually, according to a recent Kaiser Women's Health Survey, and that number is growing. A study conducted by George Washington University in 2001 found the number of uninsured women has grown three times faster than the number of uninsured men over the past five years. If this pace continues, the number of uninsured women will exceed the number of uninsured men for the first time in 2005.

Make finding a job that offers you medical benefits a priority. Your health is your greatest asset right now, and it pays to insure it. The cost of an emergency appendectomy, a broken leg, or car accident can wipe you out financially. Just when you're starting to become financially independent, a huge medical bill could burden you with a huge debt for many years to come.

The reality is that many of you will start out without any medical plan. The number of people between the ages of 18 to 34 without health coverage has grown to 19.9 million, accounting for 41 percent of the country's 43.6 million uninsured. Studies indicate that one-half of high school graduates who don't go to college and two out of five college graduates will spend time without insurance during their first year after graduation.

If you're one of them, look into short-term insurance options—kind of a health-insurance band-aid. They are not as comprehensive as regular health plans but they are more affordable; some can be purchased for as low as $25 per month. Two companies that offer such plans are Humana (www.humanaone.com) and Fortis (www.fortishealth.com). Compare rates and plans at www.HealthInsurance.com.

Another option to consider is the new Health Savings Account (HSA), introduced as part of the Medicare reform bill passed in 2003. These plans, previously limited to self-employed people and small business owners and their employees, are now open to virtually everyone. Think of them as medical IRAs; they are tax-deductible savings accounts linked to high-deductible (at least $1,000 for singles; $2,000 for families in 2004) medical plans, where the money saved (up to a maximum of $2,600 per year for singles; $5,150 for families in 2004) is earmarked to cover out-of-pocket expenses until the coverage from your health plan kicks in. You get the tax-deduction, health coverage, and enforced savings to cover interim expenses. Money not used continues to earn interest until it is withdrawn, tax-free, for medical reasons. Visit www.msahealthplans.com for more information.

As you progress in your career, if your employer doesn't offer it, you'll want to look into disability insurance to cover your monthly living expenses in the event that you become ill and are out of work for an extended period. Even if you are covered by your employer, ask yourself, would the amount of the coverage be enough? You might want to purchase more. Look into professional association or other group policies for the best rates.

Holly purchased a supplemental individual disability policy when she was working for a corporation. She knew it would be difficult to get it later, if she left the company and became self-employed. It turns out that she became ill and was unable to work for 14 months. Her individual policy continued to pay even when she returned to work on a part-time basis. Holly says, "I would have had to liquidate my retirement assets if I didn't have the coverage. Every working woman should consider an individual disability policy. As far as I'm concerned, it is more important than life insurance." (See "Don't Make a 'Grave' Mistake: What You Need to Know About Insurance" in Chapter Four for a discussion of policy options and what to ask before purchasing disability insurance.)

If you own a car, automobile insurance is essential. In most states, the law requires this. Shop around. Auto insurance is high-priced stuff, but there are many insurance companies competing for your business. A good approach is to work with an independent broker to get the best coverage for the lowest premium. Auto insurance rates have been rising, and premiums are often tied to your credit report as well as your driving record. So keep your credit score in good shape. Another way to reduce your rate is to opt for a high deductible.

When you are buying auto insurance, or reviewing what you have, keep these important points in mind: Like all other insurance, policies must be reviewed and updated regularly. Nothing stays the same. Premium rates vary according to age, gender, marital status, type of car, driving record, where you live, and the amount of risk you are willing to handle yourself by taking higher deductibility. Rates in big cities are usually higher than in small towns, presumably because the heavier the traffic, the more likely an accident. Married couples are charged less than singles. One advantage: men statistically have more accidents than women, so the rate you will receive as a young single woman should be less than comparable coverage for a man.

As your car ages, its value depreciates. Watch its cash value. If you keep a car for several years, there comes a time when you may consider dropping collision coverage altogether, because the annual premiums approach the replacement value of the car.

A word about buying your first car: for many women, this will be the first big-ticket item purchased. Financial expert Mark Wolfinger points out in "Are You About to Commit Vehicular Budget-cide?", an article on www.makingbread-magazine. com, that the simple act of choosing a low-priced ($10,000) car over a higher-end ($30,000) car, "will have a major impact on the rest of your financial life." Check his math: "If you buy the much less costly new or used car, your finances will look like this at the end of four years," says Wolfinger. "You invested the $422 difference in monthly payments in a savings account paying 3 percent interest, and you've accumulated $24,316. You use $7,824 (plus trade-in) of that amount to pay cash for another used car and invest the remainder in a retirement account. Maintaining the account for 41 years (until retirement), you will have $386,930, if your investments grow at 8 percent per year, and $821,029, if your investments grow at 10 percent per year."

Moral of that story: Buy a Ford, and pretend you're driving a Beemer.

As for homeowner's insurance, if you own your own home, your mortgage lender will require coverage, and you will want it. If you are renting and can afford it, consider both personal property and liability coverage. A person who falls and is injured can sue the tenant as well as the landlord. Consider also how much it would cost to replace your stolen or damaged belongings.

MY CURE FOR SHOPAHOLICS: CRAVE SAVINGS!

I shudder to confess this: I almost bought a $1,000 chess set a few years ago. What was I thinking? I don't even play chess! It had a gorgeous, sleek, ultra-modern board with a stately king and queen lording it over rows of gleaming crystal pawns, rooks, knights, and bishops. But beyond that, I can't remember for the life of me now why it captured my imagination or what made it an object of such obsessive desire for me. What I do know is that I'm *very glad* I didn't buy it. If I had, it would have sat unused on a corner table in my living room gathering dust, when instead that $1,000 could have been nesting in some bank vault gathering interest for me.

Others might boast about buying a house, getting a college education, or selling high tech before the bottom fell out of the stock market as their smartest money decisions. All of those are good choices, but, for me, resisting temptation—not buying that chess set—was one of the wisest money decisions I've ever made; it was a life-changing, "ah-ha" moment for me. To this day, I remind myself of that chess set whenever the urge to splurge strikes. You see, I'm a shopaholic. I shop when I'm depressed, when I'm happy, when I want to reward myself—probably even, subconsciously, when I want to punish myself. How much of a shopaholic am I? When I hear someone say, "good-bye" I think they're talking about a good buy. If I were a stock market analyst, "strong buy" would be the only two words I'd know. But almost buying that chess set helped me to "checkmate" my addiction. For some reason, the minute I picked up the phone to place the order, all of the other things that I could do (or buy) with $1,000 suddenly flashed in front of my eyes, and I hung up before the harried catalogue sales operator could pick up.

Now, before every major (or even minor) purchase I make, I stop and think about what else I could be doing with the money I'm about to part with so cavalierly. "On a scale of one to ten," I ask myself, "how much do I *really* want this THING? And what other THINGS do I want even more? If I buy this THING now, will I have the money later for that other THING that I want so much?" It doesn't matter if it's a $10 lipstick or a $200 doodad; I always ask myself, *"What else could I do with the money I'm about to spend?"* If answers like "pay the mortgage" or "take a trip," or "get two of something else I've been wanting for the price of this one THING" occur to me, then I know I'm probably better off without that particular THING at this particular time. In chess, that's called a "gambit"—sacrificing a piece to gain an advantage

Desire, I've learned, is a relative and fleeting thing. Pass up this purchase now and, caught up in the rush and whirl of daily life, you'll eventually forget that you ever wanted it—or, more likely, stumble upon something else you want even more and can now afford because you didn't spend money on that THING you desired before. That's when it's time for you to consult your built-in "Desire Meter" again; ask yourself, "On a scale of one to ten, how much do I *really* want this new THING, and what other THINGS do I want even more?"

The secret of curing a spending habit is not so much in exercising restraint as it is in *exercising choice*—in knowing what you really want. Unless you have unlimited dough, you have to pick and choose your purchases carefully. Know that once the money's gone, it's gone, no matter what great deal you might run across later in the month. Not only is it gone, but if you pay on credit, it keeps on costing you money in the form of interest long after you've lost interest in whatever it was you thought you couldn't live without. Which brings me to my second "ah-ha" money moment. The day I looked at one of my credit card-bills and noticed that only $8.63 was going towards the balance and the rest of the $100-plus dollars I was paying each month was going towards interest, I realized it was time to stop paying just the minimum and get serious about paying down my debt. Now, even if all I can afford is $5 more than the minimum, I pay it. And I'm making progress.

More and more, lately, I realize that what really makes me happy is Money in the Bank. It's the best thing I can give myself. Once you understand that money in the bank buys you freedom of choice and freedom from worry, you'll crave savings like a drug. Money in the bank buys you the freedom to say yes to opportunity, no to oppression. It bought a friend of mine the freedom to walk away from a job when he felt his principles were being compromised. It gives some women the freedom to walk away from marriages that aren't working. It allows others to help relatives, friends or strangers, if they choose. It buys everyone a secure retirement. Now, when I pass up the latest "chess set" that is tempting me (fill in your own obsessive desire of the moment), I don't tell myself that I'm not buying it because I'm broke or I'm poor. I tell myself that I'm not buying it because I *choose* to be rich. I'm not depriving myself; I'm giving myself more options, more choices, down the road.

What did I do with that $1,000? I wish I could say that I put it in the bank. That part of the lesson came later. But it did go toward buying something that I use much more often than I would have used that gleaming chess set—it went toward buying the gorgeous, sleek, ultra-modern computer I'm working on right now.

Advantage: Me. —G.H.

Female Finance Checklist:
Starting Out on Your Own

☐ **Goals:** You're on your own and must earn money now, ideally doing something you love. You've opened checking and savings accounts, established your financial identity and are exploring your relationship with money as you spread your wings in the world. What do you value most—the things that money can buy or the power and security it gives you?

☐ **Career:** You find your first job, and begin testing your skills and talents. You create or tap into a network that will be there for you throughout your working life. Don't be afraid to ask for more on your first job offer. Getting just $5,000 more per year on your first salary could increase your lifetime earnings by nearly half a million dollars.

☐ **Investments:** You've consolidated and begun to pay off your college loans—an investment in yourself—and created a spending plan, or budget. Save first for an emergency fund, then to secure your retirement and accumulate money for personal goals and dreams.

☐ **Real Estate:** Virginia Woolf said, "A woman must have money and a room of her own, if she is to write fiction." MAKING BREAD says *all* women must have money and a home of their own. Start saving to buy a starter home as an investment and a hedge against the rising cost of rents.

☐ **Insurance:** Cover yourself. Investigate short-term health policies until you can find a job with medical benefits. Or consider a medical savings plan. Once you have a job, purchase supplemental disability insurance to protect your finances in the event that you are injured and can't work. Insure your car and belongings, if you have any of significant value.

☐ **Wills:** Not necessary at this time, but it wouldn't hurt to have one. Start thinking about whom you want to inherit your estate. Whom or what are you working for? Your parents, siblings, a favorite niece, best friend, even a charity could be named as your beneficiary.

CHAPTER THREE:
GETTING REAL ABOUT MEN, MARRIAGE, MONEY AND MORTGAGES

Okay, so you've been in the workforce for a few years, you're putting money in an IRA or your 401(k) and making progress, saving toward your mid- and long-range goals. You may even have experienced a layoff already. But because you had an emergency fund, you survived and bounced back, finding another job with the help of a network of friends, a lot of persistence, and a little luck. Perhaps you've been the bridesmaid at a few weddings, and you're beginning to think about marriage and children yourself, but you're worried about balancing career and family.

It's easy to get caught up in the jumble of daily life as it rolls along, carrying you willy-nilly, like a twig, downstream. But tough choices lie in wait for the 25-to-35-year-old woman. Now is a good time to stop and take stock of what you've achieved and think about where you're headed. What's working in your life—and what isn't? Are you using everything that you have—talent, intelligence, contacts, money—to its best advantage? Is your debt under control? Are you saving for a home or investment property? How's your career going?

Use MAKING BREAD's "Calculate Your Net Worth" Checklist on the next page to measure your assets and think about how to harness them to get what you want out of life.

TIME FOR YOUR ANNUAL FINANCIAL PHYSICAL.

Your net-worth checklist will tell you whether you own more than you owe or vice versa. Perform this exercise once a year—think of it as an annual financial physical. Use it as a starting point, a baseline against which to measure future progress, and as a microscope to identify current weaknesses; then seek solutions. If you find you've accumulated a heavy load of debt, it's time to stop bingeing and go on a credit diet. Focus on debt reduction, using our 7-Step Debt Loss Plan, which you'll find in Chapter Nine. If you own a home (good for you!), and mortgage rates have come down even a couple of points since you got yours, do the math and see how much you could save by refinancing. If you have money sitting in a low-interest savings account (or no-interest checking account), move it. Put it to work for you in a higher-interest money-market account or short-term CD. That way you'll preserve a certain amount of liquidity or easy access to it, in case of emergencies, but still earn money. Never let more than one month's worth of income sit around not working hard for you. Most important of all, if you don't have three to six months' worth of income saved in a "just in case" emergency account, start saving now!

CALCULATE YOUR NET WORTH: 'MATERIAL GIRL' ASSETS

STUFF (FAIR MARKET OR ASSESSED VALUE)	MONEY (LIQUID OR NOT)	RETIREMENT ACCOUNTS	LIABILITIES
Value of your house, if you own one _____	Bank accounts _____	401(k)'s, Roth IRA's traditional IRA's, SEP, SIMPLE, KEOUGH plans, etc. and annuities _____	Personal loans (money owed to relatives, etc.) _____
Other properties, if any (second home, rental property, vacation timeshare, plot of land) _____	Savings accounts _____	Pension plan value _____	Loans co-signed for relatives or friends _____
Car, motorbike or other vehicle _____	Certificates of deposit _____		Mortgage _____
Home furnishings (furniture, antiques, rugs, etc.) _____	Employee savings plans _____		Home equity loan _____
Electronic equipment (computers, cameras, etc.) _____	Cash value of life insurance policies _____		Lines of credit (portion used) _____
Jewelry and works of art _____	Value of shares or equity in business _____		Car loan(s) _____
Rare books and other collectibles _____	Stocks _____		Credit-card balances (full amount owed, not what is paid each month) _____
Furs, designer clothes or vintage outfits _____	Bonds _____		Business loans (if you are personally responsible for them) _____
Miscellaneous stuff _____	Mutual funds _____		Student Loans _____
	Educational savings plans _____		Any taxes owed _____
	Medical savings plans _____		Other debts _____
	Money owed to you or deposits (rent, etc.) that might be repaid _____		
	Mad money hidden in your lingerie drawer, under your mattress or in a shoe box _____		

CALCULATE YOUR NET WORTH

Add up your assets (stuff, money, and retirement accounts) and your liabilities—what you own and what you owe—then subtract your liabilities from your assets.

$ ASSETS _____ - $ LIABILITIES _____ = YOUR NET WORTH _____

WHEN MAYBE MAKES TWO

Becoming part of a couple—with or without benefit of matrimony—creates new financial challenges. Let's say you're about to enter into a live-in relationship—as about half of us have by the time we hit our thirties. Have you thought about what you need to do to protect your financial interests in such an arrangement? Or you may have found your one true love and are contemplating marriage. Have the two of you talked about money?

Don't let passionate attachments cause you to lose sight of one crucial fact that too often gets lost amid the wedding tulle, lilies, rice, and cake frosting: Marriage is a financial contract between two people. When the preacher says "for richer, for poorer," what isn't stated is that women who divorce generally suddenly become much poorer than their former spouses. What also goes unsaid is that if you enter into a relationship with good credit and your intended has bad credit (opposites do attract), you will share responsibility for any debt he incurs during the marriage.

The choices you make now will have far-reaching effects in your life. In this chapter, all about men, money, marriage, and mortgages, we share the stories of women who learned the hard way what to do when they "play house" with a lover, and those who regret not having had that all-important money talk with their honey before marriage. We also offer expert advice on prenups, postnups, and buying your first home. First up, a report by MAKING BREAD contributing editor Elizabeth Kaminsky on the financial rules of living together. (Some names in her piece have been changed to protect privacy.)

PLAYING HOUSE:

HOW TO PROTECT YOUR HEART—AND YOUR WALLET— WHEN YOU DON'T HAVE THE RING

BY ELIZABETH KAMINSKY

Whether it happens in one fell swoop or one dresser drawer at a time, many couples have taken the plunge to share the same space without sharing a name. Statistics on living together are now tracked in the census. A report by the Centers for Disease Control says that, by age 30, about half of the women in the U.S. have "cohabitated outside of marriage." Clearly, it is a viable option for many adults who, for whatever reason, choose the comforts of home without the confines of marriage.

My first exposure to the concept was when I was in high school. My mom and I had just moved into a brand-new apartment, which, in my mind, was perfect. We had new appliances, reliable heat, and only three other neighbors in the whole building. I remember coming home from school that first week to find my mother pouting at the kitchen table. From her expression, I could tell that our new little palace was losing its luster.

"What's wrong?" I asked, innocently.

"I just met the couple across the hall," Mom said, scowling through a clenched jaw.

"Are they newlyweds? Do they have any kids?" I was eager to know whether there might be potential babysitting dollars to be had.

"They're living together!" Mom growled, and that was the end of the conversation.

My mother, like many others from her generation, had definite ideas regarding the rules of engagement, as it were. Imagine my surprise when, years later, a friend of hers was contemplating a third marriage at age 72. "I don't know what the hell's the matter with her," my mom said. "Why doesn't she just live with him? If she marries him, she'll lose Ed's pension." I looked at my mother in disbelief. Was this the same person who had so swiftly judged that young couple across the hall?

When I challenged her, she reasoned that her friend's decision was a financial one, and that she needed to look beyond love to protect herself for the future. While Mom's black-and-white judgments may have been a little harsh, she did have a point: Big decisions always have financial implications, and it is a wise woman who considers how those decisions will affect her future.

WHAT'S LOVE GOT TO DO WITH IT?

Gay or straight, couples cohabitate for a million different reasons. Some live with people for security, some for convenience. One woman I spoke with even said she lived with her boyfriend, because he was "neater than any roommate" she'd ever had. But by far the number one reason women gave for "living together" was that they were "in love."

For some women, like Erica, 26, the pink fog of infatuation tends to cloud their decision-making skills. "I wish I'd thought a lot further ahead, before I moved in with Jeff," she says of her five-year live-in relationship. "We were 18 when we met. My parents were hassling me, and I couldn't wait to get out of their house. Jeff had a good job at a chemical plant and a nice apartment, but, most of all, he had freedom and no one to answer to. I think I fell more in love with that than I did with him. It was great for a few years, until the bills started to pile up. We never talked about money, we just spent a lot of it. I charged thousands of dollars worth of furniture, curtains, and other stuff for the house. When we split up, I was so hurt and angry that I just walked away from all of it. Then I realized what I had done to myself. It's been three years since we were together, and I am still paying the bills for all that stuff."

Renata, 51, tells a similar story. "I was in my mid thirties when I moved in with Carl. We lived together in his house for about eight years. Early on, I was delighted to spend money decorating and sprucing up his home, turning it into our home. Little did I realize I was not only paying half of all his bills, but financing his redecorating as well. Without thinking, I was contributing far more, financially, than I had expected. When I started to question the way things were structured, he told me that it was still his house and I was free to leave any time I wished. I was hurt on so many levels. I put my heart, soul and money into living with him, and it turned out to be a very bad investment for me."

These two stories illustrate an excellent point: any living arrangement is as much a financial decision as it is an emotional decision. One way to ease the surprise factor is to make a solid plan. Financial planner Elizabeth Lewin advises couples to get their own financial house in order and be willing to discuss things with their partners. Her advice includes figuring out your net worth, together and separately, reviewing your income and expenses, and deciding who pays for what. She emphasizes that couples should be sure to put all of the important things in writing, like making out wills, designating ownership of property, medical powers of attorney, estate planning, and the like.

While societal attitudes may have changed to accept and recognize unmarried couples, the law offers them no more protection than it does to gay couples. "Unmarried couples do not have many of the financial advantages and legal protections that married couples enjoy, and they have few legal rights when it comes to medical or estate decisions," cautions Lewin. "If your significant other is in a car crash, expect the emergency room to treat you like a stranger when it comes to getting information, let alone giving permission for testing. And, if your partner dies without a will, it doesn't matter how long you may have been together or what your arrangements were. Unless you have legal documents in place, you don't have a leg to stand on."

AND BABY (OR PUPPY) MAKES THREE . . .

Many couples enter relationships with children. Some unmarried couples adopt, or become pregnant together. Other couples choose to dote on a mutually acquired pooch or parrot, whom they love as much as they would a baby. Additions to your family require careful consideration.

With children in the picture, financial planning becomes critical. In some cases, getting pregnant prompts the couple to get married. "Pete and I were really happy with our arrangement, but when I found out I was pregnant, we started looking at the future," says Jeanne, 27. "There was so much pressure from our families, too. We wrestled with what was best for us, but ultimately decided it would be better if we did get married. I wanted to stay home with the baby for at least six months, and Pete's health insurance wouldn't cover us unless we were married. Mine would stop when I left my job. So, we felt like it made sense."

Sometimes, things can get messy, even when the "kids" are grown men and women in their fifties. "Stan's kids were horrible to me," says Anna, 78. "He and I moved in together after my husband died. We made the choice not to get married, because I would lose my husband's Social Security and some other benefits from his pension. I moved into Stan's home, but we used my furniture, because it was in better shape. We split the bills, and we even had a joint travel fund for our trips together."

Anna became Stan's primary caregiver when his health began to fail. "When his prostate cancer spread to his spine, Stan needed constant care. I did it all—learned how to give him shots, bathed him, fed him, everything. I did it out of love, and I'd do it all over again. He hadn't seen his son or daughter in more than 15 years. One day he had a stroke and ended up in the hospital. It was looking like he might not make it much longer, so I called his kids to let them know. I figured they might want to see their dad, to make peace or whatever. His daughter showed up and started making funeral arrangements. She came in like a whirlwind, going through his drawers, demanding to see his bank records and other important papers. The fights were terrible. My love was dying, and his ungrateful kid was looting our house, piece by piece."

Unfortunately for Anna, Stan's good intentions didn't hold up after he died. "It was one of those things we said we'd get around to someday," she says, sadly. "He said he'd make sure I was taken care of and that I'd be able to stay in the house for the rest of my life. His money-grubbing children took care of that, selling the house right out from under me. There was nothing I could do about it."

HAVING "THE TOUGH CONVERSATIONS"

Lewin stresses that a situation like this doesn't have to happen. "The key is having the tough conversations. If you love each other enough to live together, you should love each other enough to protect one another." Getting the conversation started involves asking the right questions. She suggests starting with the following:

Who is better at paying bills, being organized? Who likes to do it? How and when will it get done? Who owns what, and who owes what: Are the CDs mine? Is the couch yours? What assets am I bringing into the relationship that I want to stay mine? How will this loan affect both of our credit ratings? We have a child together; do you intend to help support her, if we don't stay together? We bought Fido together, but who gets custody, if we split up? Am I going to leave you the china and silver in my will? Do I want to leave money to my kids? Who makes decisions for me, if I'm ill and can't make them for myself? Then put it all in writing, and get any contracts or agreements notarized. Create legal protections for yourself wherever possible.

If it all seems a little distrustful and unromantic, think about it this way: Knowledge is power. When you know where you and your partner stand on all the important issues, you have a firm, powerful foundation upon which to build your relationship. What a wonderful way to honor one another!

MARRIAGE INSURANCE

The financial agreements described above are like a "prenup without the nup," as Elizabeth Kaminsky so aptly puts it. Having candid talks about finances and future goals with "roommates" is good practice for taking the next step, tying the knot, with this—or another—partner. But even for those who enter into marriages based on open communication and sharing, divorce is a 50-50 possibility, according to the U.S. Census Bureau.

Women as a group tend to suffer far greater damage financially than men do from divorce, experiencing a 30 to 45 percent decline in their standard of living in the first year after the break up, compared with a 10 percent *increase* in standard of living for men, according to the U.S. Labor Department. One simple document—the prenuptial agreement—could protect women from this eventuality, but it is rarely entered into. Only an estimated 16 percent of couples sign prenups, according to The Equality in Marriage Institute (www.equalityinmarriage.org), founded by Lorna Wendt. Wendt made news by arguing for the corporate wife's right to a 50-50 split of marital assets during her high-profile 1995 split from Gary Wendt, the former CEO of General Electric Capital. (She got 20 percent, double the amount initially offered.)

Contrary to popular belief, prenups are not just for the rich and famous, and entering into one before marriage does not in any way indicate a lack of love for or trust in your partner. MAKING BREAD asked family-law attorney Cheryl A. Young to give us the lowdown on this document: what it can accomplish, how to go about crafting one, and why *every* engaged woman should at least consider having one. Simply put: you can't afford not to. Prenups help to keep divorce costs down, in the event that couples face a break up. If you're already married, never fear: Young and Wendt both say postnups could become the next new trend.

Wedding don't

Spotted on TheKnot.com—the mother of all bridal sites—a Wedding Plan calculator. Enter the amount of money you want to spend on your big day plus the number of months you want to take to pay off your loan, and the calculator will not only tell you what your monthly payments will be but also take you to a page where you can apply online for a Wedding Plan loan.

The wedding vows say "for richer, for poorer." But why start off poorer by going thousands of dollars into debt—without even a mortgage (and a house) to show for it? MAKING BREAD suspects you'll remember your wedding day fondly no matter what it costs, so you're better off planning a wedding that you can afford. Nothing kills passion like the pressure of worrying about paying the bills!

SOMETHING OLD, SOMETHING NEW, SOMETHING BORROWED, SOMETHING BLUE . . .
AND DON'T FORGET THE PRENUP!

BY CHERYL A. YOUNG

Donald and Ivana (and, later, Marla and Melania) had one. So do Catherine Zeta-Jones and Michael Douglas. Maybe you should, too. Most people think prenups are just for the rich and famous—those people whose financial statements include professional sports teams, TV networks, or 43-story commercial buildings. But, actually, that piece of paper is just as important as the "something old, something new, something borrowed, something blue" that brides traditionally wear when they're walking down the aisle. The protection they offer makes such a difference that these days some women who didn't sign prenups are creating a new tradition by negotiating postnuptial agreements.

What too often gets lost in the flush of romance is the fact that marriage is, at heart, a financial contract. When you marry, you sign a piece of paper that will determine ownership and disbursal of assets (and debts) accumulated during the marriage (and, in some cases, even those you bring with you into the marriage), in the event of death or divorce. While the incentive to nail down details of who gets what if things don't work out seems more compelling when multimillionaires marry, in fact, prenups may actually be more helpful to couples whose incomes fall well within the national average, who may not be able to afford heavy legal fees to sort things out later on.

That's not to say, of course, that every couple embarking on a happily-ever-after life of wedded bliss needs or wants a prenuptial agreement. Whether or not to have one is an extremely personal decision. Many people shy away from prenups, feeling that requiring one indicates mistrust on the part of one or both partners. When Paul McCartney married his second wife, Heather Mills, she volunteered to sign one, and he gallantly declined. Catherine Zeta-Jones (who reportedly will receive $2.8 million for every year of her marriage to Michael Douglas in the event of a divorce), on the other hand, told *Vanity Fair*, "I think prenups are brilliant, because it's all sorted out. . . . If I were marrying someone of lesser fortune who was twenty-five years younger, I'd be doing exactly the same thing." There are equally compelling reasons that couples with lesser fortunes should consider them, too.

NOT JUST FOR RICH FOLKS

Handled with tact, consideration, trust, and openness, the process of drawing up a prenuptial agreement can be an affirmation of the strength of a relationship, rather than a foreshadowing of its doom. The process can also be a constructive time to have a realistic discussion with your future spouse about money management. A prenuptial agreement can detail how bills will be paid during the marriage and whether all income will be put in a joint account or spouses will maintain separate accounts. It can clarify expectations regarding employment, including under which circumstances job relocation will be considered, and it can set priorities regarding work/family balance issues. Prenups can stipulate that bills will be paid by each partner on a basis that is proportionate to income. Alternately, spouses-to-be could agree to divide costs equally. Or one spouse might pay all the expenses relating to the home, while the other covers living expenses. They can even be used to stipulate how much will be saved annually.

I negotiated one prenup where the bride was a saver and the bridegroom a spender; their agreement mandated savings of no less than $25,000 per year in a joint account. In this way, they guaranteed that, in the event of divorce, there would be some marital property.

Whether or not you choose to address these issues in a formal way within the context of a prenup or simply come to an informal consensus, it's good to bring them to the forefront and make sure that everybody is on the same page. There are, however, certain circumstances when the traditional prenup is a must—not a luxury.

WHEN PRENUPS ARE A PREREQUISITE

Almost any woman who has children from a previous marriage should consider a prenup for the protection of her children. To understand how important this is, consider what could happen in the event of death or divorce if you don't have a prenup. Divorce laws dictate that all assets acquired during marriage, including increase in value from assets that you bring into the marriage

(property, or stocks, for instance), are marital and subject to some form of division between the spouses. With regard to death, if there is no prenuptial agreement waiving a spouse's right to receive an inheritance, the surviving spouse is entitled to at least one-third of the deceased's estate. Your children stand to lose something in either case. Under the terms of a prenuptial agreement, however, your spouse can agree that any assets you bring into the marriage will remain yours, regardless of increase in value, if you divorce. Likewise you can obtain a waiver in the event of death so that your assets can pay to your children.

Similarly, business owners, or those who are about to marry business owners, have special concerns that should be addressed in a prenup. One of my most difficult cases dealt with a bridegroom who owned a business where the bride worked. We agreed that she would receive 5 percent of the business every year on their wedding anniversary, up to 40 percent. In exchange, she waived any other interest in the business. However, that was only the beginning of the negotiation. He had children from a prior marriage, so we needed significant life insurance and corporate documents to provide the wife the ability to buy out his children's interest in the business upon his death.

PRENUP POSSIBILITIES

What other situations can a prenup handle? How about loss of income as a result of motherhood? Many career women may know that they will want to stay at home with their children, but they worry about losing income and career momentum during that time. A prenuptial agreement can be negotiated guaranteeing that, if there are children and the mother decides to stay at home to raise them, she will be entitled to alimony and won't have to fight for it in the courts. Her alimony can be negotiated down to the exact dollar or as a percentage of income she forfeited. Doing so makes any possible future divorce settlement much less painful.

Another of my favorite tactics is utilizing a sliding scale. For example, with regard to asset division, I often draft the document so that the percentage of the asset varies, depending on both length of marriage and size of the estate. If the couple is married for one to five years, the wife may receive 30 percent; if the marriage lasts five to 10 years, she gets 50 percent, etc. I just resolved a prenuptial agreement whereby the wife will receive 60 percent if the estate is less than one million dollars, 55 percent if the estate is between one million and one and a half million dollars, and 50 percent if the estate is larger than two million dollars. The same technique can apply to alimony.

Agreements have been drafted to include so-called "bad-boy" provisions, in which a dollar amount is put on a husband's infidelity. "Bad girls," take note; such provisions can be drafted to protect the husband, as well. Other prenuptial agreements stipulate that the dependant spouse is entitled to nothing in the event of death or divorce. Whether it is wise to marry somebody who presents you with such a "take it or leave it" document, offering you no protection whatsoever, is open to question. The best agreements are negotiated in good faith and provide adequate protection for both husband and wife.

PUTTING A PRICE ON PEACE OF MIND

Prenuptial agreements can cost anywhere from $2,500 to $10,000 or more, depending on their complexity and the amount of negotiation required. But, considering many women spend that much on a wedding gown, the price is insignificant. The amount of money spent on a prenuptial agreement pales in comparison with the amount that can be spent on an ugly divorce.

It is possible to draft a prenup inexpensively, using forms available on the Internet. Legalzoom.com (www.legalzoom.com) is one source for just such a document. My advice, however, is not to try to negotiate a prenuptial without firsthand legal advice. The laws in any given jurisdiction are complicated, and there are very specific requirements that must be met to ensure that the agreement will be valid. It's imperative that you fully understand the ramifications of the terms and conditions of the document before you sign it.

Certainly, the act of negotiating a prenuptial agreement is not romantic. However, given the divorce statistics, you cannot afford to overlook the fact that marriage is, in some respects, a business arrangement. Deal with the business aspect, and then lock that piece of paper away in a safe-deposit box and hope that you never have to take it out. Don't wait until the last minute to negotiate a prenup. I have had clients who executed the document on the way to the final fitting for the wedding gown. Get it out of the way early, so that you can relax and focus on your wedding plans and your future together.

POSTNUPTIAL BLISS— AND AGREEMENTS

If you are already married and don't have a prenup, it's not too late to execute an agreement. You and your spouse can enter into a postnuptial agreement long after your "I do's" have been exchanged. Of course, it may be more difficult to come to an agreement without the leverage of the wedding hanging over everyone's head. But, if you are a dependant spouse, it's worth considering, because it may put you on more even footing. Postnuptial agreements can be handled easily in the context of estate planning. I suspect we will see more of them in the future.

One final note: prenuptial agreements can be amended—or even terminated—as circumstances change. When Erica Jong, author of *Fear of Flying* and many other bestsellers, married her fourth husband, a divorce lawyer, they signed a prenup. Ten years later, they burned it in a wok at a dinner party. This ultimate display of trust and love may become a 21st century ritual, says Jong in an essay she wrote for the now-defunct *Talk* magazine. At some point in their marriages, she suggests, couples may ask one another: "Darling, do you love me enough to burn the prenup?" No attorney, however experienced, can help you answer that question.

Cheryl A. Young is a partner in the Family Law Practice Group of Wolf, Block, Schorr and Solis-Cohen LLP, concentrating in matrimonial law, including divorce, custody, support, property distribution, and abuse actions.

For More Living-Together Resources

SURF ON OVER TO THESE WEB SITES.

American Association of Retired Persons (www.aarp.org): There's lots of good financial advice here, even if you don't think you're old enough to need it!

NOLO "Law for All" Law Center (www.nolo.com): An online "encyclopedia" of all things legal— wills, powers of attorney, real estate, etc. They even have specific information on living-together contracts and the rules pertaining to so-called "common law" marriages, which are recognized in only a handful of states.

Social Security Administration (www.ssa. gov): Check this out for advice on your benefits and how they are affected, if you marry, divorce, remarry, etc.

THE FINANCIAL RULES OF LIVING TOGETHER:
AGREE TO AGREE ON THESE THINGS

When you take the leap to live with your lover, make sure that, along with the slamming sofa and the killer curtains, you have the right stuff to stay financially and emotionally "fashionable." Savvy women will accessorize themselves with the following.

A Net-Worth Statement: Know what you are bringing to the table. It sounds complicated, but it's really nothing more than a snapshot picture of your assets and debts. Have your partner do one, too.

A Spending Plan: You and your partner should agree to a spending plan that states who pays for what. It makes good sense to know what the household bills will be, as well as what each individual's bills are. Maybe you have student loans and credit-card bills, and he just bought a new Mustang. Those payments need to go into the mix, as they will certainly affect your lives together.

Ownership and Guardianship Agreements: Is it yours, mine or ours? For live-togethers, that little detail must be spelled out. If you are going to buy a house together, and you want it to pass to your partner in the event that anything happens to you, it must be titled as "Joint Tenancy with the Right of Survivorship."

What If You Have a Child? Who will care for and support that child? Remember, the law sees your situation very differently than if you were married. For something as important as this, get legal advice and put agreements in writing! Some couples consider a type of "prenup without the nup." That kind of living-together contract may work for you.

Wills and Insurance Policies: Each of you needs a will. Maybe you have children to provide for, or a favorite niece to whom you wish to leave a necklace. Perhaps you want your partner to be able to stay in your house when you're gone. None of that is likely to happen, unless it is outlined in your will. In most cases, a will doesn't cover your insurance policies, pensions, or other retirement funds, so check to see whom you have designated as your beneficiary and change it, if necessary.

Powers of Attorney: In order for your partner to be able to make medical decisions for you, you need a Health Power of Attorney. If you have strong feelings about what you want done to prolong your life, make out a Living Will. Give your physician a copy of each, and discuss your decisions with any blood relatives. A little planning can make your wishes be the ones that come true. For financial matters, you may want a Durable Power of Attorney. The person named here has the ability to act for you in money matters, if you can't. This power can rest with one person or several people. Maybe you trust your partner to handle the bills, but you'd rather have your sister sell any real estate. Know that you can always change these documents. You are in control. Get legal advice, if you are unsure of what's best for you.   —E.K.

FORGET THE WEDDING PLANNER AND HIRE A FINANCIAL PLANNER

Women are waiting longer to get married than in past decades. According to Bankrate.com, today's newlywed couples are usually between 25 and 27 years old, making $65,000 a year in combined income. The average bill for a wedding is now $22,000 (nearly 30 percent of the average couple's gross salary), and almost three-quarters of weddings are financed, all or in part, by the bride and groom. If you charge the wedding on credit cards and only plan to pay the minimum, the cost of a $22,000 wedding will cost you $33,000 in interest alone, assuming an annual percentage rate of 18 percent, and it will take thirty-eight years to pay it off. So your big day would actually cost you $55,000. In other words, you could still be paying for the wedding after the marriage has been dissolved. That is far too much debt for anyone just starting out to take on. Doing so will delay saving for future financial goals—and is it really fair to saddle your parents, who should be focused on growing their own retirement nest egg, with the cost?

Our advice: fire the wedding planner, keep your wedding plans simple and inexpensive, and invest the money you save in a few visits with a financial planner. Get advice on investing for your future together. Use your wedding plans as a conversation starter to discuss joint financial goals with your fiancé. What obligations do each of you have regarding student loans, car payments, unpaid balances on credit cards? Your spouse's debt is going to be part of your financial life, whether you like it or not, so become intimately familiar with it before you say 'I do."

Once you've shared your dreams and identified the goals—career, home, education, family, travel, charitable giving—that you hope to accomplish together it will be easier for you to put the cost of your wedding day into perspective. Keep your eye on the big picture, and if you still want a lavish wedding, budget for it months in advance. Figure out the amount you can afford to spend. Be realistic: if you are carrying too much debt already, then you might have to settle for a less expensive wedding. But that doesn't mean it can't be something truly special. There are any number of ways to plan a wedding day that will be both memorable and a money-saver.

On the following page, MAKING BREAD contributing editor Sharon Sorokin James offers some tips on how to be a "Frugal Bride."

VOW TO TIE THE KNOT CHEAPLY—
AND YOU'LL HAVE MORE TO SPEND ON YOUR FUTURE

BY SHARON SOROKIN JAMES

Ladders are cheaper than weddings. My father constantly and gently reminded me of that fact as I was growing up. He often teased me by saying, "I'll give you half the cost of a wedding—in cash—if you elope." He didn't exactly mean it, of course, although I'm sure he would have made good on his offer, so long as he could be present at the elopement. He wouldn't have missed my wedding for the world.

But his point was well-taken. Weddings are expensive, and often the price escalates as the planning continues. It is easy to let one's spending get out of hand, using such rationalizations as, "It's my only wedding"—a fallacy, since at least 50 percent of American marriages end in divorce, and of those who divorce, about 55 percent remarry within five years. Or "My friend had a black-tie wedding. I have to have one, too." Or "No one cooks for their wedding."

Each of these rationalizations will set you back a pretty penny. And money spent on your wedding probably means less money for a mortgage or for your tuition loans or even your retirement account.

So how can you make your wedding a special day without going broke? Here are three simple rules. Follow them, and you will undoubtedly save money and add meaning to your wedding.

1. Don't keep up with the Joneses.
2. Remember the true meaning of your wedding—the public commitment of two people to each other, in front of their community of family and friends.
3. Keep it simple.

How can you do these things? By being your own woman, and looking beyond conventional ideas of what a wedding should be. I have attended weddings in cathedrals and on docks, in public parks, and in the undecorated meeting rooms of churches, in fancy resorts and in the bride's backyard. And I can tell you that, in each case, the only thing that mattered was that the couple was getting married.

To plan a wedding that won't wreak financial havoc on your future, you need a budget. Decide how much you can afford to spend overall, then divide your wedding budget into six categories: apparel; reception; photography; flowers and other accessories; the honeymoon; and most important, your savings account for the future. Decide what your priorities are and base what you spend on each category on what's most important to you. Then vow not to exceed your limits. Below are some suggestions for saving money in each category:

Apparel. A lovely, new wedding gown purchased at an elegant retail store will easily cost you $2,000 or more. The very same dress, purchased at a large discount store, will likely be half the price. A copy of the same or a similar dress, purchased at a lower-end store, most likely in a somewhat less luxurious fabric, will probably halve the cost again. But the best alternative, the one with both the most savings and the most meaning, is to wear your mother's wedding dress, if she still has it and if you can fit into it. You may have to pay $75 to $125 to clean it and perhaps another $50 for alterations. But for that modest price, you will have an heirloom wedding.

If your mother didn't keep her wedding dress, or you hate it or can't fit into it, look for a second-hand dress in the newspaper, on Ebay, or in a resale shop. Or wear a special outfit that you wore when you first fell in love with your fiancé, to recall where it all began. Remind yourself of the adage, "Something old, something new, something borrowed, something blue," and let your dress be the old item. There is no shame in recycling; in fact you can take pride in it.

When it comes to attendants, the rule of thumb has always been: the bride picks their gowns, but the attendants pay for them. This rule has ruined many a friendship, as well as strained many a pocketbook. Be a true friend and don't make your dearest female friends wear something unflattering or something that can't be reused. Be budget-conscious and fashion-thoughtful. For my wedding, I chose, and purchased for my attendants, a bolt of blue-on-blue patterned silk at a discount textile store. I picked out a simple pattern by Laura Ashley, a mid-calf-length dress with a sweetheart neckline, fitted bodice, and draping skirt, and sent my two attendants the pattern number, along with the silk. One of my attendants sewed her dress herself, the other hired a seamstress to do it for about $25. Best of all, they were able to wear the dress again later. I simply told the flower girls to choose a dress that they liked. Two of them, sisters, arrived in identical flowered dresses. The third, who "volunteered" to become a flower girl on the morning of the wedding, wore what she already had on—a pale blue smocked dress. They all looked great and happy, and their parents didn't have to spend an arm and a leg.

Reception. Pick your site carefully. Do they require you to use their caterer? Will they provide linens? Tables? Chairs? Or do you have to rent those items? Do they require you to purchase an insurance policy? If so, how much will that cost you?

Consider having your wedding reception at a restaurant. You might find it to be much less expensive than other alternatives, particularly if you have a buffet and if you select a time when the restaurant is ordinarily closed. For instance, my family recently held a 75th birthday party for my mother at a restaurant, after looking around at caterers and halls, all of which were more expensive. We planned a mid-morning affair—a time when the restaurant wasn't open. At $30 per person, not including the open bar, but including a champagne toast, we were able to have 80 people dine on smoked salmon, French toast, eggs, various homemade pastries, strawberry shortcake and birthday cake, as well as a variety of hors d'oeuvres. When all was said and done, my two siblings and I spent about $900 each for the party—a far cry from the $5,000 that another site wanted to charge us, just for the use of a room, before tables, linens, chairs, china, and catering. Now translate that into a wedding reception: same location, same time, same menu, same savings.

Whether planning a reception at a restaurant or through a caterer, here are other savings strategies: Brunch or lunch is cheaper than dinner. Chicken or pasta is cheaper than beef. One entree is cheaper than two entrees. Wine and beer are less expensive than an open bar and less likely to cause problems for guests who have to drive home.

Save money on the cake by having a small, decorated cake for the ceremonial cutting, and a larger, sheet cake in the back for serving. Once it is cut and served, no one will know the difference—no one, that is, except for you and your budget.

For maximum savings, consider the potluck wedding. It is true that not everyone can do this, and it does require a very special group of friends—ones who won't be offended by being asked to participate and ones who can cook—but it can be very special. I've been to two potluck weddings and both had marvelous food. At a potluck wedding, some or all of the guests (depending upon their relationship to the bride and groom) are asked to bring a single dish to the wedding. It's best if someone coordinates what the friends bring, so that you don't end up with 12 salads, unless you want 12 salads. It also helps if the bride and groom provide the main course. Although a restaurant would not likely be agreeable to a potluck wedding, some caterers will be flexible. If you are holding the reception at home, or on a pier in Northern California (the site of one potluck wedding I attended), it is easy to arrange.

If you don't like the idea of asking your friends to bring food, or if your friends can't cook, then keep your costs down by keeping your menu simple. Roast turkey, green salad, and rice make a lovely meal, especially when followed by champagne and wedding cake. You don't have to impress everyone with how much money you can afford to spend on a group meal. Instead, impress them with how much you can gracefully save.

Photography. Photography at a wedding is important. You definitely want to be able to look back at photographs or a video or both, for many years. But you don't have to pay $4,000 or more for the crème de la crème of wedding photographers. First, compare prices among several photographers. Find out if posed photographs will cost more or less than candid shots. Consider selecting a photographer who does not bill him or herself as a "wedding photographer." Canvas local art schools—you might find a professor or student of photography who is terrific. But be sure to check references and examples of previous work. Saving money is useless if you aren't happy with the result.

Consider candid photos only. One friend snapped pictures throughout my wedding, put them together in a little photo album, and gave it to me as a gift. It is one of my favorite wedding gifts, and I always think of her when I look at it. She captured many of the same moments that the professional photographer did, but with a less studied and therefore more natural eye. At another friend's wedding, baskets of disposable cameras were distributed to the guests, who were encouraged to take pictures and to turn in their cameras at the end of the reception.

Flowers and Other Accessories. Don't overdo it—at the wedding or the reception—when it comes to floral arrangements. For flowers, seasonal will always be less expensive than out of season. If you purchase loose flowers from a wholesaler or a street vendor, you will save more money than if you buy them from a florist. Arrange them simply in small glass jars purchased at a dollar store. They will look pretty and natural and will serve their purpose—providing some simple beauty to set off the real beauty of the occasion, the joining of two lives.

As for other decorations, if you are having your reception at a catering hall, resist the urge to drape the walls in silk, to erect large centerpieces on each table, which only become barriers to sight and conversation, or to bring in lighting consultants. If you are having the reception at a restaurant, the restaurant will already have its own décor; stick with it. If you or a friend or relative is hosting the reception at home, don't redecorate the entire house from top to bottom. It is not necessary. Your wedding is not meant to be held in a furniture showroom.

Finally, do not feel that your guests must depart with "goodie bags." Your wedding is not a fundraising event, and the attendees need not receive a gift or favor for attending. They are coming to your wedding to see you get married, to participate as part of your community in the joining of your life with the partner you have chosen. They don't need to be "paid" for this act of friendship.

Attendants, on the other hand, have responsibilities at a wedding, and it is polite to both thank them for their efforts and to recognize their special friendship with you by giving them a gift. The gift, like all gifts, should be one that you can afford. It is the thought, not the amount spent, that counts.

The Honeymoon. Traditionally, the groom pays for the honeymoon. But traditions change, and any money the groom spends on the honeymoon is money not spent on a house, or furniture, or paying off student loans, or buying a car. So unless you are extremely traditional, or simply want to be surprised, try to plan it together. If your groom insists on planning it himself, remind him gently, once or twice, that you will be thrilled to be in his company, and the location and level of luxury is irrelevant.

I know couples who have gone biking on Block Island, camping in Yellowstone, or even simply departed to a hotel for a night or two. My husband and I spent three weeks in France on our honeymoon, and although I no longer have the record of what it cost us (if ever I did), I do know that we spent comparatively little. Our tickets were purchased well in advance. We took a subway from the Paris airport to the Paris train station, where we caught a TGV (the fast train) to the Perigeaux. There, we found a series of small hotels (we hadn't made advance reservations).

After a few days, we rented a car and drove around Perigord, the Dordogne, and the Loire Valley, eventually returning to Paris. Our accommodations ranged from lovely to tacky. The prices ranged (in 1990) from about $100 a night in Paris (Hotel du Quai Voltaire on the Left Bank with a view of the Seine) to about $18 a night in Orleans (a somewhat seedy hotel with carpeting halfway up the paper-thin walls and a bathroom halfway down the hallway). My favorite was an 800-year-old renovated stone building in a field beyond an old house in a tiny town of about eight buildings. It was about $30 a night, and the owner cooked dinner for us at his house, which doubled as the "dining room." After dinner, we walked through the field to our room—the only fully renovated and only occupied room in the building. In the morning, we awoke to the sounds of roosters, goats, and cows. It wasn't a five-star hotel in a modern city, and we were glad it wasn't.

Your Savings Account for the Future. Remember, a wedding is a beginning, not an ending. Whatever you spend on your wedding won't be available to you to spend on something else. So practice restraint and simplicity and use your common sense. Set aside some money for your future together. Perhaps you can even set one budget, and then challenge yourselves to pare it down, within reason. Every penny saved can be put toward a joint financial goal, whether it is a house, furniture, paying off loans, or whatever else your two hearts' desire, now that you are wed.

Children's author and lawyer Sharon Sorokin James is currently working on a novel. She is a contributing editor to MAKING BREAD.

THE PRE-WEDDING MONEY TALK

DIVULGE:

>> What you earn.

>> What you own (assets).

>> What you owe (every debt obligation).

>> Your savings and investments— and investment philosophy.

DISCUSS AND AGREE UPON:

>> Your joint financial goals.

>> How financial decisions will be made.

>> How the household accounts will be handled.

One good reason to keep your name ...

It gives you one less thing to do. If you do change your name or hyphenate it after marriage or divorce, be sure to notify the Social Security Administration (SSA) and your payroll department at work. You want to avoid confusing the government's computer system and compromising your record of lifetime earnings or a tax refund because names don't match up. Let the SSA know about your new moniker by filing Form SS-5 at a local SSA office. The form is also available on the agency's Web site, www.ssa.gov, or by calling 1-800-772-1213.

Show Me Yours and I'll Show You Mine:
WHAT HAPPENS TO CREDIT WHEN TWO BECOME ONE?

BE TRULY INTIMATE—SWAP CREDIT HISTORIES BEFORE MARRIAGE. After all, your individual debts will become part of your financial life together, and you don't want any surprises after you say, "I do." Your intended's pre-marriage debt won't affect your credit rating, but it can affect joint financial goals. For instance, both credit histories will be scrutinized when you apply for a mortgage. Once you are married, any joint credit accounts, including those for auto loans, credit cards, and mortgages, will show up on both of your credit histories—and if the marriage doesn't last, you will still jointly be liable for the debt. It's a good idea to keep at least one credit card in your own name alone, which you pay out of your separate checking account.

In community-property states (Arizona, California, Idaho, Louisiana, Nevada, New Mexico, Texas, Washington, and Wisconsin), all debts incurred during the marriage are considered joint debts, even if the spouse has applied for the credit in his or her name. If your husband defaults on a car loan taken out during the marriage, the lender can come after you, whether you are still married to him or not.

FOR BETTER, FOR WORSE, FOR RICHER, FOR POORER...

HERE'S THE CONVERSATION EVERY WOMAN SHOULD HAVE BEFORE SAYING, "I DO"

BY ALLISON ACKEN, PHD

How could you do this to me?" her agonized husband asked. "You promised!" After much discussion in my office weeks earlier, this couple had set a spending limit, agreeing not to buy anything over $200 without consulting each other first. So, what went wrong?

Before they had entered into what was a second marriage for both of them, George and Lisa had worked out a precise prenuptial agreement, but they didn't think to talk about spending and saving habits. Three years later, their very different money styles had strained their emotions to the breaking point. Recently, in her excitement to furnish their new home (and her unconscious anger at being limited by George's very conservative spending style), Lisa had bought not one but two items over their agreed-upon limit. Her husband was furious. Worse, he felt betrayed. The good news is that this couple is still talking. They both want to find a common ground, and I think they will.

Helping couples define and develop their financial style within marriage is great work—thought-provoking and gratifying for me. It makes me wonder how my own marriage might have been different if my ex and I had talked about finances. Money wasn't the only problem. But we didn't discuss it at all beforehand—or very much after we were married. And we had lots of feelings about it. I wanted to buy property; he didn't. We were both spenders, but on very different things. I won't begin to speak for him, but I know that I had many negative feelings about his choices. And then it was too late; we were past the point of talking about anything constructively.

To be fair, how many engaged couples do have serious discussions about money? In an informal poll, I found very few. Even for "reality TV's" *The Bachelor*, the nuts and bolts of finances were way too real. Money's not the topic of conversation in most hot tubs. However, with the divorce rate still hovering around 50 percent and money at the top of the list as the cause of marital fights, it's not a big leap to hypothesize that a few good conversations about the subject early on might save some marriages.

Of those 50 percent of couples who divorce, approximately 75 percent will remarry. Which means that if you skip the money conversation the first time around, there's an excellent chance that you'll get another shot at it. Even within first marriages, it's never too late to deal with financial issues, as long as you're both willing to communicate and compromise. So, if you haven't taken the time to consider the meaning of the words "for richer, for poorer"—and to enrich your relationship by talking about the issues surrounding them—what are you waiting for?

Below are some tips for divorce-proofing your marriage, which I've developed in my years of counseling those who've run into marital money problems. The key strategies—talk it out and function as a team—will get you through most difficult patches in any marriage.

10 ON-THE-MONEY MARRIAGE-SAVERS

Discuss! Discuss! Discuss! Learning to talk about money is the antidote to a lot of future struggles. Be as honest as you can with each other from the start. Men often feel pressure to be the expert. You're better off establishing right away that you will have some answers, and that he may have others; this is a partnership. Understand both the general principles about your individual approaches to money (conservative, impulsive, risky, etc.) and the tiny details—like how often you balance the checkbook or pay the bills. Have fun, laugh. Enjoy the experience of talking about money, about love, about your future together.

Impart your values to each other, and set your goals for the future. What is really important to you? Is it buying property or buying jewelry? Do you think it is critical to make donations to charity? Do you want a flashy new car, or are you the used-car type? How do you feel about spending or saving and debt? How much of a cushion do you need to feel safe? Where do you want to be in five years—or—25?

When the. young director of marketing for my Web site, www.womentalkmoney.com, was first engaged, she and her fiancé had a serious conversation about money. Her college sweetheart and husband-to-be said to her, "We want to be the people who earn interest, not the people who pay interest." This simple but clear concept set the tone for their marital spending. Eight years later, they have three beautiful little girls and no debt.

Share your credit scores. If you have never checked your credit report, this is the perfect time to do it. You can see just where you stand. And you can pick up any errors that might appear; these errors do happen and can stop you from getting a home loan or other credit, if you don't correct them. Repeat that process every year or so. Just in case either of you is not being upfront about your debt, for whatever reason (embarrassment, fear, worry, shame), the credit report will keep you honest. If your betrothed refuses to share his credit report, it is a safe bet that something is very wrong. Pay attention.

Organize your accounts. Include debts, assets, insurance policies, and any necessary passwords into one binder so that either partner can access the information in an emergency.

Clarify who is responsible for what. Joan Lightfoot, a marriage and family therapist in Pacific Palisades, California, says, "Never marry someone with the same interest in money as you have." She thinks it takes two people with varying interests in different aspects of money management to make a marriage work smoothly. And she has a point: if both parties are focused on the high-tech stocks, but nobody is watching the day-to-day accounts, the imbalance can be a set-up for competition and blaming when something goes awry. Divvy up the tasks and make sure you keep your partner informed about what's going on.

Now is the time to talk about generating income, sharing expenses, and handling accounts. Are your expectations that there will be one or two incomes? Will you work full-time or part-time? How will lifespan issues, such as children or retirement, affect those expectations? Will you share expenses 50-50 or proportionately, based on income, and what feelings do those choices raise? Do you want joint accounts or separate, or some combination? The joy is in these details—if you can both agree on the course of action.

Eliminate debt as soon as you possibly can. Iron out the good-debt, bad-debt wrinkles. A mortgage is often thought of as good debt, and if the property is appreciating at a healthy rate or generating income, it's worth it. Credit-card debt, on the other hand, is mostly bad debt incurred for stuff and experiences that are past. Debt gets heavier and heavier over time and arguments about debt become more and more unpleasant.

To eliminate your bad debt, operate on a budget that makes sense to both of you. With a realistic plan, "budget" can be a friendly word. It can even leave a little money left over, if you do it right: Find ways to live below your means. But remember that his tickets to the game may be as important to him as your manicures are to you, so don't nix your spouse's items just because they don't make sense to you. Be fair.

Observe a spending limit. A lot of arguments can be avoided by deciding on a dollar amount above which you will not spend without consulting your spouse. Stick to it! The amount will differ for each couple, but the concept is important. Even though that leather jacket is a great buy at 50 percent off, it can become a source of grief if it is above the limit. If you are both out there spending like mad, unless there are unlimited funds, there will be hard feelings, not to mention hard times.

Review your progress on a regular basis after the wedding. Plan on an interval (weekly, monthly, yearly) that works for you as a couple. Goals are made to be achieved, and then it's time to set new ones. Congratulate yourself on what is working. Introduce changes that make the unmet goals more attainable.

Respect each other's wishes. The whole point in having the divorce-proof conversation is to voice wishes, fears, and goals. Pay attention to what your partner is saying and treat your fiancé as well as you wish to be treated. Ongoing respect is a major factor in long-lived marriages.

Function as a team. A marriage is the ultimate two-person team, and the goal is to win. Talk, talk, talk about what is working and what needs tweaking. You picked this person because you wanted a lifetime together. Go for the exceptional—and winning—marriage. And don't forget to take a break every once in a while to have a good time and to remember how much you love each other and why you are willing to join together in this bond called marriage. Talking about money can be fun, if you remember why you are doing it.

Allison Acken, PhD, is a clinical psychologist, publisher and author of It's Only Money: A Primer for Women, *as well as a contributing editor to* MAKING BREAD.

TAKE OUR MARRIAGE & MONEY QUIZ:

How Compatible Are You on Matters That Count?

Talking about money issues ahead of time may be one of the best ways to strengthen your marriage. Use this quiz as a conversation-starter. What do you think of the following statements? Rate your agreement from 1 (strongly disagree) to 5 (strongly agree).

Next ask your partner to take the quiz. Then compare answers and discuss the differences.

1 STRONGLY DISAGREE .... 5 STRONGLY AGREE

1. Sharing your financial issues (even previously held secrets) in open dialogue with your spouse is necessary for a financially healthy relationship. _____

2. No matter who earns the most money, each partner should have an equal say in financial decisions. _____

3. Saving at least 10 percent of income is absolutely necessary. _____

4. Marriage is a partnership in earnings, too. It is important for both spouses to generate income. _____

5. A full-time, stay-at-home parent is contributing as much to the family's income as the parent who brings in the paycheck. _____

6. If you and your spouse make a financial agreement (for instance, about spending, saving, or budgeting), it's like a promise made, and both of you need to stick to it. _____

WHAT'S YOUR SCORE?

The higher your score on these items, the more ready you are for a financially divorce-proof marriage. If you have a preponderance of 3s, you probably haven't thought about these issues much. It's a good time to talk about them and form your opinion.

WHAT'S HIS SCORE?

Ask your fiancé or husband to take the quiz. Compare your overall scores and your ratings for each individual item. Talk about where you agree and disagree and why you feel the way you do.

HOW DIVORCE-PROOF IS YOUR MARRIAGE?

You will probably not be in perfect agreement (all 5s or all 2s), and that's okay. If your scores are vastly different, you have a lot of talking to do. You can bet you'll get to know each other a lot better in the process. Some financial issues are easily ironed out before marriage, and some issues you will continue to work on throughout your marriage. There is a chance that one of these issues might be so crucial as to be a deal-breaker. If you run up against one of these big differences, it's time to seek professional help to see if you can work through it together before you set the wedding day.

HOW TO 'DIVORCE-PROOF 'YOUR MARRIAGE

"Why is it so hard to talk about money?" we asked Marcia Eckerd, Ph.D., the psychologist who writes MAKING BREAD's "The Working Mom's Shrink" column. "We grew up in different families, watching our parents pursue different financial goals and habits. Nine times out of ten, we've also learned different styles of communicating about everything from love to money," she explains. "Too often, first attempts at discussing the highly charged topic of money (who controls the check book, how much should we save, what are we saving for, how much can we spend on having fun) end in tears and acrimony. After that, the subject is avoided as much as possible. Why? Because we don't fully understand the financial messages we each learned at home, and we tend to take personally any negative comments and criticism directed at us during discussions about money.

"Arguing about money is a leading cause of divorce," Eckerd points out. "Learning how to talk about it constructively, calmly and supportively, so that you can begin to manage it as a team, is the first step to a long-lasting, happy and financially secure union."

HIS, MINE, AND OURS

As Allison Acken points out, one of the first financial decisions most couples make is how they will handle the household expenses. Should you pool your money, or keep everything separate? Every couple have their preferences, but most experts agree that the "three-pot" method works best: A personal account for each of you, and a joint account, into which you each agree to deposit a set amount every pay period (perhaps a

One thing you can do right now ...

BE WHEEL SMART

When you buy a new car, take out a loan for three years, pay it off, and drive the car for three more years, redirecting the same amount each month into savings for your next one. The couple that commits to putting away enough dough to buy a car out of savings (which earns interest), rather than by borrowing—and paying out interest—ends up thousands of dollars ahead of the game.

percentage of your salaries) and from which you will jointly pay the household bills.

The joint checking account should be used to handle those items that are truly joint—rent or mortgage, homeowner's insurance, real estate taxes, vacations. Use your personal account to pay for those items that are not joint, such as clothing, gifts, lunch out, car expenses, education, medical bills, or any joint expense that you both have agreed you will take responsibility for individually. One of you might pay for groceries, for instance, and the other for entertainment.

It's vitally important for women to have their own checking account in marriage—and not just for discretionary-spending purposes. Every woman needs to establish her own financial identity and independence, whether she is working outside the home or not. Don't stop with a checking account; apply for a credit card in your own name (if you don't already have one), so you establish your own credit history, and create a "just in case" savings account, stashing away money every chance you get, even if it's just a couple of dollars here and a couple there. You'll feel more secure knowing that money is there in case you need it. One of the prime reasons women don't leave unhappy or abusive marriages is that they can't afford to; having such an account gives you freedom of choice. It changes the dynamics of any marriage for the better, putting both partners on a more equal footing.

WHEN YOU MAKE MORE THAN HE DOES

The wage gap still exists, but a growing number of women are earning more than their spouses; 15 percent of wives and 28 percent of women who live with unmarried partners now earn at least $5,000 more than their spouses, according to the U.S. Census Bureau. Among dual-income couples, 32 percent of women now earn more than their husbands. It's not a contest; the more one brings into the household the better for the entire family. In fact, if the wage gap didn't exist, it's estimated that every married household would earn an average of $4,000 more per year, cutting the poverty rate in half.

Men today tend not to feel as threatened by successful spouses than in previous generations. Still, if you do earn more than your spouse or fiancé, discussing his—and your own—attitude about that fact should be part of your "money talk."

MAKING BREAD believes that every woman must be a breadwinner for her own sake. She should have her own career—her own way of making a living—not just as insurance for a time when she will most likely be on her own, but as a means of self-expression and satisfaction. That doesn't mean you can't afford to be a stay-at-home mom. But even stay-at-home moms these days are keeping connected to former jobs through telecommuting or job-sharing arrangements, or they're starting their own small businesses to create an income stream—and a creative outlet—for themselves. (Read Chapter Seven for a series of "Choice Career" profiles—interviews with women who have found jobs they are passionate about—plus a report on which professions expect the largest growth in coming years and "Success Guide" strategies from a career coach to help you make the most of the job you have. In Chapter Eight, we offer compelling "Biz Whiz" interviews with women who have achieved financial independence by starting their own small businesses.)

SOFA TO GO

YOU'RE MOVING IN TOGETHER, and you want to get rid of the old furniture and start fresh. It's easy to be seduced by those "No interest payments for twelve months!" pitches. They sound great, until you read the fine print (you'll probably need a magnifying glass). That's where you'll learn that if that terrific promotional purchase price is not paid in full by the indicated due date, finances charges will be assessed *from the transaction date*—and the interest charged will be high.

You can make these promotional offers work for you, but it takes discipline. To avoid being hit by finance charges at the end of the promotion period, don't just pay the minimum amount on the bill they'll send you each month. (*Never pay just the minimum amount on any loan!*) Divide the total bill by 11 and pay that amount each month. That way you'll get the item paid off a month in advance, and there's no chance you'll trigger an interest charge just because you missed the final payment date by a day.

KISS THE MARRIAGE PENALTY GOODBYE—FOR A WHILE, ANYWAY

Prior to 2003, two single taxpayers with similar incomes paid less in income taxes than a married couple, filing jointly. The effect of this "marriage penalty" often pushed couples filing jointly into a higher tax bracket. The Tax Reform Act of 2003 removed that penalty, at least temporarily. Beginning in 2003, taxpayers who were married, filing jointly, and claiming the standard deduction rather than itemizing, could claim a $9,500 deduction—exactly twice the amount that two single taxpayers would receive. In 2005, the deduction has been increased to $10,000 for marrieds and $5,000 for singles.

> **Tip:** If you don't add your spouse's name to your personal account, he will not be able to tap those funds in an emergency, should you become incapacitated, for instance. And the same goes for his personal account. A side note: if divorce is in the offing, the first thing you want to do is remove your spouse's name from your account, denying him access to your money.

GET REAL—ESTATE: THE BEST INVESTMENT A WOMAN CAN MAKE

Women are postponing marriage until they're in their mid-twenties these days. The median age of a woman at her first marriage is 25.1 versus 20.8 in 1970, according to the U.S. Census Bureau. But you don't have to postpone becoming a home-owner. Married or not, as your salary and savings grow, owning your own home should be at the top of your goals list. The National Association of Realtors reports that one out of every five home-buyers is a single woman these days. It's probably the best single investment available for most people. A house purchased for $30,000 some 30 years ago (if it has been maintained well) is now worth $150,000 or more, depending on location. That's a 400 percent return on investment.

Real estate, in the form of a "fix-her-up" starter home, rental property, or vacation home, is the best investment any woman can make, according to many experts. Every mortgage payment you pay buys you equity, or ownership, in an asset you can use in any number of ways, from collateral for a small business loan to a source of rental income—and always as a tax advantage. Plus the equity in your home can be turned into a reverse mortgage, and a steady stream of income, after age 62—a time when women often require additional revenue.

Owning a home gives you three basic advantages:

1. First, obviously, it takes care of one of your most basic needs—shelter, or a roof over your head. It does this while it is accumulating capital for you. Plus it is an asset that can be added onto and improved upon, enhancing its value. Enron investors had virtually no control over the valuation of that company's stocks in their retirement portfolios; you are the CEO of your home, protecting and improving on its value.
2. Investing in real estate is one way to shield your money from inflation. (Home values tend to rise with inflation; in fact, home values have beaten the rate of inflation in the last eight years.)
3. Real estate gives you tax advantages. Uncle Sam provides an indirect subsidy for your house by allowing you to lower your income taxes through itemized deductions of the interest you

pay on your mortgage and the taxes you pay on the property.

Don't think you can afford a down payment? Putting your own roof over your head is easier than you might think, and you don't have to wait until you have a spouse's income to help cover the mortgage. Investigate lease-with-the-option-to-buy arrangements, check the newspapers for tax sales, and don't overlook properties in low-rent districts that are on the verge of being rediscovered. Ask whether your city or munici-pality offers buyer-assistance programs or incen-tives for purchasing properties in certain neighborhoods. One woman bought a row home in Delaware for $47,000 under just such a program; 10 years later, she sold it for $100,000.

For those who've been in the military, 100 per-cent financing is available through the Veteran's Administration. Also, ask your realtor about county or municipal down-payment assistance programs, which might be available to those in your area who are willing to attend money-man-agement classes. So-called "piggy-back" loans—

CREATING A PAPER TRAIL: TIPS FOR STAYING ORGANIZED

Organize important papers and records for safe-keeping and easy access, so you and others can find them quickly when you need them. Those that can't be easily or cheaply replaced belong in a safe-deposit box in a bank. Others should be stored in a fireproof box or file at home (even a collection of shoeboxes will do). What counts is not what your filing system looks like, but how well it's organized.

For tax purposes: Keep a record of stock and bond transactions, so you can figure out your gain or loss on a sale when preparing your income-tax returns.

Keeping track of the amount you invest in home improvements can save you considerable money when you sell a property. You'll have to pay a tax on your profit, but you are allowed to deduct from that profit every permanent improvement you have made over the years. That includes landscaping, converting a garage to an additional room, installing insulation and other energy-saving devices, putting in a swimming pool, adding a room or a wing, a deck or patio—anything that adds value to the house. However, you must be able to prove what you spent, so create an accurate record of bills paid and checks canceled. Always remember that the IRS does not understand the words, "I can't find it." If you want to prove you made a tax-deductible expen-diture, you must be able to document it.

Two good reasons to keep all tax records for three years: The IRS is allowed to audit you any time within three years after the date you file a return. You also have the right to file an amended return within that time frame.

For insurance purposes: It's a good idea to keep receipts (and photos) of big-ticket items. Maintain a record of who paid for what (in case of divorce), along with a detailed list of valuable possessions.

Place in a bank safe-deposit box: birth certifi-cates, stock certificates, citizenship papers, bonds, automobile certificates of title, real-estate deeds, copies of wills (but not originals), divorce decrees, death certificates of parents, passports, discharge papers from military service, Veteran's Administration papers, adop-tion papers, etc.

essentially second mortgages taken out to pay the down payment on the primary mortgage—are also becoming popular, particularly among single women and newlyweds who don't have enough money saved for a down payment. Realtors know what mortgage lenders are looking for, and they can offer advice on how to get your credit in shape before applying for a mortgage. They'll "pre-qualify" you and give you an idea of just how much you can afford to spend. In the meantime, start "window-shopping." Looking at homes will give you the incentive to increase the amount you're saving each month towards your down payment.

HOLD-YOUR-BREATH TIME: PREQUALIFY OR BUST!

Once you have an idea of how much you can afford to spend, find a broker you can trust, preferably one who represents you alone. If the broker in any transaction represents the seller as well, that fact must be disclosed. You are not required to use a broker, but a broker's services can be invaluable, particularly to first-time buyers: he or she can provide information about local real estate values, financing, and standard sales agreements. Real estate brokers are licensed by the state.

The first thing your broker will do is pre-qualify you. Read "Rent-Free at Last!", Allison Acken's account of how she bought her first home, in this section, and you'll know what a difference a good broker can make in your real-estate search.

Today, it is almost imperative that you prequalify before you make a bid on a house.

There's a difference between pre-qualifying and being pre-approved for a mortgage. Prequalifying simply means that the lender has estimated your borrowing ability. It's really more of a verbal guesstimate of how much money a lending institution will approve when you find a house you are interested in purchasing.

When you seek pre-approval, you actually go through the lengthy process of formally applying for a mortgage. You may trigger upfront fees (which may or may not be refundable), but you will be able to lock in a particular interest rate (sometimes for as longs as 90 to 120 days). Pre-approval guarantees you'll be eligible to borrow a specified amount of money, provided that the appraised value of the home comes in on target. Being pre-approved for a mortgage allows you to move quickly when you find the house of your dreams. It also gives you a solid figure on which to base your home-buying decisions, rather than a best guesstimate.

A good credit rating is key to both pre-qualification and pre-approval. So before you prequalify, take steps to ensure that your credit score is as high as you can get it. Moves to make: Consolidate high-interest debt into one or two low-interest loans; establish a consistent record of paying your bills on time and pay more than the minimum; cut back spending and make a concerted effort to pay down your debt, if it makes up more than 20 percent of your gross income. The reporting agencies look at how your total debt stacks up against your total available credit, so try to keep your revolving debt to 50 percent of your available credit. They also consider length of credit history, which is why, when closing accounts, it's best to close the most recent first—and make sure the record indicates that the accounts were "closed by the consumer."

HOW MUCH HOUSE CAN YOU AFFORD:
10 QUESTIONS TO ASK YOURSELF

1. How large a down payment can you make? Obviously, the more you can put down, the lower your monthly payments will be. Mortgage calculators are available at a variety of Web sites, including www.bankrate.com and www.quicken.com, which will instantly figure your monthly payment, given a specific home price, interest rate, down payment, and term.

2. How large a monthly payment can you comfortably make? Calculate out how much money you need to cover monthly non-housing expenses (including savings and an emergency fund). What is left is what you have to work with for housing. The general rule of thumb is that you shouldn't spend more than 28 percent of your gross income (before taxes) on housing. Don't forget to factor in the cost of insurance, utilities, property taxes, and maintenance when estimating your fixed monthly housing expenses.

3. How long a mortgage term should you accept? Mortgages can be set up to span fifteen, twenty, twenty-five or thirty years. The shorter the time, the less you spend on interest—but the higher your payments will be. You can also cut your interest costs by paying more than the minimum mortgage payment each month, or making thirteen or fifteen payments per year, instead of just twelve.

4. What will the location of the home do to your budget? Will you be increasing commuting costs? Mileage on your car? Where are the stores? Services? Recreation facilities? How far will you have to drive to get a quart of milk?

5. How will your utility bills (electric, oil, gas, water) compare with what you are currently paying? Find out from the fuel company that supplies the house you are considering how much fuel was used the last two or three winters, so you can average out the cost. Do the same with the other utilities.

6. How much more will insurance cost? Rates can change if you are moving to a new area. Check auto insurance rates, as well; city rates will be higher than suburban rates.

7. How much will your property taxes be? Find out when the last reassessment occurred. If one hasn't been done in a while, you could be hit with an unexpected hike after you move in.

8. What local services are available? Are they free? Do your local taxes pay for garbage collection, or will you get a monthly bill from the garbage collector? What about child-care facilities? How far away are they? How about schools? How good are they? This could be the most important question on your list.

9. What about closing costs? At the time of the closing, you may have to pay some points. Each point equals one percent of your mortgage (e.g., $1,000 on a $100,000 mortgage). Most lenders charge two to three points. A lender who wants a higher interest rate may demand fewer points than one charging lower interest rates. And don't forget about other closing costs, such as title and mortgage insurance, attorneys' fees, title search, prepayment of taxes and insurance, credit report, and appraisal. Altogether, you should figure closing costs of 2.5 to 3.5 percent of the amount of your mortgage.

10. Do you have enough reserves to pay moving and other miscellaneous costs? These will add up as you actually start to live in the house: new carpeting, draperies, appliances, painting? How about landscaping? If you are buying a brand-new home, it is likely to come with a minimum of trees and shrubs.

THERE'S A HOME SWEET HOME MORTGAGE FOR ALMOST EVERYONE:
A Real Estate Attorney Offers Three Tips for Finding Yours

BY SHARON SOROKIN JAMES

To buy a house, it is generally necessary to have sufficient cash for a 10 to 20 percent down payment and closing costs, as well as a credit rating sufficient to gain approval for a loan. However, there are federal and state programs—and even some commercial lenders—that will lend 95 percent to 100 percent of the purchase price and closing costs of a house to qualified buyers. You can find out about these programs through your real-estate agent, or your financial institution, or check with Fannie Mae, the nation's largest source of financing for home mortgages, at its Web site (www.home-path.com).

To decide how much home you can afford, prepare a budget covering your current expenses and your estimated future expenses, including your anticipated mortgage.

First, Select an Affordable Price Range. Based upon your budget, you will be able to test whether the price range you are looking in is appropriate for you. You will do this by looking at your weekly take-home income, after taxes, and comparing it against the housing expenses and other household expenses that you would have. The rule of thumb is that your monthly housing expenses (i.e., rent or mortgage) should not exceed 28 percent of your gross pay (before taxes). I have found, however, that you probably don't want to spend more than 25 percent of your monthly take-home income (after taxes), unless you are willing to be "house-poor."

Second, Come Up with a Down Payment. If you or your spouse are in the military or are a veteran, you're in luck: 100 percent financing is available through the Veteran's Administration to active and retired members of the military service, and their unmarried widows. All branches of the service, including the Coast Guard, are eligible. Some commercial lenders now also offer no-down-payment mortgages to borrowers who have good credit. The downsides are that the interest rate will be higher than the norm, plus you'll have to tack on the cost of acquiring required private mortgage insurance. There is a risk with these loans: If the price of real estate in your area takes a downturn, you could end up owing more than the home is worth.

You might consider "borrowing from yourself" for a down payment by withdrawing money from an IRA or 401(k) plan. Tax laws allow you to use up to $10,000 in IRA funds as a down payment, if you haven't owned a principal residence in the last two years. If you're married and you and your partner are both "first-time buyers," (i.e., haven't owned a principal residence in two years), you each can withdraw $10,000 without paying an early-withdrawal penalty—that's a potential $20,000 down payment, though you may owe taxes on that amount. And, in the case of a 401(k) withdrawal, you will have to pay yourself back—with interest.

Another option to consider: A "piggy-back" loan, or second mortgage to cover your 20 percent down payment. This way, you escape the cost of carrying the private mortgage insurance that is required for a 100 percent mortgage—and your interest payments for the second loan will be tax deductible.

However you come up with your down payment, remember that, until closing—that is, until the house is legally yours by delivery of a deed—all down payments should be deposited in a separate account managed by a reliable, neutral third party under a written escrow agreement, for delivery to the seller only after all contracts are signed or specified conditions met.

Third, Look for a House That Can Pay for Itself. I still regret not buying an old stone home that I fell in love with. The interior needed a lot of work, which frightened me, but the back lot could have been sold to finance renovations. And the renovations would have allowed us to resell the home at a considerable profit. That's a perfect example of a property with hidden potential.

There are other ways in which a house can pay for itself. You can look for a house that has a rental apartment to help defray costs, or one that could be turned into a bed & breakfast. One woman who now runs a very successful bed & breakfast in Philadelphia purchased the building she had identified as suitable for such a business by entering into a lease-with-the-option-to-buy arrangement with the owner. Under such an arrangement, the seller agrees to a price that he will sell the house for at some future date, and the buyer usually pays a monthly amount several hundred dollars above what the home's rental payment would be. It's like having a "down payment" savings plan. Be aware, though, that, if you decide not to purchase the house at the agreed-upon time, you will forfeit the extra money you have put down. VA and HUD foreclosures, some of which can be had with little or no money down, are other options to look into. Ask your real estate agent or financial institution about them.

Finding the right home—and the money to purchase it with—can be a long process, but the time you spend searching could well turn out to be one of the best investments you'll ever make!

GOING MORTGAGE SHOPPING: UNDERSTAND YOUR OPTIONS

What are banks looking for? Julia Ribeiro, a mortgage broker with National City Mortgage in Trumbull, Connecticut, says, "We look at debt-to-income ratios. We believe that mortgage debt, which includes property taxes and homeowner's insurance, should not exceed 28 to 33 percent of total gross household income. We also look at total debt—that is mortgage debt, plus such other monthly debt obligations as car payments. We don't like this ratio to get any higher than 36 to 38 percent." These ratios usually apply to buyers who have at least 5 percent of the purchase price available for the down payment.

Just what is a mortgage? It is a secured loan—a pledge of property to a creditor as security for a loan. As the borrower, you are the mortgagor. You give the mortgage to the lender, or mortgagee, who takes the mortgage and holds it (or sometimes sells it to another party) until you have paid the debt.

A mortgage has three elements: The amount

the lender provides, the rate of interest, and the repayment period. Where once you were locked in for a certain number of years at a certain rate of interest and that was it—period—today you may choose between the old-fashioned, conventional, fixed-rate mortgage, and a newer type, the adjustable-rate mortgage (ARM). And even if you choose a fixed rate mortgage, you always have the option of refinancing.

THE CONVENTIONAL FIXED-RATE MORTGAGE

Here, you pay a fixed monthly payment, at a fixed rate of interest, for the life of the loan—as long as 30 years. Many banks still offer the fixed-rate mortgage, but today the cost is likely to be as much as 2.5 percent higher initially than the cost of an adjustable-rate mortgage. If interest rates do go up over the long haul, you get the advantage, and the bank, or lender, finds that it has loaned you money at a lower rate of return, or profit, than it might have gained by some other investment.

THE VARIABLE OR ADJUSTABLE-RATE MORTGAGE

With this type, the initial cost is lower, because you start off at the lowest interest rate the bank dares to offer in order to get your business, in competition with other lenders. But you agree to abide by regular review and escalation or de-escalation as interest rates are adjusted up or down by the lender to meet the conditions of the money market. Under strict government guidelines, the rates may change every month. In practice, however, the adjustment is usually scheduled every six months or once a year, with the rate permitted to increase no more than a

maximum of 2 percent a year. The rate changes are tied to a number of interest-based indices published by the federal government, and generally the mortgage specifies a cap, or ceiling, beyond which the rate may not be raised, as well as a downward floor. In theory, however, there is no limit on how high or how low the rate may go over the life of the loan.

While the interest rate on an ARM is generally lower at first than the rates available on fixed-rate mortgages, it could eventually equal or even exceed those rates. If, on the other hand, the adjustable rate holds steady or goes down, you may come out ahead. If you are hit with a rate

Tip: With so many flexible mortgage options available these days, and with the relatively low rates of recent years, you may be tempted to take on more mortgage than you can really afford. Always try on a mortgage payment for size by saving that amount for a month or two, before committing to it, to be sure that you can manage it. If it's an adjustable rate mortgage and interest rates rise, will you be able to make the payments?

increase that is more than your spending plan can stand, ask the bank if it will keep the payments the same and extend the life of the loan, instead. Some ARMs set no cap on the interest rate they may charge you. Avoid them.

Read the fine print carefully and ask questions to be sure you fully understand how your ARM is structured before you sign up. Look for one with infrequent adjustments and a cap on increases in the interest rate or in monthly payments. "ARMs are great for people who don't plan to stay in the house for more than three years," advises Ribeiro.

"If people are planning to live in the house for more than five years, it's usually best to lock in a rate with a conventional mortgage, especially during periods when rates are low."

OTHER OPTIONS

If you cannot get the loan you want or the amount you need, consider what is known as creative financing. Many lending institutions will handle second mortgages, also known as "piggyback" loans. Often a seller, especially if he or she is eager to close the deal, will finance part of the buyer's purchase price in a "take-back" mortgage, in effect, lending you your down payment. In a new and very creative twist, some lenders are even offering "portable" mortgages that you can take with you if you are transferred or move to another area of the country and must sell your current home and buy another. Many real-estate developers offer special financing on new homes.

Ask your broker about all of these options. Just be careful when considering them to research the trend in property values in the area. You don't want to get stuck in a no- or low-down-payment mortgage on a property whose value could drop precipitously, leaving you owing more than the property is worth. Though real estate is one of the best investments you can make, it isn't without risk. Say you borrow $145,000 on a $150,000 home. You owe $145,000 plus interest payments for the term of the loan. If the property value should decline to $135,000, you now owe more than the property is currently worth. Had you put down a 20 percent down payment, you'd only owe $120,000, plus interest, and you'd still have $15,000 in equity.

A WORD ABOUT INSPECTIONS AND INSURANCE

Speaking of risk, your next step is to protect your investment. As a first-time homeowner, you can't afford to have major disasters happen. One way to protect against the cost of major repair jobs is to have a good independent inspection done before you buy the home. You have about ten days to two weeks to have the property you've put an offer on inspected by a licensed inspector (preferably not one recommended by the seller or the seller's broker). If the inspection report indicates serious problems, you have the right to back out of the deal. If you still want the house, try to renegotiate the price with the seller, taking into account the cost you face in fixing the problem.

Two areas of concern when buying an older home are the septic system and the underground oil tank. Your dream house might have neither, but for those that have one or both, beware the potential trouble they can cause. Victoria Secunda's cautionary tale about being "penny wise, pound foolish" on page 91 could save you $50,000.

MORE MUST-HAVE INSURANCE COVERAGE

Could you afford to rebuild your home if a fire destroyed it or a hurricane blew it down? What if thieves took your TV set and computer and CD player and silver and priceless antiques? Could you buy replacements out of your financial assets? Few of us could. Property and casualty insurance shifts some of the risk to the insurance company.

Homeowner's policies usually cover:

1. Fire insurance on the house.

2. Extended coverage for damage to the house

by such things as wind, hail, falling objects, smoke, and motor vehicles.

3. Allowance for additional living expenses, in the event that you have to live in a motel or rented house while repairs are made.

4. Allowance for personal property lost because of fire, theft, or mysterious disappearance. This covers such items as clothing, books, cameras, personal computers, and household furnishings.

5. Liability, which covers claims based on any injuries suffered by others and caused by your property. Classic examples: The neighbor's kid is bitten by your dog or a friend slips on the ice in your driveway. The coverage includes payments for medical expenses.

Just how much insurance should you carry on your home? It depends on the value of the house and its contents. Review your current policy with your insurance agent and update it, if necessary, annually. Some insurance companies automatically tack on an annual increment to cover the appreciation of your property and simply bill you for the increase. Make sure that increase is enough. Do you need to take out a personal property floater for items whose value

Window-Shopping for Homes & Money on the Web

> **www.va.gov:** The Web site of the Department of Veterans Affairs has a Home Loan section, where you can find out whether you or a member of your family is eligible for a VA loan, plus information on the VA's Home Loan Program, and a list of lenders who offer these loans.

>> **www.hud.org:** The U.S. Housing and Urban Development Department Web site offers a free online homebuyers' education course that satisfies HUD requirements for public homebuyer assistance programs.

>> **www.bankrate.com:** An all-purpose credit information site, offering the latest mortgage rates and articles on financing, refinancing, and much more.

>> **www.homepath.com:** Fannie Mae's Web site is where you can search for affiliated lenders and find other useful homebuyer information.

>> **www.realtor.com:** The Web site of the National Association of Realtors offers national property, lender, and Realtor listings, plus advice on home buying.

>> **www.nbba.com:** The National Bed & Breakfast Association's Web site includes a How to Start a B&B section and will soon include a B&B Marketplace, listing properties for sale.

TO BUY OR NOT TO BUY ... OIL TANK INSURANCE

BY VICTORIA SECUNDA

Anyone who's ever bought a house knows the money jitters that can set in before the moving van guys have even finished unloading—the sense that you're a heartbeat away from debtors' prison. That's how my husband and I felt after we closed on our home in Connecticut in 1994. We needed everything—window shades, a basement office, new towels—and our credit cards were on fumes. So when my friend Janice said, "Did you get oil tank insurance?" I laughed. "Surely, you jest," I replied. "One more bill and my husband will leave me."

I knew from the home inspector's report that our oil tank was buried under the front walkway. With ostrich-like, new-homeowner logic, I figured that since I couldn't actually see it, it had to be okay. But Janice kept nagging me about this policy. "If you don't protect yourself," she said ominously, "it could wipe out your entire nest egg." To get her off my back—and on the off chance that she was right—I made some inquiries and found that I could get a Tank Protection Policy for a mere $59, and I signed on.

A couple of years later, I read an article about real-estate values being jeopardized by in-ground oil tanks. Then our furnace began making belching noises reminiscent of the Titanic going down. Our oil company suggested we get a new oil tank, to be installed in the basement (i.e., above ground), the price of which, including the removal of the old tank, would be $2,500—assuming, that is, that the old tank was intact—and so we gave the go-ahead.

On a snowy day in February of 1997, the tank digger-upper we had hired—let's call him Hank—drove his bulldozer onto our driveway, chugged to a point 15 feet from our doorway, where the intake pipe was located, and began to chomp away at our lovely brick walkway. Roughly 45 minutes later, he attached a long chain to the exposed tank, winched it out of the ground, and, in triumphant tones, screamed, "It's a leaker!"

My husband and I rushed outside and peered into the hole Hank had dug. It was swimming in black oil. Terms such as "cleanup," "contamination," "water table," "Environmental Protection Agency," "fire marshal," and "fill" fell trippingly off Hank's tongue. It could cost, he added, anywhere from $20,000 on up to solve the "problem," depending on whether or not oil had traveled (yes, oil can "travel" underground) to neighboring properties.

Hank must have noticed our gasping, ashen faces. "Say," he helpfully inquired as he dialed his cell phone to report our "leaker" to the Fire Department, "you got tank insurance?" I ran indoors and read our policy, which stated that the insurance would cover all cleanup expenses up to $100,000, but that anything more would be on our nickel.

The next weeks were a nail-biting waiting game as more machines arrived, and more of our front property was dug up and hauled away in truck after truck. As soil tests continued to show oil contamination, the chasm at our front door grew into a crater 20 feet straight down and 40 feet across the driveway. Finally, a report came back saying that we were "clean" and that the new fill, walkway, and driveway could be installed. Cost to the insurance underwriters: $55,000. Cost to us: $2,500 for the tank removal and replacement, as originally planned, plus $59 for the insurance policy.

I cannot count the times since then that I have thanked Janice for rescuing us. I have spread the word up and down our street to other homeowners, most of whom also didn't have tank insurance, and who, having seen the abyss that had been our driveway, quickly got their own policies (and replaced their own "leakers" for a relative pittance).

Moral of the story: There are times in the life of a homeowner when little things—in this case, an inexpensive insurance policy—mean a lot. If your home is heated by oil, skip the new towels and spend the money on tank insurance, instead. It could be the best investment you ever made.

Victoria Secunda is an award-winning author of several books, including Losing Your Parents, Finding Your Self. *She is the executive editor of* MAKING BREAD*.*

might exceed your policy's coverage? Have all valuables appraised. Since the floater is relatively expensive, you might want to insure only those items that would be really difficult to replace, such as heirlooms, or keep your smaller valuables, such as jewelry, in a safe-deposit box and handle the risk that way.

Mortgage insurance is available from your lender to cover your payments, should you become unable to keep up them up. Most lenders, in fact, require this insurance when you are borrowing more than 80 percent of the property's value. It is very expensive, however. So, unless you are required to purchase it, or you are relying on one income to pay your mortgage and fear a layoff, or are self-employed and can't rely on a steady steam of income, it's probably best to stash the cash you'd be paying for it in an emergency money-market account or short-term CD.

LADIES' CHOICE: WHAT YOU NEED TO KNOW ABOUT CONDOS & CO-OPS & PRE-FABS.

Many single women and young marrieds gravitate toward condominiums and co-ops when they're looking for their first home, because prices for these types of homes tend to be cheaper than standalone, or detached, single-family homes. The good news is that their resale value is rising, as aging boomers begin to downsize and demand for smaller, maintenance-free homes increases. Thus a condo or co-op, while still cheaper than its stand alone cousins, may now be a very good investment. Here are some basics:

Condos. The condominium, or condo, is a structure on the order of an apartment house or town house, in which you are deeded the title to, or ownership of, your unit. Your unit becomes your property. You also have a proportionate ownership in the common facilities, such as hallways, grounds, elevators, and recreational areas (tennis courts, swimming pools, even a golf course in some condos). You pay common charges every month to cover taxes on the property (the tax portion of your common charge is deductible on your income tax return), maintenance, heat, and utilities in the common areas. You get a mortgage on your own unit.

Warning: Common charges have a way of creeping up, so make sure your spending plan can stretch to fit these increases in. Also, you could be hit with an extra assessment, for instance, when the roofs of all the units have to be replaced. As an owner, you will join a condominium association, in which each member has one vote when decisions about the condominium must be made. (All members must agree to abide by the provisions of a condo agreement.)

As a condo owner, you have the same advantages as the owner of a house and lot. Your equity builds up as time goes by. You can itemize your property taxes on your income-tax return. You are responsible for repairs and maintenance within your individual unit, just as you would be in our own house. And, unless the condo association agreement specifies otherwise, you are entitled to sell your unit to anyone you choose.

Co-ops. Co-operatives, or co-ops, are non-profit corporations. The co-op owns your unit; you own stock in the corporation. The amount of stock you own depends on the size and value of the apartment you take. There is one common mortgage on the building (unless the corporation has bought the building outright or already paid off the mortgage). You and all the owners make monthly payments. The amount you pay is determined by the size and value of your units. These payments cover, in effect, taxes, interest payment, and maintenance. As a shareholder, you are entitled to list as deductions on your income-tax return your share of the property taxes and the interest on the mortgage. When you want to sell the apartment, you are really selling your shares in the corporation.

Note: In some co-ops, a new owner must be approved by the other shareholders. The corporation may exercise the option of buying back the shares, if the prospective buyer of your unit isn't approved.

Some important questions to ask before you buy into a co-op or purchase a condo: What are the rules and regulations? Are the other residents happy with the living conditions? Is the place noisy? Too hot? Too cold? Is it clean and well-maintained, indoors and out? Are the recreational facilities adequate and well-maintained? How's the parking? What about lighting? Are you permitted to rent your unit? What are the costs of settlement? Are there any lawsuits pending against the developer or officers of the association? Are most owners living on the premises, or have they rented out their units? If they live there, they'll be more concerned about the maintenance and upkeep.

Pre-fabs. Prefabricated homes, or pre-fabs, are an old housing trend that's making a comeback. If you're looking for a starter home but are discouraged by the high prices in your area and convinced that you'll never save enough for a down payment, consider buying a pre-fab, or manufactured home. Made popular by Sears in the early 1900s when you could actually buy build-it-yourself home "kits" from the Sears & Roebuck catalogue, many of these early prefabricated homes are still standing—and the concept is undergoing a revival. With costs ranging from $25,000 to $30,000 for the simple "mobile home" look to $50,000 to $70,000 for a larger, three-bedroom, three-bath rancher and up (you'd be surprised at the variety of designs), experts estimate that you can save 20 to 25 percent off the cost of traditional new-home construction. Even with land not included, that's a good deal. Though lenders are still a little leery of issuing mortgages on prefabs, that's changing. If you have good credit and own the land you're going to put your prefab on, you should have no problem getting a mortgage. For more information about styles, retailers, financing and lots available in your area, visit www.home-store.com.

All of the home-buying advice that we've just run through comes into play in the following story about a lifelong apartment dweller's experiences first failing, then succeeding at finally becoming a homeowner. Here's how she did it.

RENT-FREE AT LAST!

BY ALLISON ACKEN, PHD

"WOW! MINE. THIS PLACE IS MINE." Every morning, I wake up in my own bed in my own house to the beautiful sight of magnolia blossoms and the clear blue (for LA) sky outside my window and wonder, "How did this miracle happen?"

A few years ago, I accepted two probabilities: (1) I would not own property; and (2) I would not have a second marriage. That must be why it's called probability theory—even the unlikeliest of things can happen. On April 16, 2003, my dream came true: I am growing accustomed to being a homeowner.

Why is this such a big deal for me? I grew up in apartments on the East Coast, and, later, as a single mom, I raised my daughters in an apartment in Santa Monica, California. My mother is still a renter at age 85. As a self-employed, divorced woman with a good income, some debt, few assets, and even less money to put down, I knew the cards were stacked against my being able to buy property.

Does any of this sound familiar? If so, I'm here to tell you: Don't give up. With a healthy housing market, a big dose of good luck, a terrific realtor, an aggressive mortgage broker, and a little extra help from your friends, you, too, can become a homeowner. Here's how I did it.

GOING HOME SHOPPING

Tip #1: Remain hopeful. Where there's a will there's a way, as the saying goes. You just have to find it and not be put off by initial failure or discouraging words from one realtor or mortgage broker. If at first you don't succeed, ask for a second, or third, opinion. I learned this lesson the hard way.

Four years ago, my first attempt to buy was humiliating. I found an inexpensive, pretty co-op with a pool. I had a small down payment (15 percent), but also an imperfect credit report and more debt than the broker wanted to see. He told me to use my down payment to pay off the debt and that would make it easier for me to get a loan. Without double-checking, I followed his advice.

You guessed it. He still couldn't get me a loan. Co-ops (you own shares, instead of the property itself) are common in the East, but not in the West; ergo, the low price. The few lenders willing to approve a co-op mortgage in my area required 20 percent down and a top-notch applicant; ergo, not me.

I tried another broker, but she told me that paying off the debt with my savings was the worst thing I could have done. In her opinion, she could have worked around the debt, but the down payment was a necessity. So, I didn't have the debt anymore—that was good—but I couldn't qualify to buy the property. I simply gave up, convinced that I was destined to be a renter forever. I felt so ashamed and so different. All of my friends were homeowners. Of course, not one of them had been a single mom for 20 years.

Tip #2: Have one of your closest friends become a realtor. Short of that, make sure to find a realtor with a good reputation, one whom you can trust and feel comfortable with, perhaps through a referral from a friend. After all, you will be sharing a lot of personal financial information with your realtor and spending a lot of time together for several months. I didn't have to look far for mine. Last year, my friend Roxanne enrolled in real-estate school—a big undertaking for her, because she has dyslexia and severe test anxiety. Roxanne bought her first house at 18. Real estate was perfect for her, if she could only get past the learning disability to pass the exams and get licensed. At the same time, my first book was coming out. We were both struggling with our new ventures and spent much phone time coaching each other throughout the process. The result: Roxanne passed the state examination the first time she took it—a terrific accomplishment for her! She became "Roxie the Realtor" at the local office of Coldwell Banker. My book received five-star reviews—a terrific accomplishment for me!

A few months later, Roxanne said, "I met a really sharp mortgage broker. Why don't you call her?" Reliving the shame of the co-op experience, I responded, "Rox, I am not nearly ready to buy anything. Housing prices have doubled since I last looked. It will never work." Gently and firmly, she prodded me: "Just call her."

Tip #3: Work with a broker who knows all the angles. I took a deep breath and called a broker at First Capital in Santa Monica. Expecting the bad news (that I would never, ever be allowed to buy a piece of property anywhere), but hoping that she might help me plan a strategy, I explained that I simply wanted her input on where to focus: saving, continuing to pay down debt, giving up completely? I learned that initial exploratory consultations of this sort can be very valuable: brokers can pre-qualify you for a mortgage and tell you exactly how much house you can afford, as well as what you have to do to increase your chances of having your loan approved.

The broker asked a few quick, businesslike questions concerning my credit report (pretty good); income (pretty good); and money available for down payment (very little). She also asked how much I had available to cover closing costs, explaining that I'd need about 3 percent of the sale price. (I had just a bit saved for that.) And she wanted a minimum three-month history of saving/investment accounts (in which I had accumulated very little). Her response, after she crunched all the numbers, was comforting: "You are not as far off the mark as you think you are." She even called me "normal." My credit score was good, my income fine. I had built up a little history of assets (savings/investments)—more would be better. With my record, she thought that I could probably get a 100 percent loan in today's market.

The 100 percent loan was very good news. Housing prices had been going up so fast that I might never have caught up otherwise. I would have needed a down payment of at least $40,000—a lot of money for a single person to save. But with a 100 percent loan, I had a chance. I just needed to come up with enough money for closing costs and any emergencies that might crop up after the purchase.

It was a good time to enter the market, but I didn't think I was quite ready. If only current conditions would hold—but would they? I thanked her and told her I would be in touch in 18 months or so, when I'd saved more money. An impor-

tant shift had occurred. I no longer felt like a loser.

Tip #4: Let your friends and family help in whatever way they can. Now that I began to believe that home ownership was not just an impossible dream, I was more motivated than ever to make it happen. Looking over my financial history, I suddenly realized that I might have more assets than I thought, which could improve my chances of getting the loan. (Moral: know what you're really worth.) For many years, I had held an account jointly with my childhood friend, James, so that I would be able to access funds easily in an emergency. I called my broker right back; she needed copies of the statements and a letter saying that I could have access to the entire account, if necessary. Done! The only remaining obstacle was the approximately $10,000 to cover closing costs, the move, any work that might need to be done, and a little cushion, just in case. I still had to save that amount.

My friend Allen had been wishing for years that I could buy a home for all the obvious reasons: the tax benefits, the equity that I'd be building, not to mention the status and the pride that come with home ownership. He had been following this process very carefully. When I reported back to him that in 18 months or so I would finally be ready to make my move, Allen said, "You need to do it now. Interest rates are as low as they've ever been, and we have no idea when they will start to go up." I started to explain again that I needed to save more money. "No, no, you don't understand. I will give you the money. Start looking," he said.

You could have knocked me over with that proverbial feather. I know many first-timers do get help from parents or grandparents, but I was on my own. My mother simply didn't have the resources. (Her contribution was lighting candles at church.) The last thing I expected was help.

I would never have thought of asking Allen for money. To begin with, I am not very good at asking for help, or even accepting it when it is offered. Years earlier, my therapist tried to counsel me, "If you don't ask, you don't get. If you ask, at least you have a chance. The worst that can happen is someone says, 'No'." But I was taught that the poor and the meek are blessed; I should wait for my rewards; to ask for something is wrong; "no" is humiliating. Today, like my therapist before me, I try to help women to ask for what they need—even if the answer they will sometimes get is "no."

I was finally ready to say, "Yes!" I accepted Allen's offer with no shame, no blame, and no guilt—just a hesitant but simple "yes." Now it was time for the fun part: shopping.

Tip #5: Set your priorities before shopping. Roxanne asked for a list of priorities. For me, those were staying in my same neighborhood, if at all possible; space for a small office; a decent bathtub; and, in my dreams, a building with a pool or a unit with a washer/dryer or a small powder room. I knew I would never get all of these at my price, but if you don't ask. . . .

The LA market was hot, and multiple bids were common. I lost two possibilities in bidding wars. When I was outbid on the first one, I was wrecked, but Roxie assured me that there would be another. we found the second one, and I lost that to another bidder. Crushed! Then believe it or not, Rox found the perfect place, and the price had been reduced! how was that possible?

Tip #6: Remember Tip #1, and keep the faith. Sometimes it seems to take forever to find the right place. Just keep telling yourself that if you miss out on one place, another piece of property, maybe even a better one, will be right around the corner. This is where luck, or fate, or whatever, kicks in. I was very lucky; the seller's agent wasn't doing his job. He lived far away and didn't want to drive to show the place, so he arranged for keys to be available. Roxanne had trouble getting the keys, and when she finally did, they didn't work. Other buyers might have given up, but I loved the grounds—a five-acre oasis with two swimming pools in Brentwood Village, my favorite neighborhood. I really wanted to see the unit.

Roxanne was tenacious, and we finally gained entry. It was the best yet: a spacious, mid-century unit, built in 1959, over-looking a park, and with great light, a huge pink bathroom, a large pink kitchen with a blender built into the countertop, and light pinky-taupe paneling on the walls of the living room and dining room. The balcony had been enclosed—perfect for an office. Hardly anything had been updated since 1959 and I loved it; this was the era I had grown up in.

Tip #7: Don't panic when it comes time to sign the mortgage papers. Snafus are part of the process. In my case, the bidding process went fairly smoothly, mainly because Roxanne cushioned me from the difficult parts, and because the owner didn't have any other bids. I'm not sure anyone else ever saw the place. And, as Roxanne said later, the things I liked (pink, paneling, vintage design elements) were things other people didn't like.

For me, the most difficult part of the entire process was signing papers at the escrow office. It took a very long time, because the escrow officer was having a meltdown, in tears from fatigue. The closing date was pushed back a day and one piece of paper had to be rushed to the office at the last moment, but those things happen. My loan went through, the escrow closed, and I finally had the keys to my first home.

Tip #8: Throw a party! I am so excited to be living in my own home. Mine! Mine! Mine! I feel like a bona fide member of society now. I conquered the big obstacle, won the race—pulled off what my mother hasn't been able to achieve. It may sound silly, but having a home is a basic American value. Our economic system is built around home ownership, giving homeowners major tax benefits and a chance to build equity over the years as the property appreciates.

Best of all, I am not throwing money away on rent anymore. As my friend Susan said, "You're finally on the merry-go-round. And (did I mention?), it is mine. Finally, I get to change things and make my home the way I want it to be. I own it, and if I want to build bookcases or rip out the carpet or add a wall sconce in the foyer, I can do it. Of course, I can't afford to do it all right now, but that's okay, too. It's something I can look forward to.

Now, I have only one probability to accept—that I will never marry again. But who knows? After all, it's only probability theory. Maybe Roxanne knows a good matchmaker.

HOME ECONOMICS: NO DOWN PAYMENT? NO PROBLEM!

BY ALLISON ACKEN, PHD

Believe me, if I can do it, anyone can. There are more mortgage products today than ever before. As my broker says, "Everyone has a different expectation and availability of funds. We structure every loan as if it were a tailored suit." That's what mortgage brokers do. They're real-estate financing professionals who act as intermediaries between consumers and lenders. They'll study your financial situation, lay out all of your options, and find something that works for you. With the help of a good broker, you, too, should be able to find a mortgage that will put you under your own roof. Visit the Web site of the National Association of Mortgage Brokers (www.namb.org) to locate a broker near you.

If bad credit is a problem, Federal Housing Administration specialists or state housing agencies can help, and a good broker will guide you through that process as well. The bottom line is: owning real estate is the best investment you can make, particularly when mortgage rates are still low. So don't wait. Here are a few of the newer mortgage products to ask about, as well as some traditional resources to consider:

>> E-Trade Financial has just introduced the first "portable" mortgage, or "Mortgage on the Move," as they call it. Qualify for this and lock in current low rates for the house you purchase now and carry that same rate over to your next home purchase. This mortgage is useful if you're buying a starter home and plan to upgrade in the future, or if you have to relocate, or will soon retire and downsize. For more information, visit www.etrade.com or call 1-866-806-7292.

>> Fannie Mae offers flexible 97-percent and 100-percent loans and many other options to increase your chances of becoming a homeowner. Visit the Homepath page at www.fanniemae.com to locate a Fannie Mae-approved lender or a state housing finance agency in your area.

>> The Federal Housing Administration (FHA) has numerous programs, including no- and low-down-payment plans, help with closing costs and lenient credit standards. Visit www.fha-home-loans.com to find out more, and, if you are eligible, be sure to check out its Officer/Teacher Next Door loans, which offer a 50-percent discount on the appraised value of properties in revitalization areas and require only $100 down.

>> GMAC's Homestretch Plan is geared to get you into your own home, even if you can't afford a down payment. If you qualify for an FHA-insured, 30-year, first-mortgage loan, you can receive a HomeStretch loan (in essence, a second mortgage) to cover the traditional down payment and closing costs for an additional 4 percent of the mortgage amount. The bonus is that the Homestretch loan is zero-interest, no-payment and fully forgiven if you stay in the home for ten years. For more information, visit www.gmacfs.com.

>> The Home Down Payment Gift Foundation offers grants up to $30,000 to cover closing costs or down payments, based on the applicant's need. The seller must agree to donate a small percent of the sale to the Foundation. Visit www.homedownpayment.org to learn more.

>> Interest-only loans, in which buyers pay only interest for the first few years, are becoming more popular. They allow buyers to purchase more house with a smaller initial monthly payment. The downside: As long as you are paying only interest you don't build equity. The upside: Your entire monthly payment is tax-deductible, and as long as the property value rises, when you sell you'll still come out ahead.

THE ANNUAL PAY-OFF

As if accumulating equity weren't enough of a benefit to convince you to become a home-owner, consider the annual tax advantage that owning property gives you. Count the ways you can take deductions from your income tax:

Mortgage interest. The interest you pay to a lender on a mortgage loan is tax deductible, whether the mortgage is for a place that is for personal use (a place to live in), business use (a place in which to operate a business), or income-producing use (a place you have purchased as an investment to rent to others).

Your monthly mortgage payments cover interest on the principal amount you owe, plus repayment of some of the principal. In addition, some banks pay your real-estate taxes and home-owner's insurance for you and add those amounts to the total monthly payment, so you are paying one-twelfth of those costs each month. All lending institutions provide you with a year-end statement that specifies how much you have paid during the year for each item.

Points. At the closing on your mortgage, you may have to pay some points. This is a one-time expense. Each point equals one percent of your mortgage ($600, for example, on a $60,000 mortgage). If points are considered to be prepaid interest, they are usually deductible on your income-tax return. They are not deducible if they are considered a service fee. Get the answer to that question when you go shopping for your mortgage. If the points are in fact deductible, don't let the bank automatically take them out of your loan. Insist on paying for them with a separate check, so you have a record of the expense.

Real property taxes. These local taxes, imposed on all property owners, are deductible from your federal income tax. Real estate taxes pay for schools, roads, and municipal services, such as police and fire departments and trash collection. Real estate taxes have a way of increasing as the value of property increases. Your city or town will reassess property every few years and increase taxes based on the new assessments.

YOUNG MARRIED'S GUIDE TO STAYING OUT OF DEBT: HOW TO KEEP THE ROOF OVER YOUR HEAD

You're a homeowner, now what? It's important to keep up your mortgage payments and protect your investment by maintaining your home. Soon you may have college savings to worry about, and sooner than you imagine, your own retirement nest egg to manage. For most of us, sticking to a budget, like sticking to a diet, is a constant struggle.

I mentioned in my introduction that my mother's biggest piece of financial advice to me was: Marry a wealthy man. "You'll marry a rich man, and then you'll be able to buy everything you want," she would say to me every time I lobbied her for a new sweater or skirt or whatever my "I've just got to have it" item of the moment happened to be when I was in high school.

Though I watched reruns of *How to Marry a Millionaire* on the "Million Dollar Movie" religiously, I didn't marry a rich man; how many of us do? I married my college sweetheart right after graduation. Two English majors in love: a financial disaster waiting to happen. Neither of us had jobs; neither of us even knew what we wanted to do with our degrees.

Our wedding was a slapdash romantic affair; we

were married by a justice of the peace under a huge maple tree in a small community park—this was the 70s, after all. Our flower girl carried wildflowers we'd picked from the side of the road on the way to the wedding, and for dessert our guests dined on luscious, fresh strawberries purchased at a roadside fruit stand that morning. Fortunately, someone thought to bring chilled champagne.

Thirty-two years later, we're still married. But, financially, we've had our ups and downs, and money problems have strained our relationship. Looking back, I can see clearly now that, had we had the Money Talk that all the experts encourage newlyweds to have, not only would we be in better financial shape today but our marriage would be on more solid ground. Or, who knows, maybe we'd be divorced, our union unable to survive the power struggle that might have ensued.

In a recent survey taken by the Association of Bridal Consultants, more than 67 percent of married couples said that their most serious conflicts in the first year of marriage were money-related. With almost 2.5 million couples tying the knot in this country every year, that's a whole lot of arguing going on! In the interest of preserving the peace, to end this chapter, MAKING BREAD asked several long-married (sometimes more than once) women to summarize their "What I Wish I'd Known Then" advice. Do as we say (not what we did), and we guarantee you'll be wealthier and your marriage will be healthier 32 years from now.

Rule No. 1: Don't "Charge" into Marriage.

"So many couples are charging their weddings on credit cards—and some are divorced before the bills are paid off. Unbelievable!" says financial planner Elizabeth Lewin. But with the average cost of first weddings reported to be $22,000 and so-called "wedding loans" offered by banks and advertised in bridal magazines and on wedding-planner Web sites such as www.TheKnot.com, it seems that the 70s wedding ideal of KISS (keep it simple, sweetie) has fallen by the wayside.

Just think how far $22,000 would go toward a down payment on a first home, and remember that fond memories of that special day will stay with you even if your wedding only costs $220. Instead, use The Knot's "Create a Gift" service to register for American Express gift cheques toward a down payment on a house, car, or any of the other major expenses that newlyweds face.

Rule No. 2: Make Money Talk Your Pillow Talk.

"There's romance in dreaming together," says Patricia Schiff Estess, author of *Money Advice for Your Successful Remarriage.* "Hot-air ballooning in France, seeing a child graduate, buying a home, all require planning. And planning means you have to put a price tag on each of these dreams and begin saving for them. That helps curb the spontaneous purchases that drain savings and throw people into debt. In times of financial crisis, people who have communicated their money values, attitudes, and dreams are better able to support each other—emotionally and practically—than those who haven't."

All of the women interviewed for this article stressed the importance of having the Money Talk. "If you have a secret, or a fear, about money—big or little—let your spouse know about it right away. And be kind and loving when your spouse tells you about a money secret or fear of his own," advises psychologist Allison Acken, the author of *it's Only Money: A Primer for Women.*

My husband and I didn't know how we were going to make our money, much less spend it, when we married. And once the money started coming in, first from his salary as a teacher and later from mine as an editor, we made no plans to save. We never sat down and identified goals that we jointly wanted to work toward—a house, children, a million-dollar retirement nest egg, a sailboat—any goal would have been better than none.

Now I think that was calculated avoidance on our part. The few times the subject did come up, we realized that our values, priorities, and attitudes about money were vastly different—he is a saver and I am a spender—and we feared that dealing with those differences would tear us apart. The wiser course would have been to face them head on and seek a compromise. How I wish now that we'd made saving a priority!

Rule No. 3: Don't Make It About Control.

"Set up three accounts: ours, his, and hers," says Estess. "Set aside a sum of money each month for each partner to spend as he or she likes, without consulting one another. Each can spend, save, or invest all or part of that money, without checking in with the other. They can even merge their funds to buy something they both want. But it all has to be voluntarily. No coercion or criticism from the other. Having control over a limited amount of discretionary funds in your own account satisfies spending urges and curbs the impulse to get into big debt."

For me, the issue of control centered on who paid the bills. At first, my husband paid them, and because we only had one joint account, I always felt I had to ask for money when I wanted to buy something for myself. Once I took over the bill-paying (after a huge argument), I felt I had

regained my independence. Even though the amount of money coming in remained the same, I had the power to decide what bills were paid when and I always knew how much we had—and how much was left over for me to spend. If we'd set up his, hers, and ours accounts, my spending might have been brought under control in a way that didn't threaten my need for independence.

"Work together on the money issues," urges Acken. "You're building the financial foundation for this partnership called marriage and you want that foundation to be smooth, solid, and strong." Health editor Nissa Simon seconds that notion, adding: "When you decide things together, it tends to strengthen a marriage."

Rule No. 4: Mall Trips Aren't Marriage Therapy.
Furniture, dishes, sheets, towels, appliances, the marriage bed. . . the first year or two after they marry are probably the most dangerous time for couples in terms of credit-binging. Add to that the fact that this can be an emotionally charged time for many women as we settle into the role of wife and financial partner, and you can see why the malls of America are filled with couples spending to soothe their tension.

Friday nights at the mall were a regular form of entertainment and relaxation for me (after all, didn't my mother tell me I'd be able to buy whatever I wanted after I married?)—and I often dragged my husband along to help carry the packages. Did he complain about my spending? Sure. Did it stop me? Unfortunately, no. In later years, he only knew how much I'd charged at tax time, when he added up the (then) deductible interest on the credit cards. That way, we'd only have one money fight a year. But that annual fight got so bad that I finally had to hire an accountant to calculate our taxes. Problem solved! The real solution would have been to put a savings plan in place, so that I'd have had less money to spend frivolously.

I learned the hard way that credit cards aren't an extension of your salary. According to Lewin, one of the first things newlyweds should do after they marry is to "add up what you both owe on student loans, auto loans, and any unpaid balances on credit cards. Then figure out what your joint take-home income is. Your monthly debt load should not exceed 15 percent of your net income—maybe a little more, but 20 percent is the beginning of trouble," she says. "Beware adding to your debt load by buying furniture on time or purchasing an expensive new car."

As tempting as they may sound, be especially leery of those "buy now, pay later" appliance, carpet, or furniture deals. When you read the fine print, you'll find that the interest rate, once you start paying the debt down, can be exorbitant, unnecessarily increasing the total amount you're paying for something that will be obsolete or need replacing in a few years anyway. Instead of buying everything new when you're setting up house, haunt flea markets, Goodwill stores, and used-car lots for good deals.

Rule No. 5: Kids 'R' Costly. Cribs, diapers, all those adorable baby clothes, the high cost of day-care, medical bills, and the loss of the mother's income, should she decide to stay home: the birth of the first child ranks right behind the first year of marriage as a money pit. More about this in the next chapter. Try to resist spending big money on designer clothes that your firstborn will outgrow in weeks or months. Instead, trade baby clothes and furniture with your friends, check Goodwill, or shop at Target, Baby Gap, or Sears. Anywhere but Neiman Marcus.

And before you make the decision to stay home for a few years, be sure to research the financial consequences. Everything from Social Security to your pension, to your 401(k), and your salary will take a hit. Consider this: a 12-week unpaid leave equals a 25 percent salary cut for the year, which reduces the amount being invested in a 401(k) proportionally. Smart couples find ways to compensate by increasing their contributions to their 401(k) months—even years— in advance. Or they set up a spousal IRA, which allows the husband to contribute up to $3,000 toward the wife's retirement each year she's off the job.

My husband and I didn't have children, but the flower girl at our wedding is now a happily married stay-at-home mom. I've since met many young women who are more focused on saving for their future than I was at their age, and I'm always in awe of their self-discipline. I've also met many young women who could use the advice that all of us quoted in this article wish we'd known way back when we first wed. Still, of the couples who attended my outdoor nuptials, four are now divorced, and we've somehow remained together. So my husband and I must have done something right.

Female Finance Checklist:
Time to Consider Marriage and Mortgages

❑ **Goals:** Your college loans have been consolidated and are nearly paid off; you've established an emergency account to cover your expenses in the event of a layoff or other financial banana peel. Time to begin focusing on becoming a property owner. It's the smartest investment a woman can make. You may be planning your wedding or considering a live-in relationship. You understand the financial consequences of any such union, and have considered the advantages of putting a pre nup or other written agreements in place. You recognize the importance of discussing spending habits and planning for future goals together when two become one financial unit.

❑ **Career:** You're gaining recognition within your company and in your field; and you're continuing to invest in professional growth by attending conferences and seminars. You also may be planning to have children shortly, and you have begun investigating alternate job arrangements or saving to make up for lost income during the months or years you may be out of the workforce.

❑ **Investments:** You're fully invested in your 401(k) plan at work, if you have one. If not, you've opened an IRA and funded it to the max, and are tucking away even more money in CDs, stock and bond mutual funds or Treasury bills.

❑ **Real Estate:** You've checked your credit score and taken steps to improve it, if necessary, so you can pre-qualify for a mortgage that fits your budget, and you're ready to get real estate.

❑ **Insurance:** Once you purchase your home, you add homeowner's insurance to your health and auto coverage. Shop around for the best package deal. Consider purchasing extra disability or life insurance, as your income and family responsibilities grow.

❑ **Wills:** Now that your assets and responsibilities have grown, write a will to ensure that your property will pass to those of your choosing. Otherwise, the state will decide who gets what, based on a formula. (Generally, community and joint property passes to a spouse, if there is one; the remainder is divided among spouse, children, parents, siblings, nieces or nephews, and the state.) If you have no family, consider willing all or part of your estate to a charitable institution.

If you are in a long-term live-in relationship, wills, powers of attorney, and other agreements are of particular importance, to ensure that you and your partner have as many of the rights, privileges, and protections of a spouse as possible.

CHAPTER FOUR:
KIDS 'R' COSTLY: HOW TO AFFORD THEM

Having children changes everything—not least of which is your financial picture. Suddenly, college bills loom—and you've barely finished paying off your own. You're no longer responsible just for your own security; you have another person to take care of. Some women find having children an excuse for spending money; others, like contributing editor Sharon Sorokin James, find them to be a reason to start taking better care of their finances. "If you are not good at saving money (like me), teaching your daughter how to do it will teach you how to do it better," she says. "Since thinking seriously about how to teach my children about money, I've cut back significantly on spending, my husband and I have started a financial plan, paid off our credit-card debt, and organized our bill-paying. It's never too late in life to do these things, but it is better to get your children started early."

Two of the most difficult choices a woman has to make are whether—and when—to have children. A generation ago, women who wanted careers knew that, to compete successfully with men, they might as well give up all thoughts of having children. Those who chose marriage and motherhood over career often struggled with the deep-seated feelings of frustration that Betty Friedan called "the problem that has no name" in her groundbreaking book, *The Feminine Mystique*.

The daughters of those women grew up to believe they could balance motherhood and career as effortlessly as a circus performer spinning plates and juggling balls at the same time. Many of them have climbed the corporate ladder while raising children, dropping only a few plates along the way. Now, in increasing numbers, these same women are leaving the Corp'rat race to return home to spend quality time with their families and start businesses of their own. They are the lucky few—the ones who have the luxury of choice that money can buy. In the low- and middle-income brackets, dual-income families and single-mother households are proliferating. Many women simply work at jobs to make ends meet—then come home, tired, to do the more important work of raising their kids.

The juggling act isn't easy, which is why so many women are postponing child-rearing. According to Census Bureau statistics, childlessness has doubled in the past twenty years, with one in five women between the ages 40 and 44 now without children. The price women pay when they have children, early *or* late, is a stiff one. "The average college-educated woman will earn nearly a million dollars less than her male counterpart over a lifetime of work because of the wage gap and the time she takes off—an average of five years—to raise children," says financial writer Susan E. Reed, who is working on a book about activism among women in the workforce. Fewer years in the workforce = fewer raises, fewer 401(k) deposits, and smaller Social Security and pension checks.

Those who wait to get pregnant until their careers are established are finding, to their dismay, that they have to pay an added penalty—the possible loss of biological choice. In her book, *Creating a Life: Professional Women and the Quest for Children*, economist and author Sylvia Ann Hewlett details the awakening realization among women who have delayed pregnancy that they may have waited too long. Assuming that they had until their forties to conceive, they are finding that, in fact, even with the latest medical reproductive techniques, the chances of becoming pregnant after the late twenties declines rapidly.

So what's a woman to do? An increasing number of us are choosing to forego the comfortable lifestyle a dual income can buy to become stay-at-home moms—though that choice exacts other costly penalties, such as the loss of a woman's long-term security and independence. Others have found that the answer is having a stay-at-home partner. It's interesting that more than a third of the women on *Fortune* magazine's 2002 list of "The 50 Most Powerful Women in Business" had either full- or part-time stay-at-home spouses—or "trophy husbands," as the magazine dubbed them, and it is predicted that trend will grow. At the top of that power list was Hewlett-Packard chief executive Carly Fiorina, whose husband, Frank Fiorina, is a retired AT&T vice president.

A growing number of women—10 million at last Census Bureau count—are single moms, doing the hardest job of all, raising their children on their own. Most of us do our best to make the right choices for ourselves and for those we love, and still hold onto our dreams. In a commencement address at Stanford University, Carly Fiorina encouraged the graduates not to be afraid of making mistakes. "Don't let your options paralyze you. Make a decision, and then choose what happens next," she advised. The questions Fiorina asks herself when she has doubts about where she's headed are: "Am I acting out a role, or am I living the truth? Am I still making choices, or have I simply stopped choosing? Am I in a place that engages my mind and captures my heart? Am I stuck in the past, or am I defining my future? And what will I leave the planet?"

Children aren't the only gifts we can leave this planet. I am one of the growing minority of women (19 percent of women, aged 40 to 44, are childless, twice as many as in 1980) who have chosen not to have children. Interestingly, the wage gap begins to close for these women; they earn 90 percent of what their male counterparts make. But my decision wasn't based on wanting to earn more money. I simply didn't feel a strong biological urge to have a child—and I didn't think that I could give 100 percent to both career and motherhood. I'm not without regrets, but I know that I made the right choice for myself, given my personal circumstances and predilections. Unfortunately, career versus motherhood is a choice—or compromise— that our society still forces women to make. More corporate day-care centers, flex time, and paid maternity leave for husband or wife would go a long way toward making that difficult choice seem like less of a compromise.

Now, with my own mother gone and no children of my own, I find myself in the peculiar role of mothering myself. I look at photos of myself as a child and wonder, "How well have I nurtured that hopeful young girl whose future I am still shaping?" Whether we are mothers or not, perhaps that's a question we all should ask ourselves on our birthdays—and regularly in between.

How well are *you* mothering *yourself*?

To help you in weighing the financial implications of the decision to have children or not, to stay home or not, in this chapter, we'll cover how starting a family affects your earning power, your savings, and your retirement security. We'll suggest what you can do to ensure that you can afford to be a stay-at-home mom—how you can counteract the negative effects of those years away from the workforce. We'll share the stories of working moms, juggling the responsibilities of work outside the home with their children's, their partner',s and their own needs. We'll discuss the "office politics of pregnancy," go over the best kinds of insurance to meet your new responsibilities, and cover some of the inventive ways mothers are teaching their daughters and sons about money. We've also included a candid mother–daughter conversation on what it's like being raised by a working mom.

HOW MUCH IS IT GOING TO COST YOU TO STAY HOME WITH YOUR BUNDLE OF JOY—A BUNDLE! HERE'S HOW TO AFFORD IT.

The feminist Supermom, juggling briefcase and diaper bag, work and child-rearing responsibilities, is well on the way to becoming an endangered species. Thank goodness! Many women these days don't feel the need to prove they can be all things to all people. Though we may still prefer to return to work for both personal and financial reasons, we're not as militant about it as the last generation of working moms

was. More and more of us, in fact, are opting to become full-time moms, at least for the first year or two after our babies are born. Call it retro chic motherhood. According to the Census Bureau, the number of women who returned to work within a year of having their babies dropped 4 percent, from a record 59 to 55 percent, between 1998 and 2000.

The number of children being raised by stay-at-home moms has risen 13 percent in a little less than a decade. Some experts suggest that the increase in Hispanic families in the U.S. may be one factor driving this trend. Others speculate that a generation of women who were raised in day care are now becoming mothers and that these women may not want their own children to become day-care or latchkey kids.

From a financial perspective, going from two paychecks to one takes careful planning. Even a three- month maternity leave can put a big dent in the family budget. Staying at home to raise your bundle of joy for a year or more can cost you, well, a bundle. You'll be losing much more than just your salary during that time. While staying home can be very tempting, before you bid farewell to your employer, you need to be aware of the many ways that such a move will impact you, as a woman, as well as your family, both now and in the future. Then find ways to compensate for the income and other benefits that you will be giving up.

When Two Incomes Become One. No doubt you have an idea of what your income and expenses are. Take those figures and start playing "what if." What if you stayed home, and your family's resources went from two incomes to one? What if you return to work after the birth of your child? What added or reduced expenses would there be in each case? You'll want to pay particular attention to the following areas that will be affected by your decision to work or stay at home. Add up the pluses and minuses, and see where you stand.

Your income. You can expect income to drop significantly, if you decide to stay at home. You'll need to start thinking about what changes you could make in order to reduce expenses to compensate for the lost income. Can you cover all of your monthly bills with one income? Be sensitive to the fact that it can be very stressful and frightening for the remaining breadwinner to bear that responsibility alone. Would it be possible for your husband to find a higher-paying job or to ask for a raise? Could you work part-time, telecommuting from home? The decision to live on one income must be made jointly.

Lost benefits. When calculating the value of your income, don't forget to factor in the value of any benefits you currently receive through your employer. A dental plan is pure gold to a family with young children! Does your spouse's plan have similar benefits, and how much more will it cost to have the entire family covered on that plan, if it isn't already?

Child care. According to the latest figures from the Children's Defense Fund, American parents pay between $4,000 and $10,000 per child per year for full-time childcare. It doesn't take much to realize how much money you would save by staying home, as opposed to paying for full-time child care for one, two, or more children. On the other hand, you will be eligible to claim a portion of your childcare expenses as a credit, should you return to work. (See taxes, below.)

Transportation. If you stay home, you'll save on gas or commuter tickets. On the other hand, if you were only relying on one car, you may now need two—one for you to drive to the shopping mall or recreation center or doctor's appointments, while you're home. You might even need to invest in a minivan. If so, can you afford a second car payment and the additional insurance?

Food. If you stay home, you'll probably cook more meals and save money on takeout and restaurant bills.

Clothing. If your current job requires you to wear designer suits, you'll see a dramatic reduction in your expenses in this area. You'll probably be able to splurge on a diaper service with the money you save.

Extra expenses. You know that mysterious black hole in your budget where all the money seems to disappear: the café latte every day, the money for a co-worker's birthday present and the office Oscar pool, expensive lunches out. You'll find that those extras disappear once you become a single-income family. There are simply fewer places to spend your money, when you're home.

Taxes. If you decide not to return to work, you'll have no income and thus no income tax to pay. On the other hand, if you return to work and pay for child care you will be able to deduct up to 35 percent of your total eligible expenses for that care from the taxes you owe, (up to a maximum of $3,000 for one child and $6,000 for two or more) thanks to the Child and Dependent Care Credit. (If you hire a nanny, just be sure to pay her Social Security. Remember Nannygate?) Whether you stay home or return to a paying job, you'll be able to deduct a $1,000 child credit from your taxes, and you'll have an extra exemption to claim on your W-4 form.

The Hidden Costs of Staying at Home. While most of us find it relatively easy to assess the short-term costs of staying at home to raise a family, what many fail to consider are the long-term financial implications of that choice. And these are significant for a woman. First of all, there's the fact that you'll likely lose ground when it comes to saving for your retirement. Take Social Security, for starters: the amount of time you take off from work will affect the size of the benefit you get when you retire. Anyone born after 1929 needs to spend at least 10 years in the workforce to become eligible for Social Security. The more you earn, the more you will receive at retirement, because the benefit calculation is based on an average of your earnings during your 35 highest paying years in the workforce. A married woman who has never worked outside the home can claim Social Security benefits based on her husband's record upon retirement, but she will receive only one-half of his benefit. If you are both fully insured at retirement, you will each receive a retirement check based on your own individual record. Or you can elect to claim a "dependent's benefit" equal to one-half of your husband's benefit, if that is higher than your own.

The bottom line is that when women cut back on the number of years they spend earning money—they also risk reducing the size of the benefit they will receive at retirement. Various plans have been proposed to compensate women for the years they spend raising their children—by giving them credits toward Social Security for each year they stay at home, for instance—but none have made it into law. (Write your congressman—or woman—and ask them to make recognition of the value of and compensation for women's unpaid work a priority.)

If you have a 401(k) plan at work, your savings—including your employer's matching contributions—will come to an end. Your husband can open a Spousal Individual Retirement Account (IRA) in your name, while you're at home raising a family. But, in reality, there will be fewer dollars available to do so. Will that smaller nest egg result in a lower standard of living for your family, come retirement time? If both of you continued to work full-time and maxed out your 401(k) contributions, you'd have a small fortune when you retired.

Then, there are the undeniable career costs associated with dropping out of the workforce for an extended period of time. You'll miss out on promotions (and raises), and you may quickly lose touch with developments in your industry or profession, something that could necessitate a period of retraining when you decide to go back to work again. Janice is an accountant and hopes to become a partner in the firm. "That never would happen if I stayed home, and it would be impossible to keep up with all the changes in tax law, if I stopped practicing for four or five years," she explains.

Third, you may lose insurance benefits. Very often, life and disability insurance are part of a corporate benefit package. As a stay-at-home mom, you'll need to buy both life and disability insurance. Did you remember to put this in your budget? What would your husband do, if something were to happen to you? Could he afford to hire the childcare he'd need?

Fourth, as a stay-at-home mom, you'll lose your financial safety net. If your marriage breaks up or your husband dies suddenly, you could find yourself thrown back into the workforce playing a big game of catch-up.

Particularly these days, there's another reason, too, for continuing as a two-paycheck family, even if your child care costs and other work-related expenses end up wiping out the second income altogether. Two incomes can shield against the terrible uncertainties of today's economy. Job security is a thing of the past. What if your husband loses his job? How easy would it be for you to find a job in a difficult job-market?

Beyond Money Considerations. With all of this to worry about, it's no wonder a recent study concluded that two-income families are generally happier and healthier than families in which only the male partner works. They have fewer financial worries and both partners are less likely to suffer from depression. Of course, money shouldn't be the only deciding factor. If you're someone who gets a great deal of satisfaction from working and who thinks she'd be completely stir-crazy by the end of her first day as a stay-at-home mom, then it makes more sense for you to keep your job, even if you can afford to stay home. Your depression and boredom will probably have a negative impact on your child. "This was not a financial decision for us at all," says Barbara. "We both felt we needed to work for the mental stimulation. I would have gone nuts if I stayed at home."

The flip side of the coin also applies, of course. If being at home with your children is extremely important to you, you may decide that you're going to stay home with them, whether you and your partner can actually afford to lose that second

income or not. Carol and Jim commuted by train two hours each way. "I realized," says Carol, "that I would never be home to see my child if I stayed at my job. We worked and reworked our budget several times and knew that we would suffer financially when I quit, but I wouldn't change a thing."

And sometimes the briefcase still doubles as a diaper bag. At the time Matthew was born, Jeanne was earning more than Eric, so there was no way she could stay at home. Eric couldn't leave his job because he had great medical benefits. Jeanne had none. Fortunately, there was a day care center in the same building where Jeanne worked. She got to work at 7:30 A.M. and kept Matthew with her until 9 A.M., when she took him to day care, and then picked him up at 2 P.M.. He napped or played in his portable crib in her office, and when he got older he "helped" her out till she left the office at 3 P.M..

Whether you decide to stay at home with your children or continue working, what's important is how comfortable you and your partner feel about the decision that you have made and that you make that decision together, fully understanding what you're giving up and what you're gaining.

Once you and your partner have decided how you will handle your new parenting responsibilities, get ready to notify your employer. Even if you plan to return to work, you'll be taking a certain amount of maternity leave. Very few companie sin the U.S. offer paid leave, whereas all European Union countries pay at least a percent of salary during maternity leave. When is the best time to tell your boss and co-workers about your pregnancy and how you will handle it? How do you protect your standing in the company while you're on maternity leave or extended leave? Our "Success Guide" columnist, JoAnn R. Hines, a sought-after career coach, offers the following advice:

THE OFFICE POLITICS OF PREGNANCY:
HOW TO HANDLE MATERNITY LEAVE LIKE A PRO

BY JOANN R. HINES

Your pregnancy is probably a dream come true for you; but you love your job, too. While you may plan to take maternity leave, negotiate a flex schedule, investigate job-sharing arrangements or telecommuting, or perhaps even put your career on hold for a few years, you want to be sure that both your leave-taking and your return to the office go as smoothly as possible. So in between going to Lamaze class, stocking up on Pampers, and decorating the nursery, devote some time to planning how you will manage the transition from job to home and back again.

Your colleagues are a sort of family, after all, and you don't want to leave them in the lurch while you are on maternity leave, nor do you want to feel that you are out of the loop while you are away. Here are a few do's and don'ts that will help ensure that your maternity leave doesn't leave you out in the cold when you want to step back onto your career track.

SOME "MOTHERLY" ADVICE . . .

>> DO your boss the courtesy of telling him or her first. Hearing about your pregnancy via the office grapevine won't put your boss in a good mood when you start your dialogue about maternity leave.

>> DO your homework and make sure the company policies on maternity leave are clearly understood before speaking with your boss. (You're entitled to 12 weeks of unpaid leave under the Family and Medical Leave Act, if you work for a company that has more than 50 employees and you have worked there for 12 months. Your company or state may offer you short-term disability or paid family leave, covering your salary or a portion of your salary for a certain number of weeks. Or you may have purchased a short-term disability policy on your own). If you know what you are entitled to, you will be in a better position to discuss your maternity leave, absences for prenatal appointments, and other issues. Visit the Department of Labor's Web site (www.dol.gov) to learn about your rights under the Family and Medical Leave Act. Make sure you speak with your insurance company as well, to explore pregnancy coverage.

>> DO write a follow-up document or letter, stating that you are pregnant, and include your due date. Give this to your employer and personnel department.

>> DO keep your employer informed about your plans. You may not know when you want to leave yet, or you may change your mind as your pregnancy progresses. If you intend to stop working before your due date (you can start your leave up to 11 weeks before the expected week of childbirth), your employer and colleagues will need to know as soon as possible.

>> DO keep your work in order and maintain clear and up-to-date records. That way, when you are away, your colleagues will be in a better position to fill in for you and keep the workflow running smoothly.

>> DO enlist the support of a female colleague who has been through maternity leave, if this is your first time. She will be able to give advice and help to keep things in perspective.

>> DON'T feel guilty about taking time off for prenatal appointments. Schedule the appointments responsibly, and don't leave anyone hanging in a lurch. Give plenty of notice for these times away from the office.

>> DON'T turn into the office's "Professional Pregnant Woman"—the kind who takes every opportunity to work her status into the conversation or to use her pregnancy to get preferential treatment. Your pregnancy might be the most wonderful thing that ever happened to you, but for the people who work alongside you, it can be a case of too much of a good thing. The resentment will still be there when you come back to work.

>> DON'T feel you have to work doubly hard to prove to your colleagues that you're still up to the job. Stress can affect your unborn baby.

>> DON'T feel pressured into giving your employer an exact date of return right away. You have no idea how you will feel after the birth of your baby. Keep your options open about the exact date as long as you can.

>> DON'T lie about returning. If you already know you won't be coming back, you have to tell your employer. By lying, you not only hurt your credibility, but that of all the other pregnant women who follow you.

>> DON'T offer to take on any work during your leave. Your body needs time to rest and recover. Wait to see how you feel, how the baby is sleeping, and how you are adjusting, before you jump back into work.

AFTER THE BIRTH . . .

Once you're home with your baby, what can you do to stay connected, yet still enjoy the precious time with your newborn? Stay in the loop with these strategies:

>> Shoot colleagues a quick e-mail before you leave and then regularly while you are home, letting them know how you are and asking for all the "office gossip." Ask them to forward you copies of anything of interest that they might uncover while you're away and to contact you whenever something relevant happens within the company.

>> It's also a good idea to keep your association memberships current and to join listservs for your industry. Subscribe to a clipping service, where you can have industry news delivered to your in-box. You can set up these accounts through Yahoo, AOL, and other Internet service providers.

>> Most important, if your career is important to you, don't take this transition lightly. Make sure it is part of the planning process, and always handle yourself with the utmost professionalism.

A successful career coach and contributing editor to MAKING BREAD, JoAnn R. Hines is the founder of Women in Packaging (www.womeninpackaging.org), an association that promotes the professional development of its members.

As Hines mentions, alternative work arrangements, such as job sharing or telecommuting, are options to consider if you want to stay home with your baby, yet keep your career alive and healthy. Below, Patricia Schiff Estess, author of *Work Concepts for the Future: Managing Alternative Work Arrangements* (Crisp Publications), reports on the trend in job-sharing arrangements for working moms. (*Some names have been changed to protect privacy.)

Would Job-Sharing Work for You?

SOMETIMES LESS IS MORE, AS THIS CREATIVE CAREER ARRANGEMENT PROVES

BY PATRICIA SCHIFF ESTESS

"I fully intended to go back to work fulltime as Director of News Practices at the network after Eli was born," says attorney Julie Rivera*. "But after the birth, I felt a tremendous tug to be with him. I didn't like the idea of part-time work, because I thought I wouldn't be taken seriously as a professional and because my job is so demanding that I knew it wouldn't work."

Julie's boss had another idea, though. Carole Knight*, Vice President of Editorial Quality for the network and mother of teenagers, knew what she needed to operate the division smoothly. She also understood how torn new parents are between children and career. She planted an idea with Julie. What if she shared the job with Susie Moran*, a former producer and mother of two, whom Carole had lured back to work on a temporary, part-time basis to fill in for Julie when she was on maternity leave?

"I was skeptical at first, especially since I had never met Susie," Julie admits. "But I called her anyway and broached the idea." And to Susie, who wanted to read her boys goodnight stories as well as have a career, the idea was intriguing. Before they could even consider this commitment, though, they knew they had to talk about their respective philosophies—how dedicated they were to the work, how their styles meshed, or didn't mesh; and how they could make this arrangement work for them on a personal and professional basis.

Quickly, they established that they were both Type-A personalities, dedicated to excelling at whatever they do. They also agreed that, while they were willing to be flexible in their scheduling, they didn't want to be on call every day of the week—which would have subverted the purpose of the arrangement. With this common vision, they carved out and submitted a job-sharing proposal, which Carole championed and the network accepted.

Their arrangement works like this: Julie is in the office on Monday, Tuesday, and Wednesday; Susie on Wednesday, Thursday, and Friday. On Wednesday, they have lunch together to discuss any simmering issues, because they appreciate how vital communication and joint problem-solving are to the success of their arrangement. They share the title and split a salary that is slightly higher than the company would pay one person in this position, because the company is getting six, rather than five, full days from the team. In other words, Julie and Susie each earn three fifths of what Julie was originally making. Their benefits (and they both work at least 30 hours a week in order to be eligible for them), such as vacation time, are determined by the length of time each has been with the company.

No doubt about it, our colleagues are impacted by this arrangement," says Julie. "For example, I may have invested three days in arguing with someone in the legal department, and then I'm not there for the rest of the week. It leaves the lawyer feeling somewhat abandoned. I have to be sensitive to this and make it easier for her, either by making certain that Susie is up to speed and suggesting she continue the discussions with her, or by allowing her to continue dealing with me, even though I'm going to be home." Although neither Julie nor Susie want to make a practice of covering for each other when the other is supposed to be "on," it happens on rare occasions.

"When you commit to an arrangement like this," Susie explains, "you understand that, in a crunch, there must be some give and take, so you have to build some flexibility into your life." One way both women have done that is to retain their babysitters five days a week, even though they are scheduled to be at home for two of those days.

As for the network, it has been generous in its support. Julie and Susie were moved into a larger office and given desks and computers to accommodate each of them on their overlap day. They were given laptops, so that if they needed to work away from the office, they could.

Unfortunately, not all companies or managers can get their minds around the concept that two people can share an important job seamlessly. Managers often feel it's too difficult to oversee, even though, generally, less supervision is needed, because job sharers take on most of the responsibility for making the arrangement work. Companies also tend to be concerned about the added costs of benefits, which are real, but what they often forget about are the considerable savings to be gained from lower turnover and higher productivity as a result of this arrangement.

All that said, if you're convinced this arrangement will work for you, there are steps you and your job partner can take to sell the idea to management.

THE SALES PITCH

If you're toying with the idea of this arrangement, your first step would be to search out someone who might be a good partner and talk about the idea. Either one of you may have to learn some new skills to round out the position, but that will only add to your value in the long run.

Talk to your boss about the idea before making a formal, written presentation. He or she may be able to give you ideas for handling either the request or the arrangement. You will probably be asked to develop a written proposal, which should include the following:

The benefits to the company and the department. Be as specific as possible, making the point that two people dealing with a problem are often more effective than one in coming up with a satisfactory or creative solution. If others in the company have worked in such an arrangement successfully, cite them. If the combination of two people's talents will enhance the position, make that case. In every way possible, let the company know it's getting two high-level, well-trained people who can be counted on because they don't have to be brought up to speed; they already know the ropes.

A proposed schedule. Time configurations for every team vary, but the most frequently cited ones are 1) one person works mornings, the other afternoons; 2) one person works one week, the other the next week; or 3) one works Monday through Wednesday until 1 PM; the other Wednesday noon through Friday, both of them overlapping for a debriefing lunch.

A proposed division of duties. In most job shares, both of you are able to do everything the job requires. But, on occasion, you'll have a successful job-sharing arrangement that resembles a good business partnership. One of you is slow, methodical, and pays attention to detail and the other is good at broad stroking and meeting deadlines. If that's the case, you might divide duties to reflect your strengths.

A communication plan. You have to know what has happened on the other job sharer's "watch." You might arrange to leave detailed e-mail messages for each other, supplemented with face-to-face meetings, phone calls, memos, and charts of pending projects. Or you might take communication one step further and share subtleties, such as how someone sounded on the phone, what a supplier told you about his view of the world situation, or what you heard about a colleague's father's medical condition. Sharing this information may seem gossipy, but it can be useful to your job sharer, who will be able to perform her job better when she understands the nuances of what has happened and what has been said when she was out of the office.

Proposed salaries and benefits. Speak to your human resources department about whether or not you'd be entitled to full benefits (pro-rated, of course) under the arrangement you propose. Your salaries should be commensurate with the position (again, pro-rated) and any bonuses you'd be entitled to would be shared equally.

SHARING SUCCESS STORIES

Before you dismiss this alternative work schedule as too complicated (and let no one tell you it's easy to pull off, because it isn't), let me share a couple of other scenarios where job-sharing has worked.

Two administrative assistants in the legal department of an insurance company share an administrative assistant job, because one is going back to school part-time and spending more time with her two school-aged sons and the other is starting a home-based business.

An associate director of development at a large New York City hospital shares her job with a freelance writer, who temporarily took over for her while she was on maternity leave. Three months after the baby was born, the associate director wanted to come back to work—but not on a full-time basis. The writer, who enjoyed her three-month stint but didn't want full-time work because she was writing a book, also liked the idea.

A sales manager for a paper manufacturer was feeling pressured as a result of care-giving responsibilities associated with her mother's declining health. She considered resigning, until she hit on another plan. One of her recent top-notch salespeople had retired and admitted to missing the work environment. When the sales manager suggested job-sharing to the retiree, the retiree jumped at the opportunity. The retiree had a smoother and more comfortable transition out of the work force, and the manager had precious time to spend with her mother during her last days.

Julie Rivera says she has a hazy image of herself going back full time, but when asked how soon, she jokingly equivocates by answering, "When I'm very thin," or "When the house is very clean." It's pretty obvious that neither Julie nor Susie is rushing back to the crushing schedules of yore. Because they have sufficient household income, this arrangement wraps around their lives perfectly—for now. Will it last forever? Who knows?

Would job-sharing work for you? Maybe not now. But, at some stage in your career, it just might provide the personal and professional balance you need.

The former editor of Sylvia Porter's Personal Finance *magazine, Patricia Schiff Estess runs a workshop series on reinventing retirement. She is a contributing editor to* MAKING BREAD.

HOW TO SUCCEED IN (HOME) BUSINESS.

More and more stay-at-home moms are starting home businesses to supplement the family income, and with the prevalence of home computers and accounting software programs, doing so is becoming increasingly easy. For a mother who wants to be home with her children, the major advantage is obvious. It's "instant flextime," as one mother, who sells Mary Kay cosmetics from her home, told us. "I am not suggesting that this is a piece of cake, but why work 40 hours—plus, commute and be home late—when you can work 20 to 30 hours per week, have fun, be available for your children, and still make money. Life is short and uncertain; it's about choices, and I choose to be there for my family."

Then there are the tax benefits: phone lines, computer purchase, square footage in your home, percent of utilities, mileage or car maintenance, all could be deductible. The IRS rules are strict, and it pays to consult an accountant about what is and isn't deductible, as well as what records to keep, before you begin. Visit www.irs.gov for more information. MAKING BREAD asked former intern (and now a stay-at-home mom herself) Vivian Y. Shic to interview several women who have started home-grown businesses. Below is a sampling of their best advice:

"Don't grow too fast." Don't try and conquer the world in the first year. Stick to what you can do. Test the market. "You don't want to launch yourself, spend a bunch of money, then find that there are no customers," says Dawn, who started her own herb-growing business, slowly, from her garden in Bucks County, Pennsylvania.

If you're an artisan, "join a craftsman guild." That's how Karin started making contacts and receiving commissions for the furniture design shop that she started out of her garage. She considers it her smartest marketing move. Another tip she offers: "Never buy your supplies at retail."

Form a network. During her time working for two major public relations agencies in the San Francisco Bay Area, Bethany says she "realized they were charging my clients twice as much as they were paying me, and I saw little of my billing rate on my paycheck. So I thought to myself, 'I can do this independently and make more money.'" Her most valuable business asset, beating out even her computer and a fast Internet connection, has been hooking up with a network of PR freelancers. Besides sharing subscriptions to expensive media databases, she meets with them once a month to discuss the different issues or problems they're confronting.

More home-grown business advice. All agree on the following basic advice for anyone planning to open up shop at home:

>> Arrange for regular child care (what are you going to do with a crying baby when you're having a teleconference with a client?), and have a back-up plan (a neighbor or baby sitter you can call at a moment's notice) in case an unplanned meeting comes up.

>> Get up early or stay up late. Fit your household chores in around your work, and forget about perfection. If your kids are old enough, organize a schedule of chores they can help

with. Don't let your husband off the hook, either.

>> Create an office for yourself. IRS rules require that you use this space (an extra bedroom, the basement, whatever) only for your work, in order to qualify for a tax deduction.

>> Get dressed (no fuzzy pink slippers during work hours), and stick to a regular schedule of work hours. It's easy to let your work crowd out your family life (and vice versa) when you're working from home. Work to maintain a balance.

DON'T MAKE A "GRAVE" MISTAKE: WHAT YOU NEED TO KNOW ABOUT INSURANCE.

Once you have a family (and maybe even a business), it's time to get serious about life insurance. Too many uninsured women risk leaving their loved ones without a financial security blanket when they die. Life's a risky business. We learn that when we take our first steps and fall.

As we grow older, the risks become more complicated. You discover the risk of getting hurt in love, the risk of failure on the job, health risks, the risk of being in the wrong place at the wrong time. If nothing else, the events of September 11, 2001, have reinforced in us the knowledge that life is fraught with unexpected dangers—and that it's best to be prepared. It's no surprise that insurance-policy inquiries and purchases increased significantly post 9-11.

At a Mardi Gras party recently, when the conversation turned to money, a young woman blurted out her biggest concern: What would happen to me and our three children if my husband suddenly died? That thought kept her up nights, she confessed. Even as a stay-at-home mom, though, she should have been equally concerned about what would happen to her family if the unspeakable happened to her. Child-care could severely strain her husband's budget if she were gone. Despite the huge pro-

HOME-BIZ LEADS 'N' LINKS

Aquent (www.aquent.com): This site finds contract, project-based, and permanent work for a broad range of creative and information technology professionals. For small businesses, it also offers a billing service called FastCash that will, for a fee, advance money on receivables.

CareersfromHome.com (www.careersfromhome.com): For $9.95 per month, this site lets you post your resume and search its job database, plus access career advice. Its database lists a broad range of telecommuting jobs for major firms, ranging from telesales and home-based receptionist to patent attorney, web editor, computer programmer, business manager and more.

HomeCareerSearch.com (www.homecareersearch. com):

This site boasts a similar telecommuter job database and has a first-time visitor promotion of $29.95 for a lifetime membership.

International Virtual Assistants Association (www.ivaa.org): Consider joining this association and listing yourself if you want to market your services as a Virtual Assistant (VA) for small businesses. Administrative tasks that VAs perform range from word processing and translations to transcriptions and travel arrangements. The IVAA offers educational services and a Certified Virtual Assistant exam.

Small Business Administration (www.sba.gov): This U.S. government site should be your first stop for advice on starting your business, writing a business plan and finding funding. Download its Startup Kit PDF.

fessional gains made by women in the last decade, women as a group continue to be underinsured in terms of protecting their economic value. Fewer women, married or single, purchase life insurance or are covered by their employers than men. And when they are covered, their death benefits are half that of men's. It's a financial gap as potentially damaging to women and their families as the wage gap is.

We don't like to think about what would happen to those we love if we weren't here, but doing so is one of the most loving things you can do. How much and what kind of life insurance you should purchase will vary, depending on your circumstances. But purchase it you should, if others are depending on you to pay the bills or put them through college.

WHO NEEDS YOU, BABY?

"Is anyone dependent on my income?" Every woman should ask herself that question. The primary purpose of life insurance is to protect your dependents (spouse, children, or elderly parents) from your untimely death. A policy at work might provide enough benefit to pay for your final expenses, but keep in mind that the policy is canceled when you leave your employer. Moreover, it probably doesn't offer enough coverage, if your family is dependent on your income. Here are some guidelines to help you determine what your life-insurance needs are.

Single Moms. At more than 10 million strong, the number of single-mother households has tripled in the last 35 years. As a single parent, you're the sole breadwinner, so life insurance is crucial. It can provide the funds to help whoever is going to take care of your children. Your sister or brother or mother or best friend might be willing to take over the responsibility, but would they have the financial resources to add a couple of kids to their family?

Divorced Moms. You need insurance if your children are dependent on your income. It is also important to remember that alimony and child support stop when a former spouse dies. That's why many divorce agreements will require that a husband purchase a life-insurance policy.

Elizabeth's agreement provides for two policies—one with her as beneficiary. Her ex-husband can only cancel the policy if she remarries. The other policy names the children as beneficiaries until the youngest is 18 years old or has graduated from college.

If you should die before your children reach majority, an ex-husband or other family member might take care of them. If you don't want your ex to get his hands on the proceeds of your life-insurance policy, then arrange for the money to go into a trust for your children. Name a trustee who knows the children and can work with your ex.

Stay-at-Home Moms. The services provided by a stay-at-home mom are undervalued. "A mom often single-handedly performs as many as 27 occupations in the course of raising a child, from child-rearing, cooking, cleaning, chauffeuring and financial planning to resolving family emotional problems," says Andrea Buchanan, author of *Mother Shock* in an article for MAKING BREAD. One study quoted in *The Price of Motherhood* by Ann Crittenden estimates a mother's worth at $508,700 a year. What would it cost to replace those services? The younger the children the more expensive it will be.

WE DON'T HATE YOU, MOM!

TAKE HEART FROM THIS MOTHER-DAUGHTER HEART-TO-HEART
ABOUT WHAT IT'S LIKE BEING RAISED BY A WORKING MOM

BY MARCIA ECKERD, PHD

The major guilt trip for all working moms is: "Am I ruining my children for life because I'm not there for them?" We lose precious sleep, beating ourselves up over that question. Then we wake up and spend too much money, trying to make up for our lack of presence in their lives with stuff. But rarely do we think to ask them how they feel about our work and how our absence really does affect them.

In this case, our kids are the experts. So it was with crossed fingers and some trepidation that I decided to talk with my own expert, my 22-year-old daughter Lindsey, about what it was like having me as a working mom. Try having the same kind of heart-to-heart with your kids—if you dare. You might be pleasantly surprised, and gaining their perspective could go a long way toward easing your guilt trip.

What I discovered was that we working moms probably suffer more than our kids do. I've spent a lot of time feeling guilty for when I wasn't there or had to say no, and Lindsey got over those times pretty quickly. She didn't walk around with a heavy feeling, but I often did. I wish I could take back all that guilt, because it kept me from enjoying myself as much as I might have and because I felt pressured to "make it up to her." Communication, openness, and staying available to what she was into seems to have been the key to finding myself so close to her now.

Bottom line, as you'll see below: We ended up just fine.

Lindsey: You should tell them the story about how you forgot me at the bus. On my first day of first grade, you were working and you didn't know school got out early. So when all the moms picked up their kids at the bus stop, you weren't there.

Marcia: Boy, do I remember that one.

L: At first, I was really upset. These nice people took me back to their house and gave me chocolate milk with all the chocolate I wanted, and I played with their little girl. They brought me   back to the bus stop when they thought you would be there.

M: I felt like I had damaged you for life and that the other mothers must have thought I was a total loser.

L: By the time you got there, I was over it, and you felt like the worst mom in the world.

M: I suffered for weeks. I made up for it by waiting with other kids whose mothers were late. You haven't stopped reminding me about it for 16 years.

L: I'm just making fun of how you were so traumatized.

M: When did you first realize that I worked, and what was that like?

L: I knew you worked when I saw people coming into the house, and I was supposed to keep out of the way. There were areas of the house where I couldn't go when you had patients, like I couldn't talk loudly in the kitchen and stuff. It was just a part of my life. When you're 6, 7, 8, you don't know enough to know other people's moms don't do the same thing.

M: Do you remember the time you and your friend snuck in and eavesdropped on me? You were about 5.

L: I didn't understand why I couldn't listen. What's so secret? It bothered me when I'd say, "My mom has a patient," and they'd ask me, "What do they talk about?" and I didn't know. What's really going on in there? Anyway, we wanted to do something we weren't supposed to do. It was really boring, so we left.

M: You went to a school where most kids' moms didn't work. Did my working matter?

L: At some point, I realized most moms didn't work, and I began to see what kind of pressure there was on you.

To be honest, I thought the mothers who didn't work were a little "frou-frou." When I got older, I noticed the other mothers were oblivious to your needs as a working mom—they would hold meetings at noon and stuff.

M: So the fact that I worked wasn't a big deal?

L: What you did was more entertaining than the fact that you worked. As I got older, the fact that my mother was a psychologist and my father was a psychiatrist was exciting to people. Everyone still always asks, "Do they analyze you a lot?" I never feel analyzed, and if I do, I just say, "Mom, stop being a shrink."

M: You were about 12 or 13 when I went to work full time outside the house. What was that like for you?

L: It pissed me off that you weren't as available if I wanted to go shopping or to the mall. I was like, "Fine." In my initial pissed-offness, I felt like I wasn't much of a priority to you. I still get pissed at you when you can't drop everything and be with me. But I got over it; it's OK with me. You worried a lot more about it.

M: My first years in that job I was really stressed.

L: I don't feel we were as close. We were both really stressed. I had a lot going on in my life with homework and what boy liked me. Neither you nor I handled stress well then, so we both yelled more. I'd come down for dinner and then disappear.

M: Do you think that the fact that I was working so hard when you were 13 caused you to pull away from me more?

L: You could have been calmer, but we all hated our parents at that age. It was a bigger deal to you than to me. I'd get over being angry. I didn't go around with this heavy feeling all the time. It wasn't a big deal to me.

M: So largely my working has been a non-event?

L: (Laughs) It's not like you were a corporate lawyer. You're more open, and we can be closer than a lot of my friends are with their parents.

M: When you see yourself having a family, would you want to work?

L: Yes, definitely, but not for the first years. How you did it worked well for me, doing a little for the first years and then increasing your work over time. It's our communication that matters. You're still the first one I call.

A licensed psychologist, Dr. Marcia Eckerd is a partner in Associates for Children and Families, a Connecticut-based practice that specializes in working with individuals, couples, and families to enhance relationships and empower individuals. A contributing editor, she writes "The Working Mom's Shrink" column in MAKING BREAD.

Working Moms. The two-income family is now the norm, and the working mom's income is used for more than incidentals. Husbands and wives are economic partners, and many families depend on two paychecks to make ends meet. If anything should happen to you and your income were no longer available, would your husband and children be able to stay in their home? Would your children have funds to pay for their education? Would your family suffer financial loss and have to reduce their life style?

Business Owners. If you own a business or a share in one, you need to consider life insurance. The business might be the largest asset that you have. Life insurance is needed to protect that asset. It insures that the business can continue if a partner or major shareholder dies. The proceeds provide the money for the surviving members of the business to purchase the share that was owned by the partner who died. How much insurance is needed? Enough to equal the partners' or shareholders' interest in the business. This should be formalized in a buy-sell agreement between (or among) the partners. In the case of a business owned by a single individual, life insurance can provide a beneficiary with money to live on until the business is liquidated. This can save the beneficiary from the complications of taking over a business that he or she may not understand or want to run.

LIFE INSURANCE 101: A WHOLE LOT OF OPTIONS

When we purchase life insurance, we are paying another party, the insurance company, to assume part of the risk of covering our loved ones' financial needs in the event of our untimely death. Because insurance companies insure millions of people, they can predict with a high degree of accuracy how many people of a certain age will die in a given period. This helps them to set rates. There are many factors that determine life-insurance rates: your job, hobbies, habits, age, health, even your credit report. The life-insurance premiums for a non-smoking administrative assistant will be less than for a sky-diving roofer. Smokers and overweight people are usually charged more. Many companies charge women less, because we have a longer life expectancy. Term, whole, universal, variable—a smorgasbord of policies is available, but don't let the glut of options confuse you. It's not as complicated as the insurance companies sometimes make it seem. The following guidelines will help you decide which might be right for you.

Term Insurance. When you buy term insurance, you are buying "pure" protection. There's no built-in savings component; the cash value of the policy does not increase, as it does with whole life. The policy pays off only if you die during the period covered, at the end of which time, you must renew (generally at a higher rate) to continue coverage. When you buy what is often referred to as level term insurance, you are buy-

ing coverage for a specific term, or length of time—usually one to 10 or more years—and the premium (or amount you pay each month) and policy value remain the same throughout that period. Another option to consider is . . .

Annual Renewal Term. Which is just what it sounds like—you renew each year with a higher premium every year, because each year you're a year older and closer to death (at least that's how the insurance companies look at it).

When the term ends for either level or annual term insurance, your new rate will depend on the state of your health and age. If you are willing to take a medical exam, assuming that you pass it, your rate for the next term will be lower than if you choose not to re-enter (that's insurance-company jargon for taking the medical exam) because of some health problem. If you choose not to take the exam, you will still be allowed to renew, but at a higher premium than if you took the exam and passed it. Either way, in most cases, the cost will be higher than it was during your previous term, because you are now older and the likelihood of death has increased.

Term insurance is the cheapest form of insurance to purchase when you're young; it's ideal for a woman who has young children and wants to provide protection for them until they are on their own. It provides greater protection for less cost than whole life insurance. A 20-year term policy that pays $250,000 upon death for a healthy, non-smoking, 30-year-old woman can cost less than $150 a year, and the premiums are locked in for the full 20 years of the term.

Barbara, a stay-at-home mom, purchased a 20-year term policy when her first child was born. The proceeds will help if her husband needs to hire a housekeeper to take care of the three young ones.

Whole Life Insurance. This form of insurance provides you protection plus cash value, or a form of enforced savings. The amount of the premium (generally higher than term) is determined by your age and state of health at the time you buy the policy; it does not increase as long as the policy is in force. Therefore, the younger you are when you buy a whole policy (also sometimes referred to as a straight policy), the less it costs you.

Over time, the policy builds up cash value on a tax-deferred basis. During the first few years, the insurance company credits only a small amount to savings. The savings builds up as time goes on. This amount is yours even if you cancel the policy. Or you can borrow from the insurance company the amount that is in savings, paying interest on it at a rate you will find stated in your policy. You continue to pay the premium, even if you borrow against the policy, to keep the policy in force. If you die, however, the insurance company will reduce the amount it pays your beneficiary by the amount you borrowed. You can use the cash value to buy additional insurance, supplement retirement income, help provide for a child's education or to meet other financial needs.

Universal and Variable Life. Two more flexible types of whole life are universal and variable life. Universal life is an interest-rate sensitive insurance plan, whose principal earns interest from a series of fixed-income investments. Consequently, the savings you build up tends to rise and fall with the markets. One benefit is that you can vary your annual premium by adjusting the amount of the death benefit your recipient will receive. So, in a lean year, you might lower the benefit to be able to afford the premium and keep the policy active.

Variable life is similar to universal, with the added benefit that you have control (within limits) of how the money is invested. You have your choice of placing it in stocks, bonds, or mutual funds—depending on the options the insurance company offers.

In deciding whether term or whole life is best for you, consider whether the savings aspect of whole life is worth the higher initial premium. Since it takes a number of years to build up a sizable cash value, the savings tend to be eroded by inflation. Are there other ways for you to build up savings more quickly and with a greater return? Are you disciplined enough to take the difference between the cost of a whole life policy and the lower term premium and invest it? If you are, then you'll probably come out ahead buying term and investing the difference in an IRA or a mutual fund. Some agents try to convince you that whole or universal life are investments. They aren't. Agents like to push whole life policies, because they receive a higher commission on whole life than they do on term insurance.

COMING TO TERMS WITH HOW MUCH YOU NEED

The cost of term insurance is initially cheaper than other forms of insurance for the same amount of protection. It can provide the largest immediate coverage for the dollar. Before consulting with an agent, ask yourself these questions:

How much coverage do I really need now? How long will I need it (until my new baby has graduated from school and is self-supporting)? How much can I afford? Would my children and my spouse be eligible for Social Security benefits? What are the death benefits from my pension? What loans would need to be paid off if I weren't here to meet monthly payments? Does my company offer life insurance? And if I'm paying for part of it, is it the best deal for me?

Next, take a look at your assets and liabilities, and then figure out how much it will cost your loved ones to maintain their current life style. In addition to replacing income, your life insurance should cover certain cash requirements that your beneficiary might pay off in the event of your death. Be sure to include:

1. Mortgages, installment loans, and all unpaid current bills and other debts.

2. Education expenses. If you have children at or near college age, you will have to calculate your insurance needs more closely than if they are younger. If they are younger, and if an insurance policy will be counted on to cover education expenses, the amount earmarked for college should be invested at a rate of return that keeps up with the ever-increasing costs of college. In this case, a variable life policy might be best.

3. Final expenses. These include administration of your estate, probate costs, attorney's and accountant's fees, appraisal fees, taxes, final unreimbursed medical expenses, and funeral expenses. Allow 2 to 5 percent of the total estate, plus at least $5,000 in funeral expenses, to cover these.

How much is enough? A general rule of thumb is to buy coverage worth about eight to ten times your annual salary. Better yet, do a capital-needs analysis to determine how much you need. Many Web sites provide calculators to help you nail down this figure. Some recommended sites include: www.iii.org (the site of the Insurance Information Institute), www.quotesmith.com, www.selectquote.com, and www.usaa.com (which provides coverage for military families, their children, and ex-spouses).

When you have worked out a sensible figure, buy no more insurance than you need and can afford. You don't want to buy a policy you can't afford. You'll end up with no coverage, if you have to cancel the policy. Remember that how much you need will change as your life changes. So re-evaluate your coverage at least every five years or at the birth of a child.

Careful planning can give you the amount of coverage you need for the amount of money you can afford. Life insurance may seem like a necessary evil, but, in reality, it's a security blanket that will let you and your loved ones sleep soundly—and live adventurously.

Ensuring That You Get the Best Price and Coverage. Here are five steps to take:

>> 1. Ask if you are eligible for healthy lifestyle discounts on your policy. For example, non-smokers can save from 10 to 20 percent on their premiums from many insurers. Remember that you have a 10-day free-look period that entitles you to change your mind about purchasing the policy. If you do so, the company will return your premium, without penalty.

>> 2. When filling out your application form, answer all questions truthfully; insurers double-check your answers against medical and credit records. A false statement can be enough reason for an insurer to refuse to pay a claim.

Tip: If you are buying term, be sure you know the terms: Get a policy that can be renewed without having to pass another physical examination. Also be sure that it has a guaranteed rate and contains a clause that permits you to convert it into a whole policy without a physical exam. If your health changes, the ability to renew and convert will become important.

>> 3. When paying your premiums, write the check to the company, not the agent, and get a receipt. Pay premiums annually or semiannually, rather than monthly, if possible. That way the company saves money on billing, and the savings are passed on to you.

>> 4. Inform your beneficiaries about the policies you own and tell them where the paperwork is located. Keep your policy in a safe place at home and place a record of the insurer's name and your policy number in a safe-deposit box as well.

>> 5. When shopping for best prices, check whether any service organizations or professional associations you belong to offer competitive group rates.

While You're Shopping for Insurance . . .

Consider getting disability. If you're 35, the chance that you will be disabled for at least 90 days before age 65 is more than twice as high as the possibility of your dying before retirement age. Working moms (and women without children) should purchase disability insurance that insures a monthly income. Stay-at-home moms need enough to cover childcare in the event that they are incapacitated. All married women should make sure that their husbands are covered.

What about Social Security and disability benefits on the job? In most cases, you'll want more security than those offer. Social Security provides disability insurance for those who become severely disabled before they reach 65, but the coverage is limited. It will pay if you have a physical or mental condition so severe that it prevents you from working, and if it is expected to last, or has lasted, for at least 12 months, or if it is expected to result in death. To be eligible, you must be fully insured under Social Security regulations. You have to wait five months after your disability begins before Social Security starts to pay, and the amount it pays is the same as the amount you would start to get upon your retirement at age 65. (Note: Seven out of 10 disability claims under Social Security are rejected.)

You may have disability coverage as part of your benefits plan at work. But there's no guarantee you'll have it if you switch jobs. And does it cover partial as well as total disability?

What Your Benefits Package May Provide.

Many employers provide disability insurance, usually using either of two types of plans;

Short-term. This provides modest benefits for a short period. The amount you get is based on your earnings, but with a maximum that is usually quite low. The waiting period before the policy starts to pay is anywhere from seven to 21 days. Some plans pay out for as few as 13 weeks, while others may pay for as long as 52 weeks. You may be able to use this to cover some of your maternity leave.

Long-term. Designed to take care of more serious disabilities, most long-term plans provide a certain percentage of your earnings—usually 50 to 60 percent of your base salary. The maximum monthly payment may vary from $1,500 to $2,000 or more. You may have to go through a waiting period, or elimination period, as long as three to six months, but payments may continue for any number of years (5, 10, or 20) or until you reach age 65.

Your employer-provided disability coverage stops at age 65 (assuming you're with the company that long), because that is when Social Security and Medicare take over. Since these two government programs are so universal, and since most people have traditionally retired at 65, the insurance companies just don't bother to develop premium rates for employee group insurance after 65.

Why You Should Consider Taking "Supplements." Since neither Social Security nor group plans usually pay as much as you really need if you are disabled, getting a supplementary disability policy is well worth trying to fit into your budget. Carrying your own policy has several advantages: the coverage is portable and goes with you if you change jobs, the benefits are generally tax-free if you pay the premiums with after-tax dollars, and you can purchase coverage that protects you from partial as well as total disability.

Premiums will be based on your age, condition of health, occupation, and income. Since policies can vary widely, be sure you know what you are buying. The underwriting rules for a disability policy are tougher today than for a life-insurance policy.

Clauses to watch for before signing include:

Maximum benefit period. This is the length of time the benefit will be paid. Usually it is expressed in weeks, months, or years. Many insurers are now discontinuing lifetime benefits, which were once common on top-of-the-line policies.

Perils insured against. This may state accident only or accident and illness. Be sure you get coverage for both.

Elimination period. This is the time that must

Tip: Group-policy rates are affected by the occupation and average age of members covered. Young and middle-aged women can frequently get a policy at a cost significantly below that offered by an employer's group plan. One woman who worked for a utility company later found that she was paying five times the rate she could have gotten elsewhere, because the company rates were based on having workers in high-risk jobs. They were a good deal for employees in their fifties and sixties, but not such a good deal for younger women at the utility.

elapse before the company starts to pay. Usually it is 30, 60, 90, or 120 days after your disability begins. Aim for the shortest wait period that you can afford.

Definition of disability. This states the conditions under which you will be considered disabled for the purpose of collecting benefits. Some plans require only that your disability prevent you from performing your regular occupation. Others will pay benefits only if you cannot perform in any gainful employment.

Non-cancelable. It used to be that just about all policies were non-cancelable, meaning the insurance company could not cancel the policy, raise the premium, or change the benefits during the life of the policy. Now many insurers charge higher premiums if they lock in the price or they drop the locked-in premium altogether. If you are buying any disability policy, make sure:

>> 1. The period covered makes sense. It may be as short as one year, or continue until you reach age 65, or cover your entire lifetime. The longer the coverage, the higher the premium.

>> 2. The policy is guaranteed renewable.

>> 3. You know when benefits start. The longer the waiting period before they start, the lower your premium.

>> 4. A future-income option is added to the policy. This will allow you to buy additional coverage as your income increases, without presenting any evidence of medical insurability.

>> 5. You get partial disability benefits. Often, a person who has been disabled can return to work on a part-time basis. Some policies provide for partial benefits that supplement part-time earnings after a total disability.

Coordination of Benefits. In many disability policies, you will find a coordination-of-benefits provision. This means that if Worker's Compensation, Social Security, or any other policies are paying you benefits, the group policy on a long-term plan may not pay as much as it otherwise would. (Note: 80 percent of all disabilities occur outside the workplace, so they are not covered by Worker's Compensation.)

If you leave your job for any reason, you might be able to convert the group plan to an individual policy. The coverage is usually limited, and the cost is high.

HEALTH=WEALTH: FINDING THE BEST MEDICAL COVERAGE FOR YOU & YOUR FAMILY

Women tend to have more chronic illnesses, are more likely to suffer from mental health problems, and are more likely to make regular use of prescription drugs than men, according to a Commonwealth Fund study. They are also more likely to be responsible for managing their family's health care. Yet, while slightly more men than women are uninsured (in part because low-income single mothers are more likely to be eligible for Medicaid than single men), the number of uninsured women between the ages of 18 and 64 grew three times faster than the number of uninsured men between 1994 and 1998. If this trend continues, the fund predicts, the number of uninsured women will surpass men by 2005.

Nearly 16 million women, including one in five non-elderly women, are without medical insurance in the United States, and minorities are more likely to be uninsured. (Thirty-Seven percent of Latina women and 20 percent of African American women go without insurance, as compared with 16 percent of white women.) Thirty-one percent of uninsured women went without a Pap test in 2001, according to the latest Kaiser Family Foundation Women's Health Survey. And that's just one way lack of coverage hurts women. Less access to preventive medicine leads to more sick days and, for hourly and temp workers, lower wages. Even when women are covered, there are gaps in the scope of benefits relating to women's needs. For example, while almost all states require private plans to cover breast cancer screenings, other conditions, including cervical cancer and osteoporosis, are covered by considerably fewer states. Contraceptives are not covered by prescription drug plans in most states. And some health-care plans charge higher premiums for pre-natal and maternity care.

What are the reasons for this unhealthy state of affairs? Most uninsured women either don't have access to employee-sponsored insurance, because women tend to work in lower-paying jobs, which come with no health benefits; they can't afford private policies; or they earn too much to be eligible for Medicaid, the federal health plan for the very poor. Because women are more likely than men to be covered as a dependent on someone else's plan, they're also more likely to be affected by divorce, widowhood, or a layoff in the family. Complicating matters are the skyrocketing medical costs and premiums of recent years: from 2001 to 2004, the share of premium paid by employees for family medical coverage has increased 50 percent. Many women who could afford coverage before are simply dropping out. The typical employee-sponsored insurance premium cost $9,068 for families in 2003, of which employees covered 27 percent (the typical premium for individuals cost $3,383, with employees covering 15 percent).

Ways to save on health $$$: Given these rising costs, it's all the more important to find ways to get the most for your money. If you are covered by a corporate plan, you'll probably have several different types and levels of coverage. Consider opting for a higher co-pay and a lower premium, if your family tends to be healthy (and go for preventive medical check-ups so that you stay healthy.) If your husband also has a plan where he works, compare coverage and cost of both carefully. Pick the one that offers you the most coverage for the lowest premium. Look into flexible spending plans, if they're offered where you work, for the tax advantage (more about them below). And always buy generic drugs, when you have the option, to save money.
The basic types of coverage offered are:

Traditional indemnity plans. Under these plans, which are becoming as rare as telephone booths because companies can't afford to offer them anymore, you select your own doctors, hospitals and pay on a fee-for-service basis. You don't need a referral to see a specialist. The traditional indemnity plan provides:

Basic hospitalization: This is provided by private insurance companies and the various Blue Cross companies nationwide. Usually the policy pays all or part of your hospital bills, including semi-private room, food, X-rays, laboratory tests, operating-room fees, and prescription drugs. The coverage in most cases is limited to a specific number of days during any one period, with a waiting period between confinements. The better the coverage, the more you pay.

Basic surgical and medical expense: Again, private companies provide these policies, while Blue Shield companies (usually associated with Blue Cross) are best known. Fees for doctors, whether surgeons or other physicians, are paid separately from hospital fees. Usually the insurance company sets a schedule of certain fees that it is willing to pay for certain operations. If your surgeon charges more than that fee, you must pay the difference. Obviously, again, the better the insurance coverage, the more it costs. (Note: Often, basic hospitalization is combined with basic medical-surgical coverage. Everyone should have at least this basic coverage.)

Major medical: This type of policy starts where basic hospitalization and basic medical/surgical insurance leave off. It covers the big expenses that are above the maximum of those policies. Usually a major-medical policy covers extensive hospitalization, surgery, other doctors' fees, private-duty nursing, home medical care, diagnostic work, therapies, medical devices, and rehabilitation. Major-medical policies contain a deductible feature, so the patient pays a certain amount—usually from $100 to $1,000—before the insurance company pays anything. (Often, the deductible is annual: Every year, you pay the first $100 or so of claims yourself before the insurance company starts to pay your claims.) Once you have gone beyond the deductible amount, most major-medical policies pay 70 to 80 percent of each claim you file. You must pay the balance yourself. When you reach a higher level (called the stop-loss limit), the insurance company takes over and pays 100 percent of all legitimate claims. Some policies put no limit on the maximum amount of claims they will pay. Others limit you to $250,000 or $500,000. Most policies set a lifetime maximum. The amount you pay above the deductible is called co-insurance.

How can you cut down on the cost of a major-medical policy? Two ways:

>> 1. Increase your deductible. Many people today accept a deductible of $1,000.

>> 2. Ask for higher maximum out-of-pocket expenses, i.e increase your stop-loss limit. Either step means you increase the risk you are willing to take. Many people prefer not to increase their risk. They pay a higher premium, so they won't have to worry that out-of-pocket expenses might send them to the bank to borrow money if a major illness occurs.

Health Maintenance Organizations (HMOs). Most corporations now offer HMOs as an alternative to the traditional indemnity plan, and the number of HMOs is steadily increasing. The HMO is organized as a nonprofit cooperative. For a fixed fee per month, it provides medical care for a member, based on the premise that it is cheaper to prevent illness than to cure it. You usually must select a primary-care physician (PCP) from the pool of doctors offered and pay a small fixed amount each visit. The PCP must approve any trips to specialists and non-emergency visits to HMO network hospitals. Since premiums paid by members constitute its only source of income, the HMO must hold down costs. Preventive medicine is one way to do so.

The HMO owns and operates hospitals and clinics and hires doctors, nurses, and medical technicians. It pays annual salaries to its professional staffs. Thus the HMO doesn't charge patient by patient or treatment by treatment in the traditional way. If you belong to an HMO, your premium covers nearly all medical expenses and you are entitled to care in one place, 24 hours a day, seven days a week. Before you make any decision about joining an HMO, find out how near the service is to you and talk with some of its members. Find out about coverage outside your area, as well. How extensive is the HMO and what options would you have if you fell ill away from home?

Point-of-Service Plans (POS). These are plans that are administered by insurance companies and Health Maintenance Organizations. You get the coordinated care of an HMO with the ability to go to nonmember doctors, for an extra charge, if you want. You usually need a referral to see a specialist.

Preferred Provider Organizations (PPOs). These are networks of doctors. They provide discounted care to members of a sponsoring organization, such as an employer or a union. If you are a patient of a particular doctor, you pay a smaller co-payment at the time of service—usually, $10 or 10 percent of the total charge. You generally don't need a referral from the primary-care physician to visit an in-network specialist. If you go to a doctor who is not on the list, your share of the bill jumps.

Flexible Spending Accounts (FSAs). A Flexible Spending Account, or FSA, is an IRS-approved, tax-exempt account that can save you money on eligible medical expenses. Use these plans, offered by many corporations in addition to regular medical insurance, to help you pay for medical expenses not covered by your regular plan (for instance, co-payments, deductibles (but not premiums), birth control pills, x-rays, ambulance service, dental fees, hearing aids, experimental medical treatment, contact lenses, drug addiction or alcoholism treatment, in vitro fertilization, reconstructive surgery after mastectomy, etc.) with pre-tax dollars. The money you choose to deposit each pay period into your FSA is deducted from your gross pay before taxes are calculated, so it is exempt from federal income tax, Social Security, and Medicare withholding, and, in many areas, even state and local income tax. Your take-home pay increases, as the amount of money you owe tax on decreases. As you incur eligible medical expenses, you request withdrawals from your account to reimburse yourself, submitting receipts with your claim. Your employer will set a limit on the maximum amount you can save; it's generally around $2,500. Review the amount you paid in previous years for out-of-pocket expenses carefully before you specify how much you will deposit annually into an FSA. Currently, what you don't use, you lose at the end of each calendar year. In many cases, your employer will divide leftover funds equally among plan participants, but the amount left in your individual plan will not be returned to you. There are proposals being considered which would adjust the rules to allow for rollovers from one year to the next in the future.

Your employer might also offer a Dependent Care Spending Account, with the same tax-exempt status as an FSA, in which you can con-

10 Questions to Ask Before Joining an HMO

1. How does the HMO ensure the competency of its staff?

2. Are doctors rewarded for cost containment—do they have an incentive to keep you from needed visits or from seeing a specialist?

3. Who decides what is medically necessary?

4. How can you appeal a decision, and how long will it take?

5. Will you have a choice of physicians, and who will pay if you see a doctor outside your system?

6. What percentage of revenue goes toward treating patients?

7. Will you get the best drugs for your condition, or will the HMO insist on substituting drugs that may not be as good?

8. How is the decision made to send a patient to a specialist?

9. What is the process for letting the HMO know what you think about the staff and quality of care?

10. Will you get prompt care in an emergency, and if you must go to a site outside the plan in the event of an emergency, will you be charged?

tribute up to $5,000 to cover day-care expenses at home or in a day care center. But you can't do this and claim the dependent and child-care tax credit (maximum of $3,000 for one dependent, $6,000 for two or more) in the same year.

Possible side effect: Any benefit that reduces your taxable income could have a ripple effect. Your pension, life insurance, disability insurance, and Social Security are all based on your salary and could be reduced. Check with your benefits department and weigh the impact of this effect when signing up for a flexible spending plan. For more information, visit www.flex-plan.com.

Health Savings Accounts (HSAs). These tax-exempt savings accounts were introduced as part of the Medicare reform bill of 2003. Not a new idea, they are, in fact, simply extensions of the former Archer Medical Savings Accounts (MSAs), previously available only to the self-employed and small business owners and their employees. The Archer MSA pilot program expired at the end of 2003. MSAs have been replaced by HSAs and have been made available to virtually all workers under age 65 as a means of saving money to pay for future medical expenses.

Here's how they work: A Health Savings Account is like an IRA. You open one at a financial instituion, in conjunction with a HSA-approved high deductible health plan (HDHP)—one with an annual deductible of at least $2,000 for a family ($1,000 for an individual). The maximum amount that can be contributed and deducted from your federal income tax is the lesser of the amount of your plan's annual deductible or the maximum specified by law (up to $5,150 a year for a family or $2,600 for an individual) (Taxpayers, 55 and older, can contribute an additional $500 a year.) These amounts are adjusted annually for inflation. Use this money to pay your out-of-pocket medical expenses under your high-deductible health plan. In addition to covering deductible expenses under your HDHP, you may make tax-free withdrawals to pay for medical services not covered by your insurance, to pay for long-term-care insurance, or to cover COBRA payments or health-insurance premiums in the event that you become unemployed. Check out the government Web site for complete information: www.ustreas.gov/offices/public-affairs/hsa.

Once you meet your plan's maximum out-of-pocket expenses, your high-deductible insurance policy kicks in and covers expenses 100 percent. The money that you don't use just accumulates in your savings account—toward future expenses or your retirement. Earnings on your savings are tax-deferred. Withdrawals used to pay medical expenses are not taxed. However, if you withdraw money for non-medical purposes before age 65, you will have to pay income taxes and a 10 penalty. After age 65, the account is treated as an IRA and you can make withdrawals for non-medical reasons, without penalty. These are reported as ordinary income and taxed. In the meantime, your money is invested in your choice of investment fund, and interest accumulates, tax-deferred. If you contribute the maximum amount each year to an HSA, and enjoy good health much of that time, you will accumulate a sizable nest egg.

Many corporations are beginning to offer high-deductible plans to reduce their medical costs. If your employer does, it's worth considering in conjunction with an HSA. Like FSAs, you get a tax advantage on money you'd be spending anyway on medical expenses; but unlike with an FSA, you don't lose the money you don't use. It just keeps earning a healthy rate of interest for you to use now or in the future.

What do you do if you are self-employed? Think about joining an organization, such as the local Chamber of Commerce, that offers group health coverage discounts to its members. Or consider membership in a professional organization or union that provides group health coverage to its members. To keep premiums low, many such organizations offer large deductibles. Or consider the advantages of a Health Savings Account. (Read "Two Women, Two Plans, One Choice: How Much I Saved with a Health Savings Account" in this section to read why one self-employed woman made the switch from a PPO to an HSA.) If an HSA doesn't work for you, ask around; sometimes, an HMO will offer group coverage to an individual who is not otherwise eligible to be in a group medical plan. The good news: All health insurance premiums are 100 percent tax deductible for the self-employed.

When purchasing a policy, always check the cancellation clause. Some companies reserve the right to cancel at any time. If you have a non-cancelable policy, your insurer cannot cancel it during the term of coverage. Nor can your premiums be increased during this period. Usually, when the stated period has ended—and it may be as short as one year—the company must renew, if the policyholder wants to renew. The premium, however, may be increased. A cancelable policy could be disastrous to the self-employed worker: If you have an illness or uninsurable condition when it is canceled, you'll have trouble finding another insurer.

If you find yourself without coverage, know that in the event of a medical emergency, emergency rooms at all hospitals that accept Medicare (which includes most of them) must accept you and stabilize your condition, without inquiring about your ability to pay, though you will have to make arrangements to pay afterwards. Another option for obtaining routine and preventive care is to investigate community health clinics in your area.

THE SINGLE MOM'S FINANCE SURVIVAL GUIDE: A RECIPE FOR LEMONADE IN CASE LIFE HANDS YOU—AND YOUR SWEET BABY—LEMONS

"Necessity is the mother of invention." A single mom must have been the first person to make that observation. "When you're handed lemons, make lemonade" is another one of those expressions people use to explain how they got through tough times. For single moms, struggling to come up with enough money to pay for the bare necessities for themselves and their children, the lemonade can be bittersweet, and "inventing" ways to make and save enough money to keep their kids safe and still somehow realize their own dreams is the name of the game.

Nearly ten million women are raising children on their own, either as a result of divorce or widowhood or because they were never married and their partners have left them. Most rely on a safety net of family, friends, neighbors, and financial aid or loans until they can establish themselves. With the gap widening between high rents and low pay, the number of homeless people in this country—1.4 million children and 2 million adults—is growing, according to the Urban Institute, a Washington, D.C., research group; many of them are single moms. "It takes a village . . ." to raise a child, as Hillary Rodham Clinton pointed out in her 1996 book, It Takes a Village, and Other Lessons Children Teach Us.

Karen learned those lessons the hard way. Her ex-husband skipped town and never paid the alimony and child support that he owed her and their three children. Working for a deli in a corporate park during the day, she went back to school at night, attending a community college, so she would be able to get a better-paying job to support her family.

She considered herself fortunate to have a neighbor who was willing to watch her toddler during the day, accepting the minimum wage Karen could afford to pay her. Her other two children attended school, and Karen was usually at home soon after they got off the school bus. "I had a great employer," says Karen. "If I had to pick one of the kids up at school early, I could take him to the deli. He would sit quietly most of the time and do homework." Her boyfriend or mother watched the kids the three nights she took courses. "I didn't have one cent left over at the end of the week, but we got through it," she says.

It isn't easy being the sole parent and primary breadwinner, particularly when you don't have a profession to fall back on or you're blindsided by

TWO WOMEN, TWO PLANS, ONE CHOICE:
HOW MUCH I SAVED WITH A HEALTH SAVINGS ACCOUNT

Sally's Traditional Plan. Sally is a self-employed writer with two kids and has a Preferred Provider Organization (PPO) medical plan through a writer's organization. She has a primary physician, who refers her and the children to a specialist, when needed. She pays a small co-payment of $20, at the time of service, to her primary physician or any doctor to whom she is referred. For medical procedures and surgery, she is billed 30 percent of the total bill, after the deductible. If she seeks care outside of the network, the PPO only pays 50 percent of the bill.

She has a deductible of $1,000 per person, with a maximum family deductible of $3,000. The out-of-pocket maximum is $5,000 per family member and $15,000 per family, and that doesn't include the deductible. "I never reached the deductible until last year," says Sally. "I needed surgery and additional treatment afterwards, and the bills were horrendous."

Sally's premiums soared last year from $625 to $935 per month. Her out-of-pocket expenses for the year were $2,560, plus $11,220 in premiums, for a total of $13,780. The out-of-pocket payments were made with after-tax dollars. (However, since she is self-employed, her premiums are tax-deductible.)

Jessica's HSA. Jessica, a friend of Sally's, has a Health Savings Account tied to a high-deductible health plan (HDHP) with a deductible of $4,950. Even with a family, she pays a premium of only about $300 per month (or $3,600 per year), less than half of what Sally pays for her traditional plan. Jessica can choose her doctors. (Remember, Sally belongs to a PPO and must stay within its network of doctors or the plan will only pay half the bill.)

Jessica contributes 65 percent of her maximum deductible of $4,950, for an annual contribution to the HSA of $3,218. She uses the money in the account to help pay for smaller, routine medical bills, tapping into her account by debit card or check. When her maximum out-of-pocket expenses are reached (and, remember, expenses for every family member count toward this limit), the high-deductible policy will kick in and pay all covered medical expenses, 100 percent (up to a lifetime maximum of $8 million, per person). She will have enough saved to cover the maximum out-of-pocket expense at the end of her second year, assuming she pays in the same amount each year.

All told, this year, Jessica paid an annual amount of $6,818 for her health plan ($3,600 in premiums, plus $3,218 to her HSA). Remember that Sally paid $11,220 in premiums alone. Because she is self-employed, like Sally, her premiums are tax-deductible. But Jessica gets an added tax advantage, because the amount she pays into her HSA is also tax-deductible.

Why Sally Switched. After comparing the benefits of her plan with her friend Jessica's HSA/HDHP, Sally decided to switch. She took into account the tax advantages of the HSA, as well as the heavy out-of-pocket expenses she paid with the PPO—a deductible for each family member, co-payment of 30 percent (after the deductible), and an out-of-pocket maximum of $5,000 per family member.

"I paid huge premiums for the PPO and only got a small amount the year I was sick. I need catastrophic insurance, which a high deductible health plan offers me, and with this new plan I get that, plus a savings plan." She also likes the fact that her new HDHP pays for procedures that her traditional plan didn't cover—eye laser surgery, teeth implants, and "alternative" therapies, such as hair implants and dental procedures.

Other Factors That Convinced Sally to Switch. If she doesn't use the funds in her account, she doesn't lose them. Chances are good that she will build up enough savings over the years to cover any year in which she has an unexpected medical expense that requires her to pay the maximum out-of-pocket figure. And anything left over will serve as additional retirement savings for her.

Some Caveats. HDHP premiums vary greatly and are dependent on the preexisting health conditions of each person or family member to be insured, their health history, etc. Smokers are really hit hard. Where you live also counts. You might pay three times as much in Miami as you do in Gainesville, Florida. Depending on the law in your individual state, coverage for certain conditions may be excluded or modified, a higher premium may be charged or coverage denied. So you need to read the fine print, and ask questions of the agent or broker who sells you your policy.

> **Tip:** Keep a record of your hospital bills. If you have to undergo a medical procedure and you don't have insurance, you may be charged the full fee for services. But lawsuits are currently underway, claiming that because of their tax-exempt charitable status, non-profit hospitals should charge the uninsured the same discounted rate for procedures that they charge patients who do have insurance.

events that you are unprepared for. The following guideposts may help you find your way on the road to independence.

What Goes Out . . . As a single mom, supporting yourself and your children on a limited income, it's crucial to come up with a budget, or spending plan. Think of it as a cash flow problem: What goes out must come in. If you're newly divorced, your new spending plan will probably have to reflect tighter circumstances. Following a divorce, as a result of the wage gap and the loss of her husband's income, a woman's standard of living drops an average of 30 percent in five years, while a man's rises 10 percent.

Before you create a budget, you need to know how much you're currently spending. Start by keeping track of your daily expenses for several months. If you have a computer, use a software program like Quicken to help you. Make a list of your fixed and flexible expenses. Once you've recorded all your expenses, analyze them carefully. Ask yourself, "Do I really want to spend that much of my money on subscriptions, eating out, dry cleaning?" What is important to you? What are your priorities? Even small, incremental changes in your spending can make a real difference!

After you have done this for several months, you'll have a clear idea of where your money is going. Then you can compare your expenses to your income, set up a spending plan and move forward. Budgeting is not a one-time project; it's an on-going process. You're creating a road map

IS YOUR HEALTH INSURER PAYING YOUR BILLS ON TIME?

Did you know that your credit report can be affected by the late bill-paying practices of some health insurers? Though most states have prompt-payment regulations on the books, consumer experts are reporting an increase in the number of bills that health providers are sending to collection agencies, because they have not been paid on time.

Unless you monitor your credit record, you may not be aware that this has happened, until you apply for a loan or mortgage and are denied a low interest rate because of the damage that's been done to your rating.

Nip the problem in the bud by making sure, first of all, that the information on your insurance forms is correct, particularly if you are seeking care from an out-of-system provider. If you find that an unpaid charge has shown up on your credit report, write to the three credit agencies (www.TransUnion.com, www.Experian.com, and www. Equifax.com) immediately and ask them to attach a note to your report explaining that the procedure was covered by your insurance and that you are looking into the matter. Then get on the phone with your insurer and voice some healthy outrage.

00187 334 0012
Charge Express

or blueprint for where you want to go. So don't forget to budget in savings for education for yourself and your children, for a home, for whatever your long-term goals are.

If there is more month than money, let the kids know. Children do better if they know the truth and can come up with their own money-saving ideas. Karen would take home all the empty soda bottles from the deli. The two older kids would sort them, then return them to the store, keep some of the money they got for the returns, and throw the rest in the common pot. "They felt like they were contributing to something that was important for all of us," says Karen.

Must Come In . . . When you're creating your budget, do a tally of what income you can expect to receive: include salary, alimony, child support, welfare, Social Security, pension income, interest and dividends from investments. Don't count your chickens before they hatch—don't include a bonus that might or might not be paid at the end of the year or a family gift that was received

SAVE YOUR MONEY:
INSURANCE YOU CAN LIVE WITHOUT

>> **Credit life and disability.** These policies pay off a small benefit if you die with an outstanding balance. They might also provide some disability payments. Life and disability insurance are much better for you.

>> **Flight insurance.** A good life insurance policy will cover you wherever you go. Check with your credit card issuer—if you charge your ticket, you might have automatic flight insurance.

>> **Life insurance for your kids.** The premiums are low but remember they are dependent on you. Better that you spend the money to get the coverage you need.

>> **Extended warranties.** You can purchase extended warranties for your car and major appliances, but they're expensive for what you get. It's generally cheaper to pay for repairs yourself.

One thing you can do right now ...
TAKE IT OFF TWO WAYS

Have a doctor diagnose you as obese and you can deduct the expense of weight-loss programs, as long as your health insurance doesn't cover them. You can even amend your taxes to take advantage of this deduction for the last three years—assuming you kept your receipts for these programs. (Fat chance of that!) Cost of weight-loss foods not included.

last year but that, because of a declining stock market, may not be given this year. And speaking of what's coming in, try to hang onto as much of it as you can. You may qualify for the Earned Income Tax Credit (EITC); many who do don't take advantage of it, according to the IRS.

The EITC is a federal tax credit available to low-income individuals and families. Income and family size determine the amount received. To qualify, both the earned income and the adjusted gross income (for 2004) must be less than $30,338 for a taxpayer with one qualifying child; $34,458 for a taxpayer with more than one qualifying child.) The average EITC credit is about $1,800, nationally. Check IRS Publication 596 for more information.

Child Support. The Child Support Recovery Act of 1992 makes it a federal crime to willfully fail to pay a past-due child-support obligation for a child living in another state. For information and counseling on your rights and how to pursue court-ordered child support from a spouse, who like Karen's husband, skipped town, or who is chronically late in paying it, contact the Child Support Enforcement Office in your area. You'll find it listed in your phone book, or by state, on www.SingleParentCentral.com. Child support is not counted as income for tax purposes.

Another option is to submit your deadbeat spouse's name to the IRS. Under the Federal Tax Refund Offset Program, you may be able to have any refunds owed him diverted to you to pay off his obligation. To learn more about this option, contact the Federal Office of Child Support Enforcement, or visit www.SingleParentCentral.com, which has a very helpful list of frequently asked questions about this process.

If you do get child support, and he doesn't already have an insurance policy naming you the beneficiary, take out a cheap term life insurance policy on him, so that you will have some protection in the event of his death. Those contemplating divorce should make life insurance a provision of their divorce settlement.

Financial Assistance. Karen received financial assistance. "I was a welfare-to-work mom," she says. "Before I got the job in the deli, I was receiving food stamps and other allowances. While receiving assistance, I had to register for work and then accept an offer for suitable work. The amounts were decreased when I got the job, and eventually they were eliminated."

Getting assistance can be difficult, time-consuming, and frustrating, but don't let that stop you. The Administration for Children and Families (ACF), part of the U.S. Department of Health and Human Services, is the federal agency that funds state and local organizations to provide family assistance (welfare), Head Start, and other child-welfare services. To find a local office that administers these programs, check the blue pages of your telephone book under both city and state government for listings under Human Resources, Social Services, and Food Stamps. You can visit the ACF Web site at www.acf.dhhs.gov to get further information about how to apply for var-

TWO THINGS ALL FATHERS CAN DO FOR THEIR DAUGHTERS

"What is the single biggest thing a father can do for his daughter? Pay child support, if he's divorced. He shouldn't make the law track him down and he shouldn't let his child sit there thinking, 'Why doesn't he pay support for me?' According to the U.S. government, more than half [of men who owe child support] don't pay it.

The other thing a man can do is love the mother of his children and let them see that he values their mother and the work she does—particularly the work of taking care of children."

— *Linda Ellerbee, award-winning TV producer (Nickelodeon's* Nick News, *among other programs) and author of the sassy, savvy, empowering "Get Real" series of books for young girls.*

ious assistance programs, including home energy assistance, as well as the address and phone numbers of aid organizations in your area. A food-stamp hotline is available at 1-888-863-6178. Look into aid programs and food distribution centers run by local churches or community organizations.

Soup kitchens and the food they distribute to the needy have changed. According to a 2003 *New York Times* article, "the growing numbers of working poor turning up at soup kitchens and pantries—in most cases, single mothers with children—are so busy juggling jobs, commuting and child care that they have little time to cook the food they are given." The solution: volunteers are distributing premade meals—for instance frozen, family-size portions of chili and spaghetti sauce—instead of the canned goods that were the major staple of food baskets in the past.

Social Security Benefits. Betty, widowed in her early thirties, received Social Security benefits for herself and her two young sons. A benefit is paid to a widow if she is responsible for children under the age of 16, and to her children. There is, however, a maximum amount paid per family. Betty worked, and her benefit was reduced because of her earnings, but the children received their full benefits until they were 18 years old.

Pension Benefits. Audrey's husband was still working when he died. He had worked for several companies during his 35-year career. She wrote to the employee benefits department of each company. In each case, she was given the choice of receiving his pension as a lump sum or in monthly lifetime payments. If you have a choice as to how you will receive this money, ask for time to consult a financial planner prior to making this important decision. You can't change your mind if you decide on lifetime payments.

Plug the Leaks. Be a responsible credit-card user. You don't need more than two cards. Put small items on a card that you pay in full every month. Big-ticket items can be charged to the card that has an on-going balance. If you're carrying more than two cards, or are paying high interest on your cards, transfer your balances to one with lower finance charges and no annual fee. You'll be surprised at the amount you save. Don't put groceries on the card that carries a balance. Those groceries will be long gone before you've paid the bill off.

Stay Healthy. Health insurance can be a horrendous problem and a major expense for a single mom. "My first consideration," recalls Karen, "was to get a job with a company that had good benefits. I was lucky that there was no major medical crisis during the time my kids and I were uninsured."

A widow or divorcée is generally eligible for coverage under her husband's health insurance, provided by his employer, for 36 months. You will pay the group rate plus a small premium for the period, but, after that, you are on your own. Ann's children were covered under their father's policy until they were out of college, but Ann had to find coverage for herself when she was no longer insured on her ex-husband's plan. She started a consulting business. "I joined the local Chamber of Commerce, only because they offered a medical plan to their members," says Ann. The rates are cheaper if you can participate as part of a group.

Each state has a health-insurance program for uninsured infants, children, and teenagers, who are eligible for low-cost or free coverage through State Children's Health Insurance Programs (SCHIP) or Medicaid. Yet a recent survey reported that six out of 10 parents whose uninsured children qualify for Medicaid or SCHIP did not believe those free or low-cost public coverage programs applied to them. In most states, SCHIP is available to uninsured children under the age of 19, whose families earn up to $36,200 a year (for a family of four). For little or no cost, this insurance pays for: Doctor visits, immunizations, hospitalizations, and emergency-room visits. If you don't qualify for SCHIP, you most likely are eligible for Medicaid.

Medicaid is available for the very poor. Each state has its own eligibility rules. Your children might be eligible in one state but not in another. For more information, log onto www.insurekidsnow.gov and www.coveringkids.org, where you'll find eligibility requirements for each state.

The Biggest Expense. Child care is likely to be one of your largest expenses—at least until your kids start school. The cost will depend on where you live and the type of care—in home or out-of-home care.

Ellen had in-home care for Eric. In addition to paying Maria's salary, she paid Social Security withholding (FICA) for her. There are lower-cost alternatives, however, that might work for you. Karen took her toddler to a neighbor, paying her minimum wage. Other women have organized neighborhood day-care centers, run by mothers who volunteer their time. If you work for a large corporation, lobby for day-care benefits or a corporate day-care center in the building. Check whether any of the churches in your neighborhood offer low-cost day-care programs. And, by all means, investigate whether you are eligible for state child-care subsidies.

A recent report by the U.S. Department of Health and Human Services found that only 1.5 million of the 9.9 million children who are eligible for child-care subsidies under their states' eligibility guidelines receive assistance. To find out if you are eligible, contact your county Division of Family and Children Services (DFCS) office, which should be listed in the blue pages of your phone book. Your local Childcare Resource and Referral Agency (also listed in your phone book) may also be able to give you a list of day-care providers that offer scholarships.

Be Happy. When you're trimming your budget, leave just a little extra for fun for yourself and your children. Build in some play money for activities that feed your soul, reduce stress, or improve your emotional life. In your local newspaper, search for free ways to have fun with your children. Tickets to cultural events or eating out might seem extravagant, but anything that gives you a break from your kids and lets you spend some much-needed time with adult friends is worth it. Join a support group—or start one. Hold a monthly single-moms' idea exchange at your place—and serve lemonade!

WILL POWER: WHY YOU NEED ONE NOW

If you die without leaving a will, you die "intestate." That means the state in which you lived immediately before your death gets to decide who will inherit your property. What the state decides may not be what you had in mind. The possibility of inequities arising is considerable, especially in the case of people who are living together without the benefit of marriage.

Most intestate succession laws are designed to pass property only to blood relatives or to a legal spouse. It is impossible, in fact, in most states, to disinherit a legal spouse. But if you don't have a will, your spouse may end up splitting your estate with other family members when you intended for him to get everything. If one member of an unmarried couple dies without a will or other legal protection for the survivor, that survivor will not inherit anything. Your will accomplishes a number of things. If you are a parent, it lets you name a personal guardian for a child. It appoints the person you want as your executor, in charge of supervising the distribution of your estate. If you leave no will, the state names a guardian and appoints an executor. Your will also directs what kind of funeral you want, and who is to take responsibility for such arrangements.

Writing your will. Your will has only one purpose: To make certain that your property goes where you want it to go after you die. Check your list of assets, insurance policies, company benefits, household furnishings, investments, your home—you probably own more than you thought you did. Think about how you want your assets to be distributed and write down your decisions. Now you have to turn that paper into a legal document that will not be disputed in a court of law.

For that you need professional help. That means a lawyer. A good lawyer will know your state's laws and will know how to head off problems, especially if you are remarried. Your lawyer will take action to prove that you are competent and not under undue influence when you sign your will, and will make sure the will is witnessed properly.

Save time—and legal fees—by writing your own first draft, or at least a statement covering what you want the will to accomplish. Your lawyer can then review and adapt your draft, and prepare it for your signature. If you'd prefer, you can request that a standard, "boilerplate" will be prepared, ready for your name and other specific details to be plugged in quickly and easily. Such wills are also available at a very low cost on the Internet. Check www.legalzoom.com, for instance. These can be filled out, reviewed for accuracy by the service, and mailed to you for notarization and signature. They're better than nothing; however, a will prepared by a local attorney familiar with your state's laws is preferable.

When you go to see your lawyer, be ready with a list of your assets (from your net worth statement), the name of your executor, and the name of a guardian for minor children. Decide who is to get what. Make careful notes on just how you want your estate distributed, including any specific instructions on particular items.

Your executor should be an adult child or friend or relative whom you trust. This person will be fully responsible for seeing your will through probate and making sure your estate is disposed of in accordance with your will. Your executor should live nearby. It won't hurt to name two executors: for instance, a relative and your attorney, or, if you are

Been There, Done That:

SMART ADVICE FROM A THIRD-GENERATION SINGLE MOM

BY ALLISON ACKEN, PHD

I am the third in a line of single moms. My grandmother was a single mom during the Depression, my mother was a single mom during the late 1950s and '60s, and I was a single mom in the late '70s. Even though none of us had two nickels to rub together in all those decades, we all had a very good time, and we knew that we could count on each other when things were tough. That was true for my mom and her brothers, for my brother and me, and for my daughters.

What my grandmother and my mother understood and I learned from them about being a single mom is that you can't be the perfect parent—but you can be "good enough." And that is enough. You need to recognize that trying to give your kids everything they need, both emotionally and materially, is impossible, perhaps even in the best of times. The attempt can leave single mothers so stressed out that they have even less of themselves available to give to their kids.

A "good enough" single mom will accept that she can't be two parents, much less a village, to her kids; she'll realize that she is only one part of her children's lives. With this wisdom, she will do her best to provide a strong emotional base for her family and whatever she can provide materially (within reason), without burying herself in debt.

Having "been there and done that," I know it isn't easy. Here are three tips I'd offer any mother going it alone.

1. The emotional support you give your children is priceless. Remember that the relationship you have with your children and your kids' relationships with each other are primary. More important than any new toy or computer game or trendy outfit or athletic shoe is the emotional base single moms build with and for their kids.

2. If you're stressed, you can't help your kids. Understand your child's comfort is related to the stress levels in your life. If money is tight and buying a new toy is going to leave you crying over the bills at the end of the month, it really isn't worth it. What is more important to them—the new toy or having a bit more time with a happier mom to read a book or go to the park or the beach together?

3. Accept help when you need it. Too many single moms try to tough it out alone. Just because the marriage didn't work doesn't mean you can't have help or support from anybody else. Yes, the kids are your responsibility (particularly the emotional territory), but if a friend or family member offers to buy new shoes for the kids or a computer or to contribute toward their college tuition, seriously consider saying, "Yes, and thank you."

---

remarried, your new spouse and an adult child from an earlier marriage. If your executor dies or becomes incapacitated, it is important to revise your will to name someone else. In such an event, do not delay, for if you should die without replacing your executor, the state will name the replacement.

A guardian is obliged to provide proper care for your children and to manage any money left to them. (Note: Legal parents of a minor child are entitled to custody of that child. If there are two legal parents—for instance, divorced parents—each is entitled to custody. If one dies, the other, in most cases automatically gains sole custody.) What if the person whom you want to name as guardian just doesn't have good financial sense?

You can name one person to handle the money and another to care for the child. Before you complete your will and sign it, be sure to check with your proposed guardian to be sure that she or he is willing to be named.

Ask your lawyer to keep the signed original copy of your will in his or her office safe. Keep photocopies in your files at home. Don't put them in a safe deposit box, for they must be accessible the minute they are needed.

Finally, review your will regularly. Why? There are countless reasons: more children may come into the picture; a child may become an adult; a beneficiary may die; an executor may die or move far away; you may move to another state, where estate laws are different; you may experience a major change in your financial circumstances; new laws affecting estates may be passed in your state; you may simply feel the need to change your beneficiaries.

Tip: Caregivers of the Sandwich Generation, take note— you may be able to claim dependent-care credit for a parent who has become your dependent (i.e. you are responsible for more than 50 persent of his or her support). CheckIRS publication 503 for the eligibility standards

Kiddie Tax Deductions and Credits. Kids *are* costly, but happily, you can benefit financially from the happy event of having a child. Count the ways, below:

Basic Exemption. You can claim a $3,200 exemption for each child. Be sure to change your W-4 form at work to reflect your new family member, so you don't end up paying Uncle Sam more than you need to throughout the year.

Child and Dependent Care Credit. This credit is available if you hire someone (a day-care center, baby-sitter or nanny) to take care of your child while you are at work. That person must be over the age of 19 and not a dependent of yours. To qualify, you have to incur the expenses while earning an income and you must report the identifying information of your caretaker to the IRS. The credit can be as much as 35 percent of your qualified expenses, depending on your income, and it only applies to the first $3,000 of childcare expenses ($6,000 if over one child). For instance, your credit would be $750 for one child ($1,500 for two or more), if your Adjusted Gross Income were $35,000. See IRS Publication 503.

Child Tax Credit. Depending on your income (upper limit before phase out: $110,000, filing jointly; $75,000 for singles), you may be eligible to receive a $1,000 Federal tax credit for every child under age 17.

Education Tax Credits. For college-age children, the Hope and Lifetime Learning credits apply. (See Chapter One for details.)

Interest on Student Loans. This is deductible up to $2,500, depending on income.

Earned Income Tax Credit (EITC). The EITC is a federal tax credit available to low-income individuals and families. Income and family size determine the amount received. To qualify for the credit, both the earned income and the adjusted gross income (for 2004) must be less than $30,338 for a taxpayer with one qualifying

FINANCIAL BABY STEPS:
A MOVE FOR EVERY MONTH OF YOUR PREGNANCY

Here are nine smart financial moves you and your husband can make to ensure your new family's financial security—one for each month of your pregnancy.

1. **Review your new family's life insurance coverage.** Do you have enough so that, if the major bread-winner (either you or your husband) dies, the death benefit can be invested and will earn enough interest to replace the missing spouse's current and future monthly income? Chances are the insurance coverage from your employer isn't going to do the job. Compare prices of term insurance and cash-value policies; a cheaper term policy may give you the extra protection you need at a price you can afford, even though it won't accrue in value.

2. **Buy mortgage insurance.** This can be purchased from the financial institution that holds your mortgage, and will be factored into your monthly payments. With it, a surviving spouse won't have to allocate a sizable chunk of a life insurance death benefit to secure the roof over his/her head.

3. **Make sure both of you are insured.** If you are the major caregiver, you need coverage so that if something happens to you, your husband will be able to afford to pay for child care.

4. **Suggest that grandma and grandpop pay for a cash-value policy on your baby.** A $25,000 policy that matures when your daughter is 25 will give her a head start on realizing her dreams, or help her pay off her college bills.

5. **Check your employer's disability coverage.** If you haven't already taken advantage of it, sign up now, or purchase an individual policy. Insurance statistics say that people are far more likely to become disabled before age 65 than they are to die.

6. **Start saving for college tuition today.** Projected costs for a year's tuition, plus room and board, at a private college for the year 2018 are $53,790; even for a public college, it's $20,624 per year. That's nearly a quarter of a million dollars, if your star pupil attends a private college. So start investing as much as you can as soon as you can. Discuss the advantages of stock and bond mutual funds, Roth IRAs, education IRAs, and state 529 plans with a financial planner.

7. **Look for tax advantages.** Don't overlook line 43 of Form 1040, which gives eligible parents a federal tax credit, ($1,000 per child in 2004) subtracted from the amount you owe each year. Also, for each dependent child, you can claim a $3,050 tax exemption. Change your W-4 form at work, so you don't end up paying more throughout the year than you have to. More good news: If you work, you can deduct up to 35 percent of your child-care or day-care costs, up to a $3,000 for one child ($6,000 if more than one).

8. **Diversify your portfolio.** You know you should do this periodically anyway. Now that you have someone to leave your estate to, plan to leave a large one.

9. **Finally, draw up a will, or revise your existing one.** You want to include your child as a beneficiary. Be sure to name a legal guardian, too—someone who will wholeheartedly accept responsibility for raising your child should both you and your husband die at the same time. It's also a good idea to allocate "limited power of attorney" to a guardian in the event that you and your husband become incapacitated or incapable of caring for your child for a period of time. Talk to the person or persons you've chosen to be sure that they are willing to assume this parental responsibility. Share with them your values, hopes and dreams for your child's future.

After you've done all of this, you can start thinking about how to teach your child that money isn't everything.

child ($31,338 for married filing jointly), $334,458 for a taxpayer with more than one qualifying child ($35,458 for married filing jointly), and $11,490 for a taxpayer with no qualifying children ($12,490 for married filing jointly). The average EITC credit is about $1,800, nationally. Check IRS Publication 596 for more information.

Adoption Credit. You may be able to receive an adoption credit of up to $10,160 for the costs of adopting a child under the age of 18, or a mentally or physically disabled person. The credit cannot be more than your tax liability and is phased out for those with incomes between $152,390 and $192,390. Check IRS publication 968 for more details.

WHAT WE'RE TEACHING OUR DAUGHTERS ABOUT MONEY

I've spoken about the lessons—good and bad—that my mother, taught me about money. A glorious, unrepentant spendthrift all of her life, her spending habits rubbed off on me. I watched my father struggle to pay the bills my mother left in her wake, but that lesson didn't take. Your money personality, your saving and spending habits, are probably similarly rooted in your childhood experiences about money and how your parents— particularly your mother—dealt with dollars and sense. One of the best gifts you can give your daughters and sons is to teach them the value of money in the bank. We sent contributing editor Sharon Sorokin James out to ask other women to share their money experiences growing up and what they're doing to give their children a financial head start.

One thing you can do right now ...

DON'T PASS THE BUCK—BE THE ONE WHO TEACHES YOUR KIDS ABOUT SAVING & SPENDING WISELY

>> Talk about money with your children—not about spending it, but about earning it.

>> Either give your child an allowance or pay your child a modest amount for individual chores. Either way, require your child to save at least half of everything he or she makes.

>> Open a passbook savings account at your local bank and take your child there at least once a month to deposit allowances, earnings, or gifts.

>> If you can afford to, match your child's savings, dollar for dollar.

>> Help your child to set definite financial goals and to meet them. Keep the goals small enough that your child can easily succeed at meeting them. For example, maybe your daughter wants the latest Beanie Baby. Help her figure out how much it will cost (don't forget the tax), and then help her develop a plan to save up for it.

>> Don't let financial-consumption goals (i.e., buying that Beanie Baby) cut into required savings. Encourage your child to pay for such items out of the discretionary portion of her allowance or chore money.

HOW SOME MOTHERS ARE HANDING DOWN SMART ADVICE ABOUT CAREERS, LIFE AND THE VALUE OF A DOLLAR TO THE NEXT GENERATION

BY SHARON SOROKIN JAMES

"Every woman should have a profession." This was a frequent pronouncement by my grandmother. She was born in May, 1890, and died a few days short of her 95th birthday. She came of age during the early twentieth century. Life was certainly different then, yet she recognized, early on, the importance of education and independence for women. My grandmother was, nonetheless, in many ways a traditional wife, raising her children, waiting on her husband, and allowing, or submitting to, his decisions. But she was clear on the destiny of women. "Every woman should have a profession."

What made her think that? She was only 16 when her mother died, leaving her to care for her father and her five younger brothers. A good student, she had to leave high school to raise her siblings. Perhaps that motivated her. Or perhaps it was the example of her husband, who studied engineering in college after running a successful business and marrying. Perhaps it was the dependence she felt on her husband. Perhaps it was her realization that no matter how hard she worked—and she did work hard, both inside and outside the home—she would never earn money of her own.

My grandmother would have been an excellent chief executive officer of a large corporation. She was organized, decisive, a good delegator, a rousing public speaker, an inspiring leader, and excellent at long-range and strategic planning. She organized Jewish women across the state of Connecticut to raise money for Hadassah, her favored charity, rising to the level of the national board of this very large charitable organization. She traveled the country, speaking, fundraising, and organizing women. But she was never paid for her work.

Her daughter, my mother, led an extremely sheltered life, doted upon by her parents and much older brothers. Although she was called "Baby" until she was 12, she was also encouraged intellectually and sent to Vassar for college, where she was desultorily pre-med, following the lead of her aunt, who was one of the very few women physicians of that era, until she met my father. He changed my mother's ambitions. A poor, hardworking and highly motivated law student, my father persuaded her to attend law school after college,

(and marriage). So at the age of 21, with the blessing of her parents, she graduated from Vassar, got married, and enrolled in law school, all within the space of three months. One of only two women in her class, she was at the top of the class academically and became editor-in-chief of the law review, an exalted position. She practiced law with my father for more than 40 years, until his death at the age of 69. And she taught me that every woman should have her own money, so she has the independence to make her own decisions.

What shall I teach my daughter? I am teaching her to save her money, something that I am not very good at myself. Each of my two children is given a weekly allowance—one dollar for each grade they are in. My daughter, Julia, in 2nd grade, gets $2 a week, and my son, Levi, in 5th grade, gets $5—when I remember to give it to them. The only rule about allowance is that they must save at least half of it. They each have passbook savings accounts, and they are thrilled whenever we go to the bank to update our paltry interest and make further deposits. Whenever they deposit money, I try to match it with another deposit. I don't feel compelled to teach Julia that every woman should have a profession. She is seeing, as I did as a child, a professional, wage-earning, working woman every day of her life. She sees her friends' mothers working, and she also sees friends' mothers who don't work. I hope Julia will feel free to choose her destiny. Although my family may be unusual in that it contained more than its share of professional women, I don't think its financial lessons were unusual. To find out, I interviewed a number of women from a variety of walks of life. We talked about what their mothers taught them about money, and what they are teaching their daughters about money.

The first person I spoke with, Ellen, is a partner in a prominent law firm. When I asked her, "What did your mother teach you about money?" she laughed tersely and said, "My father taught me about money." Her father was an accountant. Ellen, at the age of 32, is single, talented and well on her way to financial independence. Brought up in a traditional, very close Italian family, she lives at home with her parents. She helps them with their expenses, I am sure, and she saves huge amounts of money, I am also sure. I suspect she will be financially secure enough to retire by age 45, if she so chooses.

Joan, a stunningly beautiful woman in her mid forties, recently founded an independent classical music recording and production company. She will tell you that her business has not yet made her any money to speak of, but her first CD was released to glowing national reviews. When I asked Jane what her mother, a painter, taught her about money, she said, "She taught me to get good buys, to try not to pay full price, and she made me earn my own money by working every summer." Joan is teaching her own daughter that money is something you have to work for, not something that just pops out of an ATM machine when you insert your card and punch a few buttons.

Some people think that frugality is genetic. Ruth claims her family is the best evidence of that theory. Ruth, also in her mid 40s, currently works as the head chef at an alternative private school. A fabulous cook, she has had many different careers and jobs, which she attributes, only somewhat facetiously, to her liberal-arts degree. At various times in her life, she has worked in retail jewelry stores, taught pre-school, been a stay-at-home mom extraordinaire, and, in early days, worked in a travel agency, which her mother founded. Ruth's mother, widowed by 40, taught Ruth by example and by giving her responsibility. By the time she was in high school, Ruth had her own checking account (although she confesses she has never, ever balanced her checkbook, a confession in which I must guiltily join) and was responsible for buying her own clothes. She has always worked. The travel agency was founded shortly before her father's death, perhaps in anticipation of it. He died when Ruth was 14. That, and Ruth's mother's teaching, taught Ruth to be responsible, to pay her bills on time and to save her money whenever possible.

Ruth owned her own home and her own car before she was married, purchased with money she had earned and saved herself. From working with her mother in the travel agency, she saw the importance of hard work. She also saw her mother saving and investing, and Ruth has followed her example. Now the mother of two daughters, she says she is teaching her daughters the same lessons. They both have allowances and savings accounts. But they each treat money very differently. Her older daughter enjoys spending her money and loves to shop, just like her father, a consummate shopper. Her younger daughter is frugal and focused on saving, just like Ruth. This, she points out, is what makes her believe that there is a genetic component to how we handle money.

Genetic or not, like everything else, saving money is also a learned skill. Even if you are not naturally inclined to it, you can be taught to be frugal. Teaching your daughters how to spend money wisely is equally, if not more, important. It is a chance to help them emulate our strengths, or develop skills in areas in which we are deficient. The more structured you can be, the better. Not only that, if you are not good at saving money (like me), teaching your daughter how to do it will teach you how to do it better. Since thinking seriously about how to teach my children about money, I have cut back significantly on spending, my husband and I have started a financial plan, paid off our credit-card debt, and organized our bill-paying. It is never too late in life to do these things, but it is better to get your children started early.

The lessons are well learned. My 10-year-old son has started going to the supermarket with me. He has an eye for bargains and is constantly checking the prices and trying to find the two-for-one sales. He will willingly turn down items that I deem too expensive, without a fuss. My daughter, too, is conscious of saving money. In addition to her passbook savings account, she has a wallet in which she hoards her allowance. She understands that she is never allowed to spend more than half of it, and she will often choose to spend less than her limit. I try to let them purchase small items they want with their own money, so that they learn the importance of saving for a goal and enjoying the fruits of their labor. Even at their young ages, I think they appreciate that saving is important.

They have not yet learned, however, the joy of work as a way of earning money. They see my job, as a lawyer, as something that takes me away from them. Although they understand, on an intellectual level, that I get paid for it, and that the income is important to our family, they view it as a hindrance. Their own career choices are not influenced by income levels. My son wants to be a history professor and my daughter an artist or architect. Neither of them has ever asked how much money they would make doing those things. They want to do them because they love them. Of that I am very proud. And I hope I am teaching them enough about managing the money they will someday earn that they will be able to choose whatever career path enthralls them, rather than feeling the need to make a choice based on income.

That, I think, is the most important money lesson of all.

Female Finance Checklist:
The Child-Bearing Years

❏ **Goals:** Whether—and when—to have a child is the question of the moment; it is either the most difficult or the easiest decision you will ever have to make. If you do have a child, saving takes on heightened importance, as you begin to accumulate money both for your child's future and your own security—making up for the earnings, retirement benefits, and Social Security vesting you may lose during your time away from the workforce.

❏ **Career:** Discuss with your spouse how you will share child-rearing and career responsibilities. Do the math to see whether you can find ways to afford to live on one salary, and consult your heart to determine whether leaving your career in mid-stream is what you really want to do.

❏ **Investments:** Single and married women alike continue to stash away the maximum in their 401(k)s, IRAs, or other investment vehicles. With every raise, increase the amount you pay yourself first. Stay-at-home moms, roll over any vested 401(k) savings into an IRA when you leave your job; consider having your husband open a spousal IRA to compensate for your lost 401(k) savings at work. Check your portfolios regularly to make sure you have the right balance of stocks and bonds, either individually or in your mutual funds, given the current economic climate. Parents will now investigate 529 college sav-

ings plans and education IRAs as well. A good birthday present to yourself on your 30th, 35th or 40th birthdays might be a consultation with a financial planner.

❏ **Real Estate:** If you have purchased property, a new goal may be to sell it at a profit and invest the money in another property that shows promise of escalating in value. Or you might consider borrowing against the equity in your current home to purchase a money-making rental property or vacation home as an investment.

❏ **Insurance:** Re-evaluate your life, mortgage, disability and health insurance needs as soon as baby comes on the scene. Consolidate as many of your plans with one insurance company to get the best price.

❏ **Wills:** No more postponing. Your children's and your spouse's financial security depend on you putting your wishes in writing in the form of a legal document, such as a will or living trust, which the courts in the state where you reside at the time of your death will recognize. Within the framework of the will, you can and should also name a guardian for your children—someone whom you would want to take care of them in the event of your untimely death. If you have no children, look to your relatives, friends or charitable organizations that you believe in as possible beneficiaries.

CHAPTER FIVE
SECOND CHANCES: SURVIVING DIVORCE & LAYOFFS

INCURABLE ROMANTIC?

A woman we know was in a longstanding relationship with a man who had proposed to her several times. Twice married and unsure that the third time would "be the charm," she kept putting him off. Then, one day, after she had returned from a trip to the pharmacy to pick up her costly heart medication, which wasn't covered by her health-care provider, he proposed again—this time, reminding her that his superior health insurance plan would have paid for the prescription. That convinced her: she said yes and they were married. The next time she went to the pharmacy, she was informed that her drug wasn't covered under her new husband's plan, because it treated a pre-existing condition.

That true story perfectly illustrates the back seat romance often takes in a woman's decision to wed or not to wed after a first marriage has failed. Realistic considerations—what do I (and my children) stand to lose…and to gain… financially—must be factored into any decision to change your legal status. What will the tax implications be? If you're a widow, do you risk losing health benefits under your former spouse's plan? Will you forfeit your right to a share of your ex's Social Security benefits? Then there are little things like trust, open communication, and cooperation—if money problems were at the heart of your last break-up, can you do better this time

around? Second marriages, like second chances, can often seem like blessings, but the financial issues are far more complex than they were the first time around. Protect yourself by knowing the questions to ask before saying, "I Do," Two… or Three or Four.

Second chances, like New Year's resolutions, take many forms—not all of them marriage-related. In this chapter, in addition to advice from the experts and women who've been there, done that, on divorce and remarriage; we introduce you to some hard-working, inspiring women who took a second shot at college, going back to school to get their degrees while raising families and working, and we identify scholarships for other women who want to do the same. Because layoffs are a lot like divorce, we also include advice from women who've bounced back and found even better jobs the second or third time around.

First up, some advice on how to get out of a bad marriage with your finances and future security intact. In this battle of the sexes, herewith …

THE RULES OF DISENGAGEMENT

The financial aspects of ending a marriage can be overwhelming, especially for women who have had little experience in money matters. While the divorce process is undeniably a traumatic time, too often women allow their emotions to overshadow practical considerations, like finding a lawyer and gathering together all the necessary financial information. That's an expensive mistake, because your future security and happiness—as well as that of your children, if you have any—are on the line.

"Most women do not play an active enough role in the process," says Patricia Kane, a matrimonial attorney in Stamford, Connecticut. "Their main concern is to protect the family, and they expect that kindness will smooth the way. Women need to make waves and be as assertive as their spouse is. Men often see kindness as a weakness. They tend to get to the bottom line much quicker than women do." They also fare better after divorce than their wives do: women's standard of living can decline 30 to 45 percent after divorce, according to various studies.

To mitigate that effect, Kane suggests that women interview several lawyers, and select the one they feel most comfortable with. "Ask questions and walk out on anyone who tells you, 'Everything will be all right, dearie.' You don't want someone who is condescending. You are buying the services of a professional. You're not buying a friend."

A good lawyer will be your advocate throughout the process, pointing out the financial consequences of every decision you make along the way. Below are the key points that every woman must consider as she prepares for this new beginning, as well as a few stories from women who learned the hard way what not to do.

SHOW ME THE MONEY

Protecting Assets. As soon as you know that you are divorcing, direct your bank to freeze your joint accounts, so that both signatures are required for all withdrawals. If you have a brokerage account, inform your broker in writing that all transactions require the approval of both parties.

You also need to know what your husband's assets are, if you hope to win en equitable share. Finding assets, joint or otherwise, can be difficult, especially for a woman who has had little to do with the finances. Marie never opened a bank or brokerage statement during her marriage of 35 years. When she knew the divorce was coming, she watched the mail carefully, looking for envelopes with return addresses of banks and brokerage houses. She never opened any of the statements, but she made a list. She also found copies of tax returns for the last 10 years, which had a wealth of information in them. Finding them saved time, aggravation, and legal fees. "My husband was surprised when he realized I had a lot more information than he expected," recalls Marie.

Irene came home with her two babies one day to discover that her husband had cleared out the house of all its contents. (He did leave the crib.) All joint accounts had been cleared out, too. Good planning on her husband's part left her in a terrible state.

Preventive Measure: The best way to protect your share of marital assets is to keep an individual account right from the beginning, a place where you can deposit your earnings, or your share of the household income, based on the spending plan you agreed upon when you married. You don't expect that your husband will turn out to be a monster, like Irene's, but you never know. It's okay to keep a joint checking account for the household bills, but don't keep much money in it. •

Dividing Assets. The laws governing the division of property vary from state to state. Community property states (Arizona, California, Idaho, Louisiana, Nevada, New Mexico, Texas, Washington, and Wisconsin) split property accumulated during the marriage equally between the two parties. "Equitable distribution" is the method used in most other states. This means that the court decides how to separate the assets, based on criteria such as need, earning potential, financial contribution to the marriage, and the custody of children.

Preventive Measure: Get a good lawyer who listens to your concerns and will present a divorce settlement that is in your best interests to the court.

Protecting Credit. Write to your credit-card issuers, asking them to freeze any joint accounts. Let them know that you are no longer responsible for new debt. Close any home-equity lines of credit and margin stock-trading accounts. They may be approved but not yet used. You want to avoid having your spouse abuse an equity line of credit, which could expose you to the possibility of losing your home. And you certainly don't want your soon-to-be-ex to borrow against a joint brokerage account to buy investments. You would be liable for the loan and interest.

Next, check your credit history. Your spouse's overspending might have put your credit rating in jeopardy. Write a letter to the credit bureau, detailing the circumstances, especially if there are financial problems during the divorce. It can take a long time to separate your credit history from his, but it's necessary, so don't delay.

Preventive Measure: Difficulty in obtaining credit after a divorce can be avoided, if you have your own credit card and maintain your own credit history from the beginning of your marriage. Monitor all spending while married, and be aware that you will be held responsible for any debt incurred by your spouse on joint accounts, or on your own accounts that list him as an authorized user. If you don't have any credit cards in your name and you are anticipating divorce proceedings, open an account, charge a small amount, and pay it off right away. Begin to establish a credit history.

Social Security Benefits. Hang on to your hats while we explain this: If you were married for 10 years at the time of your divorce and your ex's lifetime earnings are higher than your own, you will qualify for a spousal benefit equal to one-half of his Social Security benefit when you both reach 62, as long as that amount is higher than the full amount you would get on your own record of earnings and he is already receiving benefits. If your ex is still working at age 62, you can still receive the spousal benefit, as long as you have been divorced for at least two years and are 62. If you remarry before age 60, you forfeit the right to your ex's benefit (unless you are caring for a child of his under age 16). (Remarry after age 60, and you can still claim Social Security based on your ex's benefits, as long as they are higher than those of your current spouse.)

Your ex can remarry at any time without affecting your ability to claim half his benefit, and basing your claim on his record instead of yours doesn't reduce the amount he will receive. If you don't remarry before age 60 (or age 50 if you are disabled), and your ex dies before you do, you can claim reduced benefits based on his record, or receive his entire benefit when you reach full retirement age. (If you receive a pension from a federal, state or local government job, where you did not pay Social Security taxes, your Social Security spouse's or widow's benefits may be reduced.) If your ex dies before you do and you are caring for a child of his under age 16, you can claim a surviving-spouse benefit, no matter what your age.

Got all of that? The rules are complicated, containing a lot of if's, and's or but's; for more information, visit www.ssa.gov, or call 1-800-772-1213 and talk with a representative. Your ex won't even know you are claiming a benefit based on his earnings, so don't be shy about doing this if it means more money for you during retirement. Be sure that you keep a record of his Social Security number; though it's not essential to know it, it will help the SSA track down his earnings record. Also keep your marriage certificate and divorce decree on hand.

Good record-keeping before, during, and after a divorce, can save you a lot of grief. Granted, it can also dredge up a lot of emotions—anger, sadness, loneliness, frustration—if you are recently divorced or widowed. But, being able to put your hands on the right piece of paper when you need it is the greatest relief ever devised for an anxiety attack.

Preventive Measure: Thinking of divorcing after nine years? Stick it out another year, especially if you haven't built up a substantial earning record. And if your ex's lifetime earnings are higher than your own, delay remarrying until age 60—unless, of course, you're marrying someone who is making as much or more than your ex.

Or the combination of your individual benefits, plus other retirement savings, is enough for you to live on comfortably. (See "Five Reasons Not to Remarry" in this section for more advice on weighing the cost of love and marriage.)

Pension Benefits. Beginning in 1985, the benefits of an employee under a pension, profit-sharing, or other retirement plan became an economic resource that can be put on the bargaining table during divorce. The law strengthened the claims of divorced wives to pensions earned by their husbands during the marriage. You may be entitled to a portion of all of the retirement benefits earned by your spouse during your marriage. These include IRAs, 401(k) plans, and corporate pensions. Pension plans, however, will only honor family-support orders that award pension benefits to an employee's ex-spouse, if those orders meet the standards for a document called a "qualified domestic relations order" (QDRO), normally drawn up at the time of the divorce or legal separation.

The order must conform with the specific retirement plan as well as with state law. It must be approved by the pension-plan administrator. If a court order demands a benefit that is not provided in the plan, an employer cannot be required to comply with it. The court must identify and measure an employee's interest in a retirement plan. Such interest will not include any portion acquired after the divorce or before the marriage.

Your lawyer will petition the state court for a Qualified Domestic Relations Order (QDRO) that makes you a beneficiary. You can take a one-time payment, monthly payments at retirement, or a lump-sum payment which you should roll over into your own IRA, where your money will continue to grow tax-deferred until your retirement. Many women pass on the pension in a divorce settlement, in favor of getting the house or up-front cash, instead. Depending on your circumstances, this may not be the best choice for you. Will you be able to afford to maintain the house on one income?

The Roof Over Your Head. Staying in the house becomes an emotional issue for many women, and they are often willing to trade off other assets to keep it. Then they discover they can't maintain it and they are forced to sell. In many instances, it is better to sell the house, split the proceeds, rent or buy a smaller place, and maintain rights in the retirement accounts. It is important to discuss all options with your attorney and accountant. Put emotions aside and see what is financially best for you. "I didn't want to uproot the children. They've had enough upheaval already," said Martha. "But if I had to do it over again, I'd sell the house and buy something that had no memories and that I could decorate exactly as I wanted. The mortgage payment didn't kill me, but the maintenance and property taxes did."

Bottom line: Think seriously before you give up the pension in exchange for the house. Figure out how much your share in the pension proceeds will be worth in 20 or 30 years if you roll them over into a tax-sheltered account. Weigh that against how much the house will cost you in taxes and upkeep and how much you could get if you sold it. In many instances, it is better to sell the house before the divorce, divide the money, buy a less-expensive house without the maintenance problems with your share of the proceeds, and maintain your rights in the retirement accounts.

Take-home lesson: There is a big tax advantage to selling real estate while you are still married. For married owners, there is no tax on the first $500,000 of capital gains, as long as you lived in the house two out of the last five years. If you wait and sell the house after the divorce, when you are single again, your capital gains exclusion will only be $250,000.

Medical Insurance. If you are covered under your spouse's corporate plan, federal regulations issued by the Department of Labor (COBRA) require his company to offer insurance to you for 36 months. The premiums will be higher than you were paying as a married couple, but lower than what you would have to pay on the open market. After 18 months, you're on your own. You might be able to extend the COBRA insurance, but the premiums will be very high. You should try your best to make sure that you are covered where you work before the 18 months is up. Older women who might not have been in the workforce or who worked for an employer who didn't offer medical insurance will have a problem getting coverage on their own. Anne, a psychologist, joined the Chamber of Commerce just to get coverage through their group plan.

Protecting Your Children: Make sure the divorce settlement specifies that your children will continue to be carried on your spouse's medical plan and that he is responsible for paying for all out-of-pocket medical and dental expenses. Consider stipulating that a certain amount be paid into a 529 state college savings plan or education IRA for their tuition.

The formula for determining how much tuition aid your children will be eligible to receive is based on something called your Expected Family Contribution (EFC)—or what you can afford to pay, based on a combination of savings (your assets as well as your child's), current income, and borrowing. Your divorce will impact that figure and your strategies in a number of ways:

If the divorce agreement specifies that the father is to contribute $5,000 to education, that figure is considered part of the EFC—whether he pays it or not.

If you are divorced and looking for financial aid, it is in the best interest of the child to live with the parent who has the lesser income. (Some private schools will ask for a financial statement of the non-custodial parent, as well.)

If you remarry, your new husband's income will be included as money available for the family contribution. Consequently, in some situations, it is wise not to remarry until the kids have graduated from college.

Tax Considerations. Alimony is reported as taxable income to the recipient, while the person paying it can take a deduction for the amount. Child support, on the other hand, is tax-free to the recipient and non-deductible to the person paying it.

Bear in mind, too, that taxes play an important part in dividing assets. You pay a capital-gains tax on the increase in value of any asset, but the gain is calculated from the time it was purchased jointly and not from the time that you received it as a result of a property settlement. Therefore, assets that have increased in value are worth less than an equal amount in cash, because you have to factor in the future tax liability when you sell them.

Tax Tip: Have your lawyer or accountant calculate the net-of-tax figures before any property settlement is signed. For the purposes of the IRS, you will be considered eligible for head of household status when your spouse has not been a member of the household for the last six months of the tax year and the household is the home of a dependent child.

Final Words of Advice: Don't settle for less than you deserve. "Financial preparedness is the key," says attorney Patricia Kane, "Divorce is a process, and it takes time. Ask questions, get involved, be assertive, and hang in there. Being 'nice' might give you some brownie points, but it will not get you the best settlement. You only have one chance to do it. Make sure you do it right!"

IF AT FIRST YOU DON'T SUCCEED . . .

Hope springs eternal, which may explain why 55 percent of those who divorce remarry within five years. Before you relinquish your singlehood, go back and reread our advice for newlyweds in Chapter Three. The Money Talk is more essential now than ever—the topics to be covered are far more complex.

YOU ASKED, WE ANSWERED . . .
CAN THIS DIVORCEE'S FINANCES BE SAVED?

Q: *I am recently divorced. My lifestyle will not be the same, and I know that I'll have to reduce my expenses. I've avoided dealing with my finances until now. Where do I begin?*

A: You're not alone; on average, one year after divorcing, a woman's income decreases by 30 to 45 percent, whereas a man's income increases by at least 10 percent. "Downward mobility is a fact of life for many divorced women," says Beverly Tuttle, former CEO of Connecticut Consumer Credit Counseling Services. "We see many recently divorced women who have problems dealing with their current financial reality. They don't want to admit that anything has changed. They want to live and spend the way they used to, trying to keep up a standard of living they can't afford. They don't want their friends, especially those who are still married, to feel sorry for them. Some want to prove to their ex-husband they are doing great without him. They are in denial, avoiding the reality of their particular situation."

"My husband had spreadsheets," says Lorraine. "He counted every nickel and dime and knew where every cent went. I cringe when I hear the word 'budget.' I associate that word with scrimping and sacrificing." So, let's forget the "B" word. Everyone hates it. Instead, let's use the terms "cash flow" and "spending plan." You are not going to be able to get away from the paper work, so think of it as a tool to enable you to have financial control. Start by putting your financial life on paper; fill out our net worth form in Chapter 3. It may make you feel a little better.

Next, you'll need to keep track of your income and expenses for at least three months. After you have done this for several months, you will have an idea of your current cash flow: money coming in and money going out. You will learn where your money was spent. Then you can set up a spending plan and go forward.

Where do you start? First, figure out what income you can expect to receive: salary, alimony, child support, Social Security, pension income, interest and dividends from investments. Then figure out your fixed expenses: mortgage, real estate taxes, utilities, car payment, insurance premiums, childcare. Reviewing your checkbook can help you pinpoint your fixed expenses. Your credit card bills will help identify flexible expenses. Keep a pocket notebook in your purse or car, and jot down every single cash expenditure you make during the day.

Some Other Cents-ible Suggestions. Use round figures. Don't get caught up in the nickel and dimes. Computer programs like Quicken or Microsoft's Money can make your life easier. These checkbook programs can track your check writing and prepare reports that detail your spending by category. Focus on the essentials. Work with your children, if they are old enough, to explain the importance of what you're doing. Be flexible. Allow sufficient time to gather information about money coming in and going out. Stick with the plan.

How to Develop a Spending Plan That Will Save You Money. You will not find yourself dreading your spending plan if you let yourself think positively and practically about your lifestyle. Once you've recorded all your expenses, analyze them carefully. Ask yourself, "Do I really want to spend that much of my money on cable tv, eating out, dry cleaning?" What is important to you? What are your priorities? Any small, incremental changes in your spending can make a big difference.

Ann still empties her pockets and wallet of loose change and dollar bills, the way she did when she was a young mother. This money goes into a jar along with money found on the streets or on the floor of supermarkets. "When the kids were young and things were tight, this money paid for little treats—a dinner out, a new outfit, theater tickets," says

Ann. "It's a family joke now, but it is still fun. It pays for weekends away or flying the kids home for the holidays."

Once you have made the adjustments—by starting with small changes and working up to the big ones—you will realize how quickly the savings can add up. The important thing to remember is that you are now in charge—of your finances and your life. And that's a step in the right direc-tion. If things are really tight, investigate sources of finan-cial assistance. You may be eligible for aid, if you have children and are a single mom, as a result of your divorce. Check with the Administration for Children and Families (ACF), Head Start, and other child-welfare services. Visit the ACF Web site at www.acf.dhhs.gov to get further infor-mation about how to apply for aid.

YOU ASKED, WE ANSWERED . . .
WHEN TO SAY, "I DON'T"

Q: *I'm 50, divorced, and in love with a wonderful man. Does it make financial sense to marry again?*

A: Many divorcees and widows choose not to remarry, opt-ing instead for the live-together arrangements they may have had before their first marriages. Why? For many of us, the reasons are emotional. Once burned, twice shy… but there are also very good financial reasons to stay single. Wedding vows unite couples "for richer, for poorer," but you don't have to let them make you poorer. If you have your heart set on matrimony, you should at least know what the repercussions of those wedding bells will be. Here are five reasons not to tie the knot:

1. To protect yourself against long-term care expenses: This is probably the No. 1 reason older couples avoid mar-riage. In a marriage, the assets of both can be decimated by long-term care costs before the federal Medicaid program takes over. By not marrying, the healthy partner's assets are kept safe, while the other partner's assets are depleted.

2. To avoid losing pension benefits left by a deceased spouse and Social Security benefits or alimony from a divorced spouse: You should be eligible to collect Social Security benefits on your ex's claim, if they are higher than your own, as long as you were married for at least 10 years, you're 62 or older, and you haven't remarried before age 60.

3. To retain medical insurance: Many employer plans deny medical benefits to a surviving spouse who remarries. An individual policy will be expensive and most likely will not be as generous as the corporate plan.

4. To pay less in income taxes: There can be a tax advan-tage for couples who stay single. Tax implications are something that you should look at closely with a financial advisor before retying the knot. It's also worth factoring into your decision to wed or not to wed the fact that unmarried seniors are able to earn more income before their Social Security benefits are taxed. If adjusted gross income, plus tax-exempt interest, plus one-half of Social Security benefits total more than certain base amounts, a certain percentage of your Social Security benefits can be taxed. By not marrying, either or both partners can work without affecting the other's Social Security bene-fits, which means more money in the household pot.

5. To avoid antagonizing children from previous marriages: Some couples prefer to keep financial assets separate, in order to reassure children from a previous marriage who may resent a stepparent's gaining assets that the children feel belong to them. But experts warn that if you stay sin-gle for your children, you should protect yourself and your unmarried partner in other ways. Create your own safety net by preparing pertinent legal documents, such as naming your partner as beneficiary of life-insurance policies and retirement accounts.

More Expensive Than the Wedding?
Ways to Cut Your Divorce Costs

Seems like adding insult to injury, but getting a divorce can cost as much—or more—than the wedding. It is, in fact, the fourth leading cause of bankruptcy. But there are ways to keep the cost—and the pain—to a minimum. When the husband and wife can come to a general agreement on disposition of property, child support, if there are minor children, and spousal support, if any, before they consult their lawyers, they will lower their costs significantly.

It is possible to file divorce papers without an attorney's services. However, to protect your rights, it's wise not to scrimp on the cost of a good lawyer who can be your advocate. You and your husband should have separate lawyers, for that reason. Depending on the circumstances, you may be able to petition the court to have your spouse pay all or some of your legal fees. If you're strapped, call your local court and ask for a list of lawyers who offer pro bono services.

Uncontested divorces, those in which the parties don't have to go before a judge because both parties are in agreement, can be had for as little as $500 (using such services as www.legalzoom.com on the Internet) to $1,800 or so for the services of a local attorney, particularly if no minor children are involved and there are no property disagreements. More complicated cases, involving acrimonious asset splits, alimony and child support, can take years and upwards of $30,000 or more to resolve.

Creating a prenup addressing what will happen in the event of divorce helps to keep costs down. (Remember, prenups aren't just for the wealthy; see Chapter Three for more details.) Other cost-cutting moves include use of mediation to come to an agreement before you see a lawyer and a new trend called "collaborative divorce," practiced by some 4,500 attorneys nationwide, who claim this mediation-based method can cut the price of any divorce in half. Visit www.nocourtdivorce.com for more information.

REMARRIAGE CHECKLIST:
WHAT YOU SHOULD KNOW ABOUT EACH OTHER'S FINANCES

ASSETS: Real estate, stock and bond investments, valuable possessions.

INCOME: From all sources—earned, investment, dividends, support payments.

CURRENT FINANCIAL OBLIGATIONS: Support payments, charitable pledges, debt.

EXPECTED FUTURE INCOME: Inheritance, pensions, retirement accounts.

LIFE & HEALTH INSURANCE: Policy coverage, amounts, and beneficiaries.

HEIRLOOMS: Furniture, jewelry, art.

FINANCIAL INSTITUTIONS AND PROFESSIONALS DEALT WITH: Bankers, brokers, lawyers, accountants, financial planners.

FINANCIAL HISTORY: Life events or people who have had an impact on the way you view money.

KNOW WHAT YOU'RE SAYING, "I DO" TO

BY PATRICIA SCHIFF ESTESS

Just think of how complex saying, "I do" in remarriage is—both psychologically and financially. When you remarry, a train of family responsibilities follows you and your husband-to-be down the aisle, and you are saying "I do" to all of them. Sometimes you have dependent children, sometimes adult children who haven't quite broken the financial cord, sometimes dependent parents. You've both developed defined money personalities with definite ways of managing money. To top it off, you and your husband are bringing to the union a hodgepodge of assets, debts, and things—which are probably not equal in value.

And then you run into life. That's what happened to Rosemary after her divorce from her first husband, with whom she'd co-owned a business, which nearly went bankrupt as a result of their marital conflict. He retained control over their shell of a company and bought out her share for a pittance ($10,000). "Even though I lost my job in the divorce and was strapped for funds, I was fortunate," she says. "My parents had a retail store where I was able to work."

But then, just a few months after she met her high-school boyfriend Wayne again and fell in love, her son was in a car accident that caused serious brain damage. Even though Wayne had moved in with her at that point, "there wasn't time to talk about money, or marriage, for that matter, because all my concentration was on this child. It was financially and emotionally exhausting—a low point," she says. "We just lived as best as we could, financially separately, yet physically together."

It wasn't until they decided to get married, seven years later, that Rosemary and Wayne tackled their finances as a couple. "We knew about each other's finances, but we had never done anything jointly before. Finally, we opened up a joint account and talked in depth about how we'd make major purchases and investment decisions."

It's complex. Convoluted money situations like Rosemary and Wayne's can be a constant source of irritation, unless you share financial information and talk through the monetary issues you'll be facing. Before and continuously during the early years of a remarriage, certain subjects loom large.

FIVE QUESTIONS TO ASK BEFORE REMARRYING

1. **Where will we live?** This is often a remarried couple's first order of financial business. Do they live in the home that one of them has been living in, or do they get rid of both of their places and find a home to call their own?

   If you opt to stay in one or the other's home, because you don't want to uproot children or because one home is nicer than the other, it's important, from a psychological perspective, to neutralize the space as much as possible so that the person moving in doesn't feel like he or she is stepping onto hallowed ground. Visually, you can do this by redecorating one or two rooms with the newcomer's furniture and by shuffling bedrooms. (You can turn the erstwhile study into your bedroom and convert the old bedroom into a guest room, for example.)

   Assuming some financial obligation for the home—be that paying a portion of the mortgage or taking on some of the upkeep of the property—also gives the newcomer a sense of ownership in the other's quarters. It's what Wayne did when he moved in with Rosemary and her two children. Since there was no mortgage on the house, he took care of the utility bills. And since they didn't have a joint account before they were married, Wayne gave Rosemary $300 a week, and she paid for household incidentals and food out of her personal account.

If you choose to buy or rent something new to both of you, which is often what couples like to do, it may mean that one or both of you will have to sell something you already own. Keep in mind the tax break available to homeowners: A tax-free exclusion of up to $250,000 on capital gains (the profit you make on the sale) for single filers, and up to a $500,000 exclusion for marrieds. To qualify, you must have owned and used the property as your principal residence for at least two of the five years before the sale.

2. **Who'll pay for what?** Most remarrieds opt for a two- or a three-account system to help them manage their daily expenses. In the two-pot system, each of you maintains your own checking account—and you jointly decide who's going to pay for what, based on some system that seems fair to you both. This set-up usually works well for older, more affluent couples, both of whom have strong needs for personal autonomy. It also works best when one of you, say your hus-band, is heavily in debt at the time of the remarriage and fears not being able to pay the indebtedness off. In such cases, maintaining separate accounts can help to insulate you from having a lien placed against you. If your new spouse is coming into the marriage laden with debt, make certain to check with an attorney or a certified financial planner to see what you can do to shield your own assets from his creditors. Whatever you do, don't co-mingle your funds; keep them separate to protect your assets.

3. **What estate plan will be fair to each of us and our respective children?** As a wife, you are entitled to at least one-third to one-half of your husband's estate, depending upon the state in which you live. The only time that wouldn't be true is if you have a pre- or post-nuptial agreement with your husband that limits or defines the assets you're entitled to if your husband predeceases you. Because remarriage often involves children from a former marriage, the assets in an estate don't usually follow the more traditional route of husband to wife and then to their children. You might want to leave family heirlooms to your own children, not to your husband. You might want your grandchildren to inherit some money. If you develop a good relationship with your stepchildren, you might want them to inherit something from you.

Because estate planning reflects divided loyalties, multiple responsibilities and past legal commitments (such as separation agreements), it becomes extremely complicated for remarrieds—the paper equivalents of Rube Goldberg's mechanical contrivances. Trusts, life insurance, titling of assets, gifts before death, and wills all play an important part in an overall estate plan. Putting the pieces together requires the services of an estate attorney, preferably one who's been remarried herself. Before seeing the attorney, draw up a list of family members for whom you have financial responsibility, both legally and morally. It provides the planner with a scorecard of who's who in your family and saves time (which translates into money).

Remember that estate planning is a process that needs updating or periodic revising. Review of your estate should be triggered by changes in tax laws, your financial and health circumstances, or a change of residence.

4. **How do we define what's "fair" in financial terms?** One of the biggest thorns in a remarriage is when the financial seesaw is not evenly weighted—which happens frequently. One of you is usually the "heavy", and the other the lightweight. That imbalance may never shift—or it might. Also, what's fair at one

stage of the relationship will change in the next, so you have to be flexible and reasonable in all your "fairness" talks, taking the time to carefully listen to each other's concerns. Long before the wedding date, talk about whether you both want or need to have a prenuptial agreement drawn up, or will a prenuptial discussion on what's "fair" suffice? So what's fair? There's no absolute answer to this; everyone will see it differently. If you give up your career or turn down a promotion to spend time raising his children, should you be compensated? If your children get more money for college from your parents each year than his get from their grandparents, should you ante up more for his kids than yours? Will your joint child get more of your financial resources or a larger inheritance than children from a previous union? These are the types of fairness issues you'll have to contend with for many years.

5. **Will this marriage be more successful than our last?** Do people learn from past experiences? Some do; some don't. Ironically, problems can arise because we often learn "too well." Many women, especially, feel that they've been burned so badly, financially, that they don't trust their new spouses at all. (This can be as much of a problem as trusting too naively is in first marriages.) If financial trust was broken in your first marriage, you have to slowly and sensibly learn to trust again. But remember that marriage doesn't rotate around money. It rotates around loving, caring, and connecting on a deep level with your spouse.

Remarriages aren't divorce-proof, any more than first marriages are. But if you can figure out how to "put money in its place" by resolving financial issues caringly and good-naturedly, then, by all means, fall in love again and walk down the aisle. It's complicated, for sure. But a good remarriage is more than worth the time you spend working at it. So keep talking. Negotiate, compromise, and laugh (when you can). If money issues become a constant source of contention, seek professional guidance. The goal is to resolve money issues rationally and compassionately. Heck, remarriage has enough problems without having on-going money disputes.

As for Rosemary and Wayne, they celebrated their anniversary in April. Having dealt with their financial issues openly and fairly, they are very happily married. Rosemary's son has recuperated and is working part-time. He still lives with them. "The fact that Wayne was there for me through some of the worst times of my life," says Rosemary, "proved beyond a shadow of a doubt that he cared deeply and loved me totally."

WHEN YOUR NEW HUSBAND IS A FATHER: WHY STEPFAMILY FINANCIAL PLANNING IS A MUST

What *Leave It to Beaver* was to the nuclear family, *The Brady Bunch* did for blended or stepfamilies. Neither, of course, depicts the challenges of family life realistically. Under the laugh tracks lie sob stories. Blending families and finances doesn't always go smoothly, as Lisa Cohn, a stepmom and award-winning freelance writer, points out. Particularly where two sets of children—and their considerable expenses—are involved, money issues can threaten to split the most loving of couples. But there are steps you can take to keep things fair, protecting your own and your children's interests. Cohn talked to stepmoms and experts to get the best advice. (*Some names have been changed.)

Stuff *The Brady Bunch* Never Mentioned

BY LISA COHN

When Anna* fell in love with the man who would become her second husband, she vowed to create a stable family life for her two daughters and his five children.

"I was crazy about him and wanted to be with him," she says. "At the same time, I wanted to protect my kids and make life good for them."

He agreed to live in Nashville, Tennessee, so that her daughters could continue to reside in their hometown. She agreed to become an equal financial partner with him in their household, as well as in a new business they would start together. In addition, Anna paid half the child support for her new husband's five children. She helped pay for his kids' college educations and split the cost of his children's weddings. Her generosity extended beyond the financial realm. Every year at Christmas time, the stepfamily visited a ski resort, where Anna not only bought and wrapped gifts for all seven kids, but cooked meals for her kids, his kids and his children's five friends.

"As the woman, I felt like I had to do all that," Anna says. "I probably gave too much, financially and emotionally. But I did it for the children."

Every day, women tie the knot with men who are fathers and agree to help pay for their child support, to care for their children, and to help foot the bill for their kids' after-school activities. Like Anna, they do all this in an effort to create a stable, loving, new family unit. But, in the process, they can plant seeds of resentment that can fester and threaten to undermine the family's happiness.

"Often, she is paying for the couple's current life, and he is paying for his former life," says Jeanette Lofas, a certified social worker and president of the Stepfamily Foundation, Inc., based in New York, which provides advice and resources to stepfamilies. In some cases, stepmoms are happy enough to help foot the bill for their husband's children, especially if the stepmoms are independently wealthy. However, too often, a stepmom's generosity turns to bitterness, adding stress to already complicated stepfamily life, she points out. "She is losing money and doesn't have the partner she hoped for, and if she brings it up, it becomes an issue of contention, causing outright warfare between herself and her husband." It doesn't have to be that way.

HOW TO AVOID THE GIVE-TOO-MUCH-AND-FEEL-RESENTFUL TRAP

In order to minimize such strife, future stepmoms need to communicate openly about each partner's role in the new family and strike prenuptial agreements with their fiancés, experts say. If couples go into a marriage without such an agreement and later find themselves feeling resentful, they shouldn't allow those resentments to fester; they should hire a counselor to help them find ways to start anew and create a more rewarding partnership. For instance, couples trying to start over might sign agreements requiring the husband to repay his wife for helping with child-support payments and other expenses. Or they could forge new contracts, providing some kind of compensation to the wife for caring for her stepchildren.

Stepmothers can easily fall into the give-too-much-and-feel-resentful trap, if they enter into the marriage unaware of the realities of stepfamily life, says Margorie Engel, who is the president and CEO of the Stepfamily Association of America (www.saafamilies.org). Engel, who wrote her PhD thesis on the financial position of women in stepfamilies, explains that "many people go into a stepfamily marriage not having any idea of what they are getting into. The woman has unrealistic expectations. She thinks it's like a first marriage. That often

means she thinks it's a good idea to throw all their money into one pot." Not so.

Complicating matters, when women are dating, they're reluctant to ask questions about money matters, especially if their future husband dwells on the financial consequences of his divorce. "In the dating stages, the woman listens to the guy tell her how he got raked over the coals during the divorce. The last question she wants to bring up is: 'Am I going to be the beneficiary in your life-insurance policy?' She doesn't want to be seen as greedy," says Engel.

As a result, couples often don't discuss these issues before they get married. What's more, women often aren't aware of critical legal issues. For instance, a second wife does not automatically become the beneficiary of her husband's assets. "Not all states recognize divorce as a trigger for declaring previous beneficiary documents (not only retirement benefits, but also the beneficiary status of wills and life insurance, medical directives, powers of attorney, etc.) null and void," explains Engel. As a result, a man's ex-wife and children may likely remain the beneficiaries of certain assets, unless the change is made. In the case of pensions, says Engel, the ultimate outcome would eventually be the same, because the existing spouse must be the designated beneficiary. But if the documents aren't updated properly, as Federal law requires, the pension plan administrator could misdirect payment, leading to an expensive and time-consuming court case, in order for the legal spouse to claim her rights.

If couples fail to talk about such financial issues, they will encounter snags that are sure to undermine their relationship: She may be surprised or aghast to discover that he designated his ex-wife as the beneficiary of his life-insurance policy. Or he may assume that her child support will be used for household expenses, while she may be thinking the money should be used only for her children. To equalize such arrangements, one option is for the husband to take out another insurance policy, naming his new spouse as the beneficiary, and the wife might consider doing the same for her new husband.

"Until you talk about these concerns and issues, both people are operating on a different wavelength," says Engel. Avoiding these conversations can only lead to disappointment and bitterness, adds Lofas. "Women sometimes go into stepfamilies so blindly in love. Later, they end up wondering, 'Where is my house in the country? Where is the child I always wanted?'" Yet even if stepcouples do embrace conversation and plan carefully, they don't always avoid conflict. Enter the ex-wife.

THE EX FACTOR—AND OTHER QUESTIONS

Barbara, a stepmom who lives in the Pacific Northwest, agreed to help pay for her husband Frank's child-support payments. An attorney, she assumed that her husband's ex-wife would use the money to pay for the children's food and clothing. Instead, she says, Frank's ex uses the support payments to pay off her school loans and often fails to foot the bill for the basics.

"His ex-wife knows we won't let the girls go without coats," Barbara says. "We are paying virtually 100 percent of the girls' support, but we have no control over how the money is spent."

This is an oft-heard complaint from stepmoms, notes Susan Wisdom, co-author of the book *Stepcoupling* and a licensed professional counselor in Portland, Oregon, who specializes in stepfamilies. "Often, women want to control what's happening in the other house," she says. And they might believe they've earned the right to do so, because their money is going there.

"Stepmoms can feel as if they're getting a double whammy," agrees Lofas. "They often help pay for his child support and then have no say about how that money is spent by his ex-wife. In addition, they generally have little say in how to raise his children. When you feel resentful, you need to start retrenching. It's time for a counselor and reassessment," she says.

Barbara, however, has another solution: she'd like to see no less than a change in the child-support system, in which child-support payments would be lower and dedicated solely to the basics. "Let's say you now pay the custodial parent $2,000 a month," she says.

"Under the system I'm suggesting, you would give the parent $1,500 for the kids' basic food and shelter. Then you'd take $500 out of your pocket each month and spend it on the kids directly for activities and clothing. There would be fewer arguments and tension if the person paying the expenses could do it more directly. When resentment about finances builds up, it's bad for the kids."

Barbara has two important factors going for her: She is a mother, and she works outside the home. If a second wife doesn't work outside the home or if she has no children of her own, she's more likely to become frustrated by the financial and emotional burden her new stepfamily represents. According to Engel, the Stepfamily Association of America's membership is "heavily loaded" with stepmothers who aren't moms, because that appears to be the most difficult role to adjust to. Often, women who aren't mothers don't understand why the father is fussing so much over the children. The task of establishing financial responsibilities in such a stepfamily isn't easy, acknowledges Dr. Shirley Hanson, a marriage and family therapist and Professor Emeritus at the Oregon Health Sciences University School of Nursing. "Should a childless stepparent be responsible for fewer of the household costs? If the man makes more than the woman and she's home with her kids or his kids, what should she contribute? These are hard questions," she points out.

Such tough questions come up everyday in my own stepfamily. For example, one of my stepchildren—Bill's child—now attends a private high school. If my son or our "ours" child wants to go to a private high school, who should pay for it? Should I help pay for Bill's kids' private school? Should he help pay for my son's private high-school education, if my son wants that kind of education? What about our "ours" child? Should Bill provide the same amount for her that he did for his other biological child?

We don't know the answer to those questions yet. But we do know this: In our complex stepfamily, with two of "his" kids, one of "mine," and one of "ours," it makes a lot of sense to create individual bank accounts. In our household, we have three pots of money: One for me, one for Bill, and one for the shared household expenses. Of course, it's easy to get into arguments about "shared" expenses, and if you're not careful, you can get bogged down in the details: If Bill's kids spend about half as much time in our house as my son and "our" daughter, should I pay a larger portion of the mortgage? Since he has two kids from a previous marriage and I only have one—and we need an extra bedroom for "his" kids—should I pay a smaller portion of the mortgage? We settled this issue by simply splitting the mortgage.

"Larger stepfamilies like ours often argue less about money," says Engel. "When both partners bring children into the new family, they're less likely to have problems over spending for the children. There's more of a sense that it's all one family, partly because there are always kids around. That's why I recently agreed to pay for the lion's share of a playroom for our three teenagers. I didn't mind the expense, because I thought it was really important that all the children have access to a separate room where they could spend time with their friends. I also struck an agreement with my husband, Bill, under which I will own a larger share of our house, but that's not what's most important to me. Right now, it gives me great pleasure to see all the teens playing ping-pong in our new playroom and arranging sleepovers at our house. Will my generosity come back to haunt me in the form of resentment later? I don't think so."

As Anna, who is now divorced, says, "Sometimes mothers make decisions aimed solely at benefiting the children, and that's okay." She does resent the fact that her second husband got some of her inheritance and she didn't share in any of his (they were no longer married by the time he inherited the money). Sometimes she wishes she hadn't given so much at Christmas time.

"I should have set up more rigid ground rules and spoken out more," she says, looking back. However, she doesn't regret other aspects of her generosity, because her willingness to give benefited her children, as well as his. She's proud of the fact that, even though she and her second husband split up, she still has a good relationship with her five stepchildren.

"I know I gave too much sometimes," she says. "On the other hand, I feel so good about the fact that my kids get along with my second husband's kids even now. I worked very hard to make that happen."

Some things, it seems, really are more important than money.

Lisa Cohn, an award-winning freelance writer, is the co-author of One Family, Two Family, New Family: Stories and Advice for Stepfamilies. *For more advice visit www.stepfamilyadvice.com*

COULD YOUR RELATIONSHIP SURVIVE ON ONE SALARY...YOURS?

BY MARCIA ECKERD, PHD

If your spouse has recently been laid off, the strain on you and your marriage is twofold: The most obvious concern is economic, of course. How are you going to pay the bills? But the emotional strain of suddenly becoming the sole breadwinner in the family, coupled with your desire to offer your husband emotional support during his job search, can upset the stability of even the most solid and loving couple.

The anxiety over being unable to afford necessities is oppressive. I speak from experience. Fees for health care took a dive in the '90s, because of the limits imposed by managed care. Like most of my medical colleagues, I was working twice as hard to make half the money. With a kid in college, my husband and I went from belt-tightening to muted panic. It's during times like these that spouses need to turn to each other—not the easiest thing to do.

Couples often handle anxiety in different ways: She wants to talk, and he wants to withdraw. He experiences her need to talk as rubbing his face in his "failure"; she experiences his withdrawal as rejection or abandonment. A wife can be empathetic, but, over time, the stress of the situation can cause her to burn out or feel trapped. If your husband was the primary wage earner, you may have to pick up the slack and work longer hours, leaving yourself with less energy for your kids and home. You may find that suddenly stay-at-home Dad is the "good guy," available to help the kids. You're still the one in charge of the household, so you're perceived as the nag. Your husband may focus on finding the "right" new job, while you may feel that he should accept any job available to take the burden off you.

If your "house-husband" now takes care of the kids and household, you need to let go of control of your domain. You may be unhappy with the way he does things. Isn't it written somewhere that the laundry and shopping need to be done often enough so that we don't run out of underwear and food? You might begin to feel as though you're making unacceptable compromises—that you're a bad mother. Don't do that to yourself. Lay off the guilt trips; adapt.

When a family's financial situation changes, expectations have to change. Previous plans (vacations, purchases), after-school activities, even your choice of schools for your kids will have to be re-evaluated. That's not a disaster. Even if the bond you've formed over the years with your husband is tight, pulling together to get through this difficult time can make your marriage even stronger. The following strategies should help you get through tough economic times.

TIPS FOR MAKING HARD TIMES EASIER

1. For your own sake and your kids', maintain your normal routine as much as possible.
2. Both you and your husband are likely to be overwhelmed and short-tempered. Take time outs when you feel a fight escalating, and plan to talk when you're calmer. Reach out when you can. Hearing "I love you" and feeling a caring touch can make a big difference when you or your husband are feeling alone in your corner of the ring.
3. Respect each other's ways of handling pressure, and don't take anything personally. He may not be able to help being depressed, feeling less powerful or looking to you for support that you may be too tired to offer.
4. Don't expect him to read your mind about what needs doing. So many women think it's "obvious" that the dishes in the sink need washing or that someone should go to the market when the coffee is low.
5. Seek out family and friends, even if that's hard for you. You need their support.
6. Join a support group. It's important to recognize that many others are in the same boat, and it helps to share job leads and suggestions for handling the stress. To find a support group near you, visit www.rileyguide.com/support.html.
7. Learn to handle stress constructively. You may not be able to afford the fitness club now, but walking is free. If you notice self-destructive behavior in your spouse or yourself, such as severe depression or alcohol abuse, get professional help immediately.
8. Think realistically about what you can and can't do for your kids financially. Parents with children in college should look for low-cost student loans. We did, and it helped.

THE OTHER DIVORCE

Layoffs are a lot like divorce. Rightly or wrongly, both can fill you with a sense of rejection, of failure, of betrayal. And, too often, you don't see either one of them coming. Both have severe and frightening financial repercussions—and both are survivable, if not preventable. We start this section with a first-person report from the inside of the 1998 MCI-WorldCom merger, which led to thousands of layoffs, leaving those who survived coping with equal measures of "survivor guilt" and "Am I going to be next" anxiety. This writer, as it turns out, was part of a WorldCom couple—her husband worked at the company, too, putting them in double jeopardy.

REPORT FROM THE TRENCHES
OF CORPORATE AMERICA: A SURVIVOR'S TALE

BY GABRIELLE MADISON

The world is different now. On June 28, 2002, a large-scale layoff was announced, and I watched 50 percent of my department walk out the door. In all, the company announced 17,000 layoffs that week. I was not among them. We who survived the cuts should feel fortunate, but though we aren't unemployed yet, we are dealing with the stress of having to handle quadruple our normal workload, survivor guilt, and the constant worry that we might be next. Several months later, it is still very difficult to get up in the morning and go to work. We all have feelings of anger, fear, frustration, and betrayal.

I've watched people I have known for years take on entirely new personalities, guarding their positions, as though they were playing a complicated and strategic game of chess. I've watched people make the decision to clean out their cubicles of all their personal possessions—just in case "the doors are locked one morning." I've watched morale simply get flushed down the corporate toilet.

There aren't enough hours in the day to get everything done that needs to be done by those of us who remain. Each of us has begun doing the jobs of at least four or five people to take up the slack. For a while, most of us were coming in early, eating at our desks, working through lunch and staying late to try to get "caught up." Eventually, we accepted the fact that we will never get "caught up," that we have no control over any of this. The only way we are staying sane is by repeating to ourselves over and over again, "Tomorrow is another day, and this is not worth killing ourselves over."

Rumors of another round of layoffs have begun circulating. We each know we could be next. And we're each preparing for that eventuality in our own way.

Am I Next? What I'm Doing to Prepare. I suppose I am dealing with all of this a little bit differently than most people. Even before the June layoff was announced, I began preparing myself and people close to me by initiating an outside networking contact list. I started by asking the people in my immediate area for names. Next, I expanded it to include people in other departments within WorldCom. Then I added the names of people from other companies—people who had originally been at WorldCom and left for greener pastures (which didn't always turn out to be so green, after all). I included both employees and contractors, as well as people they knew. The list has grown to almost 200 contact names at this point.

I didn't feel it would do any of us any good to just stick our heads in the sand and pretend that it wasn't really going to happen to us. I asked people to commit to sending me updated information when necessary, so we would all have access to accurate home addresses, phone numbers, e-mail addresses, and resumes. I didn't pack anything in my cube in preparation for the day. I didn't think that doing that would make me feel any more "ahead of the game," should my name end up on the next list.

My husband, who also works at WorldCom, and I used to belong to a large group of WorldCom couples. The group was reduced drastically in number by the last layoff. We've seen how hard it is when both partners are laid off. So, realizing how dependent we both are on the fortunes of this company, we were forced to sit down and make three lists. The first involved what had to be done if just my husband got laid off; the second, if just I got laid off; and the third, if we both got laid off. Those lists were really difficult to put together. In each case, they involved identifying the basic things we would need to survive, while we were out of work and trying to find other jobs.

We decided that the first things that would have to go were assets that could immediately be made liquid. We decided we needed, at a bare minimum, a roof over our heads, one vehicle and an Internet connection. Everything else was expendable, including the Koi pond we had just built in the front yard, which had doubled our electric bill all summer long. I have begun establishing a stock of food and formulating a survival plan from information gathered at several Web sites, one of which is www.waltonfeed. com. At this point, miraculously, we both still have jobs with WorldCom.

My cube contains a lot of personal items—pictures of my husband, children, parents, pets, and memorable occasions that remind me of much happier times; awards issued for a job well done. I am not yet ready to toss in the towel. The stress is unbelievable. I try to use my headphones to listen to relaxation CDs to drown out the negative discussions that still take place as the headlines continue to hit Wall Street and CNN. Our $25-a-month credit for long distance, and an "extra" day-after-Thanksgiving holiday have made their way back into our employee benefits. But none of that will mean much if we are headed for the next layoff list. It gets a little harder each day to maintain a positive attitude. Some days, I feel like I want to just pack it all in, walk away from what is still here, and head for the mountains with whatever I can carry. I know that isn't realistic—at least not at this point.

It is very tempting to want to find another job, but I choose not to move in that direction. I have contact everyday with the people on my outside networking list who didn't survive the layoff. They ask my opinion about sentence structure or whether they should downgrade their resumes, what they should wear to a particular interview, and whether they should send a follow-up letter to an interviewer they met that day. I can see how difficult it is for them to be out there, trying to find a job when there are so few available. I miss them. How much worse would I feel if I were out there, competing with them for a job when I still have one? But that's not the only reason I haven't given up. I happen to really like my job, and I still have enough faith left to be able to focus on that light at the end of the tunnel. I can only keep my fingers crossed and hope that the light at the end of the tunnel isn't a freight train heading in my direction. Like all of those left behind, my husband and I are taking it one day at a time.

Gabrielle Madison is a pseudonym for this MCI/WorldCom employee who wished to remain anonymous while sharing her story with MAKING BREAD readers. She and her husband were both laid off several weeks after she wrote this piece. Eight months later, she found full-time employment elsewhere. Her husband has returned to work on a contract basis.

DOWNSIZED BUT NOT OUT: YOUR SECOND CHANCE AT FINDING WORK YOU LOVE

Downsizing—a more polite term for layoff—has been endemic in recent years, as corporations tightened budgets, outsourced jobs, upgraded technology, and turned to contract workers to reduce costs and increase profits. For older workers, often the bitter pill is sugarcoated with an early-retirement package. "When my company downsized me in January of 2001, it was exciting at first—a jump-start into action, I thought—since I'd been contemplating starting my own public-relations consulting business for years," reports Rosemary Rys, now, indeed, the president of her own firm, Creative Public Relations (CPR for Your Communication Needs), and a contributing editor to MAKING BREAD. Pushed out of the corporate nest, she saw it as time for her to take a crash course in using her wings—an opportunity to start the business she'd always

dreamed of starting. "I had plenty of 'coaches' I could turn to for advice—other successful friends who'd gone out on their own to prevent job burnout. I had some money to work with, plus six months of unemployment as a cushion," she says. Things haven't always gone smoothly—what her friends didn't tell her is that clients come and go. She has returned to full-time work on several occasions to allow herself the money to keep herself and her business afloat, but she hasn't crash-landed yet. (See Chapter Eight for more interviews with women who have started their own businesses.)

Some caveats: "It's a given," says Rhys, "Your home computer, and vacuum cleaner, trusted tools until now, will definitely crash, and in that order. Your car will need new tires, an expensive part, or your prayers, if it's on its last legs. But things will work out. My efforts are paying off—work is finally coming in and the future looks promising, albeit a little scary. I tell myself: If you

One thing you can do right now ...

Earn extra dough by becoming a "mystery shopper." These "undercover agents" or "shopping spies" are hired to evaluate customer service by a wide variety of retailers, from brand-name department-store chains and fast-food restaurants to your neighborhood gas station. Evaluation forms, which can be quite detailed, must be filled out; you will be reimbursed for any out-of-pocket expenses and paid a fee for your time; payment is generally made once a month. We've heard of professionals who've

been laid off using this work as a stopgap measure; some even say they're now earning almost as much as they were in their previous jobs.

Visit the Mystery Shopping Providers Association (MSPA) at www.mysteryshop.org for more information. Caveats: Make sure the company you work for is accredited by the MSPA, and do not give out your Social Security number until you have compared notes with others who have worked for the company.

don't believe in yourself, who will? And my wings grow stronger every day.

If you find yourself in the same situation, just keep telling yourself: with a little persistence and the courage to reinvent yourself, you, too, can earn your wings and fly high!

Turn your layoff into a promotion with a pay raise. Remember the first rule of surviving a job loss. "Don't take it personally," says Reginald Owens, PhD, a former vice president at Metropolitan Life, management consultant, and human-resources expert, who has given many popular outplacement workshops. "Before you can take charge of your future, you must take charge of your emotions. Understand that this layoff, closing, or downsizing is not about you. It's not about your skills, your talents, or the wonderful things you're going to be able to do in the future. It is the result of a business decision. Millions of people have gone through this process, many of them two or three times. So, even though it's hard not to take it personally, don't let your emotions get the best of you."

"It's natural to feel a sense of loss, grief, shock, anger, sadness, fear, even a sense of failure, embarrassment, or humiliation over the supposed stigma of unemployment," says Owens. "You will have legitimate concerns about money and how to handle the additional stress that financial concerns place on you and your family. These emotions are experienced by everyone in your situation, and they don't make you a freak. Once you recognize this and realize that some days will be better than others, you will be ready to move on to the next level—acceptance. From there, it's an easy jump to taking control of the situation." Follow the advice below, taken from Dr. Owens' outplacement work-

shops, and you'll be well on your way to your next job—one that may even offer a higher salary than the one you lost.

Get a handle on your finances. Your first step on the road to taking control is to count your money. Knowing what you have to draw on, now and later, should give you a level of comfort (you probably have more than you realized) and an idea of how long you have before you absolutely must find another job. Think of this "comfort zone" as a gift period—use it to determine what you really want to do next with your life.

Sign up for unemployment compensation immediately, and find out what your weekly benefit payment will be and how many weeks it will last. Next, instruct your retirement plan administrator to transfer any money you have vested in the company's 401(k) plan to an IRA or other tax-deductible account. If you take possession of the money, you'll pay a 10 percent penalty fee and taxes—and you'll probably be tempted to spend the balance. The biggest mistake you can make is to cash this money out now.

Then look at how much severance pay your company will be giving you, and how much personal savings you have to draw upon. Do you have a traditional or Roth IRA? If so, you can withdraw money from either one, without penalty or tax, as long as you pay it back into the same IRA or a new one within 60 days. (But be aware that taking it out of a tax-deferred IRA automatically triggers a 20 percent withholding deduction for tax purposes, which means that when you repay the money in 60 days, you'll have to come up with the amount withheld from your own pocketbook, or you will owe tax and a penalty on that amount. If you must take an early withdrawal without paying it back, and you have both a Roth and a traditional IRA, withdraw from the Roth. You'll pay the 10 percent penalty, but at least you'll minimize the tax hit, because you've already paid tax on the money deposited there. You'll only be liable for tax on the earnings, if those are tapped. (Check with your plan administrator or a financial adviser at your bank about these options.)

How much equity do you have in your house? A home-equity line of credit can provide a temporary source of funds to help you get by until you find your next job, if you really need it. Just keep in mind that you're putting your house on the line. (If you think that layoffs are imminent in your company, and you don't already have a home-equity line of credit, consider applying for one now. It might be easier to obtain one while you are still employed.)

Do you have a life insurance policy that has cash value? How about pension plans from previous jobs? Find out how much income they represent and how soon you can begin to collect on them. If you're not sure whether you are covered by pension plans from previous employers, check with the Department of Labor in Washington, D.C. (www.dol.gov). Its Pension Division (Qualified and Nonqualified Plans) keeps a record of pension programs and plans filed by corporations. One recently laid-off accountant, who worked for McDonald's when she was a teenager, discovered that she was covered under the fast-food chain's pension plan and was now eligible to claim her benefits.

On the health front, if you have medical insurance through your company, make sure that COBRA benefits are in place, so that your coverage continues without a lapse for the next 18 months. (You will have to pay for this continued coverage, but at a much lower rate than on the open market.) Depending on your situation, you may find that you are eligible for public healthcare or other public assistance. Take advantage of them. And be aware that you can withdraw money from an IRA without penalty to cover health insurance if you have collected 12 consecutive weeks of unemployment benefits. Another option is to look into new short-term insurance options available from some companies—some can be purchased for as low as $25 a month. They're not as comprehensive as a full plan, but they'll give you some protection until you can find a job with health benefits. Two companies that offer such plans are Humana (www.humanaone.com) and Fortis (www.fortishealth.com). Compare rates and plans at www. HealthInsurance.com.

If resources are tight, consider taking a night job while you look for work during the day, or accepting a lower-level position, at least initially in order to conserve assets, while you continue to search for a more appropriate job. Lastly, don't be embarrassed to ask for support from relatives or friends. You'll find that they most likely have already experienced layoffs themselves or know that they could find themselves in the same tight spot in the future.

Decide what you need to be happy and productive. Now that you've got your finances in order, take some time for self-reflection. Get in touch with who you are and what you have to offer, before you rush out and look for your next job. Make a "needs" list. Think about what your accomplishments are, what your strengths and weaknesses are, what your likes and dislikes are, what your values are, and what you need to do your best work in a working environment. Do you perform best in a less formally structured, more creative environment, or in one with clear lines of authority and accountability? Is a long commute out of the question? Would you be willing to relocate to an area of the country where snow is a factor in the winter? Whatever your needs are, write them down, and if any are "deal-breakers," acknowledge them, so that when you receive offers for new employment, you will be able to make an informed decision about whether this is the right career move for you.

Concentrate on what you have—*not* on what you don't have. Now that you know what you want, evaluate what you have to "sell." Then, as Gabrielle did, network, network, network.

Make a list of 10 companies for whom you think you might want to work. There is nothing scientific about how you come up with this list. It might be the place where your sister works, the place where you thought it might be neat to work when you were 10 years old, a company that produces a product you like, or a competitor to your former employer. Next, visit these companies' Web sites. (Don't have a computer? Go to your local library. Most libraries make computers available to the public, and the librarians will be happy to show you how to use them.) Explore each company's Web site. Read the mission statements, articles, press releases, and biographies of management. These will tell you a lot about who they think they are. Then, click on their "Jobs," "Careers," or "Employment" links. Is there a job there that you are qualified for and interested in?

Keep in mind that the job requirements posted here, and in other employment ads, describe the "dream" candidate. If you don't think you meet all the requirements, *don't stop.* Send a resume and a short cover letter, anyway, outlining your experience and how you think it will help this company meet its corporate needs. For example, the ad may say that a college degree in engineering is required. You don't have one, but you do have 10 years of "real-world" engineering experience. Tell them that. Remember: Concentrate on what you have.

Polish your resume. There are numerous Internet sites (www.resume.com, for one) that can give you current preferred formats and resume-writing tips. Use them. One very effective trick that Dr. Owens recommends is tailoring your resume to each job you apply for by matching your strengths to the requirements of the job. At the top of your resume, where you generally present a summary of your strengths, simply line up your skills, talents and achievements in a way that mirrors the requirements listed in the job description. This will almost guarantee you an interview.

Interconnect with the Internet. Go beyond general career sites, such as www.monster.com or www.hotjobs.com; post your resume on ones that specialize in your field (www.mediabistro.com or www.journalismjobs.com, for instance, if you are in publishing). Sign up with free employment sites, such as www.careerbuilder.com, which will search the Internet for you 24/7 and send you an e-mail with job openings after you submit certain criteria (occupation, industry, zip code, etc.)

Check out salary sites, such as www.Salary.com, to gain insight into what your talents are really worth and what you should be asking for them. You may be surprised, particularly if you have been working for the same company for some time and have fallen behind the earning curve. Here's how these sites work: You put in the title of the job you're looking for and your zip code, and you'll get the salaries that people working in that position in your area are making. Look at the list of job responsibilities and requirements given for this position. How does your experience compare? Now put in your boss's title and your zip code. Could you do that job? Do you have the experience? Then perhaps *this* is the job you should really be looking for. Go for it! If your job search isn't yielding anything promising, don't give up. Invest in yourself by going back to school to upgrade your skills and education during this "gift period" you've been given. Many people find that night-school classes and online universities are the best way to fit school into a busy work and family schedule. So go ahead and take a temporary job and study on the weekends and in the evening to prepare yourself for bigger and better things to come. (See Chapter Seven for more career advice.)

As Dr. Owens suggests, for some, a layoff can provide the impetus and the opportunity to go back to school. For Dr. Elin Danien, going back to school provided the impetus and the inspiration for giving back to society. She found the experience of going back to get a college degree after years in the work force so gratifying that she started a scholarship fund to help other working women do the same. Contributing editor Elizabeth Kaminsky interviewed this remarkable woman about her scholarship and the second chance that going back to school represents for women in mid life. (*Some names have been changed.)

FEEL LIKE A SCHOOL GIRL AGAIN!

BY ELIZABETH KAMINSKY

Last weekend, I spent an entire day with my dear friend Mary*. It feels like ages since I've seen her. We were able to spend time together, because she was on spring break from college. At 49, she's been working on her bachelor's for more than 10 years now, chipping away at her degree, one or two classes at a time. This semester, she is carrying six credits, while working a demanding job in the hospitality industry.

She isn't alone in her quest. According to Census data, 2.7 million women over 35 are enrolled in school. Each one has her own reasons for being there. For some women who delayed entering college, it was a confidence issue. It took a little life experience to make them feel able to crack the books. Perhaps it meant waiting until the kids were grown. Or maybe divorce altered their life path and thrust them in a different direction.

For many women, going part time while working was the only way they could afford college. That's how it was for me. I went for my master's as a "non-trad"—affectionate slang for adults who return to school in ways that are non-traditional. I worked 60 hours a week, spent the other 100 as a caregiver, drove hundreds of miles, and lived on coffee and junk food. For those seven years, my face was locked in a sleep-deprived, sugar-doughnut stupor.

If I were going to school today, I'd still be in fashion. The National Center for Education Statistics (2000) states that 56 percent of all undergraduates were "highly to moderately nontraditional," meaning they worked full time, had dependents (i.e., care-giving responsibilities), and were not eligible for financial aid

It's no surprise that the number of women going back to school has increased over the last few decades. As we Baby Boomers age, we can see the handwriting on the wall. More than half of future jobs will require education beyond high school, according to the Bureau of Labor Statistics, and jobs that require a bachelor's degree are expected to grow the most quickly. The Consortium for Higher Education states that employees will explore an average of four different careers during their lifetime. Making those career changes requires further education.

Women like my friend Mary know that first-hand. Getting her degree means a chance to better herself and to add to her marketability in the workplace. Undeniably, adding schoolwork to an already long to-do list is a tough task. It takes a purposeful, committed woman to head down the long halls of academia. It also takes money. Elin Danien is one such purposeful, committed woman, who determined to help others find the financial help they need.

CASTING HER BREAD UPON THE WATERS

Elin Danien started her seven-year journey toward her bachelor's degree at the University of Pennsylvania's College of General Studies (CGS) at age 46. (Call this remarkable woman Doctor Danien now; she received her doctorate at age 68.) Today, at 75, she is exuberant when she talks about her first experience as a college student. "I remember going to see my professor to find out my grade. I was so nervous. When he told me I'd gotten an A, I blurted out 'A gezundt oif dein pippick!' I assured this puzzled man that the Yiddish 'Blessing on your belly button' was a good thing. He seemed pleased, but nothing could match my elation."

In 1986, Danien put her money where her happiness was. "I wanted to help women whose education, like mine, had fallen through the cracks for a lot of reasons, mostly life getting in the way," she recalls. "I wanted my degree, but I knew I could only work towards it part time." She approached her advisers and college administrators with an idea—create a scholarship fund specifically for women over 30 who want to attend college part time and need financial help. She committed to donating $1,000 a year, but she admits to giving "a bit more than that each year since." For a name, Danien and her advisers came up with "Bread Upon the Waters," after the Biblical adage about casting your bread upon the waters, and it shall come back to you tenfold.

Today, a volunteer advisory board organizes fund-raising efforts, and the University helps raise further funds, providing guidance and steering donors in their direction. In its 18-year history, the Bread scholarship has "risen" to an endowment of more than a million dollars. It has graduated 42 scholars, more than half of them with honors. "To my knowledge, this scholarship is one of a kind, just like the women who receive it," Danien reports, with a mother's pride.

Does any scholar, in particular, stand out in her mind? "They are all my daughters," she quips. "How can you pick a favorite child?" But there is one, Linda Santoro, who, Danien says, touched her heart indelibly. "She was our first scholar, and she died of cancer just before she would have received her degree. CGS broke precedent and awarded her degree posthumously."

Danien speaks easily about each incredible scholar's achievements, but she is more humble about her own. I am fascinated when she tells me that her greatest joy in achieving her degree was "realizing I wasn't a fraud." She explains she worked successfully in business for years, and everyone assumed that she had a degree. "When I finally graduated, summa cum laude and Phi Beta Kappa, it washed away all those feelings of not being legitimate. I also realized that my years of experience were worthwhile, too—and that I wasn't giving myself credit for that."

WITH A LITTLE HELP FROM MY FRIENDS— AND LOTS OF CHOCOLATE!

Molly Cronlund, a 2004 Bread scholar, had plenty of exciting life experiences to take with her to Penn. She did a tour in the Air Force, got married, had three children, and even worked for the National Security Agency. We joke that if she tells me more than that about her past, she'll have to kill me. Cronlund says that she got the Bread scholarship "through my friends, providence, and serendipity." She clipped a newspaper article about the scholarship and tucked it away, since she was too young at the time to apply. She went to Penn anyway, got accepted and took a few classes. "I surprised myself and did fairly well, but then I met this life-affecting professor," she recounts. "I couldn't turn into a sponge big enough to hold all he was teaching me. His words were like water on parched soil. I am a psychology major as a result. His confidence in me gave me the push I needed to pursue the scholarship."

She credits the supportive community of Bread scholars for contributing greatly to her success. "The atmosphere is infectious. These women support each other and stand by each other." I wonder what her children, who are 11, 8, and 4, think of their mom, the scholar. "They've told me they think it's cool, especially when they see that I have to do my homework just like they do."

What's next for Cronlund? "I want to give my learning back, working with children as a psychologist and helping them emotionally," she emphasizes. Cronlund's "give-something-back" attitude is key with the Bread scholars, who have given back more than tenfold. They have gone on to become scriptwriters and social workers, anthropologists and chemists. They are single mothers, immigrants, wives, and breadwinners. They are driven, persistent, and tireless in their passion for learning. They share those traits with the millions of other hard-working women who have returned to school without the benefit of this amazing scholarship. A love of learning and sheer curiosity have kept my friend

Mary going in pursuit of her degree for the last 10 years, in spite of the financial challenges. Her only financial help has been partial reimbursement from her employer. "There is that 'a-ha' factor that happens in a really good course," she muses. "It's the moment when you can say to yourself, 'That's why this is the way it is.' I love that feeling."

"Who managed?" wisecracks Danien, when I ask her how she managed to keep up the hard work. "Thank God I had my husband to cheer me on. You need someone to jab you and show you how far you have come," she remarks. "There are three wonderful women, fellow PhD students, who are part of what I lovingly call the 'Old Bag Brigade.' We got together once a month, talked about our research, ate chocolate, and bitched. It was wonderful."

Rita*, 62, felt she was successful, because she had her family behind her. "My husband and children were strongly supportive. They all had their degrees. I was the last 'kid' in school," she recalls. Her degree helped give her the confidence and the credentials to go into the workforce. Her advice to women who hit the books after age 30 is "be determined, organized and flexible."

Danien agrees, "Be prepared to work hard, but don't over-schedule yourself." Mary offers, "Find a program that is geared toward working adults, with the services, facilities and schedules you need."

A DEGREE OF SELF-CONFIDENCE

What is the payoff for juggling life, family, and the pursuit of education? The women I spoke with all agreed that getting an education has delivered great rewards in their pocketbooks and in their self-esteem. I fondly remember Lena*, a former writing student of mine, whose hard-won degree took her from file clerk to human-resources manager. She was 45 when she started school, and my class was the first one she took. I still have a copy of her first assignment, which was to be an essay on writing.

She wrote: "Dear Professor, I've never really done any writing, except the letters I write to my sister in Canada. I'm afraid to write for anybody else. I know that my sister is happy to hear from me, so she won't judge what I write as good or bad. I write to her once a week, because I miss her and because phone calls are expensive. So I guess I write a lot, but probably not in the way you mean. I never really thought that much about writing, until one night when Jimmy (he's my 6-year-old) asked me what I was doing, and I told him I was writing to his Aunt Kit. He said, 'You write a lot, Mommy. You must be a good writer. I want to be a good writer, too.' I looked at his little face and I knew I had to do something to live up to that kid's opinion of me. That's why I took this class."

If that wasn't enough to rip my heart out, Lena added a postscript. "This is the first class I've taken since I graduated from high school in 1968. I don't really know how to be a college student, but I'd sure like to try. Please go easy on me."

During the semester, I watched Lena's look change from confusion to confidence, as she succeeded in her assignments. Her 19-year-old classmates looked up to her. I never gave away the secret that she was a college novice. These kids thought Lena could do anything. So did I. The important thing was, by the end of the course, so did Lena. Not only did she get an "A" in my class, she graduated with honors from the college, seven years later.

Thinking about all of these women has inspired me. For a few years now, there's been a little voice inside my head that says, "Get your doctorate." It competes with the other voices that say, "Take a vacation" and "Clean out your closet." I confess to Danien about the doctorate thing. "Wonderful!" she bubbles. "I am a perfect example that women can do anything!"

The voices in my head are chuckling now, and I feel a strong urge for some vending-machine coffee and sugar doughnuts. Stay tuned.

BACK-TO-SCHOOL "BREAD" BASKET:
SCHOLARSHIPS FOR WOMEN IN MID-LIFE

ELIZABETH KAMINSKY

To find out more about how to apply for the Bread Upon the Waters Scholarship, visit www.sas.upenn.edu/CGS/resources/ bread.php. The following organizations also award scholarships to women returning to school in midlife.

>> **The American Association of University Women's Educational Foundation** (www.aauw.org) distributes more than $3.5 million in fellowships and awards, including part-time and full-time Career Development grants for women seeking to advance their careers or return to the workforce.

>> **The American Nuclear Society** (www.ans.org) awards one Delayed Education scholarship each year to a woman over 30 "whose formal studies in nuclear science, nuclear engineering, or nuclear-related fields have been delayed or interrupted."

>> **The Business and Professional Women's Foundation** (www.bpwusa.org) created the Career Advancement Scholarship Program to award financial assistance to disadvantaged women who want to further their education or return to work full time. Scholarships are available to women over 25 with financial needs and clear career goals.

>> **The Ethel Louise Armstrong Foundation, Inc.** (www.ela.org) works to "Change the Face of Disability on the Planet" by advocating the total inclusion of people with disabilities in society. Scholarships are available for disabled women seeking graduate degrees.

>> **Microsoft** (www.microsoft.com/college/scholarships) offers scholarships to women interested in studying computer science. Scholarships are for one year and have some internship requirements.

>> **Talbot's** (www.talbots.com and click on "About Us") awards small scholarships for part-time students and larger amounts for full-time students who have earned their high-school diploma more than 10 years before applying and "are determined to finally get that college degree."

>> **Wyndham Hotels & Resorts** (www.wyndham.com), in partnership with United Airlines and Meetings Professionals International, offers the WLI Wyndham International-United Airlines full or part-time scholarship for meeting planners who want to pursue academic degrees in areas related to the meeting profession, such as marketing, finance, food service, hospitality, etc.

Female Finance Checklist:
Years of Change, Challenge & Opportunity

❑ **Goals:** Supporting yourself and your children on one salary becomes the paramount concern if you have gone through a divorce or are widowed. Don't be afraid to ask for help and advice from others who've been through the same thing. Find a good lawyer, and consult a financial planner to help you sort through your many options. Consider going back to school if you can, to improve your job skills and salary level after a divorce or a layoff. Use your emergency fund to help you get through both, and have faith that the best is yet to be.

❑ **Career:** Happily marrieds may now have children in their tweens and teens. Stay-at-home moms may be considering returning to the work force. The second income will help you save for your kids' college and it will serve as insurance for you in the event that you are widowed or divorced. Professional women, perhaps it's time to evaluate your career progress and consult an executive recruiter or look into starting your own business, if you feel you've hit the glass ceiling where you are currently employed or you fear a layoff.

❑ **Investments:** Laid off? Roll over any 401(k) funds that you take from one job to the next immediately so that you don't trigger an early-withdrawal penalty fee or taxes.

Resist the temptation to withdraw from a tax-deductible account to avoid paying taxes and an early-withdrawal penalty. Too often, the wife's 401(k) is used as just such an emergency account, leaving her with nothing upon retirement. In between jobs, know that you can borrow from your IRA without paying a penalty or tax as long as you reinvest the money in 60 days. You can also tap into your IRA, penalty-free, to cover health insurance costs, if you've collected unemployment for 12 consecutive weeks. Divorced and receiving a portion of your husband's retirement fund? Consult a financial planner to see whether a lump-sum distribution now or monthly payments when you reach retirement age are best in your circumstances and where to invest your lump sum, if that's what you elect to take.

❑ **Real Estate:** Paid off your mortgage yet? As your household income increases, consider making larger monthly payments or an extra payment per year to pay it off more quickly and save thousands of dollars in interest over the life of the loan. Accumulated a lot of credit-card debt? Use your equity to your advantage; consider taking out a low-interest home equity line of credit to pay it off, and save money. If you are faced with a divorce, think seriously about the consequences of keeping the house versus taking a share of your husband's pension or retirement funds. Will you be able to afford to maintain the property alone? Would you do better to sell the house before the divorce, claiming a double capital-gains exemption as a couple—then split the profit and buy a smaller property for yourself?

❏ **Insurance:** Faced with divorce or layoff, health insurance becomes a major challenge. In both instances, maintain your coverage under COBRA, if you can afford it. In the event of divorce, make sure that your children continue to be covered under your husband's plan, and, if you aren't working, find a job that offers medical benefits for yourself as soon as possible. In the meantime, investigate the short-term policies that are available from some insurers. In the event of divorce, re-evaluate beneficiaries named on your life-insurance policies and change them, if necessary.

❏ **Wills:** Not all states recognize divorce as a trigger for declaring previous beneficiary documents null and void; make sure they reflect your wishes. Check beneficiaries and executors named on wills, medical directives, powers of attorney—any legal document that might name you or your former spouse. If you remarry, consult a financial planner to create an estate plan that protects your children's interests and the assets you bring into the marriage. And make sure your new husband notifies his retirement-plan managers of your new status as spouse.

CHAPTER SIX:
WILL YOU HAVE ENOUGH GOLD TO ENJOY YOUR GOLDEN YEARS?

My mother was a profligate spender, until the day my father died. When she became a widow and had to balance the checkbook and pay the bills herself, the term "fixed income" took on new meaning. Her transformation from spendthrift to thrifty was startling and ultimately impressive. Taking control of her finances was a point of pride for her. Born in Russia, raised in Poland, and married to an American during World War II, she lived the last 50 years of her life in the United States, always mindful of her heavy accent (she spoke six languages) and how others perceived her because of it. Smart, independent, a survivor, she fled the Nazis when they bombed Warsaw in 1939 and made her way through unimaginable horrors to relative safety in Vienna, where she met my American father.

Her survival skills (she taught herself English in a matter of weeks so that the U.S. Army would hire her as a translator in Vienna) bred in her a self-confidence that could, at times, be intimidating. She was a curious mixture of entitlement, generosity, avarice, and practicality. Either through nature or nurture, her sense of entitlement (*I deserve to get everything I want*), was passed on to me. Unfortunately, I didn't inherit her practical side.

I have been successful in my career; I make enough money to be comfortable, and I count myself fortunate. But there are always dresses I wish I could buy and sometimes do—on credit when I can't afford them. And when the bills come, and I sit signing checks and balancing my checkbook, I think about my mother and how she taught herself to be responsible about money. When my father was alive, she would whine and wheedle and charm and strong-arm him into buying the Hummel figurines, the ton of mushroom soil she needed each spring for her garden, the Rosenthal china she loved. And he usually did—how could anyone say no to her?—on credit. But when she had to make ends meet on Social Security and a military pension, she counted her pennies.

What was the secret of her radical transformation? Always fun-loving and high-spirited, she made a game of saving money. She discovered the appeal of shopping at Wal-Mart. When she lunched with "the girls" on Tuesday afternoons, she bragged about how much she saved by ordering the Senior's Special. She always paid her credit-card balances in full and on time. When she bought a new car a few years before she died, she'd saved enough so that she could pay half the price up front in order to reduce her loan and interest payments.

In a few words: she simply stopped being frivolous. Once, when on a lark I took her to lunch at a local "Turf Club," featuring off-track horse betting on tableside screens, she couldn't even enjoy putting $2 on a horse to win, place or show, calling it too much of a gamble. Only once, after my father died, do I remember her splurging on something special for herself. She bought a "pre-owned" baby grand piano, whose ivories had once tinkled in the smoky nether regions of a local cocktail lounge. She said she wanted to learn to play again (she had owned a piano when she was young in Warsaw), and she did take lessons briefly. But eventually, the baby grand stood, unused, like a beautiful black sculpture, taking up a corner of the living room, adding a touch of elegance, a reminder of the luxury she had left behind one frightening day in Warsaw.

Thinking about it now, I realize that my mother's ability to adapt, to shape her behavior to her altered circumstances, was probably the secret of her survival during the War. Her latter-day frugality and practicality are qualities I aspire to. But a lesson I treasure even more is the one she taught me when she splurged on that grand piano. In her wisdom, she knew that we all have to treat ourselves to the things we want every once in a while. Because, you know what? We deserve it.

"Woman freezes to death in bread truck."

The 53-year-old woman who was the subject of that news story didn't deserve the fate that befell her. I was sitting comfortably at my computer, a cup of hot coffee by my side, deep in the heart of the bitterly cold winter of 2003, when I heard the newscaster deliver that sound bite. She was an ex-Marine captain. And I wondered what sad set of circumstances had led her to make her home in this unheated, abandoned bread delivery truck parked behind a restaurant. The irony was hard to ignore: She died in a bread truck for lack of bread—lack of enough money to pay for a heated room and whatever other help she might have needed.

Her story vividly illustrates the need for women to follow MAKING BREAD's three principles of financial independence: be a breadwinner; the best gift you can give yourself is money in the bank, so save, save, save; and get real estate. She had been a breadwinner. Unfortunately, like many women (and men), she had worked in a low-paying job. (The military is not known for its high pay.) Even with base housing, she no doubt had trouble finding ways to stretch her paycheck and put money aside for her future. It isn't easy, but we must try our best, because the quality of our life depends on it.

The Financial Triple Whammy Comes Home to Roost. If you're reading this and you're in your twenties or thirties, give yourself the biggest gift you can by paying yourself first with every paycheck. Treat yourself to a secure retirement—one where you'll be able to afford to buy yourself a grand piano (or whatever splurge item your heart desires) someday. Make sure you have a (paid for) roof over your head, quality health insurance that will pay for your prescriptions (and long term care, if you need it), and enough money coming in monthly to meet your needs, with a little left over for the good things in life. It's during our so-called golden years that the effects of the triple whammy women face really begin to be felt, if we haven't taken steps to compensate for them earlier in life.

If you delay saving, be prepared to work longer or retire on less. But even if you are a procrastinator—or life just gets in the way of saving—don't give up hope. Often, when faced with the sudden realization that they only have 10 years to retirement—or, like my mother, experience the death of a spouse—women hear a deafening wake-up call and start making small changes that add up to big differences in their lives later on.

For a quick calculation of how much you should be saving a year in order to maintain a comfortable standard of living in retirement, visit the Web site of the American Savings Education Council (www. asec.org/ballpark/), fill out its online BALLPARK ESTIMATE worksheet, and let your computer do the math.

TEN YEARS TO RETIREMENT AND NOTHING SAVED? DON'T WORRY—BUT HURRY! HERE'S WHAT TO DO TO AVOID BECOMING A "BAG LADY"

Erica worked for several years after she was married, but, like many women, she left the workforce for 10 years to raise her children. Now divorced and 55 years old, she has a job with a company that provides a 401(k) plan. "I was trying to make ends meet, so I didn't take advantage of the plan when I first returned to work," she admits. "I've been contributing for the last 12 years, and the fund has about $45,000 in it. That's my entire retirement savings, and I only have 10 years until I retire."

For Erica, it is catch-up time, and she knows it. The "bag lady" syndrome—that frightening specter of the old woman reduced to poverty, carrying her belongs in shopping bags as she wanders the streets, searching for shelter—is something that many women fear, and that fear is no mere bugaboo. "I've told my children," she says, "gift-giving is going to be minimal from now on. The money I would have spent on them will go into my retirement account. I don't want to be dependent on my children when I'm older."

What are the chances that she'll be able to afford to retire at age 65? Currently, she is earning $50,000 a year. If she contributes 6 percent of her income ($3,000), the company will match one-half ($1,500), for a total contribution of $4,500 a year. In 10 years, the account will have a value of about $175,000. If she works an additional five years, she'll have saved about $296,000, assuming a 9 percent rate of return. Erica wisely plans to invest more than six percent, even though there will be no matching contribution by her employer for anything over the six percent mark. Even with this aggressive savings plan, however, given the rising cost of health care and her own life expectancy (a 65-year-old woman has a life expectancy of almost 20 years these days), she may have to continue working, at least part-time, well into her seventies to ensure a secure and comfortable old age.

Finding Money Now for Later. Whether you're 30 or 55 when you start saving for your nest egg, you'll need to find the dollars to put away. Like Erica, you may have to make some tough decisions. If you feel like you're depriving yourself, train yourself to think of saving as deferred spending. Tell yourself you are saving money now so that you'll have it to spend when you retire. And start putting yourself before your children.

Here are a few suggestions for finding the extra cash now for later:

She Conducted a "Great Accounting"— and Saved Ten Grand!

DO YOU KNOW WHERE YOUR MONEY WENT LAST YEAR? BY VICTORIA SECUNDA

With the hot breath of tax time upon them, every year millions of Americans collect the paperwork for their income-tax returns, sweating over how big a bite Uncle Sam will extract from their so-called wealth, and how they'll come up with the dough on April 15.

Five years ago, my husband and I—both self-employed, for whom the year 2000 had not been generous—met with our accountant, who informed us that the last thing we needed was more deductibles. What we needed was either more income, or a much, much lower standard of living. Something had to give, or we would never be able to retire.

With that chilling thought in mind, I pored through all my checkbook ledgers, credit-card bills, and cash receipts to determine exactly how much it had cost us to live in our Connecticut house for the year 2000 and where we could slash our expenses. I made a list of 46 categories, covering everything from property tax to garden supplies, dry cleaning to video rentals. Just making this exhaustive list was sobering; it exposed how little I knew about the cost of living and how easily money can evaporate, in increments, like the morning dew.

There is a very big difference between how much it costs a person to live and how much, and on what, one actually spends—and therein lies the trick of making and sticking to a budget. Figuring out what is an essential need (housing, food, medical); what is a frill (manicures, vacation trips, dinners out); and what, depending on whom you talk to, falls into the grey area of semi-negotiable (monthly hair coloring, cleaning help, premium cable TV) makes all the difference.

It is now two Great Accountings later and I can tell you, to the penny, how much we spent in the years 2000 and 2001, and where we saved money. What follows is a summary of these three categories— needs, frills, and semi-negotiablescomparing and contrasting our expenses for those two years.

Needs. Several years ago, when our daughter graduated from college, we "downsized" by moving to a less expensive community and using our real estate profits to buy a mortgage-free house and pay off our car loans. This move still left us on the hook for such expenses as property tax and homeowner's insurance. Between 2000 and 2001, these items went up a smidgen. Electricity went down a smidgen, because we removed some overhead light cans and were vigilant about turning off fixtures. Phone bills also took a dip, because I changed phone plans and eliminated one of our phone lines. Heating oil went way up—by $600—for reasons best known in the Middle East.

But medical expenses went way down. My husband, through one of his professional memberships, found a dental HMO, which, since I have numerous and varied tooth problems, ended up saving us approximately $2,000. And Shel's barbershop expenses were eliminated; I learned how to cut his hair (no, he is not allowed to cut mine; read on), an annual savings of about $140.

So far, a no-brainer. But here was the big surprise:

In 2000, food and other supermarket expenses—for two people, with occasional dinner parties and takeout Goodies, such as desserts, were a whopping $7,112. My husband, upon hearing this alarming figure, immediately usurped the grocery shopping. He's a speed shopper, I am a lingerer with a yen for hearts of palm, buying store brands of many items. My contribution to this cost-cutting exercise was to stay away from fancy food emporia (no takeout) and to finally become a decent cook. Despite these measures, our grocery bills for 2001 rose to $7,384—an increase of roughly $270. This I blame on inflation.

Frills. Okay, so there's a limit to how much one can save on essentials, assuming living in a tent is not an option. It's the "wants" (for which one can only blame oneself), when confused with "needs," that can put people knee-deep in sleep-deprived hock.

In this category, I cut out or greatly reduced several income-ravaging non-essentials. First, I got rid of our tree service (think bugs and borers), thereby saving $3,000. Then I found cheaper lawn-cutting guys—$2,000 cheaper. I also cashed in one of my husband's life-insurance policies and stashed the cash value of the policy in a money-market account, saving the $1,900, cost-ineffective annual premium. In addition, I canceled a couple of magazine subscriptions; resigned from one professional writers' association; and cut way back on entertainment—a savings, collectively, of roughly $1,500.

But there was one item, under the heading "household repairs," that, in my mind, was a need, and in my husband's (and my accountant's) mind was a frill: getting the interior of our house painted. My argument was that cracks honeycombed the walls and window frames, leaching heat in winter, and that the place looked truly shabby. To shore up our real estate investment, I reasoned, a facelift was mandatory. My husband had another argument: A decent paint job for an eight-room house would cost anywhere from $10,000 to $15,000, and would I tell him, please, where we'd find the money? (Talk about your conversation-killers.)

My solution: I'd paint the house myself. After culling through various do-it-yourself Web sites and books and talking to a couple of pros, I developed a working knowledge of spackling, caulking, and painting techniques. My husband has pointed out that, notwithstanding my noble and gorgeous efforts, this three-month labor was not exactly a freebie—it cost us roughly $1,000 in supplies and kept me from looking for writing assignments. But he only said this once (he does not have a death wish). Turns out that this endeavor is a win-win situation: My husband beams when his clients come to the house and admire its sparkling interior, and I didn't have to visit my therapist, not once, all winter.

Semi-Negotiables. I confess: I spend a ton at the beauty parlor—about $1,600 yearly—for monthly wash/cut/dye jobs. Every time I suggest to my hairdresser that I stop coloring my hair, she says, "Never. Your gray hairs are yucky, not the pretty kind." My friends, none of whom get their hair colored, are mum on the subject, as is my husband. You could say, then, that this expense is negotiable, and if push comes to shove, I'll let the yuckies prevail and only get haircuts. Meantime, I think of it as a mental-health expense.

So, too, are the lawn guys. On our acre, mowing is beyond me, and my husband's business would go down the drain if he had to spend a day each week cutting down the veldt. Some would argue that this cost is semi-negotiable. Again, if push came to shove, we'd move to a smaller place with only a bit of lawn, which I, do-it-yourself-er that I have become, could manage.

Moreover, in recent years, I have been inflicted by the gardening addiction and have spent a shameful amount on plants to fix up our formerly disgustingly overgrown property (doing most of the work myself, I hasten to add). Nevertheless, trees and shrubs are now a fully negotiable expense, by which I mean I've stopped buying. But I have indulged in occasional perennials. Negotiable? Yeah. But only somewhat. **Bottom Line.** What you really want to hear is how much less money we spent last year as a result of my Great Accounting. The grand total is $10,000 over the previous year. But here's the thing: I don't know why it isn't more. Call it the cost of living where we do.

That said, we were able to bank the entire 10 grand last year, an amount that we must increase in order to bankroll our pension funds. So, if worse really does come to worst, our plan is to move someplace even less expensive, by which time I'll be too tired to maintain an acre of gardens, and I won't give a damn what my hair looks like.

A shack in Provence would be nice....

WATCH YOUR 401(K) MONEY GROW

When you combine the power of compounding with the magic of matching contributions from your employer, the result can be a tidy nest egg at retirement, if you start early. The examples below reflect an 8 percent annual investment return, annual salary increases of 4 percent, contributions made annually until age 62, and matching contributions from your employer equal to 50 cents for every dollar, up to 6 percent.

	6% ANNUAL CONTRIBUTION	10% ANNUAL CONTRIBUTION
25 year old, earning $25,000	$797,788	$1,152,650
35 year old, earning $40,000	$506,556	$731,692
42 year old, earning $70,000	$433,923	$626,777
53 year old, earning $80,000	$122,163	$176,457

Take on a second job. Use the extra income from your part-time or second job to fund an IRA for yourself, if you don't have a 401(k) at work. You don't have to put in the maximum amount (see the box "Best Places to 'Retire' Your Money"). Put aside whatever you can. If you work beyond age 65, you can (and should) keep on making contributions to your IRA.

Rent out those extra bedrooms. Put your empty nest to work for your nest egg. Val has been doing this for years. There are corporations in her area where employees are transferred for long-term temporary assignments. "They're great tenants," she says. "They work long hours, so they come in fairly late and are rarely here on weekends." Barbara remodeled her basement and has a large studio apartment, which she rents out to a law student. Some older women rent rooms to younger people at a reduced rate in exchange for services, such as help with grocery shopping, lawn care, etc.

Tighten your belt. You can almost always find ways to cut back, giving yourself more money to save. Read "She Conducted a 'Great Accounting'—and Saved Ten Grand!" in this section, in which MAKING BREAD executive editor Victoria Secunda describes how she and her husband, Shel, spooked by the specter of retirement looming, adjusted their spending and saved a lot of dough.

BEST PLACES TO "RETIRE" YOUR MONEY

Because we're playing a game of catch up with our money, not only must we save as much as possible, but we need to look for ways to shelter as much of our money from taxes as possible.

For most of us, the best option, beyond deductible interest on a home mortgage, is the variety of tax-advantaged savings accounts available to us, including FSAs, HSAs, and, of course,

Tip: Regardless of who makes the contribution, it's the person whose name is on the account who has control of it. This is an important point to remember, if you and your spouse separate. If you divorce, it is possible to claim a portion of the spousal IRA as part of your settlement. Do so, and transfer it into an IRA in your name.

retirement accounts. Don't start investing in mutual funds until you've exhausted your tax-deferred options. The most common of these are 401(k) plans and individual retirement accounts.

The 401(k) plan is a voluntary retirement savings plan offered by your employer to which you make contributions from your gross income (i.e., before taxes), up to a maximum amount allowed by the government. Your employer is permitted under law to make matching contributions, which may be as much as 100 percent of your contribution—up to a certain dollar limit. A typical plan may say, "The company will match $0.50 for each $1.00 of the first 6 percent of your pay." The amount you contribute, as well as any matching amount, is tax-deductible. In other words, that amount is subtracted from your income before taxes are calculated, thereby reducing the amount of tax you will owe at the end of the year. You only pay tax on the money when you withdraw it upon retirement. If you take an early withdrawal, you will be subject to tax and a 10 percent penalty. Under certain circumstances, it is possible to borrow from a 401(k) and pay yourself back, with interest.

You're generally given several investment options, such as mutual funds, company stock, or other, more conservative savings funds, to choose from. According to Gerry O'Connor of The Spectrem Group, the average amount contributed to 401(k) plans is 8.4 percent. The figure is the same for both men and women, but the average balance is lower in a women's account—$37,700 versus $56,500 for men. Why? Lower salaries and fewer years of employment.

Maximum allowable contributions to 401(k) plans are:

Tax year	If you're under 50	If you're over 50
2004	$13,000	$16,000
2005	$14,000	$18,000
2006 and after	$15,000	$20,000

Warning: Think Enron, before you invest all of your 401(k) contributions in company stock. (Many of Enron's employees lost their life savings, which had been invested in the company's stock through its retirement plan, after the company went bankrupt as a result of company mismanagement in 2001.)

What If My Employer Doesn't Offer a 401(k) Plan?

If you're not covered by a pension plan or a 401(k) plan (or the equivalent, such as a 403(b) plan for employees of educational institutions and nonprofits) on the job, open an Individual Retirement Account (IRA). The deductibility of IRA contributions depends on your income level and whether you are covered by a retirement plan at work. You must have earned income or alimony to qualify, and you can't contribute more than you earn. To qualify for the full deduction on a traditional IRA, your adjusted gross income (AGI), or income after deductions, can't exceed $55,000 (singles) and $75,000 (married, filing jointly) in tax year 2005. If you are not eligible for a tax-deductible contribution, you can still make IRA contributions up to the maximum amount listed below, without the deduction.

At that point, however, you might want to consider a Roth IRA, where contributions are taxed but earnings aren't. To qualify, your AGI must be no more than $110,000 for single filers; $160,000, if married filing jointly; reduced contributions are allowed if you earn between $95,000 and $110,000 (for single filers) and $150,000 to $160,000 (married filing jointly). Among the advantages of Roth IRAs: you can continue to contribute to them after 70½, and you aren't penalized if you don't begin withdrawals at that age. MyFICO.com (www.myfico.com) has a calculator to help you determine what kind of IRA is best for you}. Once your income reaches $110,000 (singles) and $160,000 (marrieds), you are no longer eligible to contribute to either kind of IRA.

Maximum allowable annual contributions to IRAs are:

Tax year	If you're under 50	If you're over 50
2002-2004	$3,000	$3,500
2005	$4,000	$4,500
2006-2007	$4,000	$5,000
2008 and after	$5,000	$6,000

You can contribute to both a traditional and a Roth IRA—if your income doesn't exceed the limit—but total annual IRA contributions must not exceed the amounts on the previous page. You also can't contribute more than you earn.

What's a Stay-at-Home Mom to Do? If either you or your spouse is not working, the employed spouse can contribute to an IRA in the other spouse's name (this is cleverly called a spousal IRA), as well as in his/her own. That way a couple can stash away up to $8,000 (or $9,000 if over 50) annually. It's not as much as you could contribute to a 401(k) if you were working, but at least you'll be putting something away for the future, tax-deferred. So take advantage of it if you can. Women generally spend a period of five to 10 years during their prime working years at home raising children, and "the stay-at-home mom will have to work five extra years to recover lost income, pension coverage, and career promotion" during that time, says NCWRR's Christopher Hayes. But she can still save money toward her retirement while at home if her husband can find the money to invest in a spousal IRA.

Tip: If both you and your husband have 401(k) plans at work and you can only afford to contribute to one, pick the one that offers the highest matching contribution.

Self-employed Retirement Accounts. There are various flavors of tax-deferred retirement options available to self-employed individuals and small business owners: Keogh accounts, SEP-IRA's, Simple IRAs and self-employed 401(k) accounts.

A Keogh Plan is a qualified retirement plan for sole proprietors or partners. It allows a contribution of up to 25 percent of earned income to a maximum of $42,000 annually, tax deferred. Certain types of Keoghs require the self-employed to contribute a fixed percentage of income every year. Annual filings are required by the IRS.

The SEP-IRA, or Simplified Employee Pension IRA, is an employer plan, and only the employer contributes, with a limit of 25 percent of earned income for each employee and the owner, up to a maximum of $40,000. There is no limit to the number of employees eligible. These plans are easy to set up and maintain, since there are no annual filings to make. You don't have to make a contribution every year.

Simple IRAs are available to employers with one to 100 employees. The maximum contribution per employee is $10,000 annually. As the name implies, these plans are easy to set up and administer.

Self-employed or solo 401(k) plans are a new retirement vehicle for the self-employed. Multiple owners and spouses (no employees) are eligible to contribute. You can contribute up to $14,000 per year. You don't have to contribute each year, and can move money into the plan from other IRAs.

Contributions to all of these plans are tax-deductible; some permit loan withdrawals, some do not. In the case of self-employed people, the contribution is based on the net profit from the business (not the gross income).

An individual IRA is also an option for the

self-employed. If you qualify for a tax-deductible IRA, you'll have to decide which is the better vehicle for you: a plan that offers you a tax deduction now (a traditional IRA) or one that offers a tax-free withdrawal later rather than a deduction today (a Roth IRA). There is no easy answer, of course: you have to consider such factors as your age, your current income, and your expected tax brackets during your working and retirement years. As a rule of thumb, you'll do better with a Roth IRA if you expect to be paying a substantially higher tax rate after retirement than you are currently paying. Discuss these plans with your tax adviser before deciding which one is best for you.

BEYOND 401(K)S AND IRAS: WHY WOMEN SHOULD CONSIDER ANNUITIES

Annuities. Do you own them? Should you own them? Do you even know what they are? If you're confused about them, you're not alone. But in today's economic climate, with so many of us worried about whether Social Security benefits will run out before we can claim them and whether our retirement savings will stay safe from the Enron Effect, annuities—which are insurance contracts offering guaranteed lifetime income—may be worth investigating. Because women are at risk of outliving their savings, they, in particular, should look into what annuities can do for them.

That being said, annuities aren't for everyone. They come with certain tax advantages, but they carry high management fees, so you have to do the math to be sure they're right for you. And they are a long-term investment. They make good sense if you have 10, 15, 20, or more years till retirement, if you are looking for a pretty sure

thing, and if you expect to live a long, long time. The wild card in the deck: monthly payouts are based, in part, on life expectancy, so if you beat the odds, the insurance company loses and you come out ahead of the game financially.

So, what exactly is an annuity, and how does it stack up against other retirement investments? Basically, it's an investment contract with an insurance company. You pay the company a sum of money (the minimum is generally $5,000), and eventually receive a lump sum or periodic payout of the principal and interest earned. Interest rates on annuities are generally higher than those available for CDs. However, CDs are FDIC-insured and annuities are not. Still, most annuities protect your principal and, in some cases, even guarantee a specified level of return.

Your investment is made with after-tax dollars. However, the interest it earns is reinvested and keeps on growing, tax-deferred, until it is withdrawn. You only pay taxes on the money you take out when you take it out. That means that, if you opt for monthly payments instead of a lump-sum payout, you can stretch the tax hit over the lifetime of the payout and, in many cases, you end up paying taxes on that money when you are in a lower tax bracket.

If you've just received an inheritance or a divorce settlement, an annuity might be one place to stash it, as long as you've already maxed out your tax-deductible IRA and 401(k) contributions. Unlike 401(k)s or IRAs, there's no limit on how much you can invest in an annuity, and you don't have to begin taking withdrawals (and paying taxes) at age 70½. Two other advantages: in some states, annuities are protected from creditors, and as, an inheritance, they can escape probate.

Annuities are complex investments, with many options and consequences for both you and your heirs. Before buying, you should discuss your choices with a financial planner.

UNDERSTANDING YOUR CHOICES

Single or flexible payment? You have the choice of making one lump-sum payment to purchase a single-premium annuity or making ongoing contributions over a period of time. The single payment might come from proceeds of a life-insurance policy on the death of a spouse or parent. Or the money might come from a lump-sum payment from your corporate retirement plan.

Fixed or variable annuities? Fixed annuities earn a guaranteed rate of interest for a specific time period, such as one, three, or five years. A new interest rate is set once the guaranteed period is over, so it is similar to a Certificate of Deposit. However, unlike a CD, you don't have to pay taxes on your earnings until you withdraw them.

DON'T WORRY, BUT HURRY:
TEN RULES FOR A WRINKLE-FREE RETIREMENT

1. Think benefits—medical and retirement—when deciding which job to take.

2. Start saving early. Begin with small deposits, and increase contributions every time you get a raise.

3. Take advantage of pre-tax savings that 401(k) and other tax-advantaged plans offer.

4. Study your 401(k) investment options carefully, and weigh the kind of return that can be expected with each. Choose aggressive growth strategies while you are young. The worst mistake is being too cautious. Generally, the greater the risk, the greater the reward. Over time, the stock market has outperformed all other investments.

5. Protect your real estate investment. Your equity is there for you to tap into when you need it—but don't think of it as your everyday emergency fund. Any mortgage balance or equity line of credit you owe when it comes time to sell your house will reduce the size of the profit you cash out in the process.

6. Invest in an Individual Retirement Account (IRA), if you don't have a matching 401(k) plan. You don't have to put in the maximum each year. Make it automatic by having money withdrawn monthly from a checking account.

7. Even after you retire, keep some of your savings in growth funds so that it can keep on earning as much as possible for you.

8. Postpone retirement as long as you can in order to maximize your 401(k) earnings, profit sharing, and any other benefits you might have on the job. Besides, if you file for Social Security at 62, you permanently and significantly reduce your monthly check.

9. Downward mobility is a reality for many divorced women. If you are receiving alimony, contribute to an IRA. Put in what you can, because it is important to invest for your future. And, before you sign the divorce agreement, consult a good attorney to be sure that you are getting your fair share of all hidden assets, such as pension plans, 401(k)s, IRAs, and other retirement investments.

10. In good times and bad, stick with your plan. Given monthly or yearly contributions, retirement accounts can grow rapidly.

Your 401(k) plan may offer a fixed annuity as one of your investment choices. If it does, it's probably the most conservative choice, and, within that framework, it's generally not considered a good investment choice. Why invest in a tax shelter within a tax shelter? One exception might be to avoid the 10 percent penalty on early withdrawals; investing in an immediate annuity (see below) within your 401(K), should allow you to draw immediate payouts without penalty.

Variable annuities offer a choice of growth investments, such as stocks, bonds, and mutual funds. The return on variable annuities can go up or down, so your earnings are not guaranteed, as they are in a fixed instrument. You can, however, select a variable annuity that offers a combination of a fixed account with a guaranteed return and a stock account. This type also allows you to move money from one account to another to protect your assets from negative market conditions. Variable annuities tend to carry higher fees, because they require more management.

Tax-deferred or immediate annuities? These terms refer to when you start taking the money out. Immediate annuities are usually purchased with a one-time payment and payments start immediately. In a deferred annuity, you delay payment until you need it, usually at retirement. Unlike IRAs and 401(k)s, you can postpone the payout indefinitely—even leave it untouched so that your beneficiary receives all proceeds after your death.

Consult a financial expert about the tax consequences for your heirs of inheriting an annuity versus some other sort of investment, such as a mutual fund. Ask yourself: is this an investment for your security or your children's future? The advantage of a mutual fund inheritance is that the beneficiary is taxed on gains after transfer only and not on the whole amount.

Always put the maximum pre-tax contributions into retirement plans, such as your 401(k), IRA, or SEP, before you consider an annuity. An annuity is an additional way to save for retirement after all other pre-tax retirement vehicles have been used. Below, we sum up the advantages and disadvantages of this type of retirement savings:

ADVANTAGES OF AN ANNUITY

>>All earnings are tax-deferred, so you postpone paying income taxes until you withdraw the money during retirement. This is also true of a 401(k) or traditional IRA. However, with those, you must begin withdrawals by April 1 of the year after you turn 70½.

>>You can invest as much money as you want. There is no restriction on the amount that can be contributed annually with your *after-tax* dollars, with this exception: you must operate within the dollar limits established by federal law if you are using an annuity to fund your IRA.

>>You can provide death benefits to your heirs. Your beneficiaries will never receive less than you contributed (minus any withdrawals). However, the tax hit is higher than it would be for a mutual fund. A surviving spouse can become the new owner of an annuity, if payments have not begun.

DISADVANTAGES OF AN ANNUITY

>> Expenses can be high and could outweigh the tax benefits, especially during the first few

years, so your time horizon should be at least 10 years. In addition, the insurer may impose a surrender charge if you cash in your annuity within, let's say 7 to 10 years. This fee could be as high as seven percent during the first year and is reduced over the time specified in the contract. Do the math and consider your personal situation: How soon will you want to begin taking withdrawals? What will your tax situation be at the time? What are your mutual fund alternatives and how do those fees compare?

>> You face penalties for early withdrawals. With some exceptions, if you withdraw money before age 59½, the IRS will apply a 10 percent penalty in addition to income taxes. You may also be hit with withdrawal charges if you switch annuities, usually done to obtain a higher interest rate (or to benefit the salesperson). Don't let a broker talk you into switching just so that he/she can earn a commission.

>> With a fixed annuity, there is no cost-of-living adjustment when you begin withdrawals. Payments will remain the same, so there is the danger that inflation can erode the future value of your payments.

>> The payments from a variable annuity fluctuate based on the performance of the investment option you choose. If the market drops, as it has in the last couple of years, then payments will drop. This can be very unsettling, if you were depending on a certain amount with each withdrawal.

CASHING OUT YOUR ANNUITY

You can receive the money in a lump sum, take it out as needed, or receive it in a steady stream of regular payments, which is called "annuitizing." The size of the payments is based on the amount of money in the annuity, your age, interest rates, and life expectancy. There are several withdrawal methods:

Lifetime Income Payments, or Straight-Life Annuity. With this option, payments are guaranteed by the insurance company, no matter how long you live. If you die before reaching your life expectancy, the insurer keeps the balance in your account. If you outlive your life expectancy, the insurer loses the bet by having to continue payments for your lifetime.

Lifetime Income with Guaranteed Period. You'll receive income for life or for a fixed number of years, whichever is greater. Let's say you decide on "life or 10 years certain." The insurer makes regular payments for 10 years to you, if you live that long, or to a beneficiary if you die before the period is up. If you die after the guaranteed period of 10 years is over, you continue to receive payments until your death, but your beneficiaries receive nothing.

Lifetime Income for Two, or Joint and Survivor. You get payments for the rest of your life and the life of another person. The amount of your check will depend on what your beneficiary will receive after your death. Half of your check? Two-thirds of your check? The more you leave to your surviving spouse, the less you will get while both of you are alive.

Installment Payments. You pick a period of 10 years, 15 years, or whatever, in which you will receive payments, but not exceeding your life expectancy. The danger: You might outlive this income. If you die before the money is paid out to you, your heirs will get the funds, not the insurance company.

Tax Implications: As long as you choose an option that provides a steady stream of income instead of a lump sum, your tax liability is spread out. Each payment includes some of the earnings, and only those earnings are taxed. What remains continues to grow on a tax-deferred basis. By comparison, if the same amount of money were withdrawn from a qualified, or pre-tax, retirement plan, the full amount of each withdrawal would be taxed.

HOW TO GET THE MOST OUT OF AN ANNUITY

Annuities are great insurance for people who are in good health and are afraid of outliving their savings. Don't consider a straight-life annuity if your health isn't good, or the insurer could end up with the balance in your account when you die. Comparison shop. Different annuities offer a wide range of choices, prices, and flexibility.

Leave an annuity alone for as long as you can. The older you are when you begin payments, the higher they will be. Jill, a widow at age 65, has $100,000, from her husband's life insurance policy. She has decided to purchase a single-premium fixed annuity. Right now, she would receive about $664 per month on a straight-life payment and $650 if she chose lifetime income with a 10-year guarantee. If she waits until she is 75 years old to begin her payments, the monthly payments will be about $852 for a straight life and $780 for lifetime

with a 10-year guarantee. "I don't like a lot of risk," she says, "and I want to have regular income. So I'll defer payments, using income from others sources first."

Annuities are long-term savings, so you'll want to make sure the company you pick will be in business 20 or 30 years from now. The annuity contract is issued by an insurance company and not by the broker or agent that sold it to you. Is the company financially secure? Does it have a good claims-paying record? What is its rating? Check A.M. Best (www.ambest.com) and look for companies with an A or better rating.

Switching annuities can be tricky. You may incur withdrawal charges, so calculate whether the benefits of the new annuity offset the charges. And be sure the salesperson isn't benefiting from the switch at your expense. If you do switch, complete IRS Form 1035 to make sure it's treated as a tax-free exchange.

You don't have to purchase an annuity from the same company that holds the proceeds from a spouse's insurance policy or your retirement funds. Leave the money in place and shop around before you roll your money over. Stick to highly rated insurers. Choose carefully, because once you've begun annuitizing with one company, you can't get a "divorce." You're stuck.

Bottom line: Annuities are investments to make *after* you've maxed out your pre-tax retirement choices. If you're eligible for a Roth IRA, which is paid for with after-tax dollars but carries no tax burden on withdrawal, put as much money as you can there next. Then, if you've still got money to invest (lucky you!), weigh mutual funds and annuities carefully. Study your needs and your risk tolerance. Use annuities as your *added protection* for a long and comfortable retirement.

LAST-MINUTE SURVIVAL STRATEGIES, IN CASE YOU HAVEN'T SAVED ENOUGH

We hope you love your job, because, unless you began saving for retirement in your 20s, you may have to work longer than you expected to supplement a meager Social Security benefit, reduced from your years away from work, or to obtain health insurance until you are old enough for Medicare. In fact, if your husband is older than you are, chances are he'll retire before you do, making you the primary breadwinner in the family. According to the U.S. Census Bureau, in 2000 there were more than two million couples in which a man 55 or over had not worked in the previous year but his wife had. That figure represented 10.9 percent of couples involving a man 55 or over, up from 1.6 million such couples (or 9.6 percent of the total) in 1990.

Sometimes the wife flees the empty nest to find a job when her husband retires. As writer Jane Resnick so aptly wrote in a MAKING BREAD article, "Any honest wife will tell you that having a newly retired husband around is like your first encounter with a cockroach. You turn on a light, and there he is, in rooms you never expected to see him during the day… It's not all bad, of course. She goes on to comment that "he thought the hours when I normally start my day were perfect for recapturing the dimly recalled romance of our youth. And that's how I became the poster girl for midlife sex."

Then there's that mysterious factor anthropologist Margaret Mead dubbed "post-menopausal zest"—that surge of energy and drive to make our marks on the world that many of us feel after a certain age. All of those factors hold us in good stead as we enter our retirement years, helping us to find ways to make ends meet as we try to make the most of the years ahead. Below, are some last-minute retirement strategies, in case *you* haven't saved enough. You retirement-savings procrastinators know who you are.

Continue working beyond 65. Your Social Security benefits will not be reduced if you work after you reach full retirement age. Between age 62, when you can begin claiming benefits, and your full retirement age, $1 will be deducted from your benefit for every $2 you earn above $12,000. During the year you reach retirement age, $1 will be deducted for every $3 you earn, until the month of your birthday. After that, there are no limits on earnings. (See "When Not to Lie About How Old You Are: Calculating Your Full Retirement Age" in this section to figure out your full retirement age, based on your year of birth). So don't be afraid to keep working; become a consultant in your field, or apply to teach at a local community college or university. Your years of experience have value; share them with others and get paid for them!

Many service companies are looking to employ people who are reliable, experienced, and polite. Mary works as a receptionist in the physical-therapy department at a local hospital. She works about 20 hours a week and is paid on an hourly basis. Kathryn, who's now 81, did "live-ins" for years. She moved in, taking care of children when the parents took a vacation. Her former clients still have her stay in their homes to take care of their pets and plants, now that the kids are grown.

Sell your home and downsize. Remember MAKING BREAD's third principle of female finance—get real estate? Now is when you'll be glad that you did. That house you bought 20 or 30 years ago, raised a family in, loved, laughed and cried in, was an investment. Because, historically, real estate values have outpaced inflation, because of its tax advantages, because owning a home gives you an asset you can leverage (and because paying rent is like throwing your money

away), your home forms the linchpin of your retirement strategy. Buying it was as important as investing in a 401(k) plan or IRA. So don't get too emotionally attached to your home, sweet, home. There will, undoubtedly, come a time when you will want to "downsize" to a smaller one and cash out investment capital to help you pay for a more comfortable and secure retirement. It's the reason you bought the house in the first place.

Warning: Older Americans have been tapping into their home equity, using lines of credit to retire high-interest credit-card debt or simply to make ends meet—paying for rising health-care costs or to help their adult children who may be struggling financially—in record numbers. One in four families headed by someone over 65 still had a mortgage to pay in 2001, and the amount they owe has nearly quadrupled since 1989, according to Federal Reserve Board data, *The New York Times* reported in 2004. People over 65 have the fastest growing home debt—and fastest growing share of personal bankruptcy. Don't become one of them; it's important to protect your home equity so that you can cash out and downsize when you need to.

Selling the home in which you've raised your family can be a very emotional and difficult decision to make, yet there are times when it makes an abundance of sense. Figure out how much it is costing to maintain the house—lawn care, snow removal, repairs (if you are lucky enough to find someone to do them). How soon will it need repainting? A new roof? The list goes on. Once you see how much you'd be saving by selling, the decision will be made for you. After the house is sold, consider renting or use the proceeds to buy a less expensive condo, perhaps in a warmer—and cheaper—area of the country. Invest the balance to provide needed income.

Bev lived in a charming old home that required a lot of maintenance. When her husband died, she took the proceeds from his life insurance and added to a portfolio of stocks. But she had to invade the principal of the portfolio to maintain the house. As the funds began to dwindle, she was forced to face the reality that she couldn't afford to stay there. "I played with figures and did 'what if' scenarios—if I stay here, if I sell and rent, if I sell and buy, etc.," she says. "This produced a tremendous amount of anxiety." During the pre-sale clean-out period, she relived the grief of her husband's death. But she is now living comfortably in a condominium, which she purchased, paying substantially less than the amount she received for the house. She has invested the balance to produce more retirement income.

Look into subsidized housing. If you don't own a home, and you're feeling the pinch of high rents, look into low-cost housing for the elderly.

It is independent living, and rent is based on income. Look up the local Area Agency on Aging in your phone book to find out about options in your community, or visit the Web site of the National Association of Area Agencies on Aging (www.n4a.org).

Find a roommate. If you are living alone, invite one or more compatible female (or male) friends to share living expenses, rent, or mortgage payments. Remember *The Golden Girls*? It wasn't just a TV series; women in real life are finding companionship and cost savings in similar arrangements. Be sure to get an agreement in writing regarding who pays for what, who owns

what, and what will happen in the event that someone moves out.

Consider a reverse mortgage when you retire. The reverse mortgage is basically a loan that you take out against the equity in your home. The reverse mortgage lender sends you a check each month, with the amount dependent upon several factors, including your age (you must be at least 62), the value of your home, and current interest rates. You remain the owner of your home while you are alive, and you pay no taxes on the money you receive from the lender. You continue to pay property taxes and homeowner insurance. The loan is paid off when you

WHEN NOT TO LIE ABOUT HOW OLD YOU ARE: CALCULATING YOUR FULL RETIREMENT AGE

To find out how much your monthly benefit will be—something you should do when you turn 50 so that you can start serious planning for retirement—request a Personal Earnings and Benefit Estimate Statement from the Social Security Administration (www.ssa.gov, or call 1-800-772-1213). And don't forget to check with every company you ever worked for—including those summer jobs you held way back when you were a teen-ager—and ask whether you were covered by a pension plan. You might discover some pleasant surprises.

Check the chart at right to figure out at what age you can begin to receive your full Social Security retirement benefit.

If you were born in …	Your full retirement age is …
1937 or earlier:	65
1938:	65 and 2 months
1939:	65 and 4 months
1940:	65 and 6 months
1941:	65 and 8 months
1942:	65 and 10 months
1943–1954:	66
1955:	66 and 2 months
1956:	66 and 4 months
1957:	66 and 6 months
1958:	66 and 8 months
1959:	66 and 10 months
1960 and later:	67

sell the house or die. At that time, any appreciation in the value of the property goes to you or your heirs. Reverse mortgage proceeds are available as a lump sum, fixed monthly payments (for as long as you live in the house), or as a line of credit, or a combination of these three options. Depending on the option you choose, if you outlive the value of your home, you may continue to receive monthly payments, and your estate will never owe the lender more than the value of the home.

Marty is considering one. Her condo is appraised at $208,000. She would be able to get a $140,000 lump sum payment, after closing costs. Monthly payments would vary depending on the type of program, but could be about $900 per month.

The downside: The closing costs and other charges are high on reverse mortgages, so it only pays to take one out if you expect to remain in the house for at least two to three more years. Reverse mortgages also reduce the equity in your home, depleting the estate you might want to leave to your children. But you need to take care of yourself first. (If you have a wealthy child, he or she might want to be the reverse mortgage holder.) And they may affect your eligibility for Medicaid or other government assistance. Check with your financial adviser to fully understand how these mortgages work before you apply for one. For more information, consult www. aarp.org /revmort or www.eldercare.gov.

Start collecting Social Security. Women reaching age 65 in 2003 are expected to live, on average, an additional 20 years, compared with 16 years for men. For unmarried women, including widows, age 65 and older, Social Security comprises 51 percent of their total income, versus only 37 percent of unmarried elderly men's retirement income and 34 percent of elderly couples' income. Social Security is the only source of retirement income for 26 percent of unmarried elderly women, according to the Social Security Administration. At the end of 2002, women's average monthly retirement benefit was $774. Men's average benefit was $1,008.

When you begin collecting Social Security is a decision not to be taken lightly; it will impact the income you have to work with for the rest of your life. The longer you wait, the more you'll receive, until age 70, when the amount becomes fixed. However, if you need the money, you can start collecting reduced benefits at age 62. Remember that once you claim reduced benefits, you will continue to receive this lesser amount for the rest of your life. (Check "When Not to Lie About How Old You Are: Calculating Your Full Retirement Age" in this section to find out when you are eligible for full benefits.)

If you have been married, you can collect Social Security benefits on your own employment record or receive one-half of your husband's benefit—whichever provides the higher amount. Even if you are divorced, you can collect on your ex's earnings, as long as you were married for at least 10 years, don't remarry before age 60, and he is already collecting benefits. Widows can receive reduced survivor benefits at age 60 (or age 50 if they are disabled), if they haven't remarried at that time, or their deceased husband's full benefits when they reach full retirement age. Call the Social Security Administration at 800-772-1213 and talk with a representative to find out how much you will be eligible to receive at certain ages.

HEALTH=WEALTH: MEDICARE PROVIDES RELIEF FOR MANY WOMEN

While many corporations formerly extended health coverage to retirees, those benefits are rapidly becoming a thing of the past, as those same companies look for ways to cut costs. Add to that the fact that health costs are skyrocketing, and it's easy to understand why healthcare is becoming the major expense for many retirees. Making the transition from health coverage at work to going it alone is made slightly less painful by COBRA (the Consolidated Omnibus Budget Reconciliation Act of 1986). COBRA provides extended coverage under your former employer's group health plan for 18 months when you leave work, coverage to a married spouse (i.e., a widow or widower) for 36 months after a death, and coverage to a divorced spouse for 36 months after the divorce. You pay less for this coverage than you would if you had to purchase a new policy.

Of course, COBRA doesn't help the one-third of women between the ages of 18 and 64 who are not covered by employer-sponsored health insurance (either theirs or their husband's). For them, retirement may actually provide some relief; becoming eligible for Medicare is a major reason why every woman should work for a minimum of 10 years in order to qualify for Social Security. If you're eligible for Social Security benefits—either on your own record or on your husband's—you will receive Medicare hospital insurance (Parts A and B) protection at age 65. (Mark your calendars: You must sign up for it; the sign-up period begins three months before your 65th birthday and lasts until three months after your 65th birthday.) If you're not eligible for benefits, you can still pay a monthly premium to buy

hospital insurance coverage and Medicare medical insurance (Part B), which may be less expensive than a policy you might purchase outside of the Medicare system. Low-income women over 65 who meet certain stringent income eligibility requirements can qualify for Medicaid, the state and federal program for low-income individuals. Visit www. medicare.gov for enrollment information.

Below, are the basics about Medicare and Medigap insurance:

Medicare. This national health insurance covers everyone age 65 or older who pays Social Security taxes or is eligible for Social Security or Railroad Retirement benefits. It is also available to those under 65 who are disabled or who have chronic kidney disease.

Medicare is divided into parts. Part A is free of charge. It pays for hospital stays and care in a skilled nursing home as part of after-hospital care. Part B covers physicians' fees and outpatient services at a hospital, as well as certain medical services and supplies. It costs a small monthly fee, and pays for 80 percent of reasonable medical costs. You are responsible for paying the balance. Part B does not pay for eyeglasses, dentistry, prescription drugs, private nursing, custodial nursing-home care, treatment in a foreign country, or routine physical examinations.

Private health insurance plans offer additional coverage over and above A and B and are commonly referred to as "Part C." Starting in January 2006, Medicare Part D, a new benefit created by the Medicare Prescription Drug Improvement and Modernization Act of 2003, will offer some coverage for prescription drugs. Under this option, beneficiaries will pay the first $250 in drug costs;

25 percent of the total drug costs between $250 and $2,250; 100 percent of drug costs between $2,250 and $5,100; and the greater of $2 for generics, $5 for brand drugs or 5 percent coinsurance, after they reach a $3,600 out-of-pocket limit. The premium, which will vary depending on which private plan is purchased, is expected to cost around $35 per month. This with incomes under $12,123 ($16,00, married filing jointly0 pay no premiums or deductibles. Until December 31, 2005, Medicare-endorsed drug discount cards are available, costing $30 per year and offering estimated savings of 10 to 25 percent per prescription. The cards are free for those who fall in the above low-income group, and this group may also be eligible to receive $600 towards prescription costs. Visit www.medicare.gov for more information.

It's important to register for Medicare, even if

you decide not to take Social Security benefits at 65. You have a limited window of opportunity to do that, or you risk a delay in starting your coverage. Among the regulations are these:

If you apply up to three months before your 65th birthday, your coverage will begin as soon as you reach 65.

If you enroll in the month in which you turn 65, your coverage will begin on the first day of the following month.

If you enroll within three months after you turn 65, you'll end up waiting for two months

after the date you enroll before coverage starts. In the meantime, Medicare will not cover any of your Part B claims.

If you miss the latter deadline, you must wait until the next general enrollment period—January 1 to March 1 each year—to sign up. Say, your 65th birthday is in April and you do not apply by the end of July. You may not enroll until the following January, and your coverage will not begin until the July after that. You've lost a year of coverage.

To help pay for the 20 percent not covered by Part B, as well as for expenses that go beyond what Medicare is willing to pay, you should seriously consider carrying some form of supplemental policy. Your retirement nest egg could be wiped out by medical costs that Medicare doesn't cover. Medigap insurance bridges the gap between your medical bills and the amount that Medicare is willing to pay, which is usually less than the total bill from your doctor, hospital, or laboratory.

Medigap. Gaps occur because Medicare includes a deductible clause, and because your doctor is charging more than Medicare thinks the particular treatment should cost. The largest gap comes in the area of physicians' excess fees, as Medicare likes to call them. You are responsible for such excess charges, up to a payment limit that the government sets.

You should buy medigap insurance in the first six months after you begin coverage under Medicare Part B. During that time, insurance companies are required by law to sell you any policy sold in your area. This timing becomes particularly important if you have a health problem that may put you in a high-risk category and

YOU ASKED, WE ANSWERED . . .

CAN I GIVE MY MONEY AWAY TO BECOME ELIGIBLE FOR NURSING HOME COVERAGE?

Q: *How does Medicaid work, and is it possible to transfer assets to become eligible for nursing-home coverage?*

A: Medicaid is a joint federal and state program that pays for medical care for individuals who cannot pay their own medical bills. Medicaid pays for physician-approved hospital stays, medical care, prenatal care, vaccines for children, family planning services, x-rays, prescription drugs, and skilled nursing home care. However, to qualify for Medicaid, a person must have limited income and few assets, or resources. The rules are complicated, and each state operates its own Medicaid program.

In nearly every state, Medicaid eligibility is limited to children, pregnant women, families with dependent children, persons who are blind or disabled, and persons 65 or older. A few states cover single healthy adults who fall within certain income and eligibility guidelines. The guidelines for qualifying for Medicaid are based on two factors:

Income Levels: All states impose an income cap to restrict eligibility to people who have monthly income below a certain level. The income that your spouse earns is not considered. In most states, if you spend all of your income on nursing-home costs—minus a small personal-needs allowance; usually about $100 per month—Medicaid will cover the balance of the nursing-home charges. Some states are more generous than others; in South Carolina, for instance, the income limit is $1,656 per month.

Assets: Before Medicaid applicants can qualify for Medicaid, they must "spend down" their assets, such as cash, stocks, and most other items, until only a certain amount remains. This amount will vary from state to state. Most set the limit at several thousand dollars for one person and more for a couple. For instance, in Connecticut the limit is $4,000 or less per individual and $6,000 or less for a couple. You do not need to factor in certain valuable assets: the home where you live, home furnishings, a car, and the amount in a prepaid burial account.

If you enter a nursing home and your spouse does not, he can keep a percent of total income and assets. Medicaid eligibility considers all assets owned by each spouse, then allows the spouse still living at home to keep half of the couple's assets to a state-by-state limit. Any assets above that limit have to be spent down before your eligibility kicks in. In determining Medicaid eligibility, the couple's assets are evenly divided. The nursing-home patient spends his or her half down to the state's criteria (i.e., $1,656 In South Carolina), and the at-home spouse will usually get to keep the remaining 50 percent of the assets.

Can you transfer assets to qualify for nursing-home care? Many people think that in order to qualify for Medicaid they need to falsely impoverish themselves by giving their assets away. This is not always the case. Moreover, doing so to preserve assets can be tricky; timing is everything. When you apply for Medicaid you must disclose any gifts you have made to people other than your spouse within the last 36 months. Assets transferred during this period will result in a period of ineligibility for Medicaid.

The government calculates the waiting period by dividing the value of the asset given away by the average monthly cost of nursing-home care in your state. For instance, someone who gifts $45,000 can't receive Medicaid for the next 10 months, if the average monthly cost of the nursing home is $4,500 per month. Applying for Medicaid during that 10-month period is illegal.

Be aware that federal law requires the Medicaid program to "look back" 36 months prior to the application for Medicaid nursing-home benefit to see if assets have been transferred for less than fair market value. The look-back period is 60 months if the assets were transferred to an irrevocable trust. You will need to make copies of *every* financial document—bank statements, brokerage statements, etc.—to send to the Medicaid office in your state. It takes time. They don't accept "I can't find that." You might have to call banks or other financial institutions to get copies of the required documentation.

Under legislation passed in 1993, the federal government requires states to begin recovery of Medicaid money from estates of recipients who have passed away. In other words, after the death of Medicaid patient the state can lay claim against and force the sale of exempt assets, such as a house. So without proper planning, Medicaid eligibility may not save family assets from being exhausted on Medicaid cost.

Call your local or state Medicaid office for information. Better yet, consult an Elder Care attorney in your area prior to applying for Medicaid, especially if there is any question about eligibility—either financial or medical.

make it difficult for you to get coverage.

Altogether, 10 different standard medigap plans have been created, labeled A through J. They are sold as "medigap supplements." Each state decides which of the plans may be sold to its residents, so you may not find all 10 plans available where you live. But wherever they are sold, all A plans are alike in the coverage they provide. So are all Bs, all Cs, and so on, right down the line. The only differences is cost; you'll find a wide range of prices. Some companies insure healthier people. If you didn't apply during the six-month window, some companies will use health factors to weed out people who are considered higher risk.

When evaluating the 10 supplemental plans, consider what you need and what you can afford. That will help determine what medigap plan is best for you. Call Weiss Ratings, Inc. (1-800-289-9222) to order a list of medigap policies and premiums in your area. Weiss also rates Medicare HMOs and long-term care insurers.

How do Medicare and medigap fit in, if you are still working past age 65? Your employer will coordinate its health-insurance program with Medicare. In many companies, upon your retirement, the health plan turns into a medigap plan, so you don't have to buy your own medigap insurance. You must, however, enroll in Medicare Part B in order to get basic coverage. Other companies instruct you to buy your own medigap policy, but they'll cover the cost of the premiums.

Bottom line: Medicare may ease the plight of women who didn't have employer-sponsored health coverage before they retired. But health costs are still expensive and growing more so every year. Take care of yourself; the longer you stay healthy the more money you'll save. (Read "Long Term Care: Who's Going to Take Care of You When You're Old and Gray?" later in this section for a buyer's guide to how long-term care insurance can provide extra health protection for your old age.)

MANAGING YOUR RETIREMENT ACCOUNTS: WHEN DO YOU START SPENDING WHAT YOU'VE SAVED?

After 45 years of deferred spending, you no doubt feel like you're due for a mega shopping spree—or at least a cruise to the Bahamas. But wait! You've got to make that money last at least another 20 years, so make a plan. Just as you did when you were starting out, figure out what you have coming in and going out, how much interest your money needs to earn and how much more money you should be investing in order to keep enough coming in to live comfortably. A visit to a financial planner can help you understand your options and the changes you may need to make.

Financial experts generally predict that you will need 60 to 80 percent of pre-retirement income after you retire. This formula assumes that most debts will be paid off (and that's tending to be less and less the case; home debt among older Americans is growing at a faster rate than any other group), your children will be independent, income taxes will be lower, and certain work-related expenses (designer clothes and commutation) will be unnecessary. Other expenses may go up: medical, travel, and entertainment. There's no getting around the fact that things will not be the same; you will have to tighten your belt considerably.

Some Pre-Retirement Strategies. Try living for a month on 75 percent of what you spend now. If you find it difficult to do, start thinking about how you can bring more money in. Second job? Turning a hobby into a money-making venture? Starting a home business or consulting practice? Teaching?

Learn to take advantage of all the senior discounts. You probably look much younger than your age, and you'll have to ask for your discount. Don't be embarrassed! Think about how you can spend the money you're saving.

Plan vacations to areas of the country where you think you might want to retire and get a feel for whether you would really like to live there. If you're considering following the sun to a warmer part of the country, consider how you would feel living far from your family. Many retirees who move away end up moving back to their old stomping grounds to be near friends and family.

Take a long, hard look at your portfolio of investments. You will need to maximize the income from all of them. Many retirees worry about having enough money to live on, so they cling to "safe," fixed-income investments (even in their 401(k)s and IRAs), thereby exposing themselves to the risk that their assets might not

Tip: There are many financial decisions to be made during your pre-retirement and retirement years. Always know what you're signing. Here's a classic example of the need for caution. The Retirement Equity Act of 1984 requires that retirement benefits be paid in the form of a "qualified joint and survivor annuity." The annuity automatically pays an employee and his spouse a certain amount. If one dies, the survivor is paid a percentage of the amount that both were getting. There may come a time when your husband presents you with a waiver to sign, regarding his pension. You see, employees have the option of selecting a straight life annuity with no survivor benefits. However, the law requires written consent of the spouse in the form of a notarized waiver. Signing that waiver will provide a higher monthly income while your husband is alive, but nothing thereafter.

appreciate to keep up with inflation. Diversification is the answer. Talk to a financial planner a few years before retirement to make sure that you have the right mix of stocks and bonds in both tax-deferred retirement and non-retirement accounts to provide steady income from dividends and continued inflation protection for years to come. Decide whether you should shift the percentages around. A portion of both your tax-deferred retirement and taxed non-retirement assets should still be invested in growth stocks.

If your husband asks you to sign on the dotted line waiving your right to a portion of his pension after he dies, think carefully. If both of you have good pensions coming in, and you have income from Social Security, investments and proceeds from life insurance to bank on, you might be able to get along without his pension after his death. But if his pension is something you will be relying on to get by, you might want to ask him whether he shouldn't perhaps be considering your best interests and tear up the waiver, instead. By signing it, you risk losing money you might need to live on, and the odds aren't in your favor: 50 percent of women over 65 outlive their husbands by 15 years.

Upon retirement, have your 401(k) funds transferred directly into an Individual Retirement Account, along with your other IRAs. Keeping everything in one account will maximize your earnings power. Don't have the money sent to you for transfer (unless you ask that the check be made out to the new plan custodian FBO—for benefit of—your name). It's safer and easier to have it transferred directly from one plan custodian to another in something called a "trustee to trustee transfer." Why is this so important? Federal tax law requires employers or custodians to withhold 20 percent of any retirement disbursements. You'll get that 20 percent back as a tax refund, *as long as you roll the full amount of your disbursal over into another IRA or retirement account within 60 days.* But here's the catch: You must roll over the entire amount withdrawn. Since your plan administrator will have already withheld 20 percent, you'd have to replace that missing amount from other savings when you redeposit your disbursal into another IRA or be taxed on it come April 15. (Besides, why give the government extra money for that length of time, when it could be earning more interest for you?) The transfer process is easy—as simple as requesting the proper form from the new plan administrator, completing it and sending it in.

Withdrawal Pains. There will come a point when you must begin depleting your hard-earned savings. You won't have a choice: spending—or at least withdrawing some of the money—is mandatory. Minimum Required Distributions (MRDs) from your tax-deferred retirement accounts (traditional IRAs, 401(k)s, 403(b)s etc.) must begin by April 1 of the year following the year you turn 70½ or the year you retire, whichever is later. Fail to do so and you have to pay a 50 percent Federal penalty on the amount you should have taken out. When you make your withdrawals, you can't roll them over into another tax-deferred account. Of course, you don't have to wait until you're 70½ to begin withdrawing money. The magic age for withdrawals without penalty is 59½. The reason the government requires withdrawals from tax-deferred savings plans is that they were established to provide you with retirement income, not as a way to accumulate an estate for your heirs. However, your assets can be passed onto a beneficiary or beneficiaries of your choice if you die before depleting them.

You figure the MRD by dividing the balance at the end of your plan's fiscal year by the distribution period assigned to someone your age. Usually the company that administers your plan will calculate the MRD amount for you. You can also find many MRD calculators online by typing "MRD calculator" into a search engine.

The Tax Man Cometh...Finally. The tax hit on your qualified retirement savings accounts has been deferred for decades; now it's time to pay up. The good news is that you may now be in a lower tax bracket. You are going to pay federal income tax, plus state, if that applies, at your regular tax rate on your withdrawals. The only withdrawals that are not taxable are any after-tax contributions you may have made to your accounts, but you can't take those after-tax contributions out first or as a lump sum. They'll be figured in as a percentage of any withdrawal you take.

Withdrawals from a Roth IRA are tax-free (you used after-tax dollars to pay into them), provided that your contributions have been in the plan for at least five years and you're at least 59½ years of age. If you withdraw from an account that is not five years old or prior to age 59½, you pay ordinary income tax plus an additional penalty of 10 percent on the earnings (but not on the contributions). There are no penalties under the following circumstances: your death or disability (very restrictive); payment for unreimbursed medical expenses over 7.5 percent of adjusted gross income (or income after qualified deductions); payment for medical insurance after receiving unemployment compensation for more than 12 weeks; payment for qualified education expenses

for yourself and qualified family members; and for use as a down payment on the purchase a home. (You're entitled to withdraw up to $10,000 for the purchase of a first home for yourself, your children, your parents, or your grandchildren.) Because there are no minimum required distributions from a Roth IRA, this type of account can be used as an estate-planning tool.

Up to half of your Social Security income is taxable if your adjusted gross income, plus non-taxable interest income, plus half of your Social Security payment exceeds $25,000 for singles or $32,000 for a married couple filing jointly.

YOUR FINANCIAL LEGACY: PUTTING ON HEIRS

Estate planning is not just for those who have accumulated large sums of money or property holdings. Estate planning is necessary for anyone who expects to leave anything—money, investments, real estate, or personal property—to anyone. It helps to preserve and protect your assets for your heirs and ensures that your wishes will be followed. It is imperative if you have remarried or are living together with someone without benefit of a marriage contract.

Your estate is everything you own at the time of your death. The actual dollar value is not the key issue. Rather, what counts is that you set up a way to pass on most (if not all) of what you have accumulated to those whom you love and whom you expect to survive you.

Think of estate planning as a four-part process: 1) preparing a living will and health and financial powers of attorney, detailing what you want to have happen if you are incapacitated; 2) drawing up a will that clearly states and legally establishes how you want your property to be distributed; 3) minimizing federal estate taxes; and 4) establishing living or testamentary trusts.

You should have completed the first two parts of this four-step process when you entered your middle years. (If you haven't, don't waste time. Get them done now.) Next, take time to look back at your accomplishments. Did you achieve the goals and dreams that the little girl you once were dared to dream? Are there goals and dreams still to be accomplished? Setting aside the wherewithal to support yourself and follow those dreams, what will you have left to pass on to your heirs? Keep in mind that your legacy isn't just financial. Many people prepare statements, diaries, audiotapes, or videotapes to pass on values and hopes and dreams to their loved ones.

Here's what you need to know about living wills and powers of attorney:

Living will. The living will, also called an advance medical directive, is now recognized in most states. It is simply a signed statement from you to any medical professional who might care for you, detailing the kind of treatment you wish to receive—and not receive—under certain circumstances, in the event that you are unable to participate in decisions about your care. You can also use the living will to state your desire to be an organ donor. Each state has legal forms for you to use in declaring your living will. The form must be signed by you in the presence of two adult witnesses. Once you've made out a living will, discuss your wishes with your family and your physician. Give a copy of your living will to all of your doctors, your attorney, and to family members. Keep the original copy at home and readily available with your other personal papers—not in your safe deposit box. Your living will stays in effect until you revoke it. (Obtain the correct form for your state at www.medlawplus.com.)

Health power of attorney. A power of attorney is a formal document that gives a specific person the legal authority to act for another person. A health power of attorney restricts that authority to medical matters. With this document, you give someone else the authority to make medical decisions for you, if you are unable to do so. That person is not usually a doctor. Rather, it is a friend or relative. It empowers the person you designate to hire and fire medical personnel, to make decisions about such matters as surgery on your behalf, and to visit you in the hospital even when visiting rights are limited to immediate family. Some of those decisions may be guided by the wishes you articulate in your living will. Important: Be sure to name an alternate designee.

Tip: If your retirement plan includes company stock, and that stock has gained in value since you received it, you may want to separate it out from the rest of the plan funds transferred. Take the stock as a taxable distribution and, if your tax situation permits, receive the long-term capital gains preferred tax rate. Your options and the tax consequences of your actions at this time are myriad, and you might do best to consult a financial planner before you make your move.

Financial durable power of attorney. Use a durable power of attorney to authorize another person to handle money matters for you if you are incapable of doing so yourself. You can limit that person's authority in any reasonable way—

only check writing or transferring money from a savings account to a checking account, for instance—or give the person total decision-making power. If the person you are appointing is to be allowed to handle real estate transactions, you must formally record the fact (in most states) in the recorder's office of the county where you live. Almost any financial institution will accept your power of attorney, as long as it is properly filled in, signed, and dated by you, witnessed by two adults, and notarized. Make sure that the person whom you appoint keeps your power of attorney in a safe place.

Where There's a Will . . . You should already have a will tucked away somewhere. As you approach retirement, sit down with a financial planner, go over your assets, and discuss best ways to pass them on to your heirs at your death. Six basic ways to transfer property, with their advantages and disadvantages are outlined in the box in this section called "Transferring Property: 6 Ways to Give It All Away." Below, we'll share some strategies for putting them to work for you.

Jointly held property. The advantage of holding property jointly with right of survivorship, is that doing so makes it exempt from probate; it passes immediately and automatically to the survivor. Among its other advantages: It is easy to set up. It assures the other joint owner of an inheritance. It can prohibit ancillary probate (i.e., a second probate, in another state). This can be valuable, for instance, if you own a vacation home in another state. Make sure the place is jointly held, so your executor avoids probate costs. Depending on the laws in your state, your creditors may not be able to seize jointly held property.

The disadvantages: Property cannot be sold without the signatures of both parties. If you and your spouse or partner split, or if one of you is absent or incapacitated and has not given a power-of-attorney to the other, a stalemate occurs. A joint bank account can be cleaned out by either partner. Because property passes immediately to the surviving partner without going through a will, neither partner has any power to make a predisposition or pass it on to another. Whoever becomes the survivor has the entire say. Gift taxes may be imposed. A bank can freeze the account, pending settlement of all claims on the estate, preventing the survivor from using the money in the meantime.

Put Your Trust in Trusts. A trust is an estate-planning tool useful for various purposes, the most common being to preserve income for yourself, your spouse, children, and/or grandchildren; to leave assets to a charitable organization; to minimize estate taxes; and to avoid probate. Basically, it is a legal contract that you create to hold title to assets, which can continue from one generation to another.

Estate tax is a federal transfer tax levied when property passes from one deceased person to the surviving heirs. There is something called the estate tax exclusion or "unified tax credit," set at $1.5 million in 2005 and scheduled to go up to $3.5 million by 2009; estates are exempt from tax up to that amount, minus any amount given away in excess of "lifetime gift tax exclusion," currently set at $11,000 per person per year. When one spouse dies before the other, the estate passes to the surviving spouse tax-free under the marital deduction; it's when the surviving spouse dies that the surviving estate becomes liable for estate tax. Other deductions used to reduce a taxable estate include funeral expenses and debts owed at the time of death.

Trusts are especially useful for women who remarry later in life, offering a secure way to provide for children from previous marriages, as well as each spouse. They are also useful for business owners who seek to limit taxable income. Creating a trust reduces your tax liability by transferring assets before your death. Types of trusts include:

Revocable Living Trust. You create and control this type of trust during your lifetime, and it continues, per your instructions, at your death, or in the event that you become incapacitated, managed by a successor trustee who is named by you. You can cancel it, amend it, or change the beneficiaries easily. At your death, the successor trustee takes over and follows your instructions regarding the distribution of your assets. Title to all assets that you want in the trust must be transferred to it, and you must notify all financial institutions about the transfers of title.

This type of trust has no immediate tax advantages; any income from dividends or capital gains must be reported on your personal income tax return, and revocable living trusts do not protect your assets from creditors or bankruptcy. But the assets don't have to go through probate, because you transferred title to the trust during your lifetime.

Irrevocable Living Trust. You can also minimize estate taxes by establishing an irrevocable living trust. Once property is placed in such a trust, you are no longer the owner and can't be taxed on it or its earnings. Create a charitable trust, and get a tax deduction on the value you've given up.

The downside: you give up control of assets that you may need in the future. And irrevocable is just that—you can't get it back.

Testamentary Trust. This type of trust is written into your will and doesn't become active until after your death. You have use of your assets during your lifetime, and they are transferred to the trust when the estate is settled, creating a stream of income for your beneficiaries. Testamentary trusts make sense for singles and single parents. They provide a way for one parent to shield assets from an estranged parent, naming the children as beneficiaries.

Bypass or Credit-Shelter Trust. If your estate is valued above the estate tax exclusion limit, avoid estate tax on the excess by placing it in a "bypass" or "credit-shelter" trust. The income from the trust goes to the surviving spouse during his/her lifetime, while the principal is directed to go to children, grandchildren, and any other beneficiary. (Ask your financial planner about how the "skip-generation tax," created to limit the amount of income that can be sheltered by passing it on to the grandchildren and beyond, will affect your estate.) The surviving spouse can be granted the right to receive funds from the principal, if needed. The assets of the trust are not considered part of the surviving spouse's estate at death. No jointly held assets can go into this type of trust. If you are creating such a trust for the benefit of your children from a previous marriage, you might want to be very specific about your new spouse's right to use the principal. For instance, specify "for medical reasons only." Many a trust has been invaded "as needed," leaving little remaining for the children.

TRANSFERRING PROPERTY: 6 WAYS TO GIVE IT ALL AWAY

METHOD	WHAT IT DOES	ADVANTAGE	DISADVANTAGE
Naming a Beneficiary to Insurance & Retirement Accounts	Transfers property after you die.	Easy to set up. Avoids probate.	None
Will	Transfers property after you die.	Only way to name a guardian for minor children. Can name specific beneficiaries.	Time and expense of probate. Can be contested.
Joint Tenancy	Surviving Joint tenant takes title after you die	Easy to set up. Avoids probate. Difficult to contest.	Does not avoid estate taxes.
Living Trust	Allows you to pass property directly to your beneficiaries.	Avoids probate. You control the property while alive. Privacy. Difficult to contest.	Attorneys' fees. Time and expense of retitling assets to go into trust. Management fees.
Testamentary Trust	Names someone to manage assets.	Protects inheritance for your beneficiaries, either children from a previous marriage or your partner. Difficult to contest.	Assets go through probate. Management fees.
Life Insurance Trust	Holds life insurance in an irrevocable trust.	Proceeds do not become part of your taxable estate. Difficult to contest.	Must be done 3 years before death if transferring trust. Difficult to contest. Can't have any existing policies.

Irrevocable Life-Insurance Trust. Set up this trust to purchase an insurance policy, and keep the proceeds of the policy out of your taxable estate. The trust uses funds that you have given it to pay the premiums. The proceeds of the policy go to your beneficiaries, free of estate tax, or can be used to pay estate taxes or for some other purpose. Because it's "irrevocable," once created you can't change any provisions, not even the beneficiaries.

Trusts aren't the only method used to limit estate tax and pass wealth on to heirs. Two other popular methods include:

Giving or buying life insurance. Under federal law, the proceeds from a life-insurance policy will not be included in your taxable estate, if you don't own the policy. So if you already own a policy, you could transfer ownership to someone else—but you must do so at least three years before your death. Before you transfer ownership of a life-insurance policy, think it over carefully. The new owner can name the policy's beneficiaries (or change any you have named), borrow against the policy, select payment options, surrender, convert, or cancel the policy.

An insurance policy can also be taken out by someone other than the insured: Adult children from an earlier marriage can own a policy on your life, and you and your new spouse can take out policies on each other's lives.

Making tax-free gifts. Federal tax law currently allows you to give as much as $11,000 a year (the gift tax exclusion) to as many people as you want, without filing a gift-tax return. The recipient does not have to declare the money as income or pay income tax on it. But if you go over the $11,000 limit to any one person in any given year, you must declare that amount, and it will be applied against your lifetime unified estate tax credit, i.e., the estate-tax exclusion. Over time, if you have the money, you can give away substantial amounts in this way—to your live-together, your children from an earlier marriage, to a favorite charity (ask your financial planner about creating a family foundation for charitable contributions), and the recipient won't owe tax on it. Anything you give (cash or stocks) is removed from your estate. You might want to help an adult child or grandchildren pay for college or buy a home. But be sure to weigh your generous impulses against your future needs.

Avoid a Paper Chase: Create an Estate File. The amount of paperwork involved in settling up an estate can be monumental. Do your heirs (and yourself) a favor and set up an estate file. Ask your husband to create it with you, or walk you through where everything is, so you won't have to scramble, should he die before you do.

Your estate file should include a list of all assets that you and your husband own, individually or jointly, as well as liabilities, owed individually or jointly; location of the safe-deposit box and a list of the contents of the box; a copy of your and your husband's will (your lawyer should keep the originals, which will be filed with the probate court); life-insurance policies; Social Security records and cards; marriage certificate; divorce agreement (if applicable); military discharge papers (if applicable); trust agreements you or your husband have set up or are beneficiary to; latest statements for all financial accounts that are held individually or jointly (including checking, money-market, brokerage, mutual-fund, employer pension and benefit plans, and retirement accounts, such as IRAs and Keoghs); a list of all credit cards held individually or jointly; title and deed to real estate, auto registration or lease agreements; tax returns for the last three years; and partnership agreements and business contracts.

Naming an Executor: Keep It in the Family. The final step in setting up your estate is to name an executor, someone who will manage the transfer of property to your heirs. It's either going to be a headache or an honor, or both, for whomever you ask to be the executor or co-executor of your estate. But if you've got a family member who's reliable, cares about your beneficiaries, is somewhat sophisticated about finances, lives in the state, and can carry out the detail work that probating an estate entails, appeal to that person to be your executor. Relatives understand the family's needs better than anyone else. And if the executor is also a beneficiary, there's incentive to complete the task quickly.

This is a time-consuming job and, unless the family member flatly turns down a fee, because he or she doesn't need it or it doesn't make sense tax-wise to get it, the executor should be paid—family member or not. Rates for executors vary from state to state, and are often limited by the probate court or by a statutory schedule of fees. They are usually 1 to 2 percent of the estate, but can go higher. Even so, this works out to far less than the $150 to $350 an hour, or the flat fee (generally 2 to 3 percent of the total value of the estate) that an attorney might charge. Don't be surprised if the executor has to hire an estate attorney at some point during the probate, which will incur an additional charge.

If you suspect there might be disagreements among your heirs, name a professional executor and a family friend to serve as co-executors. They should be able to work together more harmoniously than two grieving or feuding siblings, because they won't carry the same emotional baggage.

What exactly does an executor do? It could be more extensive, depending on the complexity of the estate, but basic responsibilities include: filing your original will with the probate court; taking an inventory of your assets and filing the inventory with the court within a prescribed time (usually two or three months after death); finding your creditors and paying all claims; filling out form after form after form, among them, filing for life insurance and Social Security death benefit, filing tax returns and distributing final accountings to interested parties; and, last and most important, distributing assets to beneficiaries.

A TALE OF TWO WIDOWS— AND WHAT YOU CAN LEARN FROM THEIR EXPERIENCE

The average age of a widow in this country is 56; she will live 27 years or more alone. Some are better prepared than others. Here are two widows with very different stories.

Natalie was left well provided for. Her husband, who died suddenly, at age 56, was a professor and researcher at a state university. The university had a 403(b) plan, which is similar to a 401(k). Contributions were mandatory; the fund had 30 years of contributions and provided a substantial retirement nest egg for Natalie. Natalie had always kept the records, so she knew where everything was located, and, as a result, her grieving process and transition into widowhood were made more bearable. Her biggest problem occurred when she found that the safe deposit box was sealed. But the bank allowed her to get the will out of it, with a bank official standing close by.

Meanwhile, Barbara, whose husband was an attorney, was left in a precarious situation. She was never involved in the family finances, nor had she ever worked, and she didn't know where any of the important paperwork was. "Alan was sick for many years. He kept on saying, 'Don't worry. Everything is taken care of, and you'll be well provided for'," she recalls. He had invested in real estate partnerships, which had taken a beating. They were almost worthless at the time of his death. He had also borrowed on the equity in their primary residence and on his life insurance to make up for some of the losses.

The house had to be sold immediately, and Barbara took a job as a sales clerk in an upscale store. "I went from being a princess to being a pauper," she says. "I didn't have an extra dollar to put into a retirement plan." Fortunately, 10 years later, the partnerships were sold at a substantial profit. Her advice to women: "Acquire a skill, or update those that you have. Don't wait until you are put in a situation where you will need to support yourself, if you don't already. And know where all the papers are hidden!"

During their marriage, Barbara had approached Alan many times, asking about their finances and the location of important papers. He would get defensive. "So I backed off. I was completely in the dark. When he died everything was different from what I expected," she says. "I thought I was going to be a rich widow. Instead, I found myself up to my eyeballs in debt. Alan's papers were in his office file, but they were in a shambles, and it took years to unscramble the mess. His real estate partner and I would find little scraps of paper with notations that meant very little to us. I became frustrated and very angry, which made me feel guilty."

Not being able to find important papers after the death of your husband not only causes unnecessary stress at a time when you have enough to worry about; it also can result in costly mistakes. For instance, if a will or copy of one cannot be found, then the estate will be settled by the laws of the state in which you live. This can hold up settlement at a time when you may badly need money. Similarly, a misplaced or lost life insurance policy can mean that a beneficiary waits months to receive the proceeds on the policy. The state can refuse to license a car or boat on which the personal-property tax has not been paid. You cannot transfer title to the car without a certificate of title. Then there are all the major medical and other insurance claims that need filing. Make a habit of getting a photocopy of all receipts and claim forms, so that you can file all claims promptly. Be sure to make and keep copies.

Records can be replaced, but it takes time, effort, and postage to do so. Take stock certificates. If you own more than one or two, you should maintain an accurate list by name, number of shares, purchase price, and date of purchase. Compiling such a list after your certificates have been lost, stolen, or destroyed can be a horrendous task, and you may end up with incomplete records. Consider this: Before any company will issue a replacement certificate, you must sign an affidavit that the certificate was destroyed. You must also put up a surety bond, which may cost as much as 3 percent of the current market price.

Widow's Survival Kit. Besides good friends and family, a widow will need to locate, as quickly as possible, her husband's will, his and her Social Security cards, the marriage certificate, any life insurance policies, his military discharge papers, and his birth certificate. She will also need to find the birth certificates for any minor children. All of these documents will be required in order to claim proceeds from life insurance, Social Security benefits, and veteran's benefits. She should request at least 12 copies of the death certificate from the funeral home; they will be needed to transfer property and as proof of death in order to receive benefits.

There will be many decisions to be made involving your home and finances; give yourself time to grieve first. An excellent first-person account of the solitary emotional journey that widows take is Ruth Coughlin's *Grieving: A Love Story*. Every expert cautions widows not to make any important decisions quickly. Take at least six months to a year to adjust to your new life situation, as a woman on her own again, and evaluate carefully what your next steps should be. If you haven't handled the family's finances before, talk with friends, consult a financial planner, and begin to get a handle on the kinds of decisions you'll soon be making—to sell or not to sell the house, whether to take your husband's pension and insurance proceeds as a lump sum or in payments, how to invest them, when and whether to return to work, and what to do about health insurance. If you relied on your husband's health coverage, relax; that will be extended for 36 months under COBRA, so you have time to research other options. If your husband owned a business, you will have another set of questions to

deal with. Again, do nothing quickly. Study your options and weigh the tax and earnings implications of every move you make—both for yourself in the near term and for your heirs in the long term.

Financial planners suggest that placing estate funds in CDs, money-market accounts, or bank savings accounts is fine in the short term. Your first priority should be to look at assets, liabilities, and expenses, and—as you did when you first started out on your own—create a spending plan, or budget. Establish an emergency fund that you can tap into for unexpected expenses and opportunities, evaluate insurance and retirement needs, set long-term goals, and begin investing for those goals. Consult a financial planner and a lawyer to help you create your own estate plan.

And stay in touch with that little girl in the photo we've asked you to look at before you begin each day, the girl, full of hopes, dreams, ambitions and ideas, that you were long before you met your husband. You've been taking care of her; now let her take care of you. Tap into her essence. She would want you to be happy. If you listen to your inner voice—her voice—you'll receive comfort and encouragement and

Tip: If you are entitled to retirement benefits on your own work record, you can elect to take reduced retirement payments based on your own record at age 62, and then switch to the unreduced widow's benefit at full retirement age, if it's higher than what you're getting on your own record. Or you could elect to receive reduced widow's benefits at age 60 (or 50 if you are disabled), then switch to your own benefit, if it's higher than your reduced widow's benefit, as early as age 62. Do the math or consult a financial planner before you decide.

the strength to go on…even to laugh and enjoy life again.

How to Handle Your Life Insurance Proceeds. If your late husband had life insurance, your first decision will be how to take the money that is coming to you as beneficiary. The proceeds of your late husband's life insurance policy might be the only money you have to live on, until the estate is settled. These funds are available to you immediately, since they do not have to go through probate.

The insurance company has several settlement options. Some insurance policies specify the choice at the outset—not a good deal for you and this option should be avoided when any policy is purchased. It locks in how the money is to go to the beneficiary, and that settlement option might not serve your needs at the time of death. The best decision a widow can make is to let the insurance company hold the proceeds of the policy until she makes an educated decision about how she wants to handle the proceeds. Do not be rushed into it, and do not let anyone else make it for you. Here are the options:

Lump sum. This means you get a check immediately for the full amount of the policy, less any amount that may have been borrowed from cash surrender values. If you have other investments, and if you are knowledgeable about investing (or have good advice and are willing to learn), this is a good option. The lump sum settlement offers many advantages—you should be able to get a better return on investment than the insurance company provides.

Interest only. This means the insurance company holds the principal amount but pays you the interest it is earning. This is a good holding position, while you decide what to do with the proceeds.

Fixed installments. At stated intervals, you receive a check for a fixed amount, until the money is all used up. The company also pays interest on the remaining balance it is holding during the process.

Fixed period. The company agrees to pay you the proceeds, plus accrued interest, over a certain period. The size of each check depends on the length of time over which the proceeds are spread. In effect, you are buying an annuity.

If you choose the fixed installment or fixed period option, make sure you have the right to change your mind and withdraw the entire sum at any later date.

If you are considering the annuity option, check out plans available from other companies in addition to what your insurance company is offering. Get the highest monthly income possible for each $1,000 you invest.

Should You Pay Off the Mortgage? It's tempting to do so, but it may not be wise, even if you have enough proceeds from the insurance policy to do so. The money you will use to pay it off could most likely be invested at higher rates of interest. If the mortgage is close to being paid off, the monthly payments are small, and the rate of interest is probably low. So take a good close look at the mortgage situation, consult a financial professional, and find out how you can use your money in the most effective way possible to maximize its earnings power. Your goal is to have it earn enough interest income to last you the rest of your life.

Check out annuity options in "Beyond 401(k)s and IRAs: Why Women Should Consider Annuities," earlier in this chapter, and read "My Money Manager—or Me?" in Chapter Ten, for a blow-by-blow description of how one woman, a financial professional herself, approached selecting a financial planner/investment broker whom she could feel comfortable with to help her invest a windfall.

LONG-TERM CARE: WHO'S GOING TO TAKE CARE OF YOU WHEN YOU'RE OLD AND GRAY?

We've said it before: Women outlive men, on average, by about seven years. If you have children, they may well live far away. So, who will take care of you when you're old and gray? What will happen if you develop a chronic illness or disability? If this question keeps you up nights worrying, long-term-care insurance might be the answer for you. Given the fact that daughters almost always end up responsible for the care of their elderly parents—and according to a recent Met Life Mature Institute study, caregivers lose an average of $659,139 in lost wages, Social Security, and pension benefits over their lifetime. If you don't consider long-term-care insurance for yourself, you might want to consider it for your mother and father, just to make things easier (and cheaper) for yourself in the long run. Here's what you need to know about it.

What Does This "Care Package'"Cover— and How Much Does It Cost? Long-term care goes beyond medical care and nursing care to include all of the assistance you could possibly need if you ever have a chronic illness or disability that leaves you unable to care for yourself for an extended period of time. Several levels of care exist:

Skilled nursing care is the sort of care provided in a nursing home. One year in a nursing home can average more than $60,000, according to the Met Life Mature Market Institute. In some regions of the country, it can cost twice that amount.

Intermediate care, or custodial care, is at-home care, which is often supervised, though not performed, by a registered nurse. Such care can range from dressing and bathing to housekeeping chores. Further help may be needed managing medications, shopping, keeping medical appointments, or paying bills. Having a nurse's aid come into your home is less expensive than the cost of a nursing home, but it adds up, too: Bringing an aide into your home three times a week (two to three hours per visit) can easily run you $1,000 a month. Most policies limit the daily amount covered to no more than four hours.

Adult day care is custodial care that is provided in a private facility, often affiliated with a nursing home. It is useful as a means of giving the primary caregiver a break for several hours a day. You can generally receive intermediate and adult day care without prior admission to a hospital or nursing home. However, you will need a letter from a physician to demonstrate the policyholder's inability to dress, bath, etc. There probably will also be a test for mental competence.

A comprehensive policy will cover both nursing-home care and home care. There are also nursing-home-only and home-care-only policies on the market. The home-care option is important for a woman who wants to remain in her own homes and has no family caregiver nearby. Another option is payment for health services in an assisted-living facility, in the event that it is no longer feasible to stay at home.

Bitter Pill. Generally, long-term care is not covered by health insurance. About one-third of all nursing-home costs end up being paid out-of-pocket by the individuals or their families. Granted, the medicine—long-term-care insurance—is a bitter financial pill to swallow. It can be very expensive; the amount you pay is dependent on the level of services you want and the length of time you need care. But the alternative—paying everything out of pocket—could be even more expensive.

Your premium will be determined, based on the following factors:

Age: According to The Health Insurance Association of America (www.hiaa.org), in 2002, a policy offering a $100-per-day long-term-care benefit for four years and at-home care, with a 20-day elimination of deductible period, cost a 50-year-old about $950 per year. (Elimination of deductible periods refers to the number of days you must be in residence at a nursing home, or the number of home visits you must receive, before policy benefits begin. Most policies offer a choice of deductible from zero to 180 days. The longer the elimination period, the cheaper the policy. If you chose a 100-day elimination period, you are responsible for the first 100 days of care.)

The same policy would cost about $1,800 for a 65-year-old and $5,800 for a 79-year-old. A 5-percent inflation rate is factored into these figures. Premiums generally remain the same each year, unless they are increased for an entire class of policyholders at once. So, the younger you are when you buy the policy, the lower your premium will be.

Benefits: The premium is based on the amount of the daily benefit and how long you want that benefit to pay. A policy that pays $150 per day for four years will cost less than one paying $200 per day for the same period.

Your medical history: Pre-existing conditions are health problems you have when you apply for insurance. Insurance companies may require a period of time to elapse before the policy pays for care related to a pre-existing condition. You may be denied benefits during that period, which is usually six months. Make sure that the information on your application is accurate; if you try to fudge the details and the insurance company finds out, future claims may be denied.

Best Policies. There are several types of policies available. The type you choose will also affect your premium.

Indemnity Policies: These pay up to a fixed benefit amount, regardless of what you need. They are also called "per diem" policies.

Expense-Incurred Policies: With these, you choose the benefit amount when you purchase the policy. You are reimbursed for actual expenses for services received, up to a fixed dollar amount.

Integrated—or Pooled-Benefit—Policies: Here, you purchase a total amount that may be used for different types of long-term services. There is usually a daily, weekly, or monthly dollar limit for all of your long-term-care expenses. For instance, a maximum benefit amount of $150,000 would provide for 1,000 days of coverage, with a daily benefit of $150.

You usually have a choice of a daily benefit amount, ranging from $50 to more than $300 per day, for nursing-home coverage. The daily benefit for at-home care may be less. You are responsible for the actual costs that exceed the daily amount purchased. No plans cover all expenses fully.

The Fine Print. Look for these terms in the verbiage to evaluate a policy before purchasing:

Inflation adjustment is important, because the per-day benefit you buy today may not be enough to cover higher rates in the future. In some policies, the benefit amount will increase each year by a specified amount (such as five percent), compounded over the life of the policy.

Renewability means that the policy you purchased cannot be canceled, as long as you pay the premium and as long as you disclosed your health on the application.

Waiver of premium allows you to stop paying premiums while you are receiving benefits. Generally, there are some restrictions, such as required time in a nursing home—typically 90 days.

Duration or dollar limitations of benefits refers to the limits most policies place on benefits, to a maximum dollar amount or maximum number of days. You may also have separate benefit limits for nursing home, assisted-living facility, and home health care within the same policy. For instance, a policy may offer $150 per day, up to five years, in a nursing home, and only $80 per day, up to five years, of assisted-living and home-health coverage.

Have a policy and considering switching? Granted, new long-term-care policies may have more favorable provisions than older ones. For instance, newer policies usually do not require prior hospital stays before benefits begin. Pre-existing condition clauses, however, will apply all over again when you purchase a new policy, and your new premium may be higher because it is based on your current age. So don't switch, if you have an older policy, before you are sure that the new one is better than the one you currently have. And never drop the old policy before the new one is in force.

Tax Benefits. The Health Portability and Accountability Act of 1996 gives long-term health insurance the same tax treatment as accident and health insurance. That means that your premiums for long-term-care insurance, as well as your out-of-pocket expenses for long-term care, can be applied toward meeting the federal tax code's 7.5 percent floor for medical expenses (medical expenses are deductible, if the amount exceeds 7.5 percent of your adjusted gross income). However, there are limits, depending on the policyholder's age, for the total amount of long-term premiums that can be applied toward the minimum. Before you buy the insurance, ask your accountant whether you will be eligible for the deduction.

What Are the Odds of Me (or My Parents) Ending Up in a Nursing Home? While we think of long-term care as something only the very old need, the U.S. Government Accounting Office estimates that 40 percent of the 13 million people receiving long-term-care services are between the ages of 18 and 64.

A study by the Department of Health and Human Services indicates that people over 65 face at least a 40-percent lifetime risk of entering a nursing home. Many of these are going into a nursing home for the 100 days that Medicare allows for the short-term skilled care needed after a hospitalization. Medicare, however, only picks up the total cost for 20 days. After that point, up to 100 days, you pay a co-payment of $101.50 per day, and Medicare picks up the rest. You are on your own after 100 days.

About 10 percent of those over 65 will stay in a nursing home for five years or longer. The odds of entering a nursing home, and staying for longer periods, increase with age. Statistics show that 22 percent of those 85 and over are in a nursing home. A large percentage of those needing long-term care are provided for at home by family members and friends. Many people require non-medical care to help with daily tasks. If you or your parents fall into this category, check www.comfortkeepers.com.

Buyers' Guide: The Long and Short of It. You have to consider many factors before you purchase long-term-care insurance: your net worth, your age, your marital status, how much you are willing to spend on health care, and how much you want to leave to your heirs. Then you have to take into account your family history. If longevity or a chronic disease runs in your family, you may well need long-term care in the future. The idea is to purchase a policy before you need it, preferably in your fifties or early sixties.

If you decide to purchase it, make sure you buy a policy you can afford. Ask yourself: Can I afford the premiums now—and will I be able to keep them up in the future? What will you do when your income drops, if you are widowed? If you have to let the policy lapse, you'll lose the thousands of dollars you already paid into it.

Next, figure out how long you could pay for your own care. This will help determine the elimination period. Take into account that 52 percent of nursing-home stays last three months or less; about one-third last one year or more.

Choosing a policy is very complicated. There are many different policies and many options to choose from, so do your homework before you sit down with an agent. For more guidance, call your State Insurance Department or write to the National Association of Insurance Commiss-ioners (2301 McGee Street, Kansas City, MO, 64108-3600) and ask for the "Shopper's Guide to Long Term Health Insurance."

Long-term-care insurance is probably not a good idea for women with limited income and low non-housing assets, since they may qualify for Medicaid assistance. A woman with high income and substantial assets can probably pay for her own care. However, she might consider the insurance as a means of protecting her assets for her children. If you or your parents fall in between these two categories, then it's wise to consider long-term health insurance. Martha is in this category; she learned by example the benefits of such insurance. Martha's mother was in a nursing home for 13 years, after suffering a major stroke. "For the last five years of her life, she didn't recognize me," remembers Martha. "She was 88 when she died. My father had little left after paying for my mom's care for 13 years," she recalls. "I don't have the assets that he had, and I don't want to depend on my children. My dad could afford the care for my mom, but I'm alone," she explained. Martha purchased a long-term-care policy when she was 60. Since then, she has had a hysterectomy and lumpectomy.

Barbara, on the other hand, is more worried about having to assume the responsibility of primary caregiver for her widowed mother. She knows that her two brothers, who live farther away, won't be able to help out much. "Mom is always telling us she doesn't want birthday or Christmas gifts anymore, but we buy them anyway. Finally, we all got together with Mom and discussed long-term-care insurance. It took a while, but she finally accepted the idea that we would pay the premiums for her, instead of buying other gifts. We split the cost three ways."

If you can afford it, long-term-care insurance will give you enormous peace of mind. If you can get your children to buy it for you, all the better!

THE CHALLENGE OF THE SANDWICH GENERATION: WOMEN SQUEEZED THE HARDEST

Women are pulled twice into care-giving situations, first with their own children and later, or sometimes even at the same time, as the primary caregivers of their aging parents. This phenomenon, called "the sandwich effect," was created as a result of a combination of factors: women have been delaying child-bearing into their 30s, and their parents are living longer. The financial costs have been measured, and they are staggering: it is estimated that each caregiver (and most of them are women) loses an average of $659,139 in lost wages, Social Security, and pension benefits, over her lifetime. That's on top of the nearly a million dollars in lost wages, Social Security, and pension benefits women lose as a result of the wage gap and years spent at home raising their children.

The emotional costs are immeasurable, and perhaps even more devastating. Below, contributing editor Elizabeth Kaminsky puts a human face—that of her mother—on the numbers as she describes her caregiving experiences and what they taught her. As difficult as they were, oh, what she wouldn't give for five more minutes, brushing her mother's hair.

If you are the caregiver ...

Don't Pass Up This Tax Deduction: If you are providing financial support to your parents or another elderly relative, you may be able to claim that person as a personal exemption on your tax return. You must be able to document that you provide more than half of the person's support for the tax year. Support includes clothing, shelter, medical expenses, and transportation. The potential dependent's gross income cannot be higher than the personal exemption for that tax year, which currently is $3,200. But Social Security and tax-free income are not included in that figure.

Isabel shared the expenses with her brother. "We each filed a multiple-support agreement," said Isabel, "which allowed me to take the deduction one year, then Bob took it the next year." Isabel is referring to Federal Tax Form 2120. Often, the sibling who would receive the highest dollar benefit from the claim, which is usually the one in the highest tax bracket, takes the deduction.

Or This Tax Credit: You may be eligible for the Child and Dependent Care Credit, to cover day care expenses for your elderly relative, if both you and your spouse work (unless the dependent is your spouse) and the dependent lives with you. The credit is a percentage, based on your adjusted gross income, of the care expenses you paid to a care provider, up to a maximum of $3,000 for one individual (or $6,000 for two or more). This is the same credit you may have taken for day-care expenses for your children.

Do You Know About the Family Medical Leave Act? This federal law requires an employer with at least 50 employees to offer unpaid leave for 12 weeks during any 12-month period to care for an immediate family member with a serious health condition. The leave can be continuous, taken intermittently or on a reduced schedule basis.

THEIRS IS A LABOR OF LOVE . . .
BUT WHO CARES FOR THE CAREGIVERS?

BY ELIZABETH KAMINSKY

Wanted: Sensitive, capable, reliable professional to act as a caregiver. Must be available to work 10 to 40 hours per week, in addition to holding another full-time job. Responsibilities may include, but are not limited to: bathing, dressing, feeding, cooking, cleaning, shopping, administering medicines, scheduling, and transporting patient to all doctor's appointments. Must also provide physical therapy, psychological counseling, bill paying, home maintenance, entertainment and recreational activities. Volunteers only need apply, as monetary compensation WILL NOT be provided.

Would you apply for that job? I certainly wouldn't, but like many other women, I ended up doing it anyway.

Overachiever that I am, I did it twice. Right now, more than 44 million people, 60 percent of whom are women, are following in my footsteps. As we baby boomers age and live longer, even more of us will take a spin on the care-giving carousel.

It's been about eight years since I was a full-time caregiver. When I was in the thick of it, I didn't have time to contemplate the toll it took on me, financially or emotionally. I was just too busy doing all those things in that job description. Now that I have a little more time to think, I've done a little digging to see what the current state of affairs is for caregivers. What I discovered knocked me for a loop.

Met Life's Mature Market Institute did a study, appropriately named "Juggling Act," to follow up on prior work by the National Alliance for Caregiving (NAC). They were able to quantify the significant loss of wealth that caregivers reported as a result of their responsibilities. Totaling up lost wages, Social Security, and pension benefits, each caregiver lost an average of $659,139 over her lifetime. Whew—that's a boatload of dough! Now I know why there's only a tiny egg in my retirement nest. The others flew the coop, along with a few promotions, a cool job in Phoenix, and an exchange program in London.

Lost wages and retirement benefits are not new problems for women. The same thing happens when we take a few years off to care for young children, to the tune of nearly a million dollars (for the college-educated professional). Nowadays, many women whose careers were interrupted once for the kids are being pulled away a second time, just as their careers are getting back on course, to care for their aging parents. Nearly one out of four U.S. households (22.4 million) provides care to a relative or friend aged 50 or older. Three out of four caregivers are women, and their average age is 57, according to the American Society on Aging. African American women are the hardest hit by this sandwich effect, according to a joint study by NAC and the American Association of Retired Persons (AARP).

A Big Bite in the Pocketbook. Something else in the NAC/AARP study struck me. In addition to all of the time spent providing unpaid care—and the cost in lost wages and benefits—caregivers shell out more than $200 each month for their recipients' care. That's a mighty big "out-of-pocketbook" expense. That information was no surprise to my friend Louise. For the last four years, she has provided care for her 83-year-old mother who lives about 30 miles away. Between the trips back and forth, often twice a day, Louise has spent her fair share on cars, gas, and tolls, not to mention food shopping and pharmacy expenses. (Her mother had just enough annual income, $19,000, to keep her from qualifying for prescription-drug assistance.)

"I estimate that I spent between $30,000 and $40,000 a year on stuff just for Mom to live, not to mention having to take care of everything myself, including managing Mom's finances and paying her bills," Louise recounts. Her brother in California is "no help, financially or emotionally." He tells Louise he wants to "remember Mom the way she used to be." Last year, her mom's dementia worsened so much that she had to move her to an assisted living facility. Louise, like many caregivers, was so overwrought that she didn't think to consult an elder law attorney or financial planner. Had she done so, she may have been able to protect some of her mother's assets and perhaps inherited something to pay herself back for all of her care-giving expenses. "When you're in a crisis like I was, there's no thinking straight," Louise says. "I found an assisted living place that would cost roughly what I was spending each month on Mom and figured it would keep her safe and give me some peace of mind. I'd tried hiring home health aides for Mom, but that just didn't work out. I agonized about placing, Mom because she always made me promise never to put her in a nursing home."

Assisted living was a compromise. For $3,600 a month, Louise's mom gets food, shelter, and supervision, so that she doesn't wander off. Louise gets to cut her daily trips to three or four, instead of seven. Mom's assets have dwindled enough so that she now qualifies for some prescription assistance. Even so, Louise still digs deep into her pocketbook to pay for Depends, facial tissues, and baby wipes for her mother. Those "incidentals" aren't included in Mom's monthly rent. They run Louise between $200 and $250 a month.

Louise and her mom are in the unenviable position of being middle class. They have too much income to qualify for public-assistance programs and too little income to provide for the kind of round-the-clock care that her memory-impaired mother needs. When she goes to visit, Louise must still spend hours doing laundry, coaxing her mother to eat, changing soiled clothing or taking her mother to the doctors. Before you say that Louise should move her mom to a better facility, hold your tongue. The one her mom lives in is rated as one of the best in a 50-mile radius. In eldercare, $3,600 doesn't buy what you think it might.

In a way, Louise is lucky that she lives fairly close to her mother. Many caregivers have the added stress of being thousands of miles away. My friend Rae lives in New Jersey, and her father lives in Florida. She thought about moving him, but they both decided it is far too cold for him to change climates at this stage of his life. "I spent a long time feeling guilty every day for not moving down there. But, our jobs are here, and our kids love their school. Uprooting my family wasn't an option," she says. For now, Rae's father is okay. His complex provides transportation, and he has a lot of friends and activities to keep him busy. Rae goes to visit whenever she gets vacation time. "It was fine for the first few years. Now the kids are getting older, and they want to do something other than get dropped off at Disney World for the day." She figures she spends $3,000 to $5,000 a year in airfare for scheduled trips and maybe another $3,000 when she's had to go down in an emergency—theme-park admissions not included.

Time Is Money, Too. Is there any help to defray the costs of caregiving? The answer is, it depends. In my mom's case, she received a great deal of assistance with medical costs, because she had no assets and essentially no income. We decided not to have her declared as my dependent, because when we looked at the aid she received versus the tax breaks I would receive for taking care of her, it didn't make sense. Louise's situation is trickier, because her mother had some assets and an income that disqualified her for certain assistance programs. Both of us would have benefited greatly from meeting with an elder law attorney to help us better understand our options. My biggest cost savings came from friends who volunteered their services to me. For a few years, a Girl Scout troop even "adopted" my mother, providing her with companionship twice a month on days when I couldn't be there. A good place to start resource shopping is the U.S. Department of Health and Human Services' Eldercare Locator (www.eldercare.gov), which can link you up with programs in your community. The biggest mistake caregivers make is not asking for help, either from family members or government programs. Time is money when it comes to caregiving, too. If your siblings can't or won't chip in some cash, maybe they can take over for a day so that you can apply for Mom's aid.

Bumping Up Against "the Caregiving" Canopy.' Both Louise and Rae felt their careers suffered because of their care-giving responsibilities. I'll second that. We all commiserate that most of the time we were either feeling guilty about taking time off from work, or feeling guilty about being at work when we should have been care-giving. Louise adds, "I always feel like I'm not where I should be. I work for someone who truly doesn't understand. I know from the way she treats me in meetings and from the fact that she never puts me on any high-profile projects." I was fortunate that I worked for people who were pretty reasonable and understanding. Even so, my career suffered. Like these friends, I found myself banging my head on the caregiving canopy, the one that hangs just below the glass ceiling.

Lessons in Grit & Grace. We all agree that caregiving is easier when you know what your loved one expects. My mom could articulate what she wanted and didn't want, sometimes a little too loudly. But at least we could negotiate and she could participate in decisions about her care. Louise doesn't have that luxury. Her mom is too far gone to help with any decisions. They never planned for this, and now they are paying the price. Rae has learned from each of us that having some well-timed conversations with her father will make things so much easier for everyone concerned. My advice to future caregivers—have a heartfelt discussion with mom, dad, or your spouse. Ask questions like: How did your family handle caring for loved ones? How do you expect to be cared for? What happens if you can't stay at home?

I admire my godmother. When she lost her third husband, she got busy preparing for her own future. At 84, she figured that a fourth husband was a long shot (although the rumor around the assisted-living coffee pot says she has a boyfriend). Like me, she was a care-giver a few times over. We speak freely to one another about the "tough" issues. I helped her "shop" for an assisted-living community where she would feel comfortable aging in place. We looked at places in her hometown and around the area, and built up a good bit of experience. She settled on a place in Florida, near her son. She based her decision on her finances and on the services that the facility will be able to provide for her as she gets older and needs increasing care. She wants to be as independent as possible for as long as possible, and she picked her new home accordingly.

Her family is so lucky. I'll remind them of that if ever I hear them grumble about how much money it costs for her to live there. She has given them an enormous gift. She's spared them from making the tough decisions that my friends and I have made. I'm following my godmother's lead. I signed up for long-term care insurance.

There's a book I read once called *The Grit and Grace of Being a Caregiver*. I think those traits apply to care-receivers, as well. Nobody had more grit or grace than my mother. She was 52 when she became disabled. There were times when she would rail with anger because she needed me to walk her to the bathroom or put on her shoes. There were times when she would swallow her excruciating pain to cheer for me in the audience of one of my plays. And then there were times, when our life was almost ordinary, like when I was fixing her hair or fastening the back of her blouse. If I hadn't been her caregiver,

I wouldn't have been able to see the beauty in those simple acts. Even with all the years of lost time and lost wages, I'd be her caregiver again without hesitation, perhaps a little more wisely now. Like anyone who has loved and lost, I would give anything to spend another hour pushing my mother's wheelchair or five minutes more brushing her hair. While preparing for this story, I visited the Web site for the Rosalyn Carter Institute for Caregiving (www.rci.gsw.edu). The former First Lady was a caregiver, and she has dedicated time and money to helping others who are performing this labor of love. I have found wonderful resources to use there in my work with support groups. A quote appears when you access the site. It scrolls slowly across your screen one line at a time, saying, "There are only four kinds of people in the world—those who have been caregivers, those who are currently caregivers, those who will be caregivers, and those who will need caregivers."

If it were up to me, that quote would have one more line: "Take heart—because we're all in this together."

A CAREGIVER'S CARE PACKAGE

"When I was beginning my caregiving, the Internet was a twinkle in somebody's eye," writes Elizabeth Kaminsky. "So much information for caregivers is now available at the click of a mouse." If your care-giving responsibilities keep you too busy to investigate all the services and programs available to you, ask a friend— or your care-receiver—to help you check them out.

First stop, if you need financial aid, should be your county or state Department of Health and Human Services. Also contact area social-service agencies, such as Catholic Charities and local chapters of voluntary-health agencies, to find out if they offer financial support to caregivers. The National Association of Area Agencies on Aging will refer you to the area agency on aging nearest to your care-receiver. Call 1-800-677-

1116 or go to www.aoa.gov or www.eldercare.gov. Many area agencies on aging offer money-management programs.

Speaking of money management, exacerbating the caregiver's worries about how the cost of caregiving will impact her own finances, often there is concern over whether the care-receiver can still handle his or her own finances. To avoid problems, with your parents' permission, review checking account statements and other financial records and stay alert for these financial danger signs: numerous payments to credit-card companies, home shopping networks, sweepstakes, or other contests; payments for bills that already have been paid; unusually large donations to charitable or fraternal organizations; failure to list or track deposits and income; failure to record checks in the checkbook; lost checkbooks or bank statements; numerous transfers from savings to checking accounts; consistent or unusual payments to a person unknown to you—a possible sign of a scam; and unusual activity in a brokerage account.

What should you do if you find something out of the ordinary? Discuss the situation with your parent and other family members—even those who live far away—before you get involved in your parents' finances. Talking about money can be difficult in families where the subject has always been taboo. If your parents are unwilling to share financial details with you, try to get them to at least tell you where they keep their important financial papers and the name(s) of their lawyer, accountant, stockbroker, and other professionals. You might discuss your concerns with some of these professionals.

If you live far away or feel you can't take care of daily money management for your parent(s), consider using a daily money manager. These professionals offer a variety of services, from organizing and keeping track of financial and medical insurance records to help with check writing and checkbook balancing, as well as many other duties. Daily money managers charge $25 to $100 an hour, depending on the client's location and the complexity of the financial affairs. Some organizations provide volunteers who perform the same function. The American Association of Daily Money Managers (www.aadmm.com) can provide names of daily money managers in your parent's community or nearby.

For help handling the logistics of daily living, home-care services are available in many communities, offering assistance to the elderly with their personal care (bathing and dressing) and health care (giving medications, changing dressings) needs. Many communities also offer free or low-cost, door-to-door transportation services to take the elderly to doctors' visits, community facilities, and other activities. Meals-on-Wheels programs are available in most areas of the United States. An organization called Comfort Keepers (www.comfort-keepers.com) provides services to individuals or couples who are capable of handling their own physical needs but may require or desire some assistance with the daily

tasks of living. Their services include: in-home companionship, meal preparation, light housekeeping, grocery shopping, and transportation services. For legal questions, an excellent starting point is www.elder-lawanswers.com. Other useful resources include:

Consumer Consortium on Assisted Living
PO Box 3375
Arlington, VA 22203
703-841-2333

Medicine Program
PO Box 520
Doniphan, MO 63935
573-996-7300
www.themedicineprogram.com

National Association of Professional Geriatric Care Managers
1604 North Country Club Road
Tucson, AZ 85716
520-881-8008
www.caremanager.org

National Citizens Coalition for Nursing Home Reform
1424 Sixteenth Street, NW Suite 202
Washington, DC 20036
202-332-2275
www.nccnhr.org

National Council on the Aging, Inc.
409 Third Street, SW
Washington, DC 20024
202-479-6675 or 202-479-6672
www.ncoa.org

Well Spouse Foundation
30 East 40th Street PH
New York, NY 10016
800-838-0879
www.wellspouse.org

"I WAS AT A LOSS":
A CAREGIVER SHARES EIGHT AFFORDABLE SOLUTIONS TO THE ELDERCARE DILEMMA

BY PHYLLIS STAFF, PHD

"I'm one of the lucky ones. I can afford to do it," says Jan Smart (not her real name). Smart cared for her 96-year-old aunt in her home until three years ago. Then her aunt broke her hip, and caring for her at home became more than Jan could handle with her full-time consulting business.

At 82, Jan still maintains a crowded schedule, consulting with organizations all over the United States. "I have to net about $100,000 a year to pay for my aunt's care in a small adult family home. After I pay my own expenses, there's nothing left over to save for my retirement. Even though we include her Social Security in paying for her care, it takes every available penny. I'm glad I can still do it, but I wonder what would happen if I couldn't work."

Many caregivers, not as fortunate as Jan, ask similar questions. Eldercare is expensive. Costs routinely exceed $40,000 a year in the United States. In some areas, yearly nursing-home-care costs are more than $100,000. Few elders have set aside enough money to cover such expenses during their last years. And how many families have the financial means to pay for the high costs of eldercare. How do they manage?

That question suddenly became very personal, when my father was diagnosed with Alzheimer's disease. I was at a loss. When I began to look for an affordable place where my father could be well cared for, I couldn't find the kind of information I needed. I'd expected to be able to access at least as much information as I'd have available to me before buying a new car. I ended up doing the legwork myself. Below are the results of my search for affordable eldercare. One or more of these eight options might help you face the enormous financial challenge of caregiving. There's no doubt that the expenses associated with eldercare can be overwhelming, but I've found that, if you persevere in looking for something that works for you and your loved one, affordable solutions can be patched together.

1. Select the Most Suitable Care. Inappropriate levels of care ask too much or too little of the elderly resident and may increase the overall cost of care. Either can significantly reduce your loved one's quality of life, health, and finances. The assessment tools found on the following Web sites will help you determine the best level of care for your loved one: www.thebestisyet.net, www.carescout.com, and www.eldercareservices.com.

2. Look for Care Provided by Nonprofit Organizations. Research performed by Thebestisyet.net shows that, on average, nursing homes run by nonprofit organizations have about one-third fewer deficiencies and cost less than homes run by for-profit organizations. Homes run by large corporations, especially those that manage many facilities, have the greatest average number of deficiencies. By finding a nonprofit facility that provides suitable care, you could save thousands of dollars over the course of a year, and your elder may get better care.

A word of caution: I do not mean to imply that all nonprofit organizations provide good care or that all corporate homes offer poor care. It depends on the particular organization. Once you have visited a specific facility several times, you'll have a reasonably accurate notion of the quality of care offered there.

3. Investigate Low-Cost Housing and Housing Supplements for Seniors. Many large U.S. cities provide low-income housing for senior citizens. Because these housing units usually offer limited or no special services, many are appropriate only for seniors with no disabilities. Some cities offer a housing supplement (financial assistance) to income-qualified seniors. The supplement can be used for certain specified care services only, so make sure you fully understand the terms of assistance. Ask your city about the senior services available and qualification requirements.

4. Take in a Boarder. Consider exchanging a room in your home for part-time caregiving or other household chores. Try advertising in the local college paper or a small weekly publication. There are tax implications when you do this, however: the IRS considers such arrangements to be income to the senior. It requires the fair-market value of renting that room to be added to the senior's income. However, the security of having another person around the house can vastly outweigh the costs of added taxes for the senior. For more information about shared housing, check the National Shared Housing Resource Center's Web site: www.national-sharedhousing.org.

5. Share an Eldercare Apartment. Elderly couples and siblings often reduce costs by sharing an apartment in an eldercare facility. Usually the fees for a second person are only $300 to $500 a month more than the fees for one person alone. Roommates need not be related. You might find an elderly friend, or the facility itself may help you find a compatible roommate.

6. Qualify for Medicaid. Low-income seniors may receive Medicaid nursing-home care. Assisted Living care is rarely covered. Your state's Medicaid office will give you the most up-to-date information.

7. Ask for Volunteer In-Home Companion(s). Although volunteer companions may be harder to find in 2004 than in earlier years, they're still available. Check Senior Corps (www.seniorcorps.org) and Visiting Nurse's Associations of America (www.vnaa.org). Don't give up if you don't find a companion immediately: Ask your local government about senior volunteers. Post your request on bulletin boards in your church, in senior centers, and, as appropriate, with disease-specific organizations, such as the Alzheimer's Association (www.alz.org). Check with home health-care agencies. Many offer reasonably priced ($10 to $12 an hour) in-home companions.

8. Use Hospice Services. Medicare provides hospice care for patients nearing death. Many nursing and maintenance-care services and some medications are provided. A physician will determine whether your elder is eligible for hospice care. For the caregivers, hospice workers provide grief counseling and much-needed emotional support, as they come to terms with the fact that their caregiving days are coming to an end.

An experimental psychologist, Phyllis Staff, PhD, is the author of "How to Find Great Senior Housing: A Roadmap for Elders and Those Who Love Them." For more information, visit www.thebestisyet.net.

Female Finance Checklist: Your Golden Years

❑ **Goals:** Visit with that little girl in your favorite photograph—the one taken of you at 5 or 6 or 7 or 8, staring into the camera's lens with that "Look out, world. Here I come!" sparkle in your eyes—your whole life ahead of you. Look back on that life, so rich with experience. Surely, there are things that little girl dreamed of doing still left to be done. Tap into the "post-menopausal zest" that Margaret Mead wrote about and set the world—or your community—on fire with your passion and ideas and commitment to values and programs that are important to you. Run for political office, take up painting, write a book, go back to school, travel. It's now or never.

❑ **Career:** Chances are you're on a second or third career by now, or have launched your own business. Successful women have the ability to reinvent themselves to fit the times. Former stay-at-home moms who returned to work after their children were grown may now be hitting their stride, reaching for the top rung of the career ladder (or hitting the glass ceiling) just as their husbands begin to talk about retirement. Be prepared to be the sole breadwinner of the family now. Others may be called back to the home to care for ailing parents. Reach out to friends, family and social agencies for help. The caregiver's job is the toughest of all.

❑ **Investments:** Don't worry, but hurry, if you haven't saved enough for retirement. Step up your saving, take on a second, or part-time job, or a boarder to bring in extra cash to stash in your retirement kitty. Now is the time to find out what your Social Security and pension (if any) payments will be and decide which age you will begin to take them. If you've been married for at least 10 years, even if you are now divorced, compare the payment that your work record entitles you to with that of your husband's, and claim the higher of the two. Familiarize yourself with the laws regarding minimum required distributions from your tax-deferred retirement accounts. Meet with a financial adviser to evaluate your nest egg and, if necessary, reposition investments for continued growth to ensure that you will have enough to live comfortably. If you are a widow, you face many decisions now about pension rollovers, life insurance payouts and what to do with your home. Don't make any hasty decisions. Take the time to consider all of your investment options with an adviser.

❑ **Real Estate:** Now is when your real estate investment pays off. Your house, purchased 20 or 30 years ago, may have doubled or even tripled in value. You can now downsize to a smaller home and place the return on your investment in a high-interest mutual fund or annuity. Discuss your options with your financial planner. Alternatively, you could take out a reverse mortgage, if you need extra cash to make ends meet. Avoid reducing your equity through imprudent use of a home equity line of credit; otherwise, when you do sell, you won't come out ahead.

❑ **Insurance:** Invest in long-term care insurance for yourself (and your parents, if you and other family members can afford it). If you're eligible for Social Security on your own or a husband's work record, you're now also eligible for Medicare. Don't miss this deadline: Mark the date (from three months before to three months after your 65th birthday) when you must sign up. If you are a widow, you may have to decide how to take and invest the proceeds of your husband's life insurance policy.

❑ **Wills:** Schedule an estate planning session with your lawyer and a financial planner to evaluate your assets and look for ways to preserve their value for your heirs. Consider transferring assets before death into a trust, or giving a portion away to your heirs or charitable institutions, to escape estate tax, if the value of your estate warrants such moves. Review your will, living will, financial and medical powers of attorney, and make changes, if necessary. Sit down with your heirs and talk to them about your wishes. Let them know where all your important papers are. Most importantly, leave them a written or taped record of your hopes for them, as well as your own summation of what life for that little girl was like. Share your joy and wisdom, gained over the years. That's the best legacy of all.

PART TWO:
Success & Savings Strategies

CHAPTER SEVEN:

ESCAPING THE WAGE-GAP TRAP: HOW TO ASK FOR A RAISE AND OTHER SMART CAREER MOVES

Wear red on Equal Pay Day to symbolize how far women and minorities are "in the red" with their pay!

—Dress-for-success advice posted on the Web site of the National Committee on Pay Equity (www.pay-equity.org), a coalition of women's and civil right's organizations working to eliminate sex- and race-based wage discrimination

Mark this red-letter day on your calendar: April 19 is Equal Pay Day—the day on which women's earnings catch up to the amount men earned the year before. According to the committee, "Tuesday symbolizes the day when women's wages catch up to men's wages from the previous week." Every year, Equal Pay Day is observed on a Tuesday in late April to call attention to the wage inequity experienced by women and minorities.

Various activities, including protests, seminars, networking events, and public demonstrations are held to call attention to the problem. In Jacksonville, Florida, one year, for instance, the Women's Center sponsored a luncheon called "But I'm Worth It . . . How to Talk about Salary and Market Value." Minnesota activists sponsored an

"UnHappy Hour" event, in which attendees received ¾ of a cup of latte, ¾ of a muffin, and ¾ of a napkin to symbolize the almost ¾ of a dollar women are paid for every dollar men earn. In Washington, D.C., committee members handed out leaflets and PayDay candy bars to subway riders.

"Why all the fuss?" some of you may be wondering. The truth is that many women and even more men believe that equal pay—that rally cry of the Feminist Movement in the 1960s and '70s—has already been achieved. The wage gap isn't an issue in most women's minds any longer. They believe it doesn't exist—or at least it doesn't affect them. In fact, the daughters and granddaughters of those women's movement activists are still facing a wage gap that robs them and their families (yes, even men are hurt by this wage gap) of more than $4,000 per household annually, or $200 billion a year.

Today—42 years after the Equal Pay Act of 1963 was passed, making it illegal to compensate women less than men for the same work—women who work full time are paid 76 cents for every dollar men earn. What's worse—African American women earn 67 cents and Hispanic women earn 55 cents, according to the National Committee on Pay Equity (NCPE), which bases its figures on Census Bureau and U.S. Department of Labor statistics. (Only Asian-American women, who find their way into managerial or professional positions in greater numbers, manage to earn 80 cents per dollar men earn.) True, in 1963, we were only earning 59 cents, so some progress has been made. But, as the NCPE points out, that gain amounts to less than half a cent per year, and studies reveal that progress has come in large part as result of a lowering of men's wages, not an increase in women's wages. At the current rate of change, women won't achieve equal pay until 2050, predicts the AFL-CIO.

In "Still a Man's Labor Market: The Long-Term Earnings Gap," an exhaustive report released by the Institute for Women's Policy Research in 2004, the authors, Stephen Rose and Heidi Hartmann, note that across the 15 years—from 1983 to 1998—examined by the study, "women's total earnings are dramatically lower than men's . . . The gender earnings gap is bigger than many people think." Taking into account the long-term impact of lower earnings on a woman's lifetime worth—the ripple effect of lower Social Security and pension benefits—this study reports that women *actually* earn only 38 cents for every dollar men earn. How can this shocking inequity persist—and why aren't more women (and men) protesting it?

Rep. Carolyn Maloney (D-NY), who, along with Rep. John Dingell (D-MI), released results of a Government Accounting Office (GAO) report on women's earnings in November 2003, sums this sad state of affairs up nicely: "After accounting for so many external factors, it seems that still, at the root of it all, men get an inherent annual bonus just for being men. If this continues, the only guarantees in life will be death, taxes and the glass ceiling."

True, not every woman experiences job discrimination. Occupation, education, race, years in the work force, geographic region, and age all are variables that affect how much we earn. Some groups fare better than others. "Women age 35 to 44 with psychology degrees working as social scientists earn 101 percent as much as their male equivalents," reports the NCPE. Young women who work full-time year-round fare much better than older women, with 16-to-24 year olds earning 93 cents for every dollar men of the same age earn. Those gains are to be applauded, but they don't reflect the experience of the majority of working women, 50 percent

THE HALF-A-CENT SOLUTION

1963: Year Congress passed the Equal Pay Act, making it illegal to compensate women less than men for the same work. At that time, women were earning 59 cents for every dollar men earned. Today, they earn 76 cents—a gain of less than half a cent per year in the last 42 years.

1975: "You're both equally qualified, but he has a family to support." — *Excuse given this writer for being passed up for a promotion.*

1996: "Women should not be paid as much as men, because women have the option of marrying rich." — *Remark made by an "older male boss" to a woman, who submitted the comment as proof that affirmative-action programs were still necessary for women.*

2004: Morgan Stanley agrees to pay $54 million to the 340 female employees of its institutional equity division (ah, the irony!) to settle a sex-discrimination class-action suit.

of whom don't even work full time. "A recent study found that nearly 40 percent of poor working women could leave welfare programs, if they were to receive pay equity wage increases," reports the NCPE.

"Work patterns only partially explain the difference between men's and women's earnings," states the GAO in its October 2003 report. Even after accounting for such key factors as occupation, race, marital status, and job tenure, the GAO report admitted that it "could not explain all of the difference in earnings between men and women. . . An earnings difference may result from discrimination in the workplace or subtler discrimination about what types of career or job choices women can make."

Among the contributing factors cited by the NCPE and others:

>> Women and minorities are often underpaid without knowing about it. Wage data is kept secret, with most of the information needed to prove a complaint held by employers, many of whom discourage or prohibit employees from discussing their salaries.

>> Traditionally female occupations (i.e., sales, clerical, and service jobs) tend to pay less than male-dominated occupations. In professional and managerial positions, women are paid considerably better, but they also experience larger wage gaps.

>> Education does not have an equalizing effect. The median income of a women with a bachelor's degree is 25 percent less than that of a similarly qualified man. A woman with a master's degree earns 28 percent less than a man with a master's degree, according to U.S. Census data.

>> Lingering misconceptions persist that women work for "pin money"—not to support a family, as men do.

>> Management often fails to give women high-profile assignments or promote women to high- paying positions. We make up 45.6 percent of the labor force. Yet, in 2004, there were only eight women CEOs running Fortune 500 companies (see the "Corporate Scorecard" box below).

CORPORATE SCORE CARD

In 2004, only eight Fortune 500 companies were headed by women CEO's: Hewlett-Packard, Mirant, Avon, Xerox, Lucent, Rite Aid, Golden West Financial, and Pathmark. You'd think that shareholders would take an active interest in calling for equitable opportunities for women. It's in their best interest to do so: In a study of 353 companies, Catalyst (www.catalystwomen.com) found that companies with the highest representation of women on their senior management teams "had a 35 percent higher return on equity and a 34 percent high total return to shareholders than companies with the lowest women's representation." The stock of the eight companies run by women, as a group, outperformed the market in 2003.

>> Many women simply can't afford to bring charges or are reluctant to risk possible retaliation. Hence, enforcement of the Equal Pay Act is spotty.

Tougher legislation has been introduced in Congress, and some states have enacted stricter pay-equity provisions. But should we wait for the politicians? Women don't ask, I've been told over and over again by experts in the field who write for MAKING BREAD. They don't ask for raises or pensions; they don't ask the hard questions about equal pay and promotions; they don't ask investors for enough money. They don't talk about money with their friends. Many simply don't realize what's at stake; they aren't aware of the long-term impact of the wage gap on their financial security.

This is beginning to change. In recent years, Merrill Lynch & Co., Morgan Stanley, Salomon Smith Barney (now part of Citigroup, Inc.), Ford Motor Co., Mitsubishi Motor Manufacturing of America, Inc., Dial Corp., and Home Depot, among others, have settled sex-discrimination suits filed by female employees. In 2004, the largest class-action sex-discrimination suit to date, alleging unfair pay and promotion practices, was filed against Wal-Mart on behalf of 1.6 million current and former female employees.

If you find yourself facing wage inequity or sexual discrimination of any kind, tell your supervisor and the human resources department, keep detailed notes, collect evidence, talk with other women to see if yours is an isolated case or part of a company-wide problem, and if the situation isn't rectified, consult with a lawyer from the Equal Employment Opportunity Commission at 202-501-0702. (To be connected with the EEOC office in your area, call 1-800-669-4000.)

In this chapter, along with expert advice for managing your career and balancing work and family responsibilities, we share "Choice Career" interviews with four women who've found great success and satisfaction in their fields. (The headline about women and money that Pulitzer Prize-winning editor Amanda Bennett would most like to see on the front page of the newspaper she works for: "Women Achieve Wage Parity Because They Achieve Job Parity.")

These women will tell you that the surest way to happiness and security is to find a way to make money doing what you love—what you're good at. Millions of women succeed at doing just that; they may not get it right the first time, but second and third careers are not uncommon these days. Be prepared to change career paths (as one of the women we interviewed did to find her perfect profession), and never lose sight of the fact that— no matter what your situation—you alone are ultimately responsible for your welfare. Married or single, you must be your own breadwinner, or be able to make money on your own, if you are divorced or widowed. Stay-at-home moms—work at least 10 years outside the home, so that you can claim Medicare and Social Security on your own record, if need be. And always ask for what you're worth. A larger base salary ensures higher Social Security and pension benefits and more disposable income to stash away for retirement.

First up, we look at where the jobs are now— the best fields to consider, whether you're just starting out or starting over—re-entering the workforce after child-rearing or a layoff, or looking for a second career after retirement. Elizabeth Kaminsky, reports on the hottest job categories in the next few years.

Where the Jobs Are Now BY ELIZABETH KAMINSKY

JOB HUNTING—ugh! For me, that task ranks right up there with capturing the dust bunnies underneath my bed. Most people I know don't relish the thought of putting together a resume, networking, beating the bushes, etc. One woman told me that job-hunting feels a lot like door-to-door sales. Another friend, however, keeps a current, updated resume on her computer at all times. She is constantly scanning for better jobs and is poised and ready to nab one whenever it comes along. She treats the job market like the hunt for the perfect pair of shoes. "It's when you're not really looking that you find the good ones," she reports.

Over the years, my jobhunting experiences have been a lot like shopping excursions at my favorite discount store. I go there in search of bath towels and come out with an evening dress. For example, when I was looking for a marketing job, a writing job emerged. I hunted for a writing job and ended up in education. The point is my searches have been a bit unconventional and have yielded interesting results. These days, though, I'm rusty. I consider myself to be starting from scratch—kind of like re-entering the dating world after a long time on the bench. But, ya gotta start somewhere, so off we go.

Shopping for Work in Today's Marketplace.

As I write this in 2004, everyone's been telling me it's a tough market. *Any* market is tough if you're the one looking for a job, so that doesn't scare me too much. I'm expecting that I'll have to work hard, be creative, and keep my sense of humor. I'd recommend that same prescription to any woman who finds herself looking for work.

So where should we be shopping for jobs these days? There are a few key professions topping the list for the foreseeable future. These hot fields include computer and data-processing services, healthcare, elder care, legal services, and homeland-security-related services.

No surprises in this list, and I know what you're probably thinking: "I'm not a computer-software-writing nurse who can run a hot shuffleboard game, draw up contracts, and watch for intruders in her night-vision goggles." OK, well, that's what I was thinking, too.

You were probably also thinking that you would need to retool your skills to go after a job in one of these fields. Maybe it's been a while since you've been in the workplace. Don't let that stop you. Once you understand the nature of these professions and the types of jobs they offer, you may find something that you're perfectly qualified to do right now.

Computing Careers. If you're reading this, chances are you already have a good set of computer skills. Feel good about that. If you have the energy and interest to get further training, the outlook for jobs in programming, creating software or troubleshooting technical problems is bright, indeed. Jobs in these areas are set to grow rapidly—more than 6 percent a year over the next several years. Salaries aren't too bad, either. A person in this field in the year 2000 made an average of between $53,000 and $85,000. People in the field must have strong problem-solving and analytical skills. They also must be team players who communicate effectively, juggle many projects, and pay attention to detail. Hmmm, sounds like every woman I know.

Can't commit to a lot of schooling? There are a number of computer-related jobs that can be done by a person who gets a little on-the-job training or who is willing to sign up for a certificate program and has a good dose of curiosity and perseverance. Perhaps you are an expert Web surfer and have seen some sites that you know could be improved. With an eye for art and graphics and some writing savvy, you could work up to designing Web pages. Web pages have become like business cards for even the smallest businesses. Even individuals have their own Web sites now. They seem to use them for everything from showing off the latest photos of the grandchildren to selling off that inventory of homemade jam. Someone has to create them.

If Web pages aren't your thing, chances are there is something else you can do involving computers. You may be just the person to take your local business or charitable organization from mimeograph to Microsoft, bringing its files and record-keeping on line.

Healthy Employment Options. The next hot field for jobs is just about anything to do with healthcare. And you don't necessarily have to become a doctor or nurse to find a good job. Several occupations are projected to grow faster than average for the next several years. Some of the more interesting and unconventional ones that I found include: medical-records technicians, physicians' assistants, and respiratory therapists. Each one requires some training, but not a full-blown trip through med school. The median salaries weren't too shabby, ringing in at $24,000, $47,000 and $37,000, respectively.

Medical-records technicians review patient charts, assign diagnosis codes, and run specialized computer programs to pull together a complete picture of a patient's medical history for the physician, or physician's assistant. Speaking of physician's assistants, these professionals are formally trained to provide healthcare services under the supervision of a doctor. If you have the aptitude for the training program, which lasts about two years, this field may be a worthwhile investment. The same goes for becoming a respiratory therapist. These individuals, once trained and certified, treat all types of patients with breathing disorders—from premature infants, whose lungs haven't quite formed, to senior citizens, whose lungs have diminished.

It Pays to Respect Your Elders. And while we're on the subject of age, with boomers and their parents growing older in record numbers these days, elder care

is quickly becoming one of the hot sectors for future jobs. The number of assisted-living facilities is steadily climbing. People want to age in place, without having to move from their home to a nursing home, and as they age, they require increasing care. These new living situations offer a variety of options for residents, and bring with them an array of jobs to be filled.

Activities directors, patient representatives, occupational therapy aides, and social workers are or will soon be in high demand. Salaries range from $30,000 up to the mid $40s, depending on the type of facility and the level of responsibility. These positions don't require medical degrees; what they do require are employees with some solid training and a nurturing, patient spirit. For the right kind of person, working in elder care may be the most rewarding and satisfying job ever. There's a real chance here to make a lasting difference in people's lives every day. Not too many jobs can offer that.

Talk About Job Security! Want a little more action in your next job? Check out organizations that support the homeland-security effort. I'm not necessarily talking about James Bond stuff here, but a number of companies and government agencies are now in the business of keeping our people and places safe. Jobs exist in just about all categories, from accountant to baggage inspector. The skills you already possess may be put to good use in a company that is developing the next generation metal detector.

Ever since 9-11, firms in the business of managing risk have been hiring researchers and investigators to track down all kinds of information for their clients, from background checks on employees to trailing unfaithful spouses. Are you curious, nosy, or just plain good at digging for facts? You may have what it takes to be a private investigator. Much of the work is done through computers, but there is the occasional need for surveillance or undercover work. It's a field to watch, to be sure, and one that offers tremendous potential. Many private investigators are self-employed, so salary details were top secret. But for the ones employed by corporations, the average PI salary was about $40K.

Good Bet. Speaking of excitement, why not consider a career in casino gaming? Opportunities in this industry cover just about every job category. And, more and more women are making their way to the top slots. According to Beth Deighan, CEO of Casino Careers Online, "The gaming industry started primarily as a male-dominated business. That has changed. Atlantic City casinos probably offer the best proof that intelligent, hard-working women can break the glass ceiling and rise to the top. The presidents/general managers of five of the city's 12 resorts are women. Women have also made significant gains in holding senior executive positions in accounting and human resources, gaming operations, marketing, and information technology."

That's good news. After all, what better field to get into? This industry stays relatively isolated from downturns in the economy. People gamble when times are good, because they have the extra money, and they gamble when times are bad to relieve their stress. Not to worry if where you live is nowhere near Atlantic City or Las Vegas. Deighan reports that "Native American gaming has led the industry in growth this year, providing career opportunities across the nation. And, with more states considering gaming as a source of revenue to support deficits, more casinos will open or expand and more jobs will become available." Salaries in the casino field run the gamut, based on job type, geographic location, and experience.

The Law on Your Side. Games of chance not your cup of tea? Perhaps becoming a lawyer or a paralegal is more your style. As a paralegal, you get to delve into facts, research cases, draft contracts, and help clients navigate the legal system. The need for paralegals is expected to grow, because many different types of companies, not just law firms, are looking to fill positions. Places like banks, real-estate offices, insurance companies, corporations, and public-sector agencies will be hiring people with legal expertise over the next several years, and there are plenty of accredited training programs where you can get the needed education and skills.

What do employers look for in a paralegal? Ted Schaer, partner with the Philadelphia firm Zarwin, Baum, DeVito, Kaplan, Schaer and Toddy, reports, "We like our employees to be self-starters. They must be able to work independently and hit the ground running. A good paralegal will be trusted to assist with all aspects of a case. They are a valuable part of our team."

If you work well on your own, have a quest for knowledge and a sharp eye for detail, you'll feel right at home as a paralegal. Median salaries for these jobs are around $35,000. But if you have an interest in the law, why not go for a law degree—and a six-figure salary.

In preparing this article, I found some good ideas for jobs I might consider as I journey through job-search land. I could picture myself doing quite a few of them actually, because my interests are broad, I'm curious by nature, and I love to learn. But, just for kicks, I decided to look up my dream job, cabaret singer, in the *Occupational Outlook Handbook*. I didn't expect to find it, but there it was, plain as day. The good news was that the Bureau of Labor Statistics projects that jobs in this profession are "scheduled to grow at least as fast as all other occupations." They are quick to caution that "only the most talented performers get regular work." I guess the people who wrote the handbook haven't listened to the radio lately. A wise woman once told me, "It's never too late to do what you really love." In that case, there's probably room for one more "chick singer" in the world. Why not me?

Before You Start Trolling the Help Wanteds . . .

To find more information on the professions mentioned in "Where the Jobs Are Now," surf on over to:

www.bls.gov: The Bureau of Labor Statistics Occupational Outlook Handbook, found on this site, describes what workers do, how much they make, the training and education they needed, and expected job prospects in a wide range of occupations.

www.ahima.org: The American Health Information Management Association site has a Job Bank, continuing education info, and more.

www.aarc.org: Go to this site of the American Association for Respiratory Care to view a six-minute video on the roles, responsibilities, and educational requirements for respiratory care practitioners, and listen to interviews with students and physicians. Then search the Job Bank.

www.aapa.org: The American Academy of Physician Assistants Information Center offers resources, information ,and career opportunities in this field.

www.casinocareers.com: From accountant to blackjack dealer, search for jobs at Casino Careers Online.

www.paralegals.org: There's a Career Center, Salary Survey, and more at the National Federation of Paralegal Association's site.

www.iccp.org: This site of the Institute for Certification of Computing Professionals lists universities, colleges, and other schools that provide continuing education courses, many available at night, to prepare for work in this field.

www.careervoyages.gov: This site, run by the U.S. Department of Labor and the U.S. Department of Education, includes a list of fastest-growing occupations by state.

THE BUCK STOPS WITH HER:

A CEO OFFERS HER VIEW FROM THE TOP, PLUS SOME SECRETS FOR SUCCESS IN CORPORATE AMERICA

BY AMBER FAIRWEATHER, LYNNEA GARRETT AND THERESA WEEMS

"WE'RE 52 PERCENT OF THE POPULATION. It's time for 52 percent of the Fortune 500 companies to have women CEOs." That was Erica Jong, speaking at a women's conference in Delaware two years ago. As a novelist and poet, Jong has broken a lot of ground, starting with her 1973 novel *Fear of Flying*.

Working women in general have made significant strides since the 70s as well, breaking glass ceilings as they climbed into the ranks of upper management at the companies where they work. Yet, though women make up almost half of America's labor force, only eight Fortune 500 companies are run by women CEOs. Carly Fiorina of Hewlett-Packard, Anne Mulcahy of Xerox, and Andrea Jung of Avon, among them. According to a recent *USA Today* article, the stocks of those companies, as a group, outperformed the market in 2003.

Given that record, more and more women should soon make it into the corner offices of the largest corporations, earning six-and seven-figure salaries. In the meantime, many women are finding opportunity and a training ground running smaller firms (if they're not leaving the corporate world to become CEOs of their own companies).

MAKING BREAD recently talked with one of these women. Lynn Nowicki, 44, who, until recently was president and CEO of a $35 million, privately held importer of kitchen gadgets that distributes to specialty and grocery retailers. She took this position after 20 years of experience in sales, marketing, manufacturing, and managing brands and divisions for Fortune 500 and mid-sized companies. As a general manager at PepsiCo, a product manager at General Mills, and the CEO of Message Link, she has led increases in company/product profitability.

We asked Nowicki to share her experiences and the lessons she's learned on her journey to the top. Her no-nonsense advice is a roadmap for success in the corporate world. For more information about opportunities in business management, visit the Web sites of the National Association for Female Executives (www.nafe.com), which lists the top 30 companies for executive women; the Women's Leadership Exchange (www. womensleadershipexchange.com); or Boardroom Bound (www. boardroombound.biz).

MAKING BREAD: How does one become a CEO?

Lynn Nowicki: Ask for more responsibility and take leadership positions. There is definitely a fast track in the Fortune 500 companies—a clear way to move from the bottom to the top. Watch others, learn from them, and know what you're good at. Then do it.

MB: What does a CEO do on a day-to-day basis?

LN: What I like most about my job is that it varies day to day. I am responsible for my company's overall profitability. I'm accountable for every single function—sales, purchasing, manufacturing, IT, human resources, marketing, warehouse/distribution, and finance. The buck does stop at my desk.

MB: Do women CEOs have advantages over men in the same position? What disadvantages do they face?

LN: We stand out because there are fewer of us. People remember you. I am underestimated. I'm thin, tall, soft-spoken;

I don't swear or raise my voice. Throughout my career, people have underestimated how tenacious I am, and that can be used as an advantage. Yet, I can't speak for all women.

In the 1980s, many Wall Street guys made questionable decisions. Was their business acumen doubted? Did everyone attack them and their companies at the time? No. High-profile women are often more closely scrutinized than their male counterparts. When Carly Fiorina of Hewlett-Packard organized a merger with Compaq, I read many articles debating whether she would fail. You don't see that media microscope focused on the men involved in most mergers, do you?

MB: What have you found to be the most helpful to you in your career: personality, education, or experience?

LN: All three were critical for me. My MBA was my ticket into a Fortune 500 packaged-goods company, where I worked in product management. This was my first step on the path to becoming a CEO.

The most important career decision I made was at PepsiCo. I was in marketing, and I knew that getting sales (line management) experience was critical to moving up, since the company was very much sales-driven and its leaders valued this background.

The difference between a line and a staff job is that a line job directly impacts the bottom line, or profitability, of the company. So, in effect, you have "to put your butt on the line" for the bottom line. The best example of a line job is sales. A staff job supports those working in line jobs—for instance, HR, marketing, or finance.

I can't emphasize this line-job experience enough. In fact, it was so important that I took a lower-level job to move into a sales-operations-manager position. Being responsible for the profit of the company is key for any person who wants to run a company. But it's particularly important for a woman to demonstrate that she has the guts to do it. You have to roll up your sleeves, get your hands dirty (figuratively speaking), and prove to people that you have what it takes to get the job done. To show my staff, as well as my bosses, that I was willing to do the hard stuff, I'd go on a route ride at Pepsi and be very willing to take cases of soda off the truck and help build displays.

As for personality, my very first boss after business school called me a "pit bull," because I don't give up. This is the most important part: you have to be willing to be tenacious.

MB: Your first degree was in journalism. Does it matter what you study in college?

LN: Women often think education is the key to success and that once you have a degree, you're done. But experience is what's really critical, as long as you have the right educational basis.

MB: Do you think it's best to play it safe in business or take risks?

LN: The best advice I ever received was to know yourself and your tolerance for risks.

MB: What advice would you give the secretary who has ambition to move up the corporate ladder?

LN: Do a really good job, no matter what your position. Self-promotion is a must. Let people know what you do. I had a great secretary. She was a hard worker and completed everything quickly, so I helped her move into sales.

How did you get As in school? You raised your hand. Women sometimes have a problem promoting themselves. We're taught to be humble. We never liked the girls who were conceited. When you work with men, you have to get over that mentality. Even now, it's hard for women to be willing to "sell" themselves—to promote what they do well. Upward career movement won't happen, unless you get comfortable doing this. If your job is to do five or six things, do more all the time and let people know about it.

MB: How would you recommend dealing with setbacks, whether financial or personal?

LN: A few years ago, I simultaneously went through a divorce, broke multiple bones, and was selling the company I ran. Everything was going wrong at the same time. How did I get out of that? One day at a time. Every day is a new opportunity. If you get stuck, reach out and ask for help. All the wonderful people in my life were there for me. I wouldn't have been able to do it all on my own.

MB: What are your goals? Would you like to be the CEO of your own company?

LN: I'd like to make a difference for the people with whom I work. Maybe that's through my own company with a culture I build, or maybe it's working for an investment group that I'm part of. Right now, I'm enjoying work and life. I'm confident the right opportunity will always be there when I'm ready.

MB: Can you tell us about any failures you've had?

LN: I don't think about failure. When you take risks, you make mistakes. Mistakes are not failures; they're opportunities to learn. It's when you don't quickly fix a mistake that you have problems.

MB: What do you consider your greatest success?

LN: So far, my greatest success has been helping the people who work for me grow and get promoted. I get a real kick out of that.

MB: Are women helping each other out enough?

LN: People do help each other out, regardless of gender.

MB: If you had to write a memo to women who want to become a CEO, what would it say?

LN: Get experience, get a line position, know yourself—and have a sense of humor

Amber Fairweather, Lynnea Garrett, and Theresa Weems were Temple University students and interns at MAKING BREAD when they wrote this piece.

Once you have a job, you want to be sure that you are paid what you deserve. Men are four-times more likely to ask for a raise on their first job offer than women, reports Linda Babcock, co-author of the 2004 book *Women Don't Ask:* *Negotiation and the Gender Divide* (Princeton University Press). Below, career coach JoAnn R. Hines, who writes the "Success Guide" column in MAKING BREAD, offers some tips for getting mo' money.

How to Raise Your Chances of Getting a Raise

BY JOANN R. HINES

The trick is to be prepared to sell your accomplishments and value to the company—and, if you meet with resistance, for whatever reason, to be ready, willing, and able to negotiate for alternative rewards. Increase your chances of getting what you want by going through the checklist below. A little advance preparation can give you all the edge you need.

1. Do You Want a Raise—or Recognition?

First, ask yourself whether you're sure that it's more money that you want and not just more recognition or better working conditions. It's imperative to know what you want before asking. Go in with realistic expectations; large raises are no longer commonplace.

2. Why Do You Deserve a Raise?

The right answer is never "because I want one" or "because I need one." Everyone falls in one or both of those categories. Your boss will not take you seriously, unless you can demonstrate why you are worth more than you are currently being paid. Prepare a solid list of accomplishments to back up your request. This list should be similar in scope to a resume. If you don't have a long list of accomplishments, proof that you've added value to the company—then cite special skills, new responsibilities, or exceptional performance evaluations that set you apart from your co-workers.

3. How Does Your Current Salary Rate?

Do you know the industry standard for your position? If not, you need to do a little homework. Find out what other individuals are being paid in similar positions. Industry associations generally have statistics available for most positions. Or you can consult a compensation Web site, such as www.salary.com, which calculates average salaries by profession, location, company size ,and professional experience. If your compensation is below industry standard, you now have powerful ammunition to use when you request a raise.

Tip: If your research reveals that you are at the top of your pay grade, be prepared for a no—and suggest alternative perks (such as a better office, more paid vacation days, stock options, a company car, or covered tuition payments or child-care reimbursal) that would satisfy your need for more tangible rewards and recognition for your hard work.

4. Will Company Policies Get in Your Way?

Companies usually have guidelines covering

annual raise rates, compensation percentages, etc. Check your employee handbook, if you have one, to see if there are written policies regarding compensation. Or ask the company personnel director what they are.

Tip: If these policies dictate specific raises at certain times, your boss may or may not have the latitude to award a compensation increase outside those parameters. That's why it's important to be prepared to ask for other rewards.

5. Is Now the Best Time to Ask?

Timing is everything. Here are a few things to consider before making the appointment to talk with your boss: external market conditions, your boss's temperament, company policies, your current workload, and your recent performance. Try to schedule an appointment during the least stressful time of the day. Work toward getting at least 30 minutes to an hour to state your case. Don't plan your meeting before an important presentation or right after your boss has returned from a business trip.

6. What Will You Do If the Answer Is No?

Given the current economic climate, chances are good that your boss will, at least initially, say no or explain why now is not a good time. Don't accept that as the last word. Stay calm. State your case as persuasively as possible. Take ammunition; clearly demonstrate your value to the company. Use your project load or performance ratings to your advantage. If you have a letter from a customer, supplier, or other senior-level rep, take it with you to the meeting.If it becomes apparent that "no" means "no raise," don't raise the roof; be prepared to suggest alternative perks that might add value to your bottom line, instead. The most important part of the art of negotiation is knowing when to compromise. If the company's financial situation will not permit a raise at this time, ask when the freeze will be lifted.

Tip: Never give an ultimatum or threaten to quit unless you have another job waiting.

7. Rehearse.

Prepare a dry run with a close friend or family member. Role-play by asking someone you trust (not a co-worker) to play your boss. Listen to your friend's comments. An outsider is likely to see a weak point or an argument that you've missed.

8. Negotiate.

Compromise. Find the middle ground. Following these guidelines may not send you into the next tax bracket, but they will improve your chances of getting something more for your hard work. Be prepared to make a solid case for yourself, but be equally prepared to negotiate. If it seems that the only answer at this time is no, find out why. Is it the economy or your performance? Ask what you can do to increase your value to the company so that, next time you ask for a raise, the answer will be yes. Then, try again in a few months!

If you find that you have hit the glass ceiling where you work, or that the company's pay and promotion policies don't meet your expectations, prepare to move on. Next, I'll suggest ways you can place your name at the top of the Most Wanted list of the major recruiters in your profession. If you're not interested in job-hopping, these same 10 steps could enhance your chances of getting a raise the next time you ask for one from your current employer.

IT'S NOT WHO YOU KNOW— BUT WHO KNOWS YOU—THAT COUNTS

BY JOANN R. HINES

The more of the following action items you apply, the more high profile—and highly desirable—you will become.

1. **Take on Speaking Engagements or Present a Workshop.** Learn to become a public speaker or develop an industry workshop in your field of expertise. Recruiters peruse industry conferences and program schedules for the names of experts in a given field.

Tip: Start small by speaking at local functions or in-house presentations. Gain training and experience by attending a local Toastmasters meeting or group. Sign up for a speaker's bureau. As your confidence grows, take on engagements at regional or national industry functions.

2. **Become an Expert.** This will take awhile to accomplish, but your ultimate goal is to become the "go-to person" in your field. You want colleagues to know your name. Recruiters call their list of contacts to find good matches. If you are widely recognized, the recruiter will hear your name repeatedly and be compelled to call you.

Tip: Make one day a week an information-gathering day or commit yourself to an hour a day to keep informed. Ask your colleagues to forward you information, if they uncover anything of interest. Subscribe to a clipping service, where you can have "customized" news delivered to your e-mail in box. You can even set up these accounts through Yahoo, AOL, Google, etc.

3. **Be Interviewed.** All major industry publications are looking for experts to interview. Recruiters will track you down because of your name and your notoriety.

Tip: Learn the key editors at the industry's most important publications, and let them know you are available to be interviewed. Go to the publication booths at trade shows and introduce yourself to them. It always helps if they know you personally.

4. **Write Articles.** Having a byline in an industry publication is an immediate signal that you are an expert. Writing for industry publications should be a regular part of your personal marketing plan.

Tip: Do some research into the publications in your field. Find out what the guidelines are for submitting content. Write short articles to get started, then volunteer for bigger writing assignments. Letters to the editor also create good visibility; you can showcase yourself as an expert. Don't expect to get paid initially.

5. **Volunteer for High-Profile Projects.** When issues are in the news, you want to be on the task force dealing with them. Say, "Yes, I can do that."

Tip: Don't volunteer for issues that are controversial. You want your image to be positive, not negative.

6. **Accept a Leadership Role in an Association.** Professional organizations are the first place many recruiters call when looking for qualified candidates. If you are an officer, you have heightened visibility and credibility.

Tip: Many search professionals attend local chapter meetings, hoping to network. Remember the No. 1 rule in networking: You have to show up!

7. Attend Trade Shows and Conferences. Recruiters are always searching for candidates at major industry trade shows. Often, they will volunteer in association booths just to meet the members.

Tip: Plan to attend at least one every six months. Be a badge scanner. When you see someone from an executive search firm, initiate a conversation.

8. Stay in Touch with Your Colleagues and Associates. Make sure your peers know where you are and what you're doing. You want them to think of you first when the recruiter calls them for a contact.

Tip: Make one day a week a telephone day, or commit to an hour a day to reconnect with the people important to you. Send regular press releases about your activities to your resource list. Remember, serious stuff only. Keep it short and to the point. Be on the lookout for ways to help your associates. They will want to return the favor some day.

9. Become an Award-Winner. Enter industry competitions. Every one loves a winner. Awards translate into major visibility, gaining you both in-house and industry press.

Tip: Send a copy of your press release to the recruiters with whom you are most interested in working.

10. Start a Personal Business Web site. This is not the place to feature friends and family or hobbies. Make it your online portfolio. List your skill sets, accolades, attributes, and areas of expertise. Showcase your success. Paint a picture that makes people want to know more about you.

Tip: Hotlink industry associations to your site. That way search pros can discover you by surfing the Web.

The beauty of the glass ceiling is that it is glass, not steel. It can be broken, and the best way to break it is to realize your potential. Market yourself. Increase your visibility. Stand tall and start cracking. And once you're at the top, help other women up the ladder!

We've all heard about the old boy's network—they hold their meetings on the floor above the glass ceiling. If you can't beat them, create your own network. Women helping other women in business (and out) is a powerful force gaining strength everywhere in the world. Next, public-relations veteran and MAKING BREAD contributing editor Rosemary Rys, who has a special talent for networking, describes how it's done by the best of them. Public-relations pro M.H. Flick co-wrote the piece with her.

NETWORK TO IMPROVE YOUR NET WORTH

BY ROSEMARY E. RYS WITH M.H. FLICK

I'm often asked how I learned to network so well. It seems, no matter where I am, I can connect people to others who might have a skill or business solution that would be useful to them. And, often, in the end, this skill pays off for me when the favor is returned.

The secret to successful networking is being what I call a "catalytic converter." Huh? Okay, so a catalyst is "a substance that decreases the time it takes a chemical reaction to occur." In other words, when you combine the right elements—"Poof!"—magic happens. Put another way, in human terms, a catalyst is somebody who, when interjected into the mix, makes things happen. Below are some rules that I follow. You'll see that the key is to use every situation to your advantage—no matter how unimportant it might seem at the time. As they say, "Ya never know…"

Connect the Dots . . . and Become Well-Connected.

Rome wasn't conquered in a day—and neither is the room you are working! If you're uncomfortable about networking, start by taking small steps. When I started networking, I attended an industry event with a stack of cards in my pocket. I made a deal with myself that I wasn't going to meet the entire room full of people that night—I just had to meet and exchange cards with five people. At the next month's event, I decided I would speak to 10 people. Well, I found I knew two people from the first event, so I went over and said hello to them. While talking to them, they, in turn, introduced me to six new people. I then introduced myself to another person who was standing alone. I went to the ladies' room and introduced myself to two people while I was waiting in line, and so on.

Before I knew it, I had my 10 new contacts. After a few months of attending this organization's functions, I suddenly realized that I had made myself a part of the community by volunteering to help with events and getting involved. Within a year's time, I was being asked to chair a committee. I guar-antee that If you start out small, volunteer and become active in associations, you'll quickly be on your way to networking (and career) success, too.

Always Carry Business Cards.
A few years ago, when I was living and working in New York, I attended a wedding in Lancaster, Pennsylvania, over Thanksgiving. I was blown away when I realized that the man sitting to my right at the reception dinner was someone I and Gaye—one of my colleagues—had been cold-calling and trying to meet. He told me that he and Gaye had arranged a time to get together. He then proceeded to fill me in on what his company needed and gave me some insights about what he thought about my company. I gathered a ton of information from that wedding, which was extremely useful to Gaye in preparing for her meeting. Getting dressed for the party, I wasn't sure why I had put my business cards into my evening bag, but all good things happen for a reason.

Become an Information-Gatherer, Not an Infomercial.
Always ask other people what they do, so that you can refer work to them. A key aspect in marketing or business development is to not talk excessively about what you do. Ask about the other person's business. Ask how she wins work in her business. Ask how she gets leads for projects. Ask about her competitors. People love to talk about their business. Don't use your sales pitch when you're networking. Remember, good networkers are information-gatherers, not infomercials.

Work for Your Network as Much as for Yourself.
Even if the people you meet can't help your business, gathering information about them may help someone else in your network. Gather as much or enough information to provide a lead to someone else. You don't have to guarantee someone that they will "get the job or win the work." A name and phone

number, and, in some instances, your name as a referral, are all that it takes to help someone else get a step closer to their goal. Continue to give back to your network, and your network will give back to you.

I was recently asked by a friend to contact his marketing representative, because she needed PR advice. I did so, and we got to talking, and she shared with me that she was concerned about her company's internal communications, so much so that she was taking an organizational- development course online with the University of Phoenix. As it happens, I'm about to teach for that online university, so we had something in common. Add to the mix the fact that I know someone who works in the same town as my new friend, and—guess what?—he helps companies turn themselves inside out to be sure that they are operating at top efficiency. I introduced the two of them, and they are going to work together soon. Need I mention that they both plan to refer me for PR opportunities that come up in the future? It really works!

'Tis Better to Give Than to Receive. I often help others find free opportunities to promote themselves, and they come back to me when their budget is in place and they are ready to hire someone to do more of the same. I also volunteer on several committees and attend many meetings in my field. It all works out very well. People see that you're interested in your industry, and, in their eyes, you become someone worth knowing.

It's definitely better to give than to receive. A friend once asked me what I thought makes a "good networker." I thought about it and finally replied: "Someone who has leads and good information to share with someone else in their network." People within your network are going to remember the person who provided them with leads faster than they will remember the person who always comes to them with a hand out. Even small leads can help others and make you shine in their eyes.

Networking Happens Everywhere. Use every single resource you have wisely. I belong to a Professional Services Group (PSG), which is a state program providing a forum for interaction with other professionals. A monthly get-together is held at a local pub. I mentioned at one of these meetings that I was going after a marketing position for the Battleship New Jersey now berthed on the Camden, New Jersey, waterfront. Someone in the PSG immediately hooked me up with an "alum" who had held a position there. Another friend shared with me that his neighbor was that non-profit's chief fund-raiser, and he offered to mention my name to her.

P.S. In case you're wondering how my co-author and I met—you guessed it—it was through just this type of thoughtful networking.

Rosemary E. Rys, APR, is the President of Creative Public Relations ("CPR for Your Communication Needs"), located in Collingswood, New Jersey. M. H. Flick is a public-relations expert who lives and works in the Philadelphia area.

where the money is:

According to the Institute for Women's Policy Research, the top five states for women, in terms of highest median annual earnings for full-time, year-round employment, are: the District of Columbia, Alaska and Maryland (tied for second), Connecticut, and New Jersey. Heading the list of states with the smallest wage gap are: the District of Columbia, California, Vermont, Delaware, and Arizona.

Do You Want Uncle Sam (as Your Employer)?

AN-INSIDE-THE-BELTWAY PERSPECTIVE ON THE BENEFITS (MONETARY AND OTHERWISE) OF WORKING FOR THE GOVERNMENT

Those ubiquitous "Uncle Sam Wants You" posters take on new meaning when America is at war. But Uncle Sam doesn't just hire soldiers. In fact, more men and women work for Sam as civilian employees than as uniformed personnel. In 2002, the federal government employed about 1.9 million civilian workers in occupations ranging from accountant to astronomer to architect to doctor . . . the list goes on; almost every profession is represented on the federal payroll. Job opportunities exist around the country and the world. (Fewer than 15 percent are based in Washington, D.C.) The average salary for all occupations in the federal government last year was $55,871, and, according to a study prepared by the Congressional Budget Office, federal benefits tend to be more generous than those in the private sector.

Not yet convinced that you might find a choice career with the government? Consider this: layoffs, called "reductions in force" by Uncle Sam, are far less common than they are in the private sector, and, on the rare occasions when they have happened, they have tended to affect relatively few workers. The CIA recently hired *Alias* star Jennifer Garner to appear in a recruitment video on its Web site (www.cia.gov). So it would seem that Sam is reaching out to women—and the CIA isn't the only department looking. Women and minorities are sought throughout the government.

"Congressional offices are very interested in increasing diversity and hiring more women," says Nina Shokraii Rees, who began her government career working as an intern for Sen. John Warner (R-VA). No one could have been more surprised to find herself working for Sam than Rees. Born in Iran 36 years ago, Rees came to the United States in 1983 at age 14, after the revolution in her country, which overthrew the Shah and brought the Ayatollah to power.

"I wanted to be a teacher when I was young," she says. By the time she was 35, she had become the Deputy Undersecretary in charge of the Office of Innovation and Improvement at the U.S. Department of Education, putting theory into practice, policy into action for President Bush's No Child Left Behind Act. MAKING BREAD spoke with Rees about her stellar career path and what it takes to be a success in Washington, D.C.

MAKING BREAD: Deputy Undersecretary in charge of the Office for Innovation and Improvement is an original job title. Did they make it up to describe you?

Nina Shokraii Rees: They did make it up for me—or at least, I'm the first person to hold the title. The name captures people's attention. Former Secretary (of Education) Rod Paige created the office as a means of focusing on innovative educational practices around the country. A lot of states aren't thinking very creatively about how to implement the goals of the Federal No Child Left Behind Act—which is aimed at closing the achievement gap between rich and poor students—and we want to encourage them to try different approaches.

MB: What are the best and worst aspects of living and working in the rarified political atmosphere of Washington?

NSR: Washington attracts many smart, ambitious people from all parts of the country, and, in fact, the world. It's exciting to work in an atmosphere like D.C., but it can also be a challenging place to work, because the pace is very fast and competitive. It's hard to build long-lasting friendships, because many people only live in the city for a short time.

MB: Were you always interested in politics?

NSR: I've always been interested in education, actually. I majored in developmental psychology in college and didn't become interested in politics until I decided to get a job on Capitol Hill. At the time, I was working on a Master's degree, while working at Neiman Marcus as a salesperson, making $16,000 a year. A client there mentioned that she knew someone who had gotten a job with a congressman. I met with her, and she suggested I apply for an internship.

That's how I got my first job in politics; I became an intern for Sen. John Warner of Virginia. Once I started working on the Hill, it was easier to get other jobs; it helps to know someone. I eventually got a full-time job as a receptionist for then Rep. Porter Goss of Florida.

MB: Whenever I go to Washington, I always find that I'm surrounded by people engaged in passionate discussions about how they're going to change the world. What were your first impressions of working on the Hill?

NSR: Washington is the kind of place that you either like or dislike. I immediately saw that it was a place where young people can rise fast in their careers. I don't mean that so much in terms of making money, but by gaining power and having a hand in the public-policy decision-making process.

MB: You speak French and Persian. Did your linguistic skills help in your career?

NSR: Spanish would be more useful in this job. But before I was appointed to this position, I worked at the White House as a deputy assistant for Vice President Dick Cheney. After 9/11, I got to use my language skills in a variety of efforts to help people in the Muslim world better understand the war in Afghanistan.

MB: You've said that it helps to get to know people to get ahead. Are networking skills a prerequisite in government?

NSR: Networking skills are a definite asset. Network and build really strong relationships—and (this is the important part) continue holding onto the contacts you make. That helped me enormously. Honing your skills or knowledge is also critical.

MB: How did that advice play out for you?

NSR: Through my graduate work, I met a professor who knew many political consultants in D.C. He suggested I meet a political activist named Grover Norquist. I didn't know much about the world of political strategy, but I thought that getting to know him would be worthwhile. Norquist ended up hiring me at Americans for Tax Reform and charged me with helping to spin the defeat of a school-choice ballot initiative—Proposition 174—in a positive way. The position eventually gave me the opportunity to write under my own byline and build name recognition as an expert on the topic.

From there, I was hired as Director of Outreach for the Institute for Justice, a public-interest law firm. Through this work, I got to know a lot of people, including Mayor Stephen Goldsmith of Indianapolis, who later became one of the lead domestic policy advisers in President Bush's 2000 campaign. Steve invited me to serve as an education adviser for the campaign, and that connection ultimately led to the position I now hold.

MB: I gather that building a reputation as an expert is a wise move.

NSR: Yes. Washington is filled with many smart generalists—people who know a little bit about a lot. Those who know a lot about a specific topic are harder to find, so it's useful to become an expert in a particular field.

MB: What are the most rewarding and frustrating parts of your job?

NSR: I've advocated for school choice and written about it for so long that it is particularly rewarding for me to be part of the implementation of several school-choice programs. But the pace of implementing policy can be slow, and the public's desire for quick fixes can get in the way of implementing a good idea, which can be frustrating.

MB: How does the pay scale compare with what you might be making in a similar position in corporate America?

NSR: I've never worked on the corporate side, so I don't have that frame of reference. The salary for my position is public information ($130,000).

MB: What's the best advice you can give other women who are considering a career in government?

NSR: I would give this advice to both men and women: It's important to come to the job (especially as a political appointee) with a clear vision of what you wish to accomplish for the official who has hired you and not get distracted by the myriad other issues that may come up.

Otherwise, the job can bring you down, because there are so many different demands coming from different corners.

MB: At your level, there must be a certain amount of job insecurity every four years. How do you cope with that?

NSR: I think it's good to know that you are only at a job for a certain period of time. It helps you focus your attention on the goals at hand and keeps you from wasting time. I suppose the older one gets, the harder it may be.

MB: Where will you go from here?

NSR: I hope to remain involved in education and continue to play a role in closing the achievement gap between rich and poor students through school choice and laws like No Child Left Behind.

I think it's important to try to change the system from within and encourage more young people to consider teaching, running schools, or working in government agencies, even if only for a short time. The pay may not be as high as what one would make in the private sector, but the work is very rewarding. I have an extremely high level of job satisfaction, and I am gaining experience that would be difficult to replicate in a non-government job.

(For more information about career opportunities in the Federal Government, visit www.usajobs.opm.gov. Two other useful sites for those interested in pursuing a career in public service are: www.pmi.opm.gov, the Web site of the Presidential Management Fellows internship program; and www.whitehouse.gov/fellows/, the site of the prestigious White House Fellows program.

Groovy Sites for New Job Seekers
THEIR JOB IS FINDING THE RIGHT JOB FOR YOU

JUST STARTING OUT IN THE JOB MARKET? Visit **www.groovejob.com** and **www.experience.com** for networking, job leads, and career advice. Experience.com specializes in networking and recruiting for college students, providing an online venue where top employers can reach out to college students who are looking for internships or their first big jobs.

Groovejob.com bills itself as "the premier job site for high school and college-age students," and lists a wide assortment of part-time and full-time jobs at such companies as Taco Bell, Fed Ex, Wendy's, and Home Depot, plus interview tips, an SAT Word of the Day, and a nifty career-assessment tool to help you identify what sort of job you're cut out for, based on your personality traits.

Beyond the biggies, **Monster.com**, **Careerbuilder.com** and **HotJobs.com**, there are other search engines that cater to specific employment markets? For instance, if you're looking for a job in the very hot pharmaceuticals or medical sector, try **www.MedZilla.com**. Looking for an editing, writing, ad sales, marketing, or designer gig? Try **www. mediabistro.com**. Another good place to look are the Web sites of professional associations in your field. Many include job-opportunity listings. Happy hunting!

Working moms have two full-time jobs. As a working mom, and MAKING BREAD'S "The Working Mom's Shrink" columnist Marcia Eckerd offers her best advice for handling the juggling act.

"TAKE MY DESERT ISLAND CHALLENGE"

SAYS THIS EXPERT WHO'S BEEN THERE, DONE THAT WHEN IT COMES TO BALANCING WORK AND FAMILY RESPONSIBILITIES

BY MARCIA ECKERD, PHD

I'm a licensed psychologist, mother, wife, daughter, friend, some-time community volunteer, and Brownie leader. Been there, done that when it comes to juggling my commitments and deadlines, children's logistics and crises, my husband's needs, caring for aging parents, and keeping the household going ("What will we eat tonight?"). My daughter is now 22, and I'm still juggling. Just last week I had to take her to the hospital for minor ambulatory surgery. In the hospital garage, she slammed the car door on her hand, breaking her finger, which required two hours in the ER. The extra hours in the ER blew my schedule, and I had to call clients to reschedule appointments. So I know a thing or two about being a working mom. I finished my PhD dissertation when my daughter was a year old, writing in two-hour slots when I could get a babysitter.

I'm no superwoman—just a working mom stretched a bit thin, as my husband and daughter will attest. Face it, mothering IS a full-time job; the term working mother is redundant. Recent studies show that it's not possible to do two jobs at once and that "Super-Mom" is a myth. Did we need a study to tell us this? Many of us are trying to strike some kind of balance between work and home. Mothers are struggling just to keep their heads above water, and many ask my advice on how to cope with all their responsibilities without crashing.

First and foremost, I help them to understand the nature of stress. The stress response is built into our bodies as a natural fight/flight reaction. However, our bodies react the same to our perceptions as they do to real threats. What does this mean?

When we are trying to keep every item on our "to do" list in our minds, we are compounding our state of being overloaded and overwhelmed. Our typical operating mode: how many things can I get done on a single trip to the drugstore, while making calls on my cell phone? Setting priorities, being realistic about our resources (including energy and time), and having reasonable standards are critical to staying sane.

How do you set priorities? Don't kids *and* work always come first? In a word, "No." When you are stressed, you're irritable and inefficient. You'll tend to blow up and forget everything you knew or learned about good parenting. Here's an exercise I give to women (and men) for priority-setting.

My "Desert Island Challenge." Make a list of what you value. Include work, kids, spouse, family, friends, your health, your outside activities, your religious or spiritual interests, and whatever else might be important to you. Now rank in order of importance the items on your list. Next, imagine you are on a desert island and you have to give up these items, one at a time.

What would go first? In different colored ink, rank the order in which you would give up each item. It can be surprising what comes to the top. Think about it: How much time is there for enjoyment? Can you be realistic about how much energy it takes to cover everything you've scheduled?

Refueling yourself needs to be high up on your daily priority list. This may mean that something else slides down or off the list, and you need to come to terms with that. You need to relax your type-A, perfectionist standards. To create balance, you need to set some limits. Do the kids really need so many activities? Can you let go of the constant sense of urgency that everything has to get done OR ELSE? The "or else" usually is inconsequential. A good measure of "how important is this?" is the question: When you're 80 and looking back at your life, will this really matter?

Distressed? Try These Ways to De-Stress!

1. Do what calms you for 15 minutes every day. Relaxation cannot be multitasked; sorry, you can't do aerobic exercise at the same time! Take a walk, listen to music, do yoga, breathing exercises, or meditate. Good information and tapes are available through the Web site of the Mind-Body Medical Institute at Beth-Israel Deaconess Medical Center (www.mbmi.org). I like the Olivia Hoblitzelle tape; there are also tapes for kids.

2. Take care of yourself—eat right and get enough sleep. A good resource: *Minding the Body, Mending the Mind* by Joan Borysenko, PhD.

3. Care out special time with your spouse or partner. Have a regular date night to enjoy each other. It is possible and necessary. Make dates with friends, too. Lots of research shows the health benefits of having a network of support.

4. Allow spiritual time in your life. This doesn't necessarily have to do with organized religion; it may be a moment to savor the good parts of your life.

5. Spend some time with your kids just having fun. Driving them back and forth from mandatory activities doesn't count as good bonding time; you're all likely to be stressed and tired.

6. Set boundaries at work. Do you take on more than you can accomplish? Is this demanded of you on the job? Try negotiating a more realistic set of expectations with your boss.

Let Them Eat Cake … And Homemade Ice Cream …

AND COCONUT PANNA COTTA! WITH A NAME LIKE MARIE ANTOINETTE, HOW COULD SHE NOT BECOME A PASTRY CHEF?

BY ELIZABETH KAMINSKY

In 2003, for our "Choice Career" column, we caught up with pastry chef Marie Antoinette Stecher of the world-renowned Susanna Foo Chinese Cuisine Restaurant in Philadelphia, Pennsylvania. We wanted to find out why she chose to head back to the kitchen for her second career, in her 30s, and what you need to do, if you want to make money satisfying your sweet tooth, too. For more information on becoming a pastry chef, visit these sites: Pastry Chef Central (www.pastrychef.com), The Culinary Institute of America (www.ciachef.edu), and The Restaurant School (www.therestaurantschool.com).

MAKING BREAD: Why did you decide to become a chef?

Marie Antoinette Stecher: For most of my life, I was trying to figure out what I wanted to be when I grew up. After college, I went to work in the marketing department of a hotel casino. While the job was fun and demanding, I knew I was capable of much more. I spent a lot of time reading and taking career-development classes. Soon after, I took a job with a local utility, working with customers and shareholders. It taught me a lot about financial subjects and about the inner workings of a corporation. After awhile, I found myself looking for what was next.

I considered going back to school for my Master's in business or teaching. But I knew I wanted the chance to do something creative, and those two fields just didn't seem to be a good fit. I did some research and found out that The Restaurant School offered a good education

and a trip to France, too. So, I quit my job, enrolled in school and moved to Philadelphia. I have never been happier.

MB: Did you have any experience with pastry before you attended The Restaurant School? And what was the training like?

MAS: I chose pastry, because I felt it would be fun, creative, and rewarding. I've always loved to bake. My mother made beautiful cakes, and her talent was a strong influence. The other strong influence is my name. With the name, "Marie Antoinette," I guess I felt destined somehow to feed people cake.

My time at the Restaurant School was an unforgettable experience. We were trained in all aspects of the culinary arts during our two-year program. We learned the science and art of food from a number of very capable and caring chefs, and I wouldn't trade the trip to France for anything. I learned so much there.

MB: You said the program took two years. How much does it cost, and what kind of jobs or salaries can a person expect after graduation?

MAS: It costs between $14,000 and $20,000 for tuition and materials. There are student loans and other sources of funding out there, if you shop around. As for salary, it's a field that you go into more for love than money, especially in the beginning. You work long hours in hot kitchens, and you have to work your way up and prove yourself. It took me about seven years in progressively more responsible positions to get where I am now. I took a longer route, in order to learn as much as I could. You have to keep your skills sharp, and you have to keep learning and growing. The field is pretty competitive.

As a pastry cook, you can average between $8 and $16 an hour, depending on your experience and skills. Pastry chefs can make between $30,000 and $75,000, depending on where they work. Most pastry chefs in the finer hotels make more than $50,000. At this point in my career, I can finally say that I'm making more than my age bracket, which is definitely more than I made at the utility company.

Besides restaurants, there are many other places to look for pastry work. For example, some students choose to go to bakeries, catering companies, or hotels. If you are adventurous, there are jobs abroad, especially if you work in a hotel. Firms like the Ritz Carlton and Four Seasons are always opening hotels in exotic locations, and they need people to fill the spots. There are even great opportunities on cruise ships.

One other place that might surprise some people is large department stores, especially those in Europe. When I was in London this winter, I had the opportunity to meet the pastry chef of Harrods. I was shopping there and admiring the beautiful cakes on display in their food court. The chef I was talking with asked if I was in the pastry business. I told him I was and that I was from Philadelphia. He said, "So is our pastry chef. Do you want to meet him?" Of course, I said yes, and I got a chance to tour their kitchen. I was impressed that they make more than 4,000 scones a day. When I worked for the Ritz, making 100 a day was a lot.

MB: What special qualities do you feel a person should have to be successful in your field?

MAS: Stamina and a thick skin leap to mind. We work some really long hours, especially around the holiday seasons, which is true of any job in the service industry—hotel, restaurant, catering, etc. You need a thick skin, because you must be able to take criticism well. Chefs will constantly be correcting you to make sure the product is perfect for the guest. Making pastry is quite scientific, and attention to detail is extremely important. Recipes must be followed to the letter, or your product won't come out. Having good organizational skills helps in the production side of the job, like when you have to make 300 crème brulées. It can be tedious at times, but the decorating or finishing part of the job is so much fun. I'm a bit of an artist with paper and pencil, so I like to carry that over into my "food artwork," as well. Most of all, you have to love what you do—it shows in your desserts.

MB: Do you ever get tired of eating desserts? What do you pick when you eat out, and how do you keep from putting on weight when you work around such wonderful goodies?

MAS: You do have to taste things, and, at times, I get tired of sweets and crave something green, like vegetables. When I eat out, I lean towards lighter desserts, like sorbet or fruit tarts. I can usually be talked into splitting something chocolate. My mother's philosophy was: "Life is too short. Eat dessert first." I'd have to agree.

Gaining weight can be an occupational hazard. It's hard not to, when you're working with things made from cream, butter, sugar, chocolate, etc. Pastry work is very physical, though, and most pastry chefs I know are actually thin, because they run around a lot and lift heavy items like dough or bags of sugar.

MB: Can you describe some of your most rewarding moments as a pastry chef so far?

MAS: I feel proud to have been one of the team who "survived" opening a new five-diamond hotel—the Ritz Carlton in Philadelphia. My co-workers and I described it as pastry boot camp, because it was the most physically and mentally demanding thing any of us had ever done. I was fortunate enough to take a course in working with chocolate at the Valrhona School in France. The French are so passionate about pastry; it was truly inspiring. I learned new ways to work with their superior confection, and I got to sample it as I went along. How can you beat spending all day eating fine chocolate?

Of course, I am thrilled to be working with Susanna Foo now. Her energy and enthusiasm inspire me to do my best work. Asian influences were new to me when I came here, so every day I learn a bit more about the culture and the food.

MB: What do you think the future holds for you?

MAS: I always thought I would like to open my own dessert café or gelato place. Gelato is my new obsession. I'd like to write a cookbook, and I would like to improve my wedding-cake decorating skills. Right now, though, I'm happy just as I am.

MB: Any chance you could share a recipe of one of your favorite sweets?

MAS: Sure. Here's my personal recipe for Coconut Panna Cotta with Tapioca Sauce. Enjoy!

COCONUT PANNA COTTA WITH TAPIOCA SAUCE
Panna Cotta
½ quart heavy cream
½ cup sugar
1 can coconut milk
1 tablespoon plus 2 teaspoons of powdered gelatin, or 5 gelatin sheets

Place sugar and heavy cream in a pot and heat until it just begins to boil. Bloom (dissolve) the powdered gelatin in ¼ to ⅓ cup of cold water. (If using gelatin sheets, use 1 cup cold water.) Add gelatin and water mixture to hot mixture and remove from heat. Stir until gelatin dissolves completely. Add coconut milk and stir occasionally. When slightly cool, pour into small dishes or wine glasses. Refrigerate and serve when well chilled. Yields four to six servings.

Coconut Tapioca Sauce
5 cups milk
¾ cup sugar
½ cup small tapioca pearls
1 can coconut milk
2 tablespoons rum (preferably coconut-flavored Malibu rum)

Combine milk and sugar in a pot and heat until almost boiling. Remove from heat and whisk in tapioca pearls. Return to low heat, stirring every few minutes. Cook for 30 to 45 minutes, until tapioca pearls are soft. Remove from heat and stir in coconut milk and rum. When chilled, spoon over panna cotta. Garnish with a dried or caramelized pineapple chip, or add a scoop of your favorite tropical fruit sorbet.

(To caramelize pineapple chips, place them on a cookie sheet, sprinkle with sugar and a little rum, then cook them in a 350-degree oven for about 10 minutes, or until the pineapple slices get bubbly and slightly browned.)

There may be times in your life when you have to take two paying jobs to make ends meet. Below, Patricia Schiff Estess, author of *Work Concepts for the Future: Managing Alternative Work Arrangements* (Crisp Publications), offers suggestions for making these arrangements work for you. (*Names of the women in her story have been changed.)

DO 2 PART-TIME JOBS = 1 FULL-TIME JOB?

HERE'S HOW ONE WOMAN MADE IT ADD UP FOR HER

BY PATRICIA SCHIFF ESTESS

Many women, at different times in their lives, choose to work part time. They may have young children and want to spend more time with them. They may have care-giving responsibilities for elderly parents or a disabled spouse and decide they can't do it all. Or maybe they're easing themselves out of the traditional workplace—either to start a business or to retire from the workforce altogether.

But out of the economic shambles of the past couple of years comes another type of part-timer—one who's had that job option thrust upon her. She's the middle or upper managerial or professional woman who has been laid off and can't find another full-time job to match the one she had. She's also the one who is asked to work part time, because the organization is so shaky that it can no longer support her full-time position.

In almost all cases, one part-time job, no matter how attractive the hourly or project-based compensation, doesn't put the lobster on the table that the previous salary did. Dinner is now canned tuna—or even more meager fare.

Follow along on this woman's path, and you'll see her looking for a second part-time job, because she needs to make up the difference in pay. While two jobs per person is not unusual for those earning minimum wage, as social commentator Barbara Ehrenreich found out when she tried living on that wage (and later wrote about in her best-seller *Nickel and Dimed: On (Not) Getting By in America*), it is on unusual development for those middle-class women whose previous salaries were padded with health-insurance coverage, corporate retirement plans, paid vacations, and sick days.

All of which raises questions: How's it going for these women? Do two part-time jobs make up for one that's full time? What are the pluses? The minuses? The trade-offs?

Pluses & Minuses. Jill*, 40, was the clinical director of deaf services at a social-service agency in Bloomington, Indiana, until about a year ago. She liked the work, but "I was sick and tired of the politics of managed care. It subverted the mission of the agency," she says.

So when the agency announced that it was restructuring, Jill decided it was time to take action. Without waiting to find out whether she would have been part of the downsizing, she proposed a part-time assignment for herself. She would be a therapist for deaf clients—and that was it. No supervisory responsibilities. "They were happy to accommodate my request, because, if I saw clients, they wouldn't have to hire an interpreter plus a therapist. I could do both," she explains. She negotiated a schedule that had her working no more than 25 hours a week.

"But I had to find another job," she says. "We couldn't live on just half my previous income." Because she wanted to expand her areas of expertise, she applied for a 20-hour-a-week counseling position at DePauw University in Greencastle. "I was initially hired to replace a counselor who left in the middle of the semester. One of the tasks I took on was coordinating Eating Disorders Awareness Week," she says. "At the same time, the University's Task Force on Women recommended hiring an eating-disorders counselor part time. I was lucky. The department was pleased with how I handled the Awareness Week and asked me to take the job." So now she's becoming a specialist in this area.

"It's been a wonderful mix, professionally," she says. "I respect the people I work with at DePauw and have had an opportunity to learn a whole new field. I go to conferences, make presentations, counsel students, run programs and groups—all without the pressure of billable hours. I know the counseling office would like me to work a bit more, but they'd have to pay me benefits if I worked even 21 hours weekly. They can't afford that, and I'm not willing to put in the extra time without the benefits. So, for the moment, we all have to make do with the situation.

"I've also changed my arrangement with the social-service agency," she adds. "I now get paid on a fee-for-service basis—which means I'm my own boss," Jill says, with a sigh of relief. She writes up clinical notes and puts them in the charts. She uses the agency's space, and it takes care of all the billing and insurance issues. "For me, it's a much better arrangement," she says.

When you take benefits into consideration, Jill doesn't earn what she did as a director of the agency, and she says she couldn't do this if her husband weren't able to insure the family under his medical plan. But because her take-home pay is a little more than it was before (no benefits or taxes taken out), her husband has been able to increase the amount he's putting into his retirement plan and their standard of living hasn't dropped significantly.

Jill's less-than-ideal financial situation is not unique among women with two part-time jobs. In a perfect world, part-time positions would offer the same degree of job security and pro rata share of the rights and benefits available to full-time employees. But that doesn't happen often nowadays. Benefit costs are skyrocketing. To bring them down, universities, for example, are hiring adjuncts rather than tenured professors. Corporations are using consultants (often former employees), who, though they may charge more per hour than an employee, are hired on a project-by-project basis and can be dropped (without severance or unemployment insurance costs) when not needed. Smaller companies are trying to reduce benefit costs by hiring two people, each on a part-time basis, to avoid the escalating costs of providing medical insurance to a full-time employee.

How to Take Full Advantage of Part-Time Work. If you're in the position of having or wanting to take two part-time jobs instead of one that's full time, here are some ways of marketing yourself most effectively, so that you don't take a big financial hit.

Know your worth. What is it you can do that others can't? What contacts or relationships do you have that few others have? What experience do you have that's unique? When you interview for a position, be very clear about what you bring to it, and, without braggadocio, highlight those special qualities.

Estimate how much you're saving the company. Even if you can't find out exactly what percentage of a full-time salary the company spends on benefits, you can guess. It usually ranges between 25 and 40 percent of salary. So a full-time responsible position paying $50,000 annually actually costs a company at least $62,500 a year. If you're negotiating for straight salary on a 20-hour workweek, reach for a little less than half the total cost of a full-time position (in this case, perhaps $30,000). You're still saving the company money.

Learn what others are charging or being paid for the same work. Because you've been in the workforce, you usually know what full-time compensation is for a position and can deduce a reasonable part-time salary. But for a woman who is consulting for the first time, for example, figuring out what to charge hourly, daily, or for a project is difficult. You need to tap into your acquaintances' experience in this area. If you ask for too much, you'll price yourself out of the market. If you ask for too little, you'll send out red flags to prospective clients that you don't know what you're doing.

If the company wants more of your time than you agreed to, renegotiate. If the company policy is to pay benefits to anyone working 25 or more hours a week, for example, don't be the "good girl" and work 30 hours with no benefits. If the extra hours are beneficial for you, renegotiate your agreement, asking for pro-rated benefits, overtime pay, paid vacation time, or whatever benefit is most important to you.

Figure business-related costs into your fee, if you're working from home. Working in an office gives you free access to many things you don't have to pay for—telephone, computer time, electricity, paper, fax, copying, postage, etc. Don't forget to factor those costs in when figuring what to charge, if the work you're engaged in is done at home. After all, those expenses are now paid for out of your checking account.

Try to use one of your part-time jobs to broaden your reach or enhance your skills. If you've always worked as a magazine editor, for example, expand beyond magazines by working on corporate publications or trade magazines. If you're contemplating a career change, use this opportunity to leave one foot in the field you've been working in and put another in a totally new arena. That's what one pharmacist did. She works three days a week at a large drug-store chain and two in an art gallery. Her goal: to learn enough about the art world to someday own her own gallery.

So does a half plus a half really add up to one satisfactory work arrangement? Jill sums up the feelings of many who have embraced it. "It fits my lifestyle well now," she says. "I have three weeks off from the counseling center in the summer, plus all school holidays—which I love because I have more time with my two preschoolers, even though it's unpaid vacation. And I've expanded professionally—all of which should work well for me in the future. But it certainly doesn't net any financial windfalls."

WHAT A BLAST!

THAT'S THE HEADLINE NEWSPAPER EDITOR AMANDA BENNETT WOULD WRITE TO DESCRIBE HER METEORIC CAREER. HERE'S THE INSIDE SCOOP ON HOW SHE SUCCEEDED.

BY JENNIFER VISHNEVSKY

The Philadelphia Inquirer *was founded on June 1, 1829. It took this major daily newspaper exactly 174 years to appoint its first female editor-in-chief. On June 2, 2003, Amanda Bennett assumed the title of editor and executive vice president of the paper, selected for this plum job, in part, because of her track record as an award-winning journalist. As managing editor for enterprise reporting at the Portland Oregonian, Bennett won the 2001 Pulitzer Prize for public service with a team of reporters. At The Wall Street Journal, where she worked as a reporter and later bureau chief, she was part of the staff that won the 1997 Pulitzer Prize for national reporting, for a series of articles about U.S. policy on AIDS. Most recently, she was editor of the Lexington (KY) Herald-Leader. A 1975 graduate of Harvard College, Bennett, 52, is also the author of several books, including* The Death of the Organization Man, *detailing the effects of new economic realities on individual career paths in corporate America.*

Journalism became a hot career after Bob Woodward and Carl Bernstein's incisive reporting of the Watergate scandal in 1974 and the subsequent publication of their best seller All the President's Men. *Female role models in the profession, however, have been scarce—though not for lack of trying. According to a recent report from the Media Management Center of Northwestern University, while women hold 44 per-cent of newspaper jobs, few are in the top positions; 86 percent of the top jobs in newspapers today are held by men.*

If you love writing about and reporting on the events that shape our lives, don't let those statistics frighten you off. For women to reach the top "is not only possible but completely likely," says Bennett.

Three months after Bennett landed in the catbird's seat at the Inquirer, MAKING BREAD *talked to her about the opportunities for women in journalism and what it takes to succeed in this traditionally male profession.*

MAKING BREAD: What made you decide to pursue journalism?

Amanda Bennet: It sort of picked me! When I was 11, I wrote my first story, and it ran in our local paper. My youngest sister had Down's syndrome, and I described learning about the disease. Writing was pretty intoxicating. After that, I continued to have an interest in it. I worked on the college paper, and I worked with the Associated Press.

MB: What was your first job as a reporter?

AB: I worked for a newspaper in Canada. I was hired as a bilingual reporter in the French-speaking part of Canada, right on the border of Quebec and

Ontario. I was only there for a short time, and then I headed to *The Wall Street Journal*.

MB: What were the most valuable lessons you learned from those early jobs?

AB: *The Wall Street Journal* had a very busy office. I had to watch the wire and then write incredibly complicated, full-length stories. I was learning everything all at once, and I knew nothing about the business. I used to cry a lot! In retrospect, though, I learned that I could do it—even with stuff where I didn't have a clue. I could do it.

MB: How did you work up the ranks to become an editor?

AB: I resisted anyone trying to get me to become an editor for almost 20 years. I loved being a reporter, and I stayed at that much longer than most people do. Then what happened is that I got the job of my dreams: I became a national economics correspondent for *The Wall Street Journal*.

I was based in New York, but I could travel anywhere I wanted. And I got bored. I kept going to the managing editor, applying for every job there was. Finally, I got offered the job of Atlanta Bureau Chief, and I agreed. I realized that I just loved being an editor. After 20 years of trying to avoid it, I realized that it was the perfect job for me.

MB: What are the most valuable skills you need to have as a journalist?

AB: Thinking critically and being able to examine a problem from all sides. In order to report on anything, especially an area where you have no

expertise, you have to start thinking critically; ask yourself what is the most important thing. You have to be able to turn the story around in different ways.

MB: What do you think are the most necessary personality traits to have as a journalist?

AB: All different kinds. Some people are very analytical, some are aggressive, some are empathetic and intellectually curious. Maybe gossipy, too; good journalists want to be where the action is.

MB: How has a career in journalism affected your family life?

AB: I had my children relatively late. They are 14 and 9, and I'm 51. We had to move a lot; my kids hated that. On the other hand, they've had all kinds of experiences they wouldn't have had otherwise. We've lived in great places.

MB: Would you want your children to get involved in journalism?

AB: Neither of them shows the slightest interest, but I think it's a wonderful job. My son is more interested in being a musician, and my daughter is only 9. I'm always encouraging people to pursue journalism.

MB: What advice do you have for women who want a career in journalism?

AB: The most important thing in the profession is that you learn a lot by doing. Find opportunities to write and get published. Just do it!

MB: What does being the first female editor at the

Inquirer mean to other women coming up in the ranks?

AB: It is possible—and completely likely. I'm the first female editor here, but we also have the most diverse masthead in the country. Three of the top positions at the paper are held by women, two of whom are African American. Not only is it possible but it is likely.

MB: Why do you think it took so long for the *Inquirer* to appoint a female editor?

AB: Some of it has to do with historical patterns; some people have been here for a long time.

MB: How hard do you think it is for women to work in a male-dominated field?

AB: When I started 30 years ago, it was an issue. I was young, and that was hard. I was one of only 10 women at *The Wall Street Journal*. There were two specific occasions when I walked into a meeting, and I was asked if I was there for a school paper. So much has changed now; we all have support groups and networks.

MB: Is there anything you would recommend that a woman never do on the job?

AB: Getting involved with someone at work. I can't say, "Never do that," though, because I have seen it work out. I think I underestimated my own potential. Don't do that! Don't throw up barriers to your own success. That's more common than exterior barriers.

MB: What are some ways to get your work noticed?

AB: When I've been really excited about it myself, and I thought my stuff was good, I wanted other peo-

ple to see how good it was! It didn't really bother people, because it was clear that I was excited. Confidence is key. People understand when you're excited about your own work.

MB: What has been your biggest career success?

AB: It sounds so obvious, but I led a team at *The Oregonian* that won the paper a Pulitzer Prize in public service. It was totally thrilling, not only to win, but thrilling to be a part of that team and that paper at the time.

MB: Your biggest failure?

AB: I think of failure as those times when I didn't fully seize my opportunities. I look back on my career, and there were times when I didn't take advantage of moments of opportunity. When I traveled to strange places, I wish I had done more aggressive foreign-correspondent's work. I wish I'd tried more ambitious stories in my life. My failures have been times when I didn't take advantage of terrific opportunities.

MB: What's the headline about women and money you'd most like to see on the front page of the *Inquirer*?

AB: "Women Achieve Wage Parity Because They Achieve Job Parity."

MB: If you had to write a headline describing your life so far, what would it be?

AB: "What a blast!"

Jennifer Vishnevsky was a student at American University in Washington, D.C., and an intern at MAKING BREAD when she wrote this piece.

CHAPTER EIGHT:

BIZ WHIZ-DOM: ADVICE FROM SUCCESSFUL FEMALE ENTREPRENEURS

"It's not enough just to get a job. Women need to create jobs for other women." I was conducting an interview with Rep. Stephanie Tubbs Jones (D-Ohio), the first African American woman to be appointed to the House Ways and Means Committee, when she made that statement, and bells went off in my head. It seemed such a powerful—and empowering—challenge. In fact, there are currently 9.1 million businesses owned or co-owned by women, and they employ 27.5 million people, according to the U.S. Census Bureau. No doubt many of those employees are other very happy women. More female business owners (54 percent of women-owned firms versus 33 percent of male-owned firms with 10 or more employees) offer flextime or job-sharing arrangements as an employee benefit, and more women-owned firms (39 percent versus 30 percent) offer profit-sharing. Small business is a big business for women in this country: employment among women-owned firms has grown by 102 percent since 1987, and sales have grown by 131 percent. The growth of women-owned businesses beats overall business growth by nearly two to one.

Every 60 seconds somewhere in America a woman is starting her own business, says trend-spotter Faith Popcorn, in her 2000 book

EVEolution: Understanding Women—Eight Essential Truths That Work in Your Business and Your Life (Hyperion). She doesn't say how many businesses fail in those same 60 seconds. But any entrepreneur worth her salt wouldn't stop to ask that question. Since founding MAKING BREAD in 2002, I've learned that the most useful character trait a business owner can have is stubbornness—the refusal to give up against tough odds. You have to refuse to lose—refuse to admit defeat. You must be inventive and resourceful, capable of figuring out ways to use what you have to get what you want. You need to be patient and willing to compromise. Above all, you must have faith in your idea and in your ability to bring it to fruition. Another businesswoman I know recently called herself a "cock-eyed optimist." Maybe stubbornness is just another word for optimism; both are necessary to help you get through the dark days when everything seems hopeless. And there will be plenty of those.

Getting practical, it also helps to have talented, supportive partners and enough money to keep you going until your business becomes profitable. We initially launched www.makingbread-magazine.com as a one-page Web site– a promotional tool to use as we went about looking for investor dollars for a print edition of the women's finance magazine we hoped to create. "What you need is a sugar mommy," someone advised me, seeming to indicate that it might be harder to convince a sugar daddy to invest in a women's finance magazine. When investor dollars from either sex proved scarce, in an economic climate when *profitable* magazines were being killed by mega-million-dollar media companies, I decided to use what I have—a brother who has an IT background and was willing to develop a larger Web presence for us and a network of talented writers, editors, and friends who believed in my idea and were willing to contribute to the magazine for the promise of future profit.

We couldn't find the dollars to go to print, so we would publish a digital magazine, instead. In late 2002, digital editions of existing print magazines and newspapers were just coming to market. The wonderful people at Newsstand.com (www.newsstand. com), the largest of the three digital distributors, agreed to carry us—their first digital-only magazine—and MAKING BREAD was born. Later, we decided to go head-to-head against print magazines, positioning our digital magazine on CD-ROM right beside *Cosmo* and *Glamour* and *Fortune* and *Forbes* on real–life newsstands. Putting the magazine where people are accustomed to go to browse for magazines was a move calculated to give broader exposure to the digital format, which I have come to love. When I pass a print newsstand these days, my first thought is, "How old-fashioned," and I look forward to the day when I have enough money to really push the envelope with what can be done graphically and interactively to enhance the reader experience on our digital pages.

I also look forward to the day when I can hire an office full of talented women and give them a forum to create and communicate. In the meantime, the women (and a few men) who are part of our management team and advisory board, the contributing editors and freelance writers who work with me, empower me every day. Coming from the "creative" side of the magazine business, I thought I might find the business side of running a business a) boring and b) intimidating. In fact, it utilizes every creative muscle my brain and soul can muster.

"I encourage women to think about starting their own businesses," Stephanie Tubbs Jones told me in our interview. I do, too. If you have an idea that you believe in, a tolerance for risk, and the willingness to work harder than you've ever worked before, go for it. Don't let no money stop you. With enough determination, you will find a way to build a business with the potential to earn more money than you'd ever make working 9 to 5 for someone else. Don't let your fears limit you. As Myra Hart, co-founder of Staples and now a Harvard Business School professor, says in one of our articles, "Aim high." Think big. This is a global economy. The world is your customer.

In each issue of MAKING BREAD, we publish a "BIZ WHIZ" interview with a successful businesswoman, in which she shares lessons she's learned about starting and building her business. The one thread that runs through all of these interviews is the joy and satisfaction each of these women takes not only from her success, but from the daily routine of meeting unexpected challenges, interacting with customers, and growing her business. In this chapter, we offer "Biz Whiz" interviews, and soundbites from others, as well as expert advice to inform and test your entrepreneurial spirit. Cut the risk factor as much as you can by giving your business a solid foundation.

First up, attorney Sharon Sorokin James lays out five basic steps you should take before starting a business.

RISKY BUSINESS? READ THIS BEFORE STARTING ONE!

Starting your own business is not for the faint of heart, nor for the risk-averse. It requires confidence, discipline, a myriad of talents (or at least skills), a smattering of luck, and perhaps a pinch of insanity. But for many women, it is well worth it for the control, independence, creativity, and satisfaction of doing your own thing and succeeding at it.

More and more of us are taking the plunge: We're starting businesses at twice the rate of men, perhaps because we feel more of a need to create a space that empowers us—where we are in charge. Today there are 9.1 million female-owned businesses, generating $3.6 trillion annually and employing 27.5 million people, according to the Survey of Women-Owned Business Enterprises, part of the U.S. Census Bureau's Economic Census. That's more than all the Fortune 500 companies in America combined.

Thinking of joining the party? Here is our best advice for giving your business a solid foundation, so that you can improve your chances of success in the risky business of starting a business. Because here's a reality check: For every one of the nearly half a million businesses that started last year, according to *The Wall Street Journal*, almost the same number called it quits. Try not to prove the naysayers—those people who are probably telling you right this minute that you must be crazy to even think about it—right. Below are five rules of successful business startups.

biz whiz-dom out of the mouths of babes

Kristine Schaefer, founder of a Loma Communications, a California-based communications-consulting firm.

MAKING BREAD: What's the single most important piece of advice you would give to women who want to start their own business?

Kristine Schaefer: Learn the language of business—in other words, numbers. Without a well-researched business plan, it's difficult to determine if a business idea is viable. Recently, I began discussions with a would-be entrepreneur whose business concept appealed to me. Knowing she'd be great at running this business, I was inclined to become an investor and adviser, until we came to discussing the business plan. "I'll hire someone to do it for me," she said. Her reluctance to delve into the numbers dampened my enthusiasm for supporting her. If she doesn't have the discipline to learn the basics of business planning, how disciplined will she be operating the company?

Know WHAT You Want to Do, WHY You Want to Do It, and HOW You're Going to Do It. Do you want to design clothes or software, manufacture widgets, boats, or ladies' hats? Sell financial services or cater special events? Try to find a way to make a business out of something you have a passion for, and be sure that you are creating real value—a product or service that people need and will pay for.

Once you know what you want to do, you must figure out why you want to do it. The why of your business will drive the decisions that you make and inform its values and priorities. For example, if your primary goal is to develop wealth, you may be more willing to undertake excruciatingly long hours, or a grueling travel schedule. However, if your primary goal is a flexible schedule to accommodate your family, you may be willing to sacrifice certain monetary rewards for psychic and emotional rewards.

Now that you know the what and the why, you can prepare for the how. How will you start this business? "You have to do your homework," says Myra Hart, and she should know. She was one of the founders of the Staples office-supply store chain and is currently a professor of entrepreneurship at Harvard Business School.

Professor Hart has just co-written a book of how-to advice for women starting their own businesses, *Clearing the Hurdles: Women Building High-Growth Businesses*. Reading it is a good place to start doing your "homework." Excellent online resources include the Small Business Admin-istration (www.sba.gov); Entrepreneur magazine (www. entrepreneur.com); The Wall Street Journal's Center for Entrepreneurs at www.startupjournal.com; SCORE (www.score. org), a nonprofit association that provides small business owners with free business counseling; and the National Association of Women Business Owners (www.nawbo.org).

Write a Business Plan and Stick to It (or Adjust It Where Necessary). Having a business plan is extremely important for several reasons. First, it will crystallize for you what you know and don't know about your business. Second, it may help you attract key employees or partners in the earlier stages of your business. Third, it is essential if you want to get investors. No self-respecting investor worth her (or his) salt would put money into a business that doesn't have a plan—a viable plan.

A business plan should state the objective of the company, describe current market conditions for its products or services, identify the competition and what distinguishes you from the competition, lay out a general pricing module and marketing strategies, contain key financial information (such as how much money the business has now, how much it is making, and how much it is spending) and financial projections, and describe the key players in the business.

Finally, the business plan should describe how the business expects to grow over the next several years and the risks inherent in both the business

---

biz whiz-dom out of the mouths of babes

Dottie Drake, founder of Miracles Fitness, a chain of female- and senior-friendly fitness clubs.

MAKING BREAD: How did you raise the money to start your business?

Dottie Drake: Thank God, I owned my home. I took out a home equity line of credit, and that's how I started my business. I took a big risk, putting my house on the line. Would I encourage someone else to do it that way? Probably not. In my situation, I felt it was a calculated risk, an educated risk. I had only myself to take care of, so I took the plunge.

MB: What was your toughest challenge in starting the business?

DD: Being a woman in the male-dominated fitness industry. No one took me seriously. Every place I called to get equipment or financing would say, "Well, I need to speak to the owner." And I'd say, "I am the owner," and they didn't believe me.

itself and in investing in it. If you expect to use the business plan to attract investors, please consult a lawyer to determine the legal requirements that must be met when disclosing the risks of investing and the proper way of presenting your financial projections.

Although it is important to stick to the plan you have made, if market conditions, financial conditions, or other circumstances change so that the plan is no longer viable as conceived and written, then change it in a way that makes sense.

Where do you get the dough to put your plan into action? First, you must know how much you require. Do you need to rent space? Hire employees? Pay for manufacturing? Buy computers, stationery, insurance? What about paying yourself? All of this must be factored into your financial projections.

Almost all entrepreneurs, according to Professor Hart, "start the business on their own money alone. Because women in the corporate world are underpaid, relative to men, and have a shorter period of time in the workforce before they become entrepreneurs," she says, "they have less of a nest egg to put into business. Nonetheless, the vast majority of entrepreneurs don't get outside capital until they have actually already developed a product, gotten something into the market, and developed proof of concept."

So how do entrepreneurs fund their startups until they can get to the point where they can approach an investor? Most often, in the form of "their own cash, a mortgage or second mortgage, and foregone expenses—such as working out of one's home, or not paying oneself—until they have developed enough credibility to get people to buy into the business concept," Hart says, then she shares this tip: "Venture capital firms with women

on board make a far higher proportion of investments in firms led by women."

Bottom line: what this really means is that most entrepreneurs, and in particular, most female entrepreneurs, who tend to have fewer resources, are strapped for cash. Although for nearly all women entrepreneurs, it will be harder to obtain loans and investors than it often is for male counterparts, Professor Hart reminds us that women should "aim high and ask often. We never get what we don't aspire to and ask for. You have to be prepared to go out and enlist the aid of others and be relentless and enduring in seeking the kinds of resources you need to make your business grow."

Excellent advice for all of life, not just for starting a business. Aim high and ask often.

Put All the Pieces in Place. What assets does your business need? There are three kinds of assets: tangible assets, such as a building, or a piece of equipment; intangible assets, such as

biz whiz-dom out of the mouths of babes

Kristine Schaefer, founder of Loma Communications, a California-based communications-consulting firm.

MB: As a media specialist, what advice can you offer women on how to publicize and market their businesses?

KS: Everyone loves to hear a good story, so if you're not comfortable talking about yourself, tell an interesting anecdote about one of your customers or how your product or service delivers value. The one story that every owner must learn to tell is why she started the business. People will learn something about you and what you stand for.

processes and formulas and protected ideas; and human assets—your employees. Be sure you have determined the full extent of all three types of assets you will need.

Will you need a physical location or special equipment? Can you work from your basement or spare bedroom of your home, or do you need an office, factory or warehouse? Should you lease or own your space? Your accountant (by now you should have selected one, preferably with experience counseling similar businesses) can help you make this decision.

Intangible assets are equally important, and can and should be protected. Intangible assets are often referred to as "intellectual property." Intellectual property may be a new method for doing something, a formula, a recipe, a source code, an article, the content of your training manuals—there are many kinds of intellectual property. These forms of property are protected through patents, copyrights ,and trademarks. You can find out more about copyright protection by visiting the U.S. Government Copyright Office at www.copyright.gov, or by consulting an intellectual property lawyer.

When considering the assets you will need for your business, don't forget the human assets. Will your business need any employees, other than yourself, during its first year of operation? Will you be paying your employees? Will they be working for a piece of the business? If so, how will that be documented? You should have clear, written agreements describing the relationships, if the employee is to be a part owner of the business. Finally, if you are hiring employees, you should consult an accountant and lawyer to be sure you correctly handle all aspects of the unemployment, Social Security, and tax issues.

Create a Marketing Plan. A marketing plan is essential, even if, in the beginning, you must create it yourself. Identify who will purchase your products or services, why they will purchase them, and how you can reach them to convince them to purchase them. Will you be serving preexisting clients from a former professional life of yours? Will you be advertising products in newspapers, radio, or on television? Will you be undertaking a direct-mail ad campaign? Will you be relying on word of mouth? The best business concept in the world, even if beautifully executed, will not succeed without customers.

Make It Official. What are you the CEO of? How you structure your business will determine how much tax you owe, how much liability you have, and how you share the profits with your partners. There are many guises under which one may conduct business, including sole proprietorships, general partnerships, limited partnerships, limited liability partnerships, limited liability corporations, and corporations. All of these entities are "creatures of state law"—that is, although they are similar in their powers and rights from state to state, they are governed by the laws of the state in which they were created, and those laws give them particular sets of rights and powers. This means that you must consult a lawyer in the state in which you plan to organize and operate to determine which type of entity is the best for you. Below, is a brief overview of the general differences among the types of entities.

A sole proprietorship is an unincorporated business owned by one individual. It's the simplest form of business organization to start and maintain, according to the IRS. What sets it apart from the other structures is that you bear sole liability. However, the profits are also yours alone. You record the income of the business and can deduct all qualified business expenses on your own tax return.

A *general partnership* is a business or undertaking in which two or more people or entities come together to do particular things (although the purposes can be extremely broad). The hallmark of a general partnership is that all of its partners are fully liable for the acts of the partnership and for the acts of the partners related to the partnership. Income and expense deductions are shared by all the partners.

A *limited partnership* is a partnership for one or more purposes, which is composed of one or more general partners and one or more limited partners. The general partner or partners are fully liable for the acts of the partnership. The limited partners are not. Under the laws of most states, the liability of the limited partners is limited to their investment in the partnership. However, the price the limited partners "pay" for this limitation on liability is that they are not allowed to have any say in the day-to-day management of the partnership.

A *limited liability company* is similar to a limited partnership, except that it has members, instead of partners, and generally all of its members are insulated from liability. Limited liability companies provide more flexibility in operations than limited partnerships, while retaining liability protection.

A *corporation* is an entity in which people (or other entities) hold ownership positions in the form of stock. The stockholders are not liable for the acts of the corporation, unless they behave as if the corporation is their own personal fiefdom—that is, if they don't observe corporate formalities. Some corporations are taxed like partnerships, as long as they meet certain criteria and make certain tax elections.

Minding Your Business. Going into business requires great vision, an almost obsessive and single-minded passion for your idea, endurance in the face of seemingly insurmountable obstacles, and resourcefulness, so that you can make the most of your initially limited resources. Doing your homework and following up by putting all the legal, marketing, logistical, and financial pieces of the puzzle in place will go a long way toward reducing the risk of any startup, but the smart entrepreneur knows one more trick.

"The good entrepreneur recognizes risk and is willing to tolerate it, but she gives most of it away," says Myra Hart. "For example, by pre-selling your product, you transfer risk to the customer. Management or partners take on risk, giving up good jobs and money in the short term to work with you, betting they will make more in the long term. The good entrepreneur sees opportunity where others do not and mobilizes energy and resources to make it happen."

If that's a job description that fits you like your favorite business suit, you're ready to mind your own business.

Plan to Succeed with Your Business Plan

A BUSINESS PLAN is a communication tool and a plan of action. If you are starting a new business or expanding an existing one, and seek funding, you have to have one. Your business plan is where you show off everything you know about your product or service (and that should be everything there is to know about it) with the goal of persuading someone to invest in you. Think of yourself as the salesperson and your business as the product you are pitching. You have to convince the reader (potential financial backers, partners, banks, accountants and lawyers) that there is a need for your product or service and that you are the one to provide it in a cost-efficient manner that will make a profit. Go to www.sba.gov for a free small-business startup guide, including an in-depth guide to writing a business plan. Basically, a business plans consists of the following main sections:

The Executive Summary. This provides a concise overview of the entire plan; it should be the last section that you write. It is a summary of all the details of your business plan.

Market Analysis. This should include an industry description and outlook, target market information, market test results, and an evaluation of your competition.

Company Description. This section should include information about the nature of your business (*why* you're in business), as well as a list of the primary factors that you believe will make your business a success.

Organization and Management. The *who* of your business, here you will provide the information about the ownership of the business, profiles of your management team, with a special emphasis on your own skills and background, and the qualifications of your board of directors.

Marketing and Sales Strategies. Marketing is the process of creating customers. What is your market strategy now and *how* will it grow in the future? Who are your potential customers? How many are there?

Service or Product Line. *What* are you selling? Include the specific benefits of your product or service, the product/service's ability to meet consumer needs, advantages that your product/service has over the competition.

Funding Request. Here you will request he amount of funding you will need to start or expand your business. Lenders will want to know how you plan to use the money—capital expenditures? Working capital? Debt retirement? Acquisitions?

Exit Strategy. What is your end game, and how will your investors make their money back, plus a return on their investment (ROI)?

Financials. The financials should be developed after you've analyzed the market and set objectives. If your business is already established this is where you will provide historical financial data—past income statements, balance sheets, and cash-flow statements. If you are a startup seeking seed money, supply prospective financial data—projected income and expense budgets, balance sheets, cash-flow statements, capital-expenditure budgets, etc.

The Appendix. This section includes resumes of key managers, product pictures or drawings, details of market studies, licenses, permits or patents, copies of leases, contracts with suppliers, business consultants, attorney and accountant, and anything else that will help to impress and persuade your target audience.

One Final Note: This is serious business. Before you begin to pass your business plan around to interested parties, have an attorney carefully review the plan to be sure that it conforms to Securities and Exchange Commission (www.sec.gov) rules regarding investment solicitations. You must accurately disclose the risk of investing in your company and identify any assumptions that you have made in projecting future success. While you're at it, have the attorney also prepare a non-disclosure and confidentiality agreement, which you will ask your potential investors and other interested parties to sign before reading your plan.

WHAT DO YOU DO WHEN YOU WANT TO SUCCEED IN A MAN'S WORLD?

REDEFINE IT AS A WOMAN'S WORLD, SAYS THIS HEAD OF A SUCCESSFUL NEW CONSTRUCTION COMPANY

BY SHARON SOROKIN JAMES

Emily Bittenbender is 37 years old and has a bachelor's degree in fine arts. She grew up in a small town in Pennsylvania and studied at an excellent art school, but never attended business school. That she is now the majority owner of a construction company that bears her name and is bidding on—and winning—multimillion-dollar contracts is proof both that she is an excellent architect of her own career and that you don't need a business degree to be a big success in business.

She will tell you that her biggest success to date is "being part of the team that designed and built the National Constitution Center," which opened July 4, 2003 to much fanfare in Philadelphia. As vice president of design and construction for the center, she led the team's efforts to build, on time and under budget, this magnificent $100,000,000 center devoted to the Constitution. Before that, her career included stints working for a large architectural and design firm in Philadelphia (where she served as construction manager for the renovation of a City-owned office building) and serving as the City's Director of Capital Projects and a member of then-Mayor Ed Rendell's cabinet.

Bittenbender is a tenacious negotiator, a very hard worker, and an excellent manager, able to coax savings out of even the most obdurate budgets. She is also outgoing, warm, stylish and fun-loving. MAKING BREAD was delighted to have had the chance to sit down and chat with her about her success in what many people consider to be a man's world and what

she and a handful of other women are redefining as a "woman's world."

MAKING BREAD: Tell us how Bittenbender Construction Company got started.

Emily Bittenbender: I started the company with two partners in October 2003. One of my partners, John Kratzinger, has a background in the construction industry. My other partner, Pierce Keating, owns a large construction company. I own 65 percent of Bittenbender Construction Company. Being very small and very young, we try to conserve dollars and do everything ourselves.

When we started the business, we planned it so that we would have enough money to carry it for the first year of operations. We each invested in the business, and there are some loans, too. Our goal was to be self-sufficient within a year. We reached our goal within three months, because we landed several contracts right away.

MB: Do you think the construction industry is a difficult industry for women?

EB: It's a good business for women. I've always been a really firm believer in that. I don't know why more women don't go into construction. Many women think construction is a male-dominated field—and it is—and women are scared off or haven't ventured into it because of that. But there is tremendous opportunity for women in this area. Lots of governmental and other public bodies require that part of their work be done by women- and/or minority-owned firms. We're certified as a female-owned firm with the city of Philadelphia, and we're going through the process of becoming certified with the state and others.

MB: What do you especially like about the construction industry?

EB: I love this work, because there's a tangible reward at the end of it. You drive by the building you helped to build and can walk up to it and touch it.

MB: Why did you decide to go into business on your own?

EB: Honestly, I didn't want to work for anyone else again. In all my previous jobs, I worked enormous hours and wasn't really benefiting myself. Also, I wanted to create something with our own culture and not have to adapt to somebody else's culture.

MB: What are your plans for growth?

EB: We will grow pretty quickly in the first two years, if my business plan is right. It's an enormous amount of work. Including marketing and all the stuff I do in the evenings, I work 80 hours a week. The idea originally was that I would just do the marketing, but I have to manage projects and be involved. As we staff up, I'll be freer to do more marketing. We've been really fortunate. We've landed a couple of corporate clients, bidding against our standard competitors. Now there are two big school projects, where we are applying with a joint-venture partner—a very large construction company. We'll be the female-owned business on the job.

MB: Other than opening your own business, what do you consider your single greatest achievement in your career?

EB: Being part of the team that designed and built the National Constitution Center.

MB: What advice do you have for women who are in nontraditional careers?

EB: I would say: Do what you love and have no fear, whether you have a place there or not. You make your own place. There's absolutely no reason to be intimidated by a man, ever.

To find out more about opportunities for women in construction, a field that is expected to grow by more than a million jobs in the next decade, visit the Web sites of Professional Women in Construction (www.pwcusa.org), the National Association of Women in Construction (www.nawic.org), or Associated Builders and Contractors (www.abc.org).

WHEN YOU NEED DOUGH . . .

As Harvard's Professor Hart indicated, most women rely on their own cash, credit, or other assets, such as a home-equity line of credit, second mortgage, or foregone salary, to fund their startups. More than half of all funding for startups comes from the founder's personal investment of one sort or another. However, between 1992 and 1996, the percent of women-owned firms using credit cards to cover short-term needs dropped from 52 percent to 23 percent, and the percent using business earnings doubled, from 38 percent to 72 percent.

In general, until you have proof of concept—in other words, demonstrated consumer appeal and existing cash flow—it is difficult to find an investor to back your product or idea. Women receive less than 5 percent of venture capital, according to Fund Isabella (www.fundisabella.com), a venture-capital (VC) firm focusing on early-stage women-led companies. As Hart indicated, your chances of success in obtaining funding increase when you approach firms that have women in management positions. Funds that specialize in funding women-owned firms are your best first stop on the road to VC dollars; besides Fund Isabella, they include Seraph Capital Forum (www.seraphcapital.com), Axxon Capital (www.axxoncapital.com), and Capital Across America (www.capitalacrossamerica.org). Check local business listings for groups that may have formed in your area, with an interest in funding regional women-owned firms.

Most states have programs designed to help women and minorities find the resources—financial and otherwise—that they need to start their own businesses. You might start your hunt for working capital by checking with your State Departments of Labor or Commerce to see what your options are locally. The federal government offers grants to certain businesses, but if you decide to pursue this route, be prepared for a very long approval process. The ultimate source for government grant information is the Catalog of Federal Domestic Assistance (www.CFDA.gov).

Applying for a loan from a Small Business Administration-approved lending source may be a better way to capitalize your business, as long as you already have demonstrated cash flow. The Small Business Administration (SBA) doesn't offer grants, but it does make it possible for small business owners to qualify for loans for which they might not otherwise be eligible. Basically, if you meet the SBA's criteria of a sound business risk, it will guarantee a substantial portion of your loan (as much as 85 percent of loans up to $150,000 and 75 percent of loans of more than $150,000, up to a maximum of $1 million) to fund your business. That can be a boon to those who don't have the necessary collateral to obtain commercial loans. Go to www.sba.gov/ financing to find information on lender programs backed by the SBA. Another source: The Commerce Department's Minority Business Development Agency offers good advice on alternative financing sources at its site, www.mbda.gov.

If your business is already up and running, one method of handling a short-term cash-flow problem is "factoring" your receivables. Factors are companies that buy your accounts receivable from you. In essence, they're betting on your customers' ability to pay. You get cash up front from the factor; it collects your receivables, charging you a fee of between 3 and 6 percent a month, until all the debts are collected and they get back the money they advanced to you.

Who else can "show you the money"? You probably know people who have taken out a second mortgage on their homes and/or hit up their relatives to get the seed money they need to plant their "field of dreams" and keep it watered until those crucial first, second, and third crops come in. There's a reason for that—even with SBA backing, it isn't easy convincing commercial banks to put up "their" money where your mouth is, so to speak.

If you've done your homework, have an accurate picture of your risks, as well as the upside (competitive advantage) of your particular business (no hype—this is the time to be honest with yourself!), then that's not a bad way to go, either. That's assuming, or course, that you're fortunate enough to have those resources to call upon. If your family comes through for you on this scale, you'll never be able to take them for granted—or miss a holiday meal with them, again!

One thing you can do right now ...

GET ON THE IRS'S BUDDY LIST

If you're self-employed or a small business owner, sign up for the IRS's free e-mail service, designed to keep you current on all tax changes that apply to you, as well as provide you with alerts regarding important upcoming tax dates, and the availability of recently added tax forms and publications. Just log onto www.irs.gov/businesses/small/index.html and submit your e-mail.

biz whiz-dom out of the mouths of babes

Marrie Hill, owner of the Thriller Clothing Company boutique in Las Vegas.

MAKING BREAD: You told us you used your savings to start the business. Would being a saver be your smartest money move, so far?

Marrie Hill: Absolutely! I am very careful with money and move slowly when it comes to making changes with the business. Not being in debt was a big plus when I started the business. I didn't feel like I was behind and had to catch up. It was more like I started at the beginning and just went up from there.

HOME SWEET HOME BUSINESS

More than a third of women-owned businesses, or 3.5 million of them, are small family affairs, operated out of spare bedrooms or basements. Most of these businesses are small, employing fewer than 10 people. Working out of the home has its advantages and disadvantages.

Pros: You get tax benefits for your home office (check with your accountant to make sure you conform to the rules), the overhead is less than if you have to rent space, and there are no commuting costs. You don't have to spend as much on clothes, and you might not need extended day care for your school-age children. You can also write off work-related expenses on your tax returns. One woman used to deduct snow removal as a business expense—how else would her clients get to her? If you telecommute, some of your expenses may be reimbursed.

Cons: Unless you're a telecommuter, paid to work at home by your employer, there's no certain paycheck. This can be nerve-racking. And it's often difficult to keep your work and home life separate. For your protection, you should consider the added cost of home-office insurance. One woman kept her files in the basement, and when the water heater exploded, she lost a lot of crucial information. Have a back-up system to protect your records in case of fire or disaster.

Often, women will start their business out of their home and move to an office setting when their business grows. Val started a booking agency for Texas musicians 10 years ago. "All I needed," she remembers, "was an extra phone line for the fax and computer. I was able to save on rent and was eligible for a partial tax write-off of the utilities and maintenance for that part of the house." But she admits it was difficult to set boundaries between work and family obligations, especially when her son came home from school. "You have to be self-disciplined to work out of the house," she adds, "and my only contact with the outside world was by telephone. I would try to meet friends for lunch just to see and talk with a live human being."

Val soon realized that she couldn't keep up with the business end of the business. "I deal with so much paperwork," she says, "Contracts, promotional material, CDs, touring schedules, billings, etc. It became overwhelming, and the trips to the post office took hours." She finally moved to an office in town and hired Gigi, who handles the paperwork plus keeps the financial records in order on the computer. She has added two part-timers and now has five phone lines and several linked computers. The part-timers help Gigi get all the materials out and keep the business organized.

"After 10 years in this business, I'm tired. I

With a Little Help from Your Friends

If you're starting a new small business and need working capital, the solution may be closer than you think. Loans made by family, friends, and colleagues amount to $65 billion annually, according to experts. But even when you're borrowing from someone you know, you need to formalize the terms and the process. To the rescue: Circlelending.com, which for a small fee will act as middleman to administer the loan process. It has a "Small Business Fundraising Kit," "Handshake Plus" contracts, and other custom-tailored loan repayment plans to help your friends feel comfortable with the arrangement. To find out more, visit www.circlelending.com.

would do anything to take two straight weeks off at any one time," Val says, "No ringing phones, no faxes, no e-mails. But that's not possible. My son finishes high school next year, so I'm thinking of moving the office back home. The money saved in rent would go to the ever-increasing costs of providing medical insurance for my family and one full-time employee." Val suggests, with tongue only partly in cheek, that small business owners would benefit from having a spouse with a corporate job and a terrific health plan to cover the family's medical insurance.

Besides health coverage, as you grow, you'll want to offer your employees and yourself a retirement savings plan. Retirement plans for the self-employed and small business owners include Keoghs, SEP-IRAs, simple IRAs, and self-employed 401(k) plans. They are described in more detail in Chapter Six. Discuss the tax advantages of each of these options with your accountant or tax adviser before deciding which one is best for you.

And speaking of taxes, a good accountant is a must for any small business owner. If you are the creative type and hate paperwork, consider hiring a part-time bookkeeper to set up all income and expenses on a computer program. If you are a sole proprietor, you will report your income on Schedule C—Profit or Loss from Business. You subtract expenses from gross income and pay tax on the net profit. Just remember that the IRS will not allow you to run a business that continually loses money. If you don't show a profit in at least three of every five consecutive years, the IRS will consider your business a hobby.

There is a lot to consider if you are starting a business or thinking of expanding an existing one. Look at your strengths and weaknesses. Concentrate on what you are good at. Hire people to handle those tasks where you are weak. Check your local newspaper for networking organizations, designed especially for you, the self-employed woman.

CHAPTER NINE:
CASH DIETING TIPS & FINANCIAL MAKEOVERS

News flash: There's a 99-cent store in Beverly Hills. Saving must be the new shopping chic.

A lady stopped me on the street, as I was walking to the office one morning. She was wearing a Burberry jacket and carrying a Dooney & Bourke handbag, and she asked me if I knew where the nearest dollar store was. "They're always around, when you're not looking for them," she complained. As it happened, there were two within three blocks, and I directed her to the closest one.

And then it occurred to me: Shopping at dollar stores has become the new shopping chic. There's even a 99-cent store in Beverly Hills these days, reports *Money* magazine. Some time between the high-flying 90s and now, when the Hilton sisters weren't looking, it became fashionable to save money, and more and more people are coming out of the closet about their frugal ways. If you haven't been to a dollar store yet, you should try it: you'll never pay full price for garbage bags or laundry soap again.

Nor should you. Why pay top dollar for anything, when you can get it for less and save the difference? That savings, however small it may seem now, will make a *big* difference in the quality of your life later on, if you let it earn interest for you.

More to the point, why pay *over-the-top* dollar for anything, when you can get it for less and save the difference? What's over-the-top dollar? The price of any purchase you put on a credit card and don't pay off before interest kicks in.

Throughout this book, we've enumerated the reasons women need to save money. We have a choice to make with every penny we earn: spend it or save it—two sides of the same coin. Flip a switch in your head and begin to view the money you don't spend as a gift you're giving yourself. That way, you won't feel like you're depriving yourself, when you pass up charging yet another pair of shoes on your Visa or Mastercard. (An Oppenheimer Funds survey a few years ago revealed that 54 percent of single women say they are more likely to accumulate 30 pairs of shoes than $30,000 in retirement savings.) Credit-card debt is one of the major obstacles to our financial security.

A couple of years ago, I was asked by a TV interviewer what my best advice for women who are worried about debt is. I said the first thing that came to my mind: "Pay your bills on time." What a boring, predictable answer that must have seemed. But, in fact, the credit climate has changed dramatically in the last five years. When interest rates dropped to new lows, financial institutions began to look for ways to make up for what they wouldn't be earning in interest payments. To make up the difference, they've raised penalty fees for late payments to $39 (and up) now—and shortened the amount of time, known as the "grace period," that you have to send your payment in before interest payments are levied. Where once you had 25 or 30 days, you may now only have 20. Make a habit of paying late and not only will you be hit with late-payment fees, your interest rates will be increased and your credit score will suffer, making it difficult for you to receive low rates from other lenders.

"Pay your bills on time." As boring and predictable as that answer may seem, given existing sky-high penalty fees and the recent rise in interest rates, there is a special urgency to getting your debt under control now. You're never going to get ahead financially, unless you pay your bills on time and pay more than the minimum required. In this chapter, we'll offer strategies for managing your credit-card debt—ways you can become the kind of person who *earns* interest, not the kind who pays it. We'll also offer first-person stories written by shopaholics and recovering shopaholics—plus a financial makeover given by two of our experts, advising a woman who wrote to MAKING BREAD for advice.

HOW MANY CARDS DO YOU HAVE IN YOUR WALLET?

Until 1975, many lending institutions discriminated against women. Creditors routinely disregarded a wife's income on the assumption that she would become pregnant and not return to work. They would ask couples of child-bearing age what kind of birth-control practices they used and whether they planned to have children.

---

6 questions to ask before you spend a dime

Ask yourself these questions every time you pull out your wallet. Try it for a month and see how much money you save. Remember, the more you save now the more you'll have to spend later.

1. Do I *need* this or *want* this?
2. What *won't* I be able to buy, if I spend my money on this now?
3. What *will* I be able to buy later, if I don't spend this now?
4. Would I buy this if I were paying cash, instead of using a credit card?
5. Is there a cheaper alternative?
6. How much interest would this money earn for me if I put it in the bank instead?

Many married women did not have credit histories in their own name, even though their husbands did. Credit bureaus did not carry histories in the name of both the husband and the wife. This created problems for divorced and widowed woman, when they applied for credit. When co-author Elizabeth Lewin was divorced in 1974, she never considered that she would have trouble getting a credit card. But with no credit history in her own name, the only way she was able to obtain a card was with the help of a close friend (male, of course) who was the manager of a bank and knew her situation.

That all changed in 1975, with the passing of the Equal Credit Opportunity Act, making credit equally available to all creditworthy people without regard to sex, marital status, race, religion, or

CHARGING INTO TROUBLE

A SPENDAHOLIC REVEALS THE CREDIT-CARD STRATEGIES THAT GOT HER WHERE SHE IS TODAY

BY LAURIE M. LESSER

"You play that thing like a slot machine," my best friend, Carol, said to me the last time I saw her in New York. She was referring to the ATM machine I had just swiped my Visa card through. She was right. It was a time in my life when I never knew what would come out—the cash I requested or the white slip that read "Insufficient funds for this transaction."

"I don't know how you can live like that," Carol said, shaking her head. She always knows exactly how much is in her checking account, which is, of course, always perfectly balanced. I told her I didn't know how she could live the way she does, but not without a tinge of envy. "You're so anal," I snapped.

I think my spending habits are genetic. My mother's like this; my father's even worse. Both of them think that if you use a credit card, it doesn't really cost you anything. That way they can afford to be as generous with their wallets as they are with their hearts.

Carol told me this story about her daughter. Hannah, being 7 years old, has very childish and naïve ideas about money. The other week, she wanted a new Barbie doll, and her mother said it was too expensive. It was just a week or two after Hannah's birthday, which is not too long after Christmas.

"I don't have any money left," Carol told her.

"Just go to D'Agostino's, and put your card in the machine and get some," Hannah said.

Makes sense to me.

When I am really broke and can't withdraw any money from an ATM (because there's nothing in the account), the solution seems obvious: charge it. Of course, charge cards have minimums, so you can't just charge a simple sandwich. You are forced to have a decent meal, maybe a glass or two of wine—but it's the only way to eat with no money. A girl can't let herself starve, can she?

Or, you go out with a friend or two and put the whole tab on your card and collect cash from your gal pals. You have a good meal with friends and leave with more money in your pocket than when you walked in. What could be more sensible?

Once Carol and I met for drinks in New York. I was totally broke at the time, but for some reason, I had invited her out. She was working across from the U.N. building, and we ended up at the Waldorf Astoria Hotel. Comfortable armchairs, piano music, and vodka gimlets that were only a couple of dollars more than in the cheap Irish bar on Second Avenue. There was one other advantage: here I could pay with my Visa card. We ordered our two vodka gimlets on the rocks and looked around, feeling really cool and classy. I told her I was hungry; I really needed to eat something. We reached for the little bar menus on the low tables between the armchairs. The cheapest thing on the menu was $15 for a small serving of caviar and blinis. We had no choice.

I put it all on my card, so it didn't cost me anything at all that night. And now I can say I've had caviar and vodka in the Waldorf piano lounge.

But there must be a better way!

Laurie M. Lesser works as a freelance editor and writer in Washington, D.C. She is at work on a novel.

age. Under the provisions of this act, creditors must now consider both part-time as well as full-time income. Alimony and child support can be used as evidence of the ability to repay. All joint accounts are reported in both a husband's and wife's name to the credit bureau. A woman can now have her own credit history. If you have been denied credit, you have the right to find out why.

Consumer credit got its start nearly 150 years ago when Isaac Singer thought up the concept of paying "on time": $5 down, $5 a month, for his $125 sewing machine. With this payment plan, Singer generated sales that would have been impossible if people, who earned on average only $525 a year in 1856, had to pay the full price of his machine up front. He never envisioned that one day almost everything—from groceries to movie tickets and college tuition—would be paid over time by credit card.

Today, credit-card issuers come up with one marketing strategy after another to lure customers to accept and use their cards—rebates, rewards, free miles, low introductory interest rates, etc. Competition is fierce to bring in new customers—and it is working. The Federal Reserve Board reports that household debt is at a record high, relative to disposable income. Consider some of the following figures: The average U.S. household carries more than $9,340 in debt, according to CardWeb.com, a company that monitors credit-card use. The average American has seven credit cards—three bank cards and four retail cards. (How many do you have in your wallet?) Total consumer debt in the United States is at more than $1.98 trillion, and over the past seven years approximately 9.5 million Americans have filed for personal bank-

ruptcy— which may explain why competition among debt-consolidation companies is even fiercer. Women have a higher bankruptcy rate than men do.

Plastic is here to stay. Used wisely, there's no doubt that paying over time offers many benefits. But, for those who can't control its use, credit carries great temptation and danger. Women can't afford to give more money to the banks and credit-card companies than they have to. Be a "controlling woman," says MAKING BREAD. Take control of your finances to take control of your life. That starts with limiting the bite out of your finances that interest rates, late-fees and other finance charges take.

Those of us who have trouble controlling our spending often have trouble prioritizing our needs and our wants. You may *want* a Jaguar or a trip to Barbados, but you need an emergency fund, and you need to save for your secure retirement. Fulfill those needs before you give yourself what you want. Better yet, stop and think about what you *really* want; you may find that it is financial security. Money in the bank. Freedom of choice and freedom from worry. The ability to do what you want.

Most of us step on a scale every morning, or at least once a week, to weigh ourselves. That way, if our weight begins to climb, we can start cutting back on our calories and carbs. Carrying around too much debt is a lot like carrying around too much weight. So count up the amount you owe on each credit card or consumer loan at least once a month, and if you see the numbers beginning to inch up, take charge (no pun intended) of the situation by cutting back on your spending and pay off those high balances. Either you control your credit, or it will control and limit you.

ABC'S OF CREDIT

There are two kinds of consumer credit (besides home mortgages, which were covered in detail in Chapter Three): installment loans and credit cards.

A personal installment loan is money lent to you, which you agree to repay in regular installments, plus interest, over a period of time. Major lending sources for installment loans are banks, credit unions, and finance companies. A car loan is a typical example of a personal installment loan.

Loans can be either secured or unsecured. A secured or collateralized loan is one in which you offer security, or a tangible pledge of goods or real estate, to guarantee repayment. Creditors have the assurance that, should you not repay the money, they will be compensated, because you will forfeit the collateral. Home mortgages and auto loans are prime examples of secured loans. An unsecured loan—and most credit cards fall into this category—is backed by your ability and willingness to repay, as measured by your current income and good credit rating.

Credit Card or Charge Card? Not all credit cards are equal. There are several basic types:

Retail credit cards are issued by department stores, oil companies, or specialty shops. They impose credit limits, charge interest on unpaid balances, and those rates tend to be higher than the rates offered by bank credit cards. Every time you open one of these accounts, you're adding another creditor to your credit report. Ask yourself: do you really need that Macy's or Bloomingdale's or Sears card? Why jeopardize your credit rating, for the paltry discounts or benefits that might be promised by these cards?

Bank credit cards are issued by thousands of banks and credit unions across the country, usually through MasterCard or Visa. Both the credit limit and the. interest rate you qualify for are based on your household income and credit rating. You have the option of either paying your bill in full each month or carrying (revolving) the balance over to the next month, paying a finance charge on the outstanding balance. In general, as you charge more money and pay it off on time, your credit limit increases. If you are habitually late in paying your monthly bills or you skip payments, your limit will be reduced (or your credit cut off) and the interest rate charged on the balance will most likely be increased.

Charge cards (think American Express or Diner's Club) are the answer, if you want the convenience of whipping out plastic and not carrying a lot of cash, but you *hate* paying interest on your purchases. Charge cards don't charge interest; they are credit cards issued by financial institutions to customers who pay an annual membership fee and agree to pay each monthly bill in full. Most also offer an extended-payment plan to cover certain travel expenses, which does charge interest. There is no set credit limit on the amount you can charge.

Even with their sometimes high annual fees ($50 and up), if you tend to use plastic a lot, the cost of a charge card is significantly less than the interest-related debt that accompanies credit cards. Most merchants accept both charge cards and credit cards. Both types generally offer perks in the form of rewards based on the amount of your purchases. The more you use your card, the greater the number of frequent-flier miles, for example. Latest wrinkle: cash-rebate cards pay the holder a percent on purchases. Don't let these incentives to spend cause you to buy things you don't need.

Then there are the affinity credit-card programs—some 1,500 of them. These set up relationships between charities and nonprofit organizations, including alumni associations and professional organizations. The organizations benefit by receiving a portion of the cardholders' annual fees and/or transaction fees. Again, don't let these feel-good cards affect your spending. If you want to donate to Greenpeace, just send them a check.

Credit-card holders get into trouble when they can't resist the impulse to max out their spending limit. Think of your available credit as insurance—not spending money, or an extension of your salary. Get in the habit of using your card only for emergencies. Look into online bill-paying and automatic payment arrangements, too, to avoid those rising late-payment fees.

The pluses: Credit cards let you buy what you need or want without carrying large sums of cash around. They allow you to keep money you've already spent in an interest-bearing account, earning money for you, until the credit-card bill comes. As long as you pay off the balance before the credit-card company charges you interest, you come out ahead. You bought what you wanted, enjoyed it now, paid for it later, and *earned* interest in the meantime.

Remember secured loans? One final type of plastic is the secured credit card. People who have had credit problems and are having trouble obtaining a credit card can generally get a "secured" card by depositing money—usually $300 to $500—with the issuer. The line of credit is the amount you put into the savings account. The finance charge will probably be very high, plus there will be other fees. Prove that you can pay on time, and eventually you will be rewarded

with a regular credit card. Read the fine print before applying for a secured card. Your deposit should be returned to you at some point. However, some scams have surfaced involving issuers handing out secured cards, then immediately charging initiation fees of $500, reducing the holders' credit limit to 0 until the money, plus interest, is paid off.

What Are Creditors Looking for? Two things: Ability to repay, and willingness to pay. They want to know what your present total income is, including such sources as alimony, child-support payments, investments, and full or part-time employment? Is your income sufficient enough to permit repayment of debt? On your loan application, do not show income that is based on overtime pay or on moonlighting. What if that income should stop? Also, before you take on the responsibility of repaying any loan or carrying monthly credit charges, make sure you have sufficient emergency funds to pay your debts, as well as other living expenses, if you are laid off.

Willingness to pay is judged by your past performance: have you repaid previous obligations and paid them on time? If you have no history of borrowing, you will need to convince the lender that you understand the responsibility and will meet it. The lender may insist that you have a co-signer. This means that the co-signer is as liable for the payments on the account as you are, even though the card is in your name and will be reported that way.

Saying Grace for the "Grace Period" Are you what credit issuers call a "convenience user"—someone who pays the full amount due every month? If you are, you can take advantage of the billing cycle to gain a free ride. Here's how:

Most credit cards allow a grace period of 20 days (down from 25 to 30 days a few years ago) after the date on which they bill you, before they begin to assess finance charges. If you make a purchase immediately after your billing date (you'll find the date on your bill), and if you pay in full when the bill comes due, you get free credit for almost two months. Say your billing date is January 1. You buy a new microwave on January 2. The charge won't appear on your statement until February. You then have until due date stated on your bill (probably around February 20) to pay for it. If you pay the full amount of your new balance by that date, no interest will be charged. You've had free use of your microwave for almost six weeks—and the price of that purchase has been earning interest in your checking or savings account.

Interpreting Those Finance Charges. If you don't pay the amount due in full every month, you are referred to as "a revolver," and your credit-card company starts tacking on finance charges. Any of several methods of calculation may be used by your company. The most common is the average daily balance method, which comes in three flavors:

The average daily balance method, excluding newly billed purchases. This is the best of all methods, but it is becoming increasingly hard to find. Under this method, you are given a grace period for newly purchased items. Your finance charge is calculated based on the previous billing period's average daily balance. (Calculate your average daily balance by adding each day's balance and dividing the total by the number of days in the billing cycle. To get your finance charge for the month, multiply the average daily balance by your card's monthly periodic rate, which is calculated by dividing your annual percentage rate by 12. For instance, a card with an annual interest rate of 18 percent would have a monthly periodic rate of 1.5 percent. If your card had an average daily balance of $500, it would be billed a monthly finance charge of $7.50.)

The average daily balance method, including newly billed purchases. In this method, you get no grace period for newly purchased items. As soon as your latest purchase goes into the computer, your average daily balance changes and your finance charge goes up. If your creditor uses this method, it is better to pay as soon as you receive the bill rather than waiting until the end of the month.

The two-cycle method. Under this method, now being used by a few credit-card issuers, your daily balance is based on your last two billing months, not just one. This method can be very expensive,

Out of the mouths of babes

"Banks, like most businesses, are in the business of making money. This is how they make a profit—charging you more and giving you less. Shopping around may help you to find banks that are a little more generous with their interest-rate payments."

—*Mandee Heller Adler, CEO of Heller Adler Consulting and co-founder and former vice chairman and COO of the Women's Financial Network at Siebert (www.wfn.com), explaining why banks pay less interest on savings accounts than they charge in interest payments.*

MY 5 BIGGEST MONEY MISTAKES

"NO REGRETS" IS A POLICY ONLY THE WEALTHY CAN AFFORD—GET RICH BY AVOIDING THESE DOLLAR DON'TS!

BY VICTORIA SECUNDA

"Rue" is one of those 20-dollar words that means "regret" or "sorrow." But "rue," when used to describe one's financial blunders—as in, "I rue the day I bought Enron stock"—can also be fancy shorthand for "that may not be the stupidest thing I ever did, but it's close."

When it comes to the question, "What are your five biggest money mistakes?, it's hard to know where to begin, because finances have a funny way of morphing into follies. I asked several of my pals to weigh in on the subject. The following are highlights of what, in the aggregate, is a list as long as all of our arms put together:

1. Racking Up Credit-Card Debt. I vividly remember the first time I ever got a charge account, way back when I started working (for pennies) in publishing. The account was at Bloomingdale's, where, after much pleading on my part, a woman in the credit department said, "I'm going to make an exception and trust you."

Now, of course, my German shepherd gets plastic in the mail. Infants do, too. And therein lies the rub: It's way too easy to get credit cards and easier still to accrue the Himalayas of interest payments and simultaneously sink into the Grand Canyon of debt.

Carrying monthly credit-card interest fees is No. 1 on the hit parade of financial dumbness. A woman I know told me, as though this were even faintly cheery news (I shuddered), that she recently consolidated her debts onto one low-interest credit card and now she'll be able to pay off the balance "in just a matter of a few years."

I used to be among the credit-card stupidistas, until the day my husband, in tones that suggested harsh consequences if I failed to heed him, said, "We are never again going to pay only part of our Visa balance; from now on, it's the entire amount. I don't care if we starve to death, we're gonna do it. I hate paying interest." It is 10 years since we implemented this pol-icy, the result being that I spend a fraction of what I used to spend on, well, let's see . . . there were so many truly forgettable purchases that I lost track. Now, on this financial score if on no other, I can sleep nights.

2. Not Saving Money Religiously. A woman I have known for more than 20 years has always man-aged to bank at least 10 percent of every paycheck she earns. She did this when she was single, when she was married, when she divorced, even when she was on unemployment (okay, I made that one up). The point is that I have never had the discipline to fol-low her gilded example; if I had, I wouldn't be so panicked about never being able to hang 'em up. She, on the other hand, was able to retire comfort-ably in her 50s.

Another friend speaks of a "rainy-day fund," which she began only after years of freaking out when sud-den mandatory expenses—such as repairing a septic system—took chunks out of her grocery budget. "I used to spend every penny I made on frivolities," she recalls, "and when I was downsized and needed the money, it wasn't there." After a long period of serious impecunity and belt-tightening, she finally has some emergency cash in the bank. (Cautionary note: lipo-suction does not count as an "emergency.")

3. Indulging in Luxuries—and Repenting in Leisure. A colleague who now works from home recently confessed to me that she has a closet full of designer suits, which she never wears. "I wish I had all the dough I blew on Diors," she said. I didn't tell her that I have a similar couturial graveyard, in my case, of Armanis, purchased to wear at one or another pro-fessional gig, such as a book tour. I actually—and I blush to admit it—spent $2,000 on a suit once, and I have been punishing myself ever since by calculating how much I would now have if, instead, I had stashed that amount in a savings account.

Shoot me. I was insane. I thought I had to have that stuff. But I didn't. If I'd possessed a scintilla of rectitude, I would have found a seamstress to run up a little something that looked just like the real thing. Or I would have imagined that there were worse things than being caught dead at Marshall's.

Merciless rule of thumb: If you see it in a store, retail, you can probably find it for 50 percent less someplace else. And if you can't, forget it, Charley. Make do, or do without.

4. Gambling on the Stock Market.

A lot of us have learned, the hard way, that putting money in the stock market is second only to playing the ponies in riskiness. The only people who can afford to invest are a) the very young, single, and unencumbered, who, in a market disaster, have a lifetime ahead of them to start over, and b) the rich, who have other assets.

It's true that during the post-1987, pre-millennial stock-market bubble—and I quote my accountant here—"you could throw a dart at the Dow and make money." But too many people, when the signs were otherwise, actually clung to that line of thinking, making disastrous decisions, such as taking second mortgages or spending their kids' college funds in order to "play" the market. Making matters worse, a little uptick went a long way to encourage people to hold when they should have folded. One chum told me that she wishes she had sold a stock that had doubled in value and called it a day; instead, she hung in, only to watch the stock plummet to less than she paid for it. My husband and I were equally boneheaded, plunking money into such dogs as the now-defunct online grocer Webvan.

Millions of other people, whose retirement funds were tied up in stocks issued by the companies for which they work, have watched their 401(k)'s tank. Their mistake was that they had no other financial ballast, such as savings, CDs, or Treasury bills, should their companies go bankrupt.

If there's a message here, it's that you only invest what you can afford to lose.

5. Lusting After Hot Wheels.

A cousin once asked me to lend her some money to help her buy a new car, since her old one had more than 150,000 miles on the odometer and looked like a truck had hit it. I charmingly and firmly demurred, adding, "Now, if you were talking appendicitis...." The next day she called to apologize and said, "I must have been out of my mind. I just talked to my mechanic, and for $800, he'll have it running like new. Who cares what it looks like?"

I used to think it was a "guy" thing to spend far too much on wheels, but now I'm not so sure. Forget that many women's magazines have auto columns and that females are not exactly strangers to the Ford/Mercedes/name-your-brand showroom. Jillions of women lust after spiffy cars, treating this particular expenditure as if it were a civil liberty or something.

There's no debt like car-payment debt to make you feel poor. Mortgage payments at least bankroll one's real-estate investment, which provides shelter from the storm. A new car, on the other hand, is worth a huge bunch less the instant you drive it off the lot, and—let's be honest—provides nothing more than transportation from point A to point B.

This year my husband bought a new car for the first time in a decade. He paid hard-earned cash for it. If he hadn't had the money in the bank, he would have struggled with the old heap because—did I mention?—there's no debt like car debt. In any case, cars don't turn us on; we log six figures, mileage-wise, before we even look at an auto ad, much less take a new car for a test spin.

So there you have it, the Rue Roundup. I could go on and on about this subject and so, I'm willing to bet, could you. While all this may seem devastatingly depressing, thoughts of financial regret are actually instructive; they point out—and this is the good news— that as poor as you think you are, you did more than your share to get that way.

Moral: This is one problem that you—yes, you—can do a whole lot to fix!

particularly if you sometimes pay in full and sometimes carry a balance; you can end up paying interest even on purchases you've already paid for.

Whatever method is used to calculate your finance charge, there's one breadwinner rule you must follow: if you can't pay the entire balance, PAY MORE THAN THE MINIMUM! The system is rigged so that, if you only pay the minimum, and finance charges keep building up, you will be in debt to this creditor indefinitely. Over the past few years, card issuers have quietly lowered the typical minimum required payment from 4 percent to about 2 percent of the balance. That means that, if you owe a large balance, your required minimum payment may well be only a few dollars more than the finance charge. You'll effectively be paying down your balance a few dollars a month. As your balance drops, your minimum will drop, too. Pay the minimum payment of two percent on a $2,500 balance at 18 percent ($50 the first month), and it will take you nearly 28 years to pay off the balance. Your interest charges will be $5,896 in interest over that time—more than double the original charge.

Picking Your Plastic. If you pay your bill in full every month, the interest rate doesn't matter. You could go with a charge card, instead of a credit card. But you'll pay an annual fee. So why not get a no-fee, low-interest card? That way, if you decide to charge a big-ticket item, you'll have the option of spreading your payments over a few months. Check the grace period, so you know how much time you have to pay your balance before interest charges kick in, and compare penalty fees before you settle on a card.

If you're a "revolver," then look for a card with the lowest annual percentage rate (APR), a figure that takes into account the total cost of the money you're borrowing, including fees and finance charges over a period of 12 months. (That 0 percent introductory rate won't last forever.) The APR is the most accurate measure of the cost of your credit. Find out if the finance charge is fixed or variable. Variable rates are usually tied to the prime rate or the Treasury bill rate. They change when the underlying rate changes. Fixed rates can be changed, too, but the bank has to give you advance notice. You then have the option of accepting the higher rate, closing your account (you'll continue to pay down your balance at the old rate), or transferring your balance to a lower-rate card.

How Many Cards Should You Have? Two multipurpose cards are more than enough for most people. Make one card a no-fee card, which you pay in full each month. This is your convenience card; use it like a checkbook—just be sure to pay the entire balance every month, or you could run into trouble. (Often, debit cards, or cards that are tied to the balance in your checking account, are used in the same way. The only difference is that with a debit card, you don't have a grace period; the amount is automatically deducted from your checking right away.) Save the second card for big-ticket purchases and emergencies. Get one with as low an interest rate as you can, and don't let a big balance accumulate. If you own a business, get a corporate card, so that you can track your business expenses and keep them separate from your personal expenses.

What's the Catch? When shopping for a card—or, for that matter, anytime you receive a notice of change of policy from your card issuer—read the fine print with great care. You're likely to find some surprises. Here are a few things to watch for:

Fickle Rates & Fees. The pitch in the letter says "no fee" and promises a delightfully low rate of interest. The small print discloses that after a certain amount of time (usually six months to a year), the interest will jump higher and an annual fee may be imposed.

Tier Pressure. Some cards offer what they call a "tier system." The issuer lowers the interest rate on larger balances. For instance, your rate may drop by a percentage point if your balance exceeds $1,000 and even further if your balance is more than $2,500. You are being rewarded for not paying off your balance. Is this a good thing? Even with the lower rate, you're probably not going to come out ahead. In another form of "tiering," higher late-payment fees are accessed on customers who have higher balances.

Playing Favorites. The bank that issued your card suddenly announces it is reducing the interest rate. Don't assume you will get the lower rate. Depending on your credit rating, or other provisions of the offer, you may first have to pay off your entire remaining balance at the old rate. If your credit rating is good enough, you could probably save money by simply switching to another credit-card issuer—a competitor that is also offering a lower rate.

Teaser Rates. Often offered to entice you to switch cards by transferring your balance from an old card. Be aware that this "teaser" rate may only apply to the balance you transfer. New purchases will be charged a higher rate of interest. But you have to read the fine print to find out what that rate is.

Mandatory Spending. The card offering that very low interest rate may also require that you charge a certain amount annually to be eligible for the rate.

Incredible Shrinking Grace Periods. Issuers are shortening or eliminating the grace period. Often, this change is announced in the fine print of a notice tucked in with your bill . . . the kind of thing you probably throw out without reading.

Incredibly Shrinking Rebate Offers. Most airlines now require 25,000 miles for a free ticket, instead of 20,000.

The Old Bait-and-Switch. You get an invitation to apply for a "pre-approved" Gold card with no annual fee. But when you apply, you are turned down. The issuer may then send you the standard non-Gold card, instead. This card has a higher interest rate, a lower spending limit, and an annual fee. You don't have to accept it; simply cut it up and send it back. But remember that you filled out and signed an application, so the account may show up on your credit history even if you never use it, leading some other creditor who is looking you over to think you are already overextended. Write the three credit reporting agencies (see box in this section) and ask that the account be removed from your record.

Penalty Fees That Pinch. Average late-payment fees are now $31.00—a 56-percent jump since 1998. In 1994, the average late fee was only $12.56, according to Cardweb.com, which tracks trends in the credit-card industry. Late fees on some

1. Get with the Picture: Return your VCR rentals on time. Blockbuster's $3.99 five-day rental fee is half as cheap as your average movie ticket, but if you keep that video an extra day you immediately forfeit the savings to your entertainment budget. Better yet, says a reader, "Don't rent videos at all—go to the library and borrow them, free of charge."

2. Buy Regular, Save Regularly: By choosing to feed my car regular instead of "Only-the-Best-for-My-Baby-Super-Duper-High-Test," at my local pump, I save $6.00 every 20 gallons I put in the tank. My car doesn't know the difference. If you're concerned about how it will affect your car's performance, compromise and select Plus, instead of Super.

3. Discover the Dollar Store: Aiming to beat Wal-Mart, Target, and other discount retailers at their own game, several chains of "dollar stores" or "99 cents" stores have sprung up around the country in recent years. Try them. You'll be surprised by what you can buy there. You can easily save $25 on your grocery bills every week by shopping there for such staples as cleaning products, soap, garbage bags, artificial sweeteners, even food items. How can they afford to sell this stuff at such a cheap price? They keep their overhead low, have streamlined distribution systems, and buy merchandise in large lots, among other reasons. Maybe we should ask why the other stores are charging so much.

4. Sample the Goods at Goodwill: True story: A friend of mine recently found a designer suit, easily worth more than a thousand dollars, for four...dollars that is. Admittedly, such finds aren't to be had every week. But at larger Goodwill stores, the inventory does change dramatically every week, so it pays to visit often. If you're just starting out after college, or setting up house on your own again after a divorce, Goodwill is great place to quickly and cheaply stock your kitchen with dishes, glasses, pots and pans. Children's books and clothes can be had for a quarter here.
Another tip: when you're doing your spring cleaning, take the contents of your closets to Goodwill and ask for a receipt. The value of your goods will be tax-deductible next year.

5. Exchange Your Loose Change: Why is it that four quarters never seem as valuable as a dollar bill? What odd principle of mathematics is that? We all have vases or coffee cans where we throw the loose change that collects in our purses and pockets every day. With change machines in many supermarkets and banks nowadays, it's easier than ever to take those pennies, dimes, nickels, and quarters in and have them converted to paper currency. (**A tip**: use your bank's change counter; those supermarket machines charge a percentage of the total.) After you've converted your change, deposit it directly into your savings account where it will earn interest. Do not detour to the mall. You'll be surprised how much money you're already saving this way, without even knowing it, every month.

special accounts have gone as high as $49, and over-the-limit fees can be just as high. Thirty-five percent of the industry's total revenue now comes from penalty fees. Adding insult to injury, card issuers now raise interest rates for cardholders who exceed their credit limits, pay late, or skip a payment. And be aware that 39 percent of card issuers will now raise your interest rate, if they find, through a periodic check of your credit report, that you have been late paying other creditors' bills.

The "Can You Count?" Award. One of the sneakiest ways to engineer a rate hike is this one: Some banks use a 360-day year, instead of a 365-day year. Those five days make a difference—a 9-percent interest rate is really 9.13 percent, when it is calculated using a 360-day basis.

If you are unhappy with the rates and practices of your current card issuer, it may be time to transfer your business—and your balances—elsewhere. First, approach your current card issuer and see if you can get a better deal. It's cheaper for them to try to keep you than it is to replace you as a customer, so they might try to accommodate you.

The Fine Art of Transferring Your Credit-Card Balances. "Many cardholders aren't sure whether it pays to switch," says Gerri Detweiler, author of *The Ultimate Credit Handbook*. " The answer is that it depends on your current balance and the rate you now pay on your card. Transfer a $1,500 balance from a card charging 19.8 percent to one at 5.9 percent, and you can save about $105 over the first six months. Transferring the same balance from a card at 15 percent can put $68 in your pocket." You also have to factor

in whether your current card will assess a balance-transfer fee. Detweiler's rule of thumb: it pays to transfer if you have at least $1,000 of debt on a card and your new rate, after the introductory rate has expired, is still lower than the one you have now.

Transferring your high-interest debt to lower-rate cards almost always provides instant savings. By doing so, you are immediately able to put more money toward your principal each month, even if you keep paying the same amount. So you cut the total amount you pay substantially. With competition among card issuers so fierce, opportunities abound to grab lower rates; the average household receives at least one offer a week.

But if you decide to apply for a low-interest-rate credit card, you could be in for a shock: getting approved isn't as easy as most people assume. Credit-card companies that issue low-interest credit cards are working on a tight profit margin. This means that they have to be very careful about who they take on as customers. The last thing they want is to have to absorb any losses incurred by customers who default on their payments or declare bankruptcy. That's why credit-card companies offering these attractive interest rates typically ask you to fill out a far lengthier and more detailed application than normal. They'll delve into every conceivable area of your financial life, so that they can make an informed decision about whether or not you're a good risk.

To improve your chances of getting approved, check your credit-card history with the three credit bureaus (see "Give Yourself Credit . . . for Checking Your Credit Score" box in this section) before making any new applications. Review it carefully, and if you find an error caused by one of your creditors (for example, one of them has reported that you pay your bills in 120 days, but you've never been late with a payment in your life), get in touch with the creditor and ask it to correct the information. Also dispute the claim with the bureaus.

It's important for newly divorced women, in particular, to check their credit rating before applying for loans or new cards. Christine, a recently divorced mom, discovered that her ex-husband's credit report was mixed up with hers. "What a mess," she said. "He had been a deadbeat when it came to his credit cards, and it took more than a year to straighten things out. It almost led me to bankruptcy, but I did not give in." Her situation is not unique; one of the first things a divorced woman should do is close any joint credit accounts, notify the credit bureaus that they have been closed at her request, and ask them to remove any accounts from her credit report that do not have her name on them.

But checking your credit rating isn't all that you can do to increase your chances of securing a low rate. Below are a few other steps you can take.

1. Plan ahead by catching up on any unpaid bills before you apply.

2. Avoid doing anything that may make you appear like a high risk. For instance, if you have four or more credit cards with outstanding balances, try to pay one or more of them down.

3. Make sure that you aren't using more than 75 percent of your credit limit; if you're using more, the credit-card company may assume that you're already overextended.

4. Reduce the total amount of credit that is available to you by canceling any credit cards that you are no longer using. Believe it or not, lenders view charge accounts or home-equity lines of credit that you are not using as a risk. After all, you could go on a spending spree at any time. Don't close these accounts all at once, however, or a lender may assume that you're running into financial troubles; just close one or two a month. And when you do close these accounts, ask each account-holder to promptly report this information to all of

give yourself credit ...

FOR CHECKING YOUR CREDIT SCORE

To check your credit history, or to dispute errors, contact all three credit bureaus: Experian (1-888-397-3742; www.experian. com), TransUnion (1-800-916-8800; www.tuc. com), and Equifax (1-800-685-1111; www. equifax.com). Under the Fair and Accurate Credit Transactions Act, signed in 2003, you are owed one free credit report a year from each of the three major credit bureaus. (They normally cost about $9.) For your once-yearly free report, go to www.annualcreditreport. com. You are also eligible to receive a free report whenever you are denied credit, insurance coverage, or a job as a result of a poor credit score; when you are on welfare or unemployed and looking for work; and whenever there is an inaccuracy as a result of fraudulent activity, such as ID theft, on your report.

00187 334 0012

the credit bureaus that it deals with, and then follow up with the credit bureaus directly to make sure that everything has been handled correctly.

5. Resist the temptation to apply for too many low-interest credit cards at the same time. When your application for a new credit card comes in, the issuing company requests your credit history. All credit requests show up on the credit bureau's computer. Too many inquiries over a short period of time can make you look like a poor risk.

Beware These Transfer Traps Tucked into the Fine Print:

>> Is there a fee involved in transferring a balance from one company to another?

>> If so, is it a one-time flat fee or an ongoing percentage of your balance?

>> Is there a limit to the amount you can transfer?

>> Will your old credit card company charge you a fee or penalty for ending your relationship with it? Will it charge extra fees on other accounts you have with it?

>> What fees and rates will the new company charge you for new purchases?

>> What changes can the new company apply to the introductory rate after the transfer is completed? Will you automatically lose your low rate if you make one late payment?

In some cases, these lurking fees can wipe out any savings that you might gain by switching to a lower-interest card. But if you can pay off your transferred balance during the low-rate introductory period, the switch will have been worth it.

Knowing Your Score. The three credit bureaus know all about you. You'd do well to know a little about them and how they work. Whenever you apply for credit, lenders check your credit history with whichever one of the three major credit bureaus, Experian, TransUnion, or Equifax, they happen to purchase their information from. Lenders, insurance companies, even landlords and potential employers, are deemed to have a "permissible reason" to see your report, because you have applied to enter into a transaction with them. Your report may differ at each bureau, so it's important to keep tabs on all three of them to ensure accuracy.

Your credit report lists all of your credit accounts. It shows whether you pay on time or are late making payments, whether you keep current on your loans or arc delinquent. It indicates how often an inquiry has been made by another party concerning your report. It may also include any civil suits, judgments against you in favor of creditors, or other information that could affect the lender's opinion of you as a credit risk.

Using a mathematical formula, credit bureaus may also sell lenders your credit "score," often called a FICO score (named for Fair Isaac and Company, the firm that devised the formula). These scores range from 300 to 850; like bowling or SAT scores, the higher your score the better. For instance, with a score of 720 or above, your application will most likely be approved within minutes, and you will qualify for the lowest interest rates available. Below 620 points, you'll probably find yourself locked out of the best rates. Anywhere in between, and lenders will take a

MUSIC YOU CAN PAY YOUR BILLS TO:
MAKING BREAD'S TOP 20 LIST OF MONEY SONGS

From 1949's "Diamonds Are a Girl's Best Friend," by Jules Styne and Leo Robin, to The Beatles' '60s classic "Can't Buy Me Love," down the ages, musicians have been eloquent on the subject of money and the things it can (and can't) buy. Just for fun, we decided to compile a Top 10 list of money songs—songs you can pay your bills to or whistle on your way to work. But we found that so many artists have written money songs that we couldn't narrow the list down to just 10.
Some have messages, others are just cheap thrills.

1. Money (That's What I Want), The Beatles
2. Money Changes Everything, Cyndi Lauper
3. A Poor Man's Roses (Or a Rich Man's Money), Patsy Cline
4. Material Girl, Madonna
5. Money Don't Matter 2 Night, Prince
6. Women Be Wise, Bonnie Raitt
7. She Works Hard for the Money, Donna Summer
8. Money Can't Buy It, Annie Lennox
9. Money Back Guarantee, Jimmy Buffett
10. I Want My Money Back, Saffire
11. When the Money's Gone, Cher

12. And the Money Kept Rolling In and Out, Madonna (from "Evita")
13. You Never Give Me Your Money, The Beatles
14. Money for Nothing, Dire Straits
15. Free Money, Patti Smith
16. Tax Man, The Beatles
17. What Is Success, Bonnie Raitt
18. Money, Tina Turner
19. Independent Women, Destiny's Child
20. God Bless the Child Who Has His Own, Billie Holiday

Of course, no list of money songs would be complete without some country-western titles, songs like Willie Nelson's "If You've Got the Money, I've Got the Time," and the following three titles found in a search for money songs on the Internet.

1. If My Nose Were Full of Nickels, I'd Blow It All On You
2. She Got the Gold Mine and I Got the Shaft
3. If Money Talks, It Ain't on Speaking Terms with Me.

We couldn't have made these up, if we'd tried! (Well, maybe, if you'd paid us....)

closer look at the risk you may represent. They might ask you to supply bank statements or tax returns before they approve a loan. The difference in the interest rate offered to someone with a score of 520 and someone who has a 720 score is 3.45 percentage points, according to Fair Isaac & Company. That difference could save you a lot of money. Bankrate.com's "credit-score estimator" offers a quick way to find out where you stand.

Credit bureaus don't make judgments. They simply provide information to their business clients, who then consider that information, along with other factors, to come to a decision about your credit-worthiness. If you discover an error and report it, the credit bureaus must investigate, delete the false data, if they find your claim to be accurate, and notify any creditors who received your report within the past six months that erroneous information has been deleted. If the dispute can't be resolved, the bureaus must allow you to provide a brief written statement, telling your side of the story, and include that statement in your permanent credit record.

How permanent is your credit history? Individual entries are kept for seven years. Bankruptcies remain on the record for 10 years.

Time for Some "Plastic Surgery"? Debt problems can sneak up on you like so many unwanted pounds. Here's how to tell when you're in trouble. Ask yourself: Do any of these statements apply to me?

I don't have any money in the checking account, and just a few bills in my purse, so I pull out my credit card. My credit-card balances have risen significantly in the last six months, and my balances are at or near my credit limit. My monthly payments cover only the minimum required, if that. My minimum payments, plus finance charges, add up to a major expense every month. I've applied for more credit in the last six months. My disposable income keeps getting smaller and smaller. I'm using my cards to take frequent cash advances. I've missed a monthly payment or two in the last year. I pay less than the minimum due. I've begun juggling bills, paying one account this month, another account the next month. I'm getting past-due notices in the mail. Collection agencies are calling. When it's time to pay the bills, my stomach is in knots, my head aches, and my ulcer kicks in. I've added up everything I owe, and my total indebtedness is greater than my annual income.

Sound crazy? It happens all the time. In almost all cases, serious debt problems evolve slowly until they overwhelm you. It's a subtle process—you pay only the minimum, you pay late fees, you go over your credit limit, your rates climb, and before you know it, you're in over your head. Debt knows no social or economic boundaries. A junior assistant on a $35,000-a-year salary owes $35,000. An executive earning six figures owes more than $100,000. They're equally bad off.

If the above statements describe your own situation, don't despair. Admitting that you have a problem is the first step to correcting it. On the next page a MAKING BREAD reader describes how she got herself into—and out of—$25,000 in debt.

My Cash Diet:

"WHAT I THOUGHT WAS THE SOURCE OF HAPPINESS TURNED OUT TO BE NOTHING MORE THAN A BUNCH OF RECEIPTS"

BY LINDA LINDSEY

I started receiving credit-card offers during my first year in college. These cards made it not only tempting but extremely easy for me to live above my means. That pattern continued after graduation and into my first marriage.

We lived in a remote college town full of expensive restaurants catering to tourists but with few corporate employment opportunities. With my college degree in marketing, I was fortunate to land the highest paying job of anyone I knew—a whopping $7.00 an hour to market the services of a local attorney. Although both my husband and I used our credit cards, the cards were in my name alone and so—I discovered when I divorced—was the debt.

In 1995, I left that small town and that marriage and headed home to Atlanta, Georgia, carrying with me $18,000 worth of debt. The first job I landed in Atlanta increased my income by 60 percent. But $21,000 a year doesn't get you very far in Atlanta (or many other places, for that matter), and the move triggered some expensive purchases. Within a month, I had to buy a new car and a new wardrobe. I knew my array of color-coordinated sweatpants wasn't going to impress corporate America. In the first two years after my divorce, I began to get my spending in check, but my basic monthly bills were still $250 more than I was earning, and I used credit cards to fill the gaps.

By the time I was 25, the debt monster had swallowed me whole. At the peak of my debt, I had 22 credit cards with balances ranging from $75 to $6,000, open accounts with more than 30 lenders and total debt of $24,638, with nothing to show for it. Like an alcoholic with a genetic predisposition to overindulge, I felt programmed to use—and abuse—my credit. And my overindulgence didn't stop there;

I weighed more than 300 pounds. I felt as though my life was spiraling out of control.

One of my darkest moments came during a visit to my doctor. I went in with the flu, but I left his office with a wake-up call. Too heavy for my weight to register on the doctor's scale, I was sent next door to be weighed on an industrial scale. The large, red number "306" flashed an undeniable message to me, informing me that I was "in the red" in more ways than one. I knew I had to get my weight, my finances, and my life under control, or I wouldn't live long enough to enjoy anything I could afford to buy.

I sought help with my weight, and it was then that I began to notice similar patterns and parallels between my out-of-control eating and my out-of-control spending. Blame it on youth, immaturity and low self-esteem, but I realized I had spent six years trying to buy happiness. I had searched for contentment in every department store, discount store, and restaurant within a 50-mile radius; but all I had found was a self-perpetuating cycle of guilt and loneliness, resulting in a backlash of overspending and overeating.

Determined to change, in a five-year period from 1997 to 2002, I obliterated my debt and lost more than 140 pounds. I accomplished both by identifying the root causes of my desire to overeat and overspend, creatively increasing my income and staying focused on my goals. It wasn't easy, but it was the best thing I ever did for myself. Now I share my cautionary tale with others every chance I get, in the hope that they will avoid falling into the same traps I did. Looking back, there were several key strategies that helped me get my debt under control.

NINE TIPS TO HELP YOU
TIGHTEN YOUR FINANCIAL BELT

1. Know where you stand. I used to think that the definition of "manageable debt" was the ability to pay the minimum balances on my credit cards every month. After learning the meaning of the phrase "debt to income ratio"—a standard way of comparing your debt to your income and measuring your financial stability—I sat down with a single sheet of paper to calculate mine, which you do by dividing your total monthly minimum debt payments (excluding mortgage or rent payments) by your monthly take-home pay. The smaller the number, the better off you are.

I was astonished to see that my total debt was $24,638. Until that moment, I had fooled myself into thinking that the amount I owed was closer to $15,000. It was more comfortable for me to turn a blind eye to the situation than to face the facts; taking the time to make a list of all my creditors and my current balances was the eye-opener I needed.

2. Make a plan. My father always told me, "If you have a good credit rating, you can write your own ticket in this world." As a result of that, no matter how high my debt climbed, I always tried to protect my credit rating. I knew that if I consulted a credit counselor, that fact would immediately hurt my credit score, so I decided to try to reduce my debt on my own.

Most of the 22 credit cards on which I owed money had annual interest rates well above 18 percent, so it didn't much matter which one I picked to begin to pay off first. Instead, I concentrated on paying off the credit cards with the lowest balances. That way, I reasoned, I'd be able to see progress quickly.

3. Communicate with your creditors. This is key. I swallowed my pride and got on the phone. Many of the lending institutions refused to lower my interest rate, because of my long history of paying only minimum balances, but that didn't stop me from calling and asking for a rate reduction every three months, like clockwork. My persistence paid off. Because I kept my creditors informed and kept every promise I made, I was eventually rewarded with lower interest rates and the ability to skip payments on occasion. Accompanying my final payment to each credit-card company was a polite letter asking that my account be closed.

4. Find places to cut back. I made a budget. I started by listing every expense I had, including rent, car payment, insurance, and utilities. I examined each bill and made some tough decisions about which services were vital and what areas could be trimmed back or cancelled altogether. I shopped around for car-insurance rates and gas providers, and I said goodbye to a $70-per-month premium cable bill and hello to a $14-per-month basic-cable service. Instead of spending close to $200 a week on eating out, I took two $50 cooking classes and cut my food budget to $50 per week.

My entertainment budget was hit hardest of all. I stopped dropping $30 for a movie ticket and popcorn or dinner every weekend and found joy in the free things in life, such as going to the park, watching planes take off at the airport, or taking a drive through the mountains. Every weekend, I would seek out new and interesting free activities. I joined a service organization and volunteered to help fill my time. I clipped coupons for movie rentals, movie tickets, buy-one, get-one-free dinners, and anything else that would help me save money and still feel normal.

5. Barter! One of the most valuable skills I refined while digging myself out of debt was the age-old art of bartering. I had to find ways around paying cash for everything, because I simply didn't have it. If I wanted take-out that I couldn't afford, I'd offer to redesign menus in exchange for free meals. To see performances at the local theater, I volunteered to be an usher or ticket taker. I even designed a brochure for an art museum in exchange for free admission to an upcoming show.

6. Earn extra money. My most valuable asset in life has been my entrepreneurial spirit. I knew that I was not going to accomplish my goal of becoming debt-free solely by trimming back on expenses; I also had to increase my income, so I sought out part-time jobs that enabled me to use my skills and abilities outside my 8-to-5 day job. My favorite part-time job was my stint performing singing telegrams; this led me to market myself to sing at weddings and nightclubs. I started offering personal diet coaching services, as well. I had always written press releases that got great response rates for my various employers, so now I marketed myself to small businesses in need of public-relations services. Although I feared rejection, my desire to be debt-free was greater than my fear of hearing "No, thank you," or "Not at this time." I treated my clients fairly and always kept in mind that I needed them just as much as they needed me.

7. Ask for help! There was no one in my life who could simply write me a $25,000 check to end my worries, but that didn't stop me from asking for nonmonetary help. When my full-time job in corporate America ended in a layoff and I made the decision to work for myself, I didn't pull out my old friend, the credit card. I pulled out my address book and called everyone I knew. Within three weeks, I had converted my second-floor bedroom into an office with a computer, printer, modem, desk, and fax machine, all obtained through the generosity of others. I do my best to pay forward my good fortune at every opportunity. I believe this keeps good things coming my way.

8. Use windfalls wisely. With only three payments left to make on my car, I had a terrible accident. Two weeks later, I deposited an insurance check for $8,600 in my checking account. Two minutes after that, I wrote checks to two different credit-card companies, totaling $8,600, and mailed them. Instead of buying a new car, I bought a used car with an extended warranty. I was able to put zero down on the car, and I got an interest rate of 9 percent—much lower than the rate on the cards I'd paid off. I'd already budgeted for monthly car payments, so I came out ahead.

9. Focus on every success. Every month or so, I'd take an inventory of my progress. I could count my successes in a number of ways—from the lowered interest rates I'd negotiated with my creditors, to a reduction in the number of open credit cards, to the shrinking balances I owed. I did my best to take pride and pleasure in every small step forward, and I forgave myself for the occasional backslide. I strove for persistence, not perfection. The exhilaration of writing the final check to the last credit card on which I owed a balance was overwhelming. (I was a little surprised the payment found its way to the credit-card company; the check, payment slip, and envelope were tear-stained.) My most satisfying moment came when I bought a house in 2002. My realtor asked me how much I owed, and I was able to answer proudly: I owe nothing.

In my journey to be debt-free, I had to address a lot of emotional issues. Overspending was a symptom of a much bigger issue for me; I constantly sought happiness outside myself through material possessions and food. Recognizing and tackling those emotional issues helped me to rid myself of my debt and 140 pounds of excess weight! It took me five years to climb out of the hole I had dug for myself, but I came out of the experience a better person. I have a new respect for the small things in life, and I have found happiness inside myself. Sharing that joy with my new husband has made my life complete.

Now my husband and I shop hand in hand at garage sales and laugh and play lovingly together, as we push our cart through discount stores. Instead of filling our home with material possessions, we fill our scrapbooks with memories that will last a lifetime. What I thought was the source of all happiness turned out to be nothing more than a bunch of receipts.

Linda Lindsey is a marketing professional who lives and works in Atlanta, Georgia. To learn about her weight-loss program, visit www.facethefat.com

DO YOU OWE TOO MUCH?
FIGURING OUT YOUR DEBT-TO-INCOME RATIO

Write down all of your current consumer debts and how much you must pay each month to meet these obligations. Is your debt level too high? To find out, figure out a debt-to-income ratio for yourself, based on your total take-home pay and your installment obligations. Your debt-to-income ratio is the percentage of your take-home pay (i.e., your net income after all payroll deductions) that you must commit to the repayment of debts. Do not include your mortgage in the total monthly credit payments.

Total monthly credit payments divided by monthly after-tax income equals your debt-to-income ratio.

How Did You Score? *You are managing credit well if your debt-to-income ratio is less than 15 percent. Most people find that they are in danger, if more than 15 to 20 percent of net income is committed to repaying consumer debts. If your debt level is more than 20 percent, you are in trouble—most likely robbing Peter to pay Paul, borrowing to meet daily expenses, lengthening the time between payments, charging items that will have a life span less than the time it takes to pay for them.*

Take This Test: Can you pay off all your debts within the next 18 to 24 months? If not, your debt ratio is too high.

Ah-Ha Moment: Clamping down on any costs that include interest payments gives you more money to spend and save. Every time you pay over time, instead of paying cash or paying off a debt before the interest payments kick in, you're spending more than you have to. Borrowing money costs a lot of money!

You should always be aware of your debt-to-income ratio. Every time you pay off a loan, of course, the ratio will change. Don't be hasty about committing your newfound money (the amount that had gone toward paying off that loan every month) to new debt. For instance, when you pay off an auto loan with an obligation of, say, $250 a month, you might decide to purchase a new car with a $325 payment. "What's another $75 a month?" you might say to yourself. But if your ordinary non-credit living expenses were to rise by $75 a month due to inflation, you'd be crying foul. Instead, think about keeping the old car for another year or so, and putting the $250 into a savings account, toward a down payment on the next car. If you repeatedly replace old debt with new debt that is larger than the debt you've just paid. off, you'll never get ahead.

IT'S MIND OVER (FINANCIAL) MATTERS:
10 EASY WAYS TO CHANGE YOUR SPENDING HABITS

BY ALLISON ACKEN, PHD

Debt is like a big weight we carry around—only no one talks about it. In this weight-conscious society, there's so much focus on our fat-to-muscle ratio, it's easy to lose sight of our debt-to-income ratio. But the more we spend, the less we have.

Every day, in magazines, on TV, and on billboards, we receive hundreds of messages, obvious and subliminal, telling us how to spend our money—on clothes, makeup and accessories, iPods, new computers, and newer, smaller, smarter cell phones. Where are the messages telling us how attractive it is for women to have money in the bank, or investments, or real estate? If Cindy Crawford came with a big, fat assumable debt, would she look as attractive?

If you're ready to buy into the concept that fiscal fitness is as attractive as physical fitness in women and want to stop overspending and tone up your financial muscle, there are some steps you can take. Here are 10 exercises that should help you improve your fiscal fitness—some of them not all that different from those you might use to lose weight.

HOW TO IMPROVE YOUR FISCAL FITNESS.

1. Decide that you want to change. Little words like "now" and "yet" have great power. When I hear women say, "I can't save money" or "I don't know anything about investing" or "I can't stop overspending," I encourage them to add one little word to the end of each sentence. Listen to the difference. "I can't save money." "I can't save money yet." "I can't stop overspending." "I can't stop overspending yet." One sentence is a dead end, finito, forget it, no possibility of change. The other has a sense of a present reality, but with an expectation of change in the future, maybe even tomorrow.

Now, I use the word "now." "I want to stop over-spending now." "I am ready to stop overspending now." "I want to, and am ready to, change my spending habits now." Now, we're getting somewhere.

2. Remind yourself of your decision often. Write one of those sentences out and tape it to your mirror, your calculator, checkbook, or your wallet. If you do a lot of online shopping, tape it to your computer monitor. Put it wherever it will serve as a helpful reminder of your commitment to yourself.

3. Use the buddy system. Tell your best friend about your decision, and involve her in the process. Maybe she's ready to change her spending habits now, too. One of the problems with money is secrecy. Most of us have been taught not to talk about money, but not talking about money digs us deeper into trouble. You and your best friend can begin to coach each other into spending less and having more now.

4. Stay away from temptation as much as possible, especially when you're feeling blue, frustrated, or angry. That temptation could be the mall, a particular store, an Internet site, or home shopping on television. Most cravings pass in a few minutes. When you feel the urge to overspend, call your best friend, and have her talk you down.

5. Use cash, not plastic, when you spend. I know a very successful businesswoman who tried this technique. She began using cash when she shopped. Even though she had a healthy amount of discretionary income, she found that it was a very different experience pulling six $100 bills from her wallet than plunking down a piece of plastic. It made her really stop and think about whether she wanted to trade her hard-earned money for that item.

6. Give yourself time to shop for bargains. When you must go shopping for an outfit for a special event, for instance, give yourself plenty of time so that you have alternatives. Try not to force yourself into buying something on short notice. It's a set-up for over-spending.

7. **Try not to buy anything impulsively**, if you can help it. Give yourself 24 hours to think about those shoes or earrings or whatever. It is entirely possible that, by tomorrow, you may have lost the desire or even forgotten about the item that seemed so compelling yesterday. If you are having a great deal of trouble fighting that impulse, ask the store to hold it for 24 hours. The salesperson may say the store doesn't hold anything and try to convince you that it will be gone if you come back later. That's her job, but it isn't necessarily true. And always, always make sure that you can return purchases for a full refund, not a store credit.

8. **Use mind games to motivate yourself.** Find a picture that represents a cherished financial goal—whether it's being able to afford to be a stay-at-home mom, going back to school, having your own business, owning a home, building an investment portfolio, sailing a yacht, or being a happy older woman with no money worries. Tape that image to the fridge or bulletin board or mirror, just as you might a picture of a dress you'd like to fit into when you're on a diet.

9. **Track your progress.** Keep a record of what you haven't spent and use it as a cushion for your real goals. Start charting the money that you are accumulating by spending less. Tina, a school secretary, calls her cushion her "God-forbid money." She says that we don't really need those six new pairs of shoes; what we need is a cushion. Keep that chart in a conspicuous place, so that you can see the positive effect of your efforts.

10. **Start talking about money with other women.** Have you ever eavesdropped on a bunch of guys, waiting for a commuter train? Chances are they're talking about money (when they're not talking about sports). Talk leads to action—and we can beat them at their own game!

MAKING BREAD'S SEVEN-STEP DEBT-LOSS PLAN

If your debt-to-income ratio tells you it's time to get serious about reducing your debt, take heart—and take control. There are a number of very effective moves you can make. Here's our seven-step plan.

>> 1. Make a list of your cards, noting the balances on each, and place the ones with the highest interest rates at the top of the list.

>> 2. Call each card issuer, and try to negotiate a lower rate and monthly payment. Be upfront with them; explain how much you can afford to pay. Almost all creditors would rather extend your loan term or reduce your monthly payments than receive nothing. Keep a detailed record of your phone conversations. Follow up with a letter. If the creditor refuses to work with you, write a letter, explaining that you are sending in a proportional payment anyway. Then contact them a few months later and try negotiating a lower rate and payment again. If you don't succeed, transfer your high-interest debt to the lowest-rate card you can obtain. Read the fine print on the offers you're considering to be sure that low rate will hold for at least six months, and be aware that if you make even one payment late, once you accept the card, the rate may convert to a higher one.

>> 3. To find extra cash to pay down the debt, write down how you spend every penny for a month. Look for things you can do without or do more cheaply. Take a second, part-time job, if you must. Use that extra money to pay off the cards, one at a time, starting with the one with the highest rate. Increase the amounts you pay on the remaining cards as well. As you pay off each card, contact the company and close your account, and notify the three credit bureaus that you have done so. Double check that this is recorded on your record as having been "closed by consumer," not the credit company.

Since credit history—or length of time that you have had credit—plays a large part in determining your credit score, it's best to try to maintain one active card while you go through this process. Charge only a limited amount on it, and pay off the balance each month; that way you won't have to start from scratch, building up a credit record once you're solvent again.

>> 4. NEVER pay just the minimum. Doing so can triple the amount you end up paying, and you'll still be making payments long after the stuff you charged is obsolete—or no longer fits.

>> 5. If you have enough money in a savings account or mutual fund to cover your credit-card debt, consider using it, or part of it, to pay down your debt. The interest it's earning is likely to be far less than the interest you're being charged by the card issuer, so you'll really be saving money by allocating it toward debt repayment. Once the debt is paid off, keep making payments—back into your savings accounts or mutual fund.

>> 6. Borrow from yourself: many 401(k) plans allow you to borrow a percentage of your savings at a rate a few points above prime, and the interest you pay goes back into your account. If you have life insurance policies that have a cash value, consider borrowing against them.

>> 7. Own a home? Another option is taking out a home equity loan or line of credit, whose interest rate should definitely be lower than the credit-card interest you're paying—and it's tax-deductible! By doing this, you will consolidate your loans at the cheapest possible rate. But shop around. Competition is tremendous, so compare rates. And be aware that you are putting your house on the line. If you revert to your old spending habits, you could lose it.

Use Step 3 to find the dough to pay the home equity line of credit off ASAP!

What Happens When You Go to a Credit Counselor? Linda Lindsey (see "My Cash Diet" sidebar in this section) found the self-discipline to pay her debt off by herself. She negotiated better terms for herself, found ways to spend less and make more money, and set up a payment schedule to systematically pay down her debt. It can be done, and, in most cases, you're better off if you do it yourself. But some people need a little help getting back on track. That's where credit counselors come in. But be careful: in recent

Wal-Mart . . . Dollar Store . . . Supermarket?

MAKING BREAD'S GROCERY COMPARISON SHOPPER FINDS THE BARGAINS IN SIX CAN'T-LIVE-WITHOUT CATEGORIES

BY JENNIFER VISHNEVSKY

Garbage bags, cereal, shampoo: every week or two, we replenish our stock of several can't-live-without items—the staples of our daily domestic routine. Most of us automatically include them on our shopping lists and toss them into our shopping carts as we cruise the aisles of our local supermarket, stocking up on our groceries for the week. Granted, there's a lot to be said for the convenience of one-stop shopping. But how much is that convenience costing us?

MAKING BREAD sent its intrepid comparison shopper—moi—off with a short list of items to see what kind of deals I could find. How much would buying no-name brands save? Do you have to buy in bulk to trim your costs? To answer those questions, I ventured to three locations to price shop for the items listed below. My stops were a local supermarket, a dollar store, and a local Wal-Mart. Here's what I found:

MAKING A LIST . . .

Cereal: First stop, the cereal aisle. To satisfy my sweet tooth, I wanted Frosted Flakes and Cocoa Puffs. But, since the name of the game was savings, I was willing to accept the cheapest brand, even a no-name, or generic, supermarket brand. I mean, are you paying for the name or the cereal?

A 12 oz. box—roughly a week's worth of cereal—cost $3.69 at the supermarket. At Wal-Mart, a larger, family-sized box of the same cereal only cost $2.33—a savings of $1.36. As I walked through the dollar store, I saw two boxes of generic frosted flakes and chocolate puffs, each priced at $1.00—$2.69 less than the supermarket— and I could have gotten two boxes for less than the price of one family-sized box at Wal-Mart.

Bottom line: The dollar store won this round, hands down.

Toothpaste: I found several varieties of Colgate at the dollar store for a buck. In the grocery store, the same Colgate product was priced at nearly three times as much, costing $2.99. Wal-Mart gave the dollar store a run for its money, pricing the same product at $1.58.

Bottom line: The supermarket takes the biggest bite out of your budget here; pass Wal-Mart, and head for the dollar store.

Shampoo: The shampoo aisle of any store is always filled with a dizzying array of choices. In the dollar store, the selection wasn't as broad. I did find two name-brand products, Alberto VO5 and Suave, at $1.00 a piece. At Wal-Mart, I was surprised to find the same two products, each costing only 88 cents. At the grocery store, smaller-sized bottles of the same products cost $1.39.

Bottom line: Lock in good prices for your tresses at Wal-Mart.

Paper Products: At the dollar store, generic brands of paper products were all available in multipacks. A buck apiece bought four rolls of toilet paper, a 250-count package of napkins, and a roll of paper towels. At the supermarket, a six-roll package of toilet paper cost $4.29, the same brand of 250-count napkins cost $1.99, and a roll of paper towels cost $1.99. That's a difference of $5.27—and all you get is two more rolls of toilet paper. At Wal-Mart, a six-roll package of toilet paper only cost $1.99, a 400-count package of napkins cost $1.86, and four rolls of paper towels cost $1.44.

Bottom line: The bulk packaging and pricing at Wal-Mart wins the day.

Garbage Bags: Basic-black, heavy-duty bags were sold in a 30-pack for $1.00 at the dollar store, a 40-pack at the supermarket for $5.00, and a 60-pack at Wal-Mart for $2.00.

Bottom line: Take your pick—Wal-Mart or dollar store—but buying trash bags at the supermarket is a waste of money.

Detergents: The dollar store sold two brand-name dishwashing liquids—Ajax and Joy—for, you guessed it, a dollar apiece. The local supermarket sold the same bottles for $3.19, while Wal-Mart sold them for $1.58 each. Laundry detergent was sold at the dollar store in bottles and boxes. One quart of a generic bottle and a one-pound box of detergent each sold for $1.00. The supermarket sold the same products for $1.29 and 3.49, respectively. Wal-Mart had the best prices, selling a three-quart bottle for $1.29 and a four-pound box for $2.43.

Bottles of 409 and Touch of Glass were available for $1.00 at the dollar store, $2.45 at the supermarket, and $1.83 at Wal-Mart.

Bottom line: Buy these products in bulk at Wal-Mart and save.

ADDING IT ALL UP . . .

Not surprisingly, given its name, overall, the dollar store won the price war, but Wal-Mart wasn't far behind—winning three categories (shampoo, paper products, and detergents) and tied with the dollar store in one (garbage bags). Setting aside some minor differences in unit pricing or quantity, it cost me $28.27 at the supermarket, $16.78 at Wal-Mart, and $10.00 at the dollar store to buy all of the items on my list. That means that if you normally buy everything at the supermarket, you're spending $18.27 more than you need to every week or two—for a possible savings of up to $75.00 a month.

You're more likely to find a broader assortment of brand names at Wal-Mart (or Target or Kmart or Costco or any of the other discount chains) than at a dollar store, though you may end up lugging home bulk packaging. You'll still save $11.49 over the supermarket each time you purchase these items at a discount store.

Sure, it's easier to do all of your shopping at the supermarket. But our advice is: save the grocery store for groceries, and make the effort to buy household goods like the ones I purchased at a discount or dollar store near you. There's a good reason these stores are always packed with people. Shopping there is worth the effort!

years, many illegitimate credit counselors have sprung up, trying to take advantage of the growing number of people in debt crisis. Always ask for references, and check with the Better Business Bureau (www.bbb.org) before you sign up with a company. Call 1-800-388-2227, or check the following Web sites, www.debtadvice.org or www.nfcc.org, to locate a reputable counseling service. For emotional support and coaching, you might also consider joining an organization called Debtors Anonymous (www. debtorsanonymous.org).

What kind of assistance will you get? Certified consumer-credit counselors act as coaches; they will go over your income and expenses, help you prioritize, and recommend solutions. They advise you in managing your money, assist you in establishing a realistic budget so that you can do more with the money you have, and teach you to manage money so that you can handle credit in the future. These services operate as nonprofits; they charge a nominal fee for their services.

About one-third of the people who seek advice from credit counselors need more help. They need a debt-management plan. Certified credit counselors work with each of these clients to come up with a debt-repayment schedule that the client can live with. They negotiate with their

KNOW YOUR RIGHTS

UNDER THE FAIR DEBT COLLECTIONS PRACTICES ACT, IT IS ILLEGAL FOR DEBT COLLECTORS TO:

>> Contact your employer or your neighbors about your debt, unless they are doing so in order to locate you. They may not mention your debt.

>> Call you late at night or at unreasonable hours.

>> Call you at work.

>> Call you repeatedly.

>> Engage in deceptive conduct.

>> Call you without disclosing the collection agency's identity.

>> Use obscene, derogatory, or insulting remarks.

>> Threaten arrest or loss of child custody or welfare benefits.

>> Publish your name.

>> Use any communication, language or symbols on envelopes or postcards that indicate that the sender is in the debt-collection business.

>> Threaten repossession without legal right or present intent to do so.

00187 334 0012
Charge Express

clients' creditors on their behalf to reduce finance charges and suspend late-payments fees. However, entering into a debt-management plan does not guarantee that your interest rates will automatically be lowered. Each creditor has different rules. One may cut your interest rate in half, another may increase your rate, and still another may leave your rate unchanged. In general, you'll have about as much luck renegotiating rates yourself as a counselor will.

What You Need to Know About Debt Management Plans. Once your creditors agree to your repayment plan, you'll hand over a certain amount of money each month to the credit-counseling agency you're working with, which will, in turn, distribute these funds to your creditors. The amount paid to each creditor is usually in proportion to the debt owed to each. For example, if you send the agency $500 per month and your MasterCard bill represents 20 percent of your total debt, then $100 will go to MasterCard. *All* of your monthly check is used to repay creditors, when you are dealing with a reputable agency. The average fee for this service is $11 a month (based on your ability to pay), but it may be waived, if necessary. Credit counseling agencies also request and generally receive money from the creditors, who pay a percent of the repaid debt.

Sounds great, but there is one very important caveat—and any reputable credit-counseling group you go to should warn you of this fact: your credit report could be affected. Although the counseling agencies won't tell the credit bureaus that you've enrolled in their program, some of your creditors might. When your creditors see that you have applied for whatever

special terms they may offer to those in a credit-counseling program, they can ask the credit bureaus to add a note to your credit file. Once that happens, it will be difficult to get further credit until your debt is cleared and you have proven that you can manage credit responsibly. Your creditors will most likely also immediately freeze or close your accounts so that you can't make further charges.

What You Need to Know About Debt Settlement. In some extreme cases, a creditor will agree to debt settlement. In this situation, the creditor will write off the debt as uncollectible or reduce the amount owned. Short of bankruptcy (and we'll discuss that in a minute), this is one of the most damaging notations to have listed on your credit report. Also, the amount forgiven is often (though not always) considered taxable income by the IRS. The bank forgiving the loan will send a 1099 form, reflecting the amount, to the IRS at the end of the year. For instance, if you owe $1,000 and the creditor agrees to settle for $500, the IRS could consider the other $500 as taxable income.

While it is possible to put together a debt-management plan and renegotiate your interest rates with your creditors on your own, going it alone is not easy. It can be very stressful. A credit-counseling service acts as a buffer between you and the creditor and isn't judgmental. All that being said, however, if you can do it yourself, you'll probably protect your credit rating to a certain extent—and, just as Linda Lindsey did, you'll have an incredible sense of accomplishment when you write that last check.

Avoid These Credit-Repair Scams. You may be tempted by advertisements from companies promising that they can help repair your credit report. Don't be taken in by these companies! They'll charge you an upfront fee of $200 to $1,000, then, maybe, they'll write the credit bureaus on your behalf, questioning one or more of your credit items. But if the item proves to be accurate, then it remains on your credit report. Meanwhile, the "repair shop" has closed shop and moved on, pocketing your money.

Never give out your bank account or credit-card numbers when you are inquiring about help from one of these companies. If they ask—hang up. They're probably trying to steal your identity, and you certainly don't need other people opening credit accounts in your name!

What You Need to Know About Bankruptcy. If all else has failed, you are left with one last option: bankruptcy. Over the past seven years, approximately 9.5 million Americans have filed for personal bankruptcy—more than a million in 2003 alone.

Congress passed the Bankruptcy Act of 1978 to make it easier for people in debt crisis to repay a substantial portion of their debt and to ease the burden of going bankrupt. This act (with a little help from a faltering economy) has produced a tremendous increase in personal bankruptcies: In the 12 months ending March 31, 2004, there were 1,618,063 personal bankruptcy filings—up 2.8 percent from the previous period—costing lenders more than $45 billion. Bankruptcies cost each household about $500 a year in higher prices and interest charges.

Before you decide to declare personal bankruptcy, talk with a lawyer about the steps you must take and how the law in your state pertains. Chapters 7 and 13 are the provisions of the Bankruptcy Act that are most commonly used by individuals filing personal bankruptcy. Bankruptcy form packages, by state, are available for a fee on www.legalzoom.com. Note that there are some debts that cannot be discharged through bankruptcy, including recent student loans, alimony, child support, and most taxes. You know what they say about death and taxes....

Chapter 13 encourages you to repay your loans. Its so-called "wage-earner plan" lets you consolidate your debts and repay a percentage of them, as approved by the court, over three to five years. During that time, your creditors must suspend interest and late charges on most debts, and they may not continue any action against you. After you file a petition with the federal bankruptcy court in your area, you must submit a repayment plan, including debts owed to each creditor and an accounting of your income and expenses. The bankruptcy judge determines how much you can truly afford to pay. Once the judge approves a repayment plan, you make payments to a court-appointed trustee, who then distributes money to your creditors. They accept whatever payment the court has approved as payment in full. You get to keep your property. If you default on Chapter 13 payments, the court will throw you into Chapter 7 proceedings.

Chapter 7 covers a straight bankruptcy. That means the court collects, sells, and distributes your assets, with certain exemptions. You are usually not released from paying delinquent federal income taxes and student loans. Depending on the state you live in, you risk losing your home, cars, and any other valuable possessions.

But let's think positively—the only chapters you'll be filing are the ones in the success story of your life. We'll end this chapter, with a MAKING BREAD Financial Makeover. In March, MAKING BREAD received a frantic e-mail from Molly Driscoll (name changed to protect privacy), asking for help: "I'm going to be 56 this month, and I've been on my own for the past 20 years. I've had to live on what I made, and sometimes I can't make ends meet. I haven't been able to save for retirement, and now I'm frightened. Can you please give me some hope?"

We were so moved by Molly's letter that we immediately asked her if she'd like to work with an MB team on a financial makeover. Our "Ask Mr. Modem" columnist, Richard Sherman (visit him at www.mrmodem.net), even got involved, offering the following pep talk: "First, she's young!" he wrote. "She has time to get on a healthier financial path. Remember, 60 is the new 40!" In his pep talk, he went on to urge her to "seize control of her life—which only she can do—and make a life plan that will incorporate some changes in her financial situation."

With financial planner Elizabeth Lewin advising Molly on her financial options and psychologist Allison Acken helping Molly examine the personal/emotional issues that might be getting in her way, Molly's makeover began. Five weeks later, the results were almost unbelievable: she was finding money everywhere—a not-so-serendipitous sea change in her circumstances that emerged as soon as she began to take control of her finances. "My whole attitude has shifted," she reported back to us.

Below are excerpts from Allison Acken's "Money Diary," which she kept to track Molly's emotional and financial odyssey, plus Elizabeth Lewin's financial Rx for Molly's complicated situation, moving forward.

IT STARTED WITH A CRY FOR HOPE—
AND NOW SHE'S FINDING MONEY EVERYWHERE!

BY ALLISON ACKEN, PHD

WEEK 1: MOLLY'S FEARS MAY BE JUSTIFIED.

Our first call: Molly is sweet, talkative, and happy to have MB's help, but even I have to admit the situation looks bleak. She has a complicated housing situation, is trying to help her daughter, and owes a huge debt to her mother for repair bills. "I am looking forward to working with you," she tells me. "I'm sort of frozen in a do-nothing pattern, because I have no idea how to save for my future, and it is coming fast."

Six months earlier, Molly had been scrambling to find a place to live on short notice. Divorced for 10 years, she decided to move in with her daughter, a struggling single mom, and her two children, who were all staying in a 150-year-old house, owned by Molly's parents—but for which Molly paid the mortgage, because she had once lived there with her ex. (You see what I mean about complicated?) The plan, when she moved back in with her daughter, was to remodel the attic into an apartment for herself.

Almost immediately, "the plumbing had to be replaced A to Z. The electrical had to be upgraded" to code, and the "cesspool started backing up—you don't want to know," she said. "It was one thing after another." Molly ended up living at her sister's, but paying for a house that her daughter lives in and her parents own.

I asked her if she talks to anyone about money. "I am usually the listener, not the talker," she says. She "gets frustrated" when she talks "with a married friend with two healthy incomes, who lectures" her about saving money. I asked her to consider whether she has a friend with whom she could talk. Perhaps she is too private for that, but she will give it some thought. On the plus side: Molly "has a good family support network." Still, she fears that if she has any health problems, she will be "out of luck with nothing to fall back on. I worry about being a bag lady." She hears about "save, save, save" and "has been trying to read about money," but she's afraid that, even if she "has the $20 to put away," she "doesn't want to lose it by doing the wrong thing." She "knows" her employer "has a 401(k)," but she "isn't in it."

Molly has a long, expensive commute. Recently, her workload has increased, because of a merger, but she has received no increase in pay. The job situation closer to home is "difficult—everyone travels at least a town or two to work."

I raised a few questions gently. Can her daughter contribute something? "No," Molly explains, "she is doing so much on her own." I asked, gently again, if her parents had thought of refinancing the house to cover some of the repair bills. She wasn't sure. Enough for one night. We arrange to talk next week.

I hang up, wondering, "Is the bag-lady fear about not having enough money or—as is often the case—not knowing what she has? She seems to have all the responsibility for, but no authority over, the house. A real double bind. And she doesn't understand that by not saving money in her 401(k), she is throwing away free matching money.

Tip: Start talking about money. Like many women, Molly is frozen by fear that is keeping her from learning more about money. One friend's well-meaning but judgmental lectures have shut her down. Our conversations may help her start talking about money more productively both with other close friends and with family.

WEEK 2: THE PICTURE BRIGHTENS.

The picture is not as bleak as it appeared initially. Elizabeth

Lewin spoke to Molly and determined that the house is held in some kind of trust and that Molly is supposed to inherit it. She has no credit-card debt. Elizabeth explained the 401(k) very effectively, and Molly will pursue it. She also confesses that she has had a long-time wish to visit Puerto Rico.

I asked if it is possible to get the house into her name, so she can benefit from the mortgage-interest deduction. She will try to ask her mom. She was unclear how refinancing and using equity in the house could benefit her, "because if you borrow on it, don't you just have a bigger loan?"

Molly has tightened her belt by a significant $500 a month to pay her mother back for the plumbing and electrical work, but it's really a struggle making ends meet. If the mortgage could be refinanced, yes, she would have a bigger loan; however, because of today's low interest rates, she might pay the same, or even less, per month—and maybe the attic costs could be added into the loan. "On a good day," Molly says, she could talk to her mother about refinancing, but her parents had been "pretty private about their money matters."

Now that she's had a few conversations with me and with Elizabeth, I ask her how it feels for her to be talking about money. "Better! A lot better!" she says. "You talk to me about what to do, and I do it." And she's passing the information on; she told a younger woman at work to think about contributing at least something to the 401(k).

We look for other possible sources of additional money for her: Usually at this time of the year, she gets a raise, but not so far. I raise the issue of asking for one, based on her increased workload. She is "not afraid to ask, and definitely would put any increase into the 401(k)," because she "wouldn't even notice it." About the 401(k), she explains, "I used to think that, if I couldn't do it all, I might as well do nothing at all." Those massive repair bills, with nothing saved to cover them, became her wake-up call.

Tip: What you don't know (and do) may hurt you. Molly was terrified and frozen into inaction, in part

because she didn't have enough information. Now that she's taken the time to look into and list her assets, things are not nearly as bad as she feared. She'll have her Social Security when she retires (and she'll continue to work at least part time beyond age 65). She will have the proceeds from her 401(k)—now that she's investing in it—and she will inherit the equity in the house.

WEEK 3: NEW DEVELOPMENTS.

Two brand-new issues came up this week: stock options and a possible job offer. Molly has some options for stock in the company she works for, which must be exercised this week or she will lose them. She thinks they may be worth $1,000 and is not sure what to do. She will e-mail Elizabeth first thing tomorrow.

On the job front, she is being recruited by a competitor much closer to home. She is excited about the possibility of a shorter commute and is ready to negotiate for more money. Even if this doesn't work out, it may give her more bargaining power in her current position when she asks for a raise.

Tip: Do ask. Do tell. When it comes to money, women have a tendency not to ask—not to ask questions, not to ask for help, not to ask for a raise. Not asking almost guarantees not getting—information, help, more money. It is true that if you ask, the answer may be no. But if you don't ask, the answer is definitely no. Molly will keep trying.

WEEK 4: FINDING MONEY EVERYWHERE!

Molly and her mom had a bit of a blow-up earlier in the week, when her mom told her, "That woman [me] is nuts!" But Molly, bravely, tried again and had a very brief and useful conversation with her mother about refinancing the mortgage. It looks like her parents are going through with it, adding $20,000 to cover the cesspool work, which should start soon, and the interest rate will be around

5 percent. (The current mortgage is for less than $30,000, at 8½ percent, and the property is worth approximately $400,000. Wow, that is big news!) The net effect is that Molly will be paying roughly the same amount per month on the mortgage, given the lower interest rate.

She spoke with Elizabeth and was advised to sell the options for $1,000. She received her tax refund. She will get the matching dollars for her 401(k) contribution. She asked for a raise, making a pitch to move to the "higher end of the scale," and she even won a few bucks on a lottery ticket. It even looks like her dream of seeing Puerto Rico may be close to coming true. Her sister has bought a timeshare there. Now they only have to come up with cheap fares and a little travel money.

Molly, her daughter, and her sister have all been talking about how they might earn additional income. Molly is fluent in Spanish and loves "anything Latin." She also enjoys writing (children's stories, letters, and poetry). Clearly, she has many possibilities to explore.

How does talking about money feel to her now? Since she's been talking and getting information, she says, "it's not as bad as it was. I'm still not comfortable, but it has made me think. Having someone to talk to—having somebody give me a kick in the butt—has really helped me deal with my money fears." We will have a follow-up call next week, and she will be speaking with Elizabeth again.

Tip: Make your assets work for you. Technically, the house belongs to her parents; they bought it to protect her, and they probably put it in the trust to protect her. But now she has no ownership or access to the equity and no decision-making power until her parents' death (which she hopes is a long time away). She's been struggling to pay off the repairs from her paycheck. But since she was able to convince her parents to refinance, because the mortgage is an old one at a high interest rate, the new loan will save her quite a bit of money and make the repairs manageable.

WEEK 5: NEW GOOD NEWS: MORE MONEY!

Although Molly doesn't have an answer about her raise yet, her boss did find out that she has not been paid for the many overtime hours she has put in since the merger (she didn't think she qualified for overtime). Now she will be getting $5,000 in back pay. What a windfall!

With all of this newfound fortune, she is feeling much better about her situation, and she is even talking about opening an investment account. She's beginning to understand that all of this good fortune only came her way, because she took an active part in looking for it.

The past few weeks have been a whirlwind for her. "Because of my family, I know I would never really be a bag lady; they would help me. But I am very independent, and I don't like feeling like a bag lady. I didn't know how to go about any of this. I guess I knew the options, but I would get paralyzed." Now she thinks she's "headed in the right direction. My whole attitude has shifted," she says.

Tip: Pass it on. When you get new information about money, talk to your friends about it. If you share the resources, you will build your information bank much more quickly than if you try to do it alone. Molly is now talking to co-workers, friends, and her family about money issues that may save them money—or make them more money.

She's got much more than hope now; she's got a plan.

THREE WISHES, NO GENIE, ONE HAPPY LADY: A FINANCIAL PLANNER'S ACTION PLAN

The good news: Molly knows what she wants, and she has no credit-card debt. In our first conversation, I ask her, "What are your financial goals?" Without hesitation, she answers: "A trip to Puerto Rico, fixing up an apartment in the house, and saving for retirement." (I'd have rather she listed them in reverse order.) Thanks to some aggressive action on her part and a little luck, it turns out that all three of her wishes are well on their way to becoming true.

Molly's financial situation is unique; she pays the mortgage and expenses on a house that her parents own and which is currently occupied by her daughter and her daughter's children. Her plan is to renovate the attic of the home her daughter lives in into an apartment for herself. But, first, old plumbing has to be replaced and the electric service brought up to code. Her parents will cover the cost of this through the refinancing of the mortgage, but she must repay them. She estimates that this debt will come to $3,500 to $5,000.

The bad news: Molly gets no tax benefit from the house, even though she pays the mortgage. And, even though her employer offers a 401(k) plan with matching funds, she has not participated in it. She covers her expenses with her monthly take-home pay of about $2,300 per month, with little left over to put into a savings account.

The happy ending: Any time you make a commitment to start saving, the first step is to figure out where your money is going. I send Molly some work sheets to help her keep track of her expenses, so that she can find places to cut back and allocate that newfound money to savings.

Next, we discuss the benefits of contributing to her employer's 401(k) plan, something she must do if she is serious about building up retirement savings. She checks and discovers that her employer matches 100 percent of the first three percent contributed and 50 percent of the next two percent contributed. Because she's playing catch up, Molly decides to contribute 10 percent of her salary, or $3,800. With the matching funds, she could have a nest egg of $47,000, assuming an 8 percent return, by the time she retires. It's never too late to start.

A week later, she e-mails me: "I must talk to you immediately." She'd gotten notification of a deadline concerning some corporate stock options; she had to decide whether to exercise them or take the current dollar value of about $1,000. I advise her to take the money and run to a money-market account, with the idea that she can use this amount to help cover the cost of the studio apartment. By paying cash instead of borrowing, she'll save on interest owed.

She asks for a raise, on our suggestion, and learns that she is eligible to receive $5,000 in overtime back pay. What should she do with this additional windfall? I suggest placing what is left, after taxes and Social Security payments are deducted, into the money-market account she's just opened. That way she'll have an emergency fund that she can tap into easily for any future crises. She could also use some of it to cover the cost of the renovation. But, since she has no credit-card debt or other outstanding loans—and thus no up-to-date credit history—I suggest she consider using this substantial sum as collateral for a loan to fix up the studio apartment. By making automatic payments on this loan, she'll be creating a credit history for herself.

Molly was toying with the idea of investing the money in a timeshare, because her sister and her niece have one in Puerto Rico. I caution her that a timeshare is not an investment. They are difficult to sell, and there's no guarantee that they will increase in value. She finally agrees with me. Besides, she can always tag along with her sister, when she goes to Puerto Rico.

As a reward for the remarkable strides she's made, I suggest she splurge on something nice for herself, like a day at the spa. Molly loves that idea—and she has earned it. She knows now that she should invest in herself, in the house that she will inherit, and in a secure retirement. She's gone from hopeless to hopeful in five weeks.

Postscript: Seven months later, Molly gave us a progress report. "I just talked to the people at Schwab, where my 401(k) funds are. I have almost $8,000, in just months, since you first talked me into investing. I always thought I didn't have enough to make it worth investing. Boy, do I wish I had started sooner!"

Making Bread's Top 10 Failed Financial New Year's Resolutions

MANY MAKE THEM; FEW KEEP THEM. WILL THIS BE THE YEAR WE ALL LEARN TO "BUCK THE TREND"?

SPEND LESS: I will count my calories AND my pennies, because I know that, when it comes to money, spending less is the *only* way that "less is more" makes any sense.

SAVE MORE: I will get a warmer, fuzzier feeling when I put $100 in my savings account than I do when I put a cashmere sweater on my back.

OWE LESS: I will give credit where it's due—to *myself* for getting serious about consolidating my loans and paying down my debt.

PAY PROMPTLY: I will remember to pay my bills on time so that I can avoid those outrageous, annoying late-payment fees that make it impossible to get ahead—and protect my credit rating in the bargain.

GET ORGANIZED: I will arrange my financial papers so that I can find them when I need them.

BECOME A BARGAIN HUNTER: I will compare prices on everything from interest rates to light bulbs. (Is it time to refinance my mortgage?) I will form a savings club with my friends and buy in bulk. Outlets will be my outlet when the urge to splurge hits!

BE PREPARED FOR ANYTHING: I will start an emergency fund so that, in the event that I am laid off, I will have at least six months' salary saved up.

THINK LIKE A MOGUL: I will form an investment club with my friends to learn about the stock market, then act on my newfound knowledge.

LOOK TO THE FUTURE: I will make a plan, outlining where I want to be in five years, in terms of my career and my financial security…and I will map out a way to make my dreams come true.

GIVE BACK: I will keep spare change and dollar bills in my pocket and hand them out daily to those in need wherever I see them, because I know that kindness pays huge dividends.

CHAPTER TEN:

WOMEN & INVESTING: TIPS FOR MAKING YOUR BREAD RISE

Three women sit at a table in a trendy restaurant, engaged in gossip and girl talk, as they wait for cocktails. The waiter serving them surreptitiously eavesdrops on the conversation, which goes something like this:

"I want a man who leaves me alone, except when I need him."

"Not me. I want someone who pays a lot of attention to me."

"Maybe I should try a woman."

The waiter raises an eyebrow at that last comment. Of course, it turns out that the ladies are talking about money—not love. Specifically, they're dishing about their financial advisers. This Charles Schwab commercial, which aired in 2004, is very funny, and its point is well-taken: well-heeled women with roomy Kate Spade bags can pick and choose their financial consultants based on their unique, even idiosyncratic, needs. But what about the rest of us—women without huge portfolios or designer totes, who may need good financial advice more than anyone else?

The good news is that we, too, have finally been discovered. Women of all income levels are being courted by financial institutions as never before, as Allison Acken found when writing an article on the stock market for us. It's about time. We are in the workplace to stay; we control 80 percent of household spending; women- owned businesses employ 27.5 million people and contribute $3.6 trillion to the economy; and women are more actively involved in their finances than ever before. Financial firms know this. Which is why they want us—large portfolios or not.

Depending on the financial institution, the minimum amount an investor must have in order to qualify for professional management can range from $5,000 to $100,000. But even if you don't have $5,000 saved, many financial institutions will offer you advice. And why not? If they can help create another millionaire—and get the business of managing her portfolio, both come out ahead.

Women's fear of investing may be one of the biggest stumbling blocks these companies face, and, surprisingly, that trepidation isn't just limited to older women. According to a 2000 Schwab/Harris poll, "GenX women were just as likely as senior women to say investing is scary for them" and that they "prefer to delegate to a professional," even though GenX women started investing much earlier than seniors (age 23 versus age 40). Results from the same poll indicate that "women are open to learning," with 64 percent saying that "investing might be more interesting, if they knew more about it."

For the woman who wants to increase her investing knowledge and experience, an abundance of resources exists these days. Most of the major brokerage houses include free information and educational resources on their Web sites, and often conduct seminars in the hope of attracting women's business. Women's investment clubs are springing up across the country and online (visit www.chickslayingnesteggs.com), where novice investors can learn the difference between a bull and a bear market together. (Animal lovers, take note: investors would love to make bears an endangered species.)

The National Association of Investors Corporation (NAIC), which provides investment education to about 28,300 investment clubs nationwide, reports that nearly 70 percent of the clubs' 327,000 members are women, with some belonging to all-women clubs, and others joining mixed groups. The average club size is 11 members, and members invest an average of $84 per month. According to the NAIC, women's portfolios outperform men's portfolios by 1.4 percent. Those power-lunchers would no doubt raise their glasses in a toast to that difference between the sexes.

Think of investing as "power saving," or "saving on steroids." If you have your 401(K) money invested in a mutual fund, you already own stocks. If you still have a little loose change burning a hole in your pocketbook after taking care of all your monthly expenses, you already have an emergency stash of cash squirreled away in a CD or money-market account, and your 401(k) and IRA options are maxed out, then consider putting money in "securities"—stocks and bonds—for your retirement. For women, who are playing catch-up with their retirement savings

because their lower earnings translate to lower 401(k) savings and Social Security benefits, investing provides a necessary boost.

To help you join the investing crowd, in this chapter, we'll cover the basics of buying stocks, bonds, and other investment products. We'll offer a first-person account by a financial expert in search of a money manager to help her invest a windfall. Along the way, she offers some entertaining insights into the different ways men and women approach investing and lets us in on what financial experts look for in a financial adviser. We even offer one woman's rationale for pulling

One thing you can do right now ...

DRIP YOUR TOES IN THE MARKET

Not an annoying problem with your faucet, rather DRIPs, or dividend reinvestment plans, are a great way for investors with small amounts of money to begin to invest in stocks. Here's how they work: You purchase a minimum number of shares in a company's stock (it could be as little as a single share, in some cases) and instruct the company to reinvest the dividends the stock earns into purchase of more of the same company's stock. Some companies even offer a discount on their stock price when you purchase it through a DRIP. Not all companies offer DRIPs, and management fees vary from company to company, though some charge none at all. Visit www.sharebuilder.com and www.dripadvisor.com for more information.

her money out of the market. Investing isn't for everyone, after all. There is risk involved. But you owe it to yourself to give it a try. Historically, the stock market has outperformed all other investments.

STOCK UP!

If you have the appetite for a little risk and are willing to devote some time to educating yourself about smart ways to minimize that risk, investing in stocks and bonds provides the quickest means of increasing your net worth and insuring your financial security in retirement. Getting the biggest possible ROI—return on investment—from their money is the best way women have to make up for wealth lost as a result of the wage gap and years spent away from the work force. Just compare the interest rate you'll get with a savings account or CD (maybe 3 or 4 percent) with the return your money might earn in a mutual fund (6 to 10 percent), and you won't have to think long and hard about where your dough will rise the fastest. Knowledge of investing will come in handy, when you sell your house for a profit, inherit a portfolio of stocks and bonds, or receive a large sum of money, such as a lump-sum payment from a pension plan, proceeds from a life insurance policy, or a cash settlement in a divorce decree. Once you get started, you may find that playing the stock market is not only fun but empowering.

THE DIFFERENCE BETWEEN SAVING & INVESTING.

Many women just tune out when they hear talk of REITs, options, book value, yield to maturity, price-to-earnings ratio, and other terms heard on the street . . . Wall Street. Don't let the men in

Getting Comfortable with Your Inner Stock Trader.

Try to avoid these common first-timer mistakes:

>> Don't blame yourself when you sell a stock at a loss. The economy or your stockbroker are more likely culprits. And don't hang on to a loser, just to avoid facing the reality of the loss.

>>Don't be too conservative; you'll risk losing purchasing power that way. The interest your money earns in a savings account or CD may not keep up with inflation, particularly after you pay taxes. That's why you're in the stock market. Sure, you can lose money, if you are too aggressive. But, over time, the potential for growth is great.

>>Don't let yourself become overwhelmed by all the investment alternatives and procrastinate making financial decisions, out of fear of making the wrong choice. Learn from your mistakes.

your life fool you; a lot of them don't understand the lingo, either. Breaking the code of Wall Street jargon is not difficult, once you get the hang of it. First rule: If you don't understand, just ask: "What does that mean?"

But even before you worry about the words (see the "How to Sound Like a Stockbroker in One Easy Lesson" box in this chapter), it helps to understand the basic principles of investing. Investing means looking ahead—far ahead—3 years, 5 years, 10 years, maybe longer. With investing, time literally is money. The longer you have to invest, the greater your return. You cannot think short-term. It requires you to sit down and seriously consider your objectives, so that you can choose your investments to accomplish those goals. You must do your homework, gaining an understanding of what investments are and how they work. If you've always saved a certain amount of money from each paycheck, that's great. But saving isn't investing. Investing takes saving to the next level. It broadens your choice of what you do with the money you've saved, and it involves some risk—how much depends on the type of investment. Unlike savings accounts, money market accounts and certificates of deposit, the money you invest in securities, or the stock market, is not FDIC-insured. You accept the risk on the premise that you will receive returns that are higher than you would get from a dependable but conservative savings account or certificate of deposit (CD). When you invest in a stock, you are assuming that you will sell your shares later on, at a price higher than you paid for them. Over the long term, you will see slumps and rallies. You may be tempted to sell when your stock hits a slump, or is worth less than you paid for it. In most cases, you'll be better off keeping the faith. Remember, investing means looking ahead . . . to the next rally . . . and it sometimes requires reallocation of your assets. So investing is active, whereas when you save, you merely put your money in one place and watch it earn a steady, predictable albeit small, rate of return.

READY, SET, INVEST.

Here are some investor basics, followed by a step-by-step guide to getting started:

Build your foundation first. Before you invest, make sure you have money put away for specific goals and rainy days. Do you have as much life and disability insurance as you are likely to need? Review cash flow for your household. How about the house itself? Will you need to pull money out of your investments later to cover major changes or improvements?

Get a good fix on your current financial situation. Do a net-worth statement and a cash-flow analysis at least once a year. Regular review is indispensable.

Check your risk pulse, and take your risk temperature. You are the only one who knows exactly how much stress you can stand. Your risk tolerance will determine what type of investment to make. Avoid risky investments such as options, commodities, futures, and new stock issues, if you're going to lose sleep over the possibility of taking a loss.

Stay well informed. Keep reading up on money matters and current affairs, expanding your knowledge of how the two interact. The stock market can seem like a woman with PMS, in the way it overreacts to current events. You need to be able to understand and predict that response, then be able to take a deep breath (or a Pamprin) and not respond yourself. Read the financial publications. The Wall Street Journal is a terrific paper, and not just for its financial coverage. It covers the human-interest side of money daily, in very entertaining and thought-provoking fashion. Talk to your broker or financial adviser regularly. Ask questions. Be prepared to take an active role in decision-making. Don't give anyone free rein over your money.

Develop an investment plan. Set your objectives, both mid-range and long-term. Is security over the long term your first order of business? Or are you out to make a fortune? If you're in it for the long term, do you have the patience to ride out bad markets?

Never fall in love with a stock. If a stock turns out to be a loser, get rid of it. Don't get emotionally attached to any one stock. Are you holding on because it's the company your late husband worked for? If your goals change, review your portfolio and evaluate it in light of your new goals, and make changes, if necessary.

Don't be afraid to sell. People say, "I can't afford to sell, because I'll have to pay a huge tax on the profit." Sell a stock, if you think it has peaked in price. Pay the tax. A drop in price could cost you more than the tax, if you don't sell at the peak. Identifying the peak, of course, is the trick. That's why it pays to keep informed about the company, its competitors and market conditions. A little women's intuition doesn't hurt, either.

Don't look for magic or miracles. You won't find any. You will have some gains, and some losses. To get high returns, if that is your goal, you will have to take risks.

Put your eggs in more than one basket. No single type of investment performs best at all times or under all conditions. Diversify, diversify, diversify.

Keep liquidity in mind. What if you need cash? What will you sell? You should always know which stocks will be the first you will let go if you have to.

Test the water first. If you have never bought stocks, and if you are a little wary about getting started, you can get a feel for it by buying shares in a mutual fund. Or "paper trade" for a few months. Pick stocks and follow them, as though you had put money down to purchase them. At the end of six months, see how much you would have made or lost, and test your risk tolerance. How do you feel about your make-believe gains or losses?

Keep it simple. A broker might try to sell you on some innovative way to take advantage of the latest tax law or a new financial product of some kind. Don't do anything you're not comfortable with or don't fully understand. Stick with what works for you.

Be patient. Most significant gains take 24 to 30 months, except in strong bull markets.

Don't be greedy. Don't be fearful. You're not always going to sell at the top of the market. Enjoy what gains you have. Don't lose faith and sell, if there's a big drop in the market. Remember you're in for the long haul, and history tells us there will always be a rebound.

INVESTING BY THE NUMBERS: A STEP-BY STEP GUIDE.

Now that you've gotten an idea of what's involved, are you ready to become a stock mogul? First, step: Identify your goals. Next: Narrow your choices to match those goals.

What's Your Goal? Ask yourselves some key questions: How important is income right now? Do I need to supplement my other income? Do I have enough current income from other sources? If so, am I willing to put money into investments that will grow steadily and, in the future, be worth a lot more? Or do I want aggressive growth—some quick bucks, so I can sell at a good profit and repeat the process? What about tax advantages? Do I want to defer taxes, or even pay no taxes at all by buying tax-free municipal bonds?

Your goals, based on the answers to the key questions above, will fall into one or more of four basic types:

1. Income return: Income-producing investments will bring you regular, current income. Use them if you want to supplement your other income or add to your retirement income. What kinds of investments produce income? Government, municipal, or high-grade corporate bonds, and income stocks, such as utilities or Real Estate Investment Trusts (REITs), that pay a substantial portion of their earnings in regular dividends.

2. Safety of principal: If you want to protect yourself against any possible loss of principal, or your initial investment, you will probably have to accept a low rate of return. You cannot expect high yields. Money-market accounts, regular savings accounts, U.S. Treasury bills, and certificates of deposit (CDs) all provide principal protection; in other words, you will always get back at least what you put in.

3. Long-term capital growth. Ideally, this is exactly what you want. When you invest for growth, you are looking ahead to the day when your investments will have increased substantially and you will be able to realize a profit, or capital gain. In short, your money is working not only to keep ahead of inflation, but to give you financial security in years far ahead. Real estate, stock mutual funds, and certain stocks that pay little or no dividends are your best bets to satisfy this goal.

4. Tax savings. Here your goal is to protect your earnings from taxation entirely, or defer it as long as possible, under laws passed for just that purpose. Municipal bonds give you income that is exempt from Federal income tax and state tax, if they are issued in the state where you live. 401(k) accounts and Individual Retirement Accounts (IRAs) defer taxation until you withdraw the funds, when presumably you will be in a lower tax bracket.

Work out your investment goals and decide upon a strategy before you start buying specific investments. Don't deviate from your objectives, unless you have an excellent reason to do so, because of some change in your life situation. Don't think about, or let yourself be influenced by, where the market is from day to day. Think about your needs for tomorrow. Consider your age, your feelings about risk, your current needs, and what you think your future needs will be. Last, but not least, think about your time frame: When do you want to take that trip to Europe, buy a new car, retire? In general:

You will invest for growth and for tax advantages . . . if you know your income level is rising and if you do not have children or other dependents to feed, clothe, and educate.

You will invest for income and high yield . . . if you are on the threshold of (or in) your retirement years; if you need income to supplement alimony or your salary; or if you have dependents— expensive teenagers, college undergrads or grad students—whose financial needs you must meet or help meet.

WHAT ARE YOUR CHOICES?

Have you looked carefully at your spending plan? Reviewed your net worth? Are you confident that you have enough income to cover your monthly expenses? Then consider the following two types of investments: fixed-income and equity.

In a fixed-income investment, such as a corporate or government bond, you lend your money to a corporation or a government agency (at the federal, state, county, municipal, or other local level) for a period of time. This makes you a creditor of the corporation or government agency, which agrees to pay you interest at a rate that is set, or fixed, when the bond is issued. In an equity investment, you buy stock, or equity, in a company. In effect, you own a piece of the company, when you buy a share in it. Why make such an investment? First, because you hope that the company will grow and that, as a result, the price of its stock will rise so that eventually you can sell your share for more than you paid for it. Second, you believe that the company will be so well managed that it will make a profit and divide that profit among its shareholders, in the form of a dividend paid to you at regular intervals. And third, you expect the company will continue to do well, increasing the dividend it pays to you. Note: Not all companies pay dividends. Start-up companies, in particular, do not. You invest in these, because you expect maximum appreciation of the value of each share, if and when they do well.

Money-market accounts and certificates of deposit, issued by banks, and guaranteed income contracts (GICs), issued by insurance companies, are common forms of fixed-income investments that provide steady, predictable, risk-free income. In general, however, though your minimum investment may be higher, you will usually get a higher rate of return by purchasing a corporate or municipal bond. These come in the following six flavors:

Corporate Bonds. Companies issue corporate bonds to raise money for a variety of reasons, from building a new plant or purchasing equipment, to expanding into new markets. When you buy any bond—government or corporate—you lend your money to that particular government or corporation for a certain length of time. At the end of that time, on "the date of maturity," the government or the corporation that issued the bond pays you back the full amount of the bond—called its "face value." In the meantime, while you hold the bond, you receive a fixed rate of interest (the "coupon rate"), which, in most cases, is paid twice a year. You can find the rate of interest printed on the bond. If the rate is nine percent on a $1,000 bond, for example, you will get $90 a year. Once the bond is issued—in other words, once you have purchased it—the interest rate does not change, no matter how much bond prices fluctuate.

How risky are bonds? Consider two factors: First, bonds are as risky as the credit-worthiness of the issuer. If the perception of the value of the issuer deteriorates, the bonds are likely to lose value. Second, if interest rates rise, the value of the bonds drops. Sometimes you can buy a bond at less than its face value. The seller is offering it to you at a discount, in effect, to induce you to own a bond that is worth less than the going rate. Such a bond is known as a discount bond.

How do bond markets work? Bond prices move up and down with changes in interest rates, because "yields," or the amount of money paid to holders, on existing bonds must compete with those on new bonds that are being issued. Yield is not the same as interest rate. Your yield may be higher or lower than the interest rate, depending on whether you bought the bond at a discount (i.e., below face value) or at a premium (above face value).

In short, bond prices increase when interest rates go down and decrease when interest rates go up. Suppose you buy a $1,000 bond that pays 9 percent. If interest rates then rise to 10 percent, no one will want to pay $1,000 for your 9 percent bond. The price of your bond will drop, so that its current "yield to maturity" will equal 10 percent. The yield to maturity takes into account the coupon rate of nine percent and any difference between what you paid for it and what you will collect (the face value) at maturity. If you decide to sell a bond before it reaches maturity, you may not get as much as you paid for it—depending on how much interest current bond issues are paying. If you are buying a bond after it has been issued (think of it as a pre-owned bond), be sure to ask the broker what the "yield to maturity" is. The yield that is reported in the newspaper is the "current yield"—or what you are receiving in relation to the current price of the bond.

Bond prices also depend on the length of time between purchase and maturity. The longer the time to maturity, the more volatile the price of the bond. If interest rates rise one percentage point, the price of a 10 percent coupon bond with a 30-year maturity is likely to fall about 8.7 percent. But, assuming a similar rise in rates, a 10 percent bond that is due in only three years will drop only about 2.5 percent. So a change in interest rates has a greater effect on the price of a bond with a long time to maturity than on the price of one with a shorter maturity. This is referred to as "interest-rate risk." What happens if interest rates go down? You'll see the opposite effect. Your bond will increase in value. You can sell it at a premium, because—when interest rates are down—buyers are willing to pay a premium to get a bond with a higher interest rate. Here's how current yields can fluctuate:

PURCHASE PRICE	INTEREST PAYMENT	CURRENT YIELD
If you buy at par: $1,000	$80.00	8%
If you buy at discount: $800	$80.00	10%
If you buy at premium: $1,200	$80.00	6 ⅔%

What's the chance that the issuer will fail to repay you? Most bond buyers get the answers to such questions by looking at rating services. The two best known are Standard & Poor's (www.standardandpoors.com) and Moody's (www.moodys.com). These companies don't report the market attractiveness of the bond. They study the financial stability of the issuer. Their job is to inform the investor about how much risk is involved in buying any particular bond. Bonds of the highest quality are rated as AAA by S & P's and as Aaa by Moody's.

Most corporate bonds have a par value of $1,000 and carry various maturity dates. Generally, these bonds pay higher rates than government or municipal bonds because they carry greater risk. However, because they provide a fixed income with the opportunity for repayment of capital, corporate bonds are considered slightly less risky than equity investments, or stocks. Purchase corporate bonds through stockbrokers, banks, or other securities dealers individually or in bond funds (more about them later). Income earned is taxable.

Government Securities. When you invest in government securities, you are loaning money to the government. With the U.S. government borrowing some $200 billion every year, new issues are often available. These investments are safe simply because they are backed by the "full faith and credit of the United States." Government securities come in four types:

Treasury bills. Sold every week, these reach maturity within three, six, or 12 months. You must invest at least $1,000, with $1,000 increments. The interest is deducted from the purchase price and paid at maturity. If you buy a three-month Treasury bill worth $10,000, you might pay $9,850, or more, or less, depending on the interest rate. After three months, you present it for full payment of $10,000. The difference between what you paid and the $10,000 is interest.

Treasury notes. These are sold every four weeks or so. Maturity varies from one to 10 years. The usual minimum purchase is $1,000, and you pay the full price of the note you buy. The government pays you interest semiannually.

Treasury bonds. You won't find a regular schedule for the sale of these. You must watch for them. If you are interested, check in regularly with your banker to see when they will be offered. These bonds are frequently issued with maturities of 30 years, although they can have maturities of 10 years or more. They are definitely in the long-range category. The usual price is $1,000 each. Like Treasury notes, you buy them at full price and then get cash interest twice a year. Treasury bonds are considered a barometer of the bond market.

Treasury Inflation Indexed Securities (TIPS). Every six months, TIPS are adjusted to reflect inflation as measured by the Consumer Price Index. If inflation occurs, the principal increases. If deflation occurs, the principal decreases. When the security matures, you are paid the inflation-adjusted principal or the original principal, whichever is greater. The maturity is five, 10, or 20 years.

TIPS pay a fixed rate of interest. The interest rate is applied to the inflation-adjusted principal. If inflation occurs throughout the life of your security, every interest payment will be greater than the one before it. In periods of deflation, the interest payments would decrease in value. You can buy TIPS directly (i.e., without a broker or middleman) at any Federal Reserve Bank, or by opening an account at www.treasurydirect.gov. You can also buy them through a bank or a broker, but both will tack on a handling charge (up to $50), and you may be charged a custodial fee, as well.

Hold onto government securities until they mature. You can always borrow against them, or sell them in the secondary market at current market prices, where you will get more or less what you paid for them—depending on whether interest rates have risen, fallen, or stayed the same since you bought them.

Tax tip: The interest you earn from government securities is taxed by the federal government, but it is not taxed at the state or local level. So if you live in a state that taxes interest income on other securities, these can give you a certain tax advantage.

Government Savings Bonds. U.S. savings bonds are not marketable; You can only buy them from the U.S. government, and they may not be traded among investors. Rather than guaranteeing a minimum interest rate, as in the past, the government now pays market-based rates and credits interest to all bonds twice a year. Series EE have a maturity value of $50 to $10,000. You purchase them at a 50 percent discount and receive the full value at maturity. Series I bonds are purchased at face value. Interest earned is exempt from local and state taxes, and you pay no federal tax until the bonds mature (10 years extendable to 30 years), or you cash them in.

Savings bonds have excellent liquidity. You may cash them in at any bank after holding them for only six months. They are extremely safe. But their yields are lower than other investments that are just as safe. Why buy them? One reason: If you cannot afford any larger form of government security. Another: To force yourself to save, by buying them through a payroll deduction plan. Interest on EE bonds can be tax-exempt if used for educational purposes, with certain income limitations.

Tax-Exempt Bonds. Issued by states, communities, or their agencies, and sold by stockbrokers, banks, or licensed securities dealers individually or in funds, these bonds are generally called municipal bonds, or "muni's" for short. Minimum investment is $10,000, unless they are purchased as shares in a larger bond fund. The interest they pay is not taxed by the federal government. Because of their tax advantages, they are usually recommended for people in high-income brackets. If you want to decide whether to buy tax-free or taxable bonds, you have to figure the tax-equivalent yield—in other words, the yield a taxable bond would need to produce *after* taxes in order to equal the yield of a tax-exempt issue. The answer will depend on your particular federal and state income-tax rates. Bonds that have longer maturities will give you extra yield.

Tax tip: When you buy a bond issued by the state in which you live, you avoid not only the federal tax but any state or local taxes.

HANDY-DANDY RULE FOR FIGURING HOW MUCH OF YOUR RETIREMENT SAVINGS TO INVEST IN STOCKS

"Subtract your age from 100, and that is the percentage you should have in equities."

—*Words of wisdom from Charles P. Kindleberger, the economist who wrote the 1978 classic* Manias, Panics and Crashes: A History of Financial Crises, *documenting the repeated boom and bust cycles of the stock market.*

Mortgage-Backed Securities. These are pools of mortgage loans. Among the most popular are those backed by the Government National Mortgage Association (GNMA)—or "Ginnie Mae," to her friends. Ginnie Maes pay interest and a small amount of principal each month. The

How to Sound Like a Stockbroker in One Easy Lesson

Basis Point: One one-hundredth of a percent of the face value of a bond. Basis point is used to measure yield differences among bonds. There is a 30 basis point difference between two bonds if one yields 10.3 percent and the other yields 10.6 percent.

Blue Chip: A company known nationally for the quality and wide acceptance of its products or services, and for its ability to make money and pay dividends.

Bond: Basically an IOU, or promissory note, from a corporation, usually issued in multiples of $1,000 or $5,000. A bond is evidence of debt on which the issuing company usually promises to pay the bondholders a specified rate of interest, for a specified amount of time, and to repay the loan on the maturity date.

Bear Market: A declining market.

Bull Market: An advancing market.

Commission: The broker's basic fee for purchasing or selling securities.

Common Stock: Securities that represent an ownership interest in a corporation. The owner of common stock is rewarded in the form of dividends and capital appreciation.

Convertible Bond: A bond that may be exchanged by the owner for common stock, usually of the same company.

Discount: The amount by which a preferred stock or bond may sell below its face value.

Diversification: Spreading investments among different companies in different fields.

Dividend: The payment designated by the Board of Directors to be distributed pro rata among the shares of outstanding stock. Dividend size varies with the fortunes of the company and the amount of cash on hand, and payment may be skipped when business is poor.

Dow Jones Industrial Average: A trademark for one of the oldest and most widely quoted measures of stock-market price movements. The average is calculated daily by adding the share prices of 30 large, seasoned industrial companies and dividing that sum by a figure that is adjusted for such factors as stock splits and substitutions.

Face Value: The value of a bond that appears on the face of the bond. Face value is usually the amount the company promises to pay at maturity. For instance, if you own $5,000 in bonds (or five bonds), the face value is $5,000.

Fallen Angel: A once popular security that has lost investor favor and has declined in value.

IPO: Initial Public Offering, or the initial sale of the common shares of a corporation to the public.

Liquidity: The ability to easily and quickly convert assets to cash.

Market Order: An order to buy or sell a stated amount of a security at the most advantageous price obtainable at the time the order is placed.

Market Price: The last reported price at which a stock or bond sold.

Option: A right to buy (a call) or sell (a put) a fixed amount of given stock at a specified price within a limited period of time. The purchaser of a call hopes that the stock's price will go up, while the purchaser of a put hopes it will go down.

Preferred Stock: A class of stock with a claim on the company's earnings before payment may be made on common stock. Preferred stock holders are usually entitled to dividends at a specified rate.

Premium: The amount at which a preferred stock, bond, or option may sell above its par value.

Price/Earnings Ratio: The price of a share of stock divided by earnings per share. As a rule, a relatively high price/earnings ratio is an indication that investors feel the company's earnings are going to grow. Price-earnings vary among companies, among industries, and over time.

Round Lot: A unit of trading or a multiple thereof. On the New York Stock Exchange, the unit of trading is generally 100 shares in stocks and $1,000 par value in case of bonds.

Stock Dividend: A dividend paid in additional shares rather than cash.

Stop Order: An order to sell at a price below the current market price. A stop order is generally used to limit loss. A stop order becomes a market order when the stock sells at or below the specified price.

Yield: Also known as return. The dividends or interest paid by a company, expressed as a percentage of the current price.

---

actual yield of a mortgage-backed security depends on how rapidly its underlying loans—that is, the mortgages held by the lending institutions participating in the pool—are paid off ahead of time. If interest rates drop, for instance, borrowers may either sell their homes or refinance them. As a result, you may receive a return of a large share of your principal, which you will have to invest at lower interest rates.

The yields on GNMAs are usually higher than on long-term Treasuries. GNMA certificates come in $25,000 lots. Many investors, however, purchase mutual funds that own mortgage-backed securities, in which they can invest in lots of $1,000 or more. Buy GNMAs through your broker. Interest is taxable.

Zero-Coupon Bonds. These pay no interest while the loan is outstanding but promise big capital accumulation at maturity. The longer the maturity, the higher the yield. The rates are locked in. Zero-coupons come in the form of Treasuries, and corporate and municipal bonds. You receive all the interest, plus your original investment, when the bond matures. Why buy zero-coupon bonds? Because you can usually get more for your money. Why are they sold? Because the issuer can keep and use its money for longer than if it were required to make periodic interest payments.

Zero-coupon bond values fluctuate more than full-coupon bonds that pay interest every six months. But you will find no effect on the value of the bond, if you hold it to maturity. And if you are buying zeros, you can take advantage of the fact that you can buy varying maturity dates that coincide with such goals as retirement or education. Of course, it is best to buy them when interest rates are up.

Tax tip: Unless you buy tax-free or municipal zeros, you must pay income tax on the deferred or phantom income you would have received, if payments had been made periodically.

EQUITY INVESTMENTS COME IN THE FOLLOWING EIGHT FLAVORS:

1. Common Stocks. Buying common stocks makes you a part owner, or shareholder, of a corporation. From its earnings, the company pays you dividends. But if earnings are slim, or if there are none, the company can reduce its dividends—or pay none at all. And if things get really bad and the company is liquidated, the holders of common stock are the last to be paid.

2. Preferred stocks. These also make you an owner of the company. But you get paid before any earnings are distributed as dividends to those who own common stock. Your dividends are fixed and stated in advance. However, they are not guaranteed. If the company is liquidated, you get paid (as a preferred stockholder) before any common stockholder—but after those who own the company's corporate bonds.

3. Stock options. These put you into a higher level of risk. You should not get into them unless your base of savings and other investments is really solid. Stock options give you the right to buy or sell shares in a certain stock at a stated price until a certain date, after which, the option expires. Your company may give you a bonus or retirement benefit in the form of corporate stock options.

If you think the stock is going to rise in value, you buy a "call" option. The call gives you the right to buy a particular stock at a specified price during a certain period. If the price of the stock goes up, you can sell the option at a profit or exercise your option to buy the stock at the specified price. If the price doesn't go up, or goes down, you will have to sell the option at a loss. If you do not, it will expire and you will have lost your entire investment in the option. If, on the other hand, you buy a "put" option, the process is reversed—you hold the right to sell the stock at a specified price during the time period. In either case, when you hold a stock option you have no legal obligation to exercise it.

4. Commodities. A commodity is any tangible property that is traded on a commodities exchange. Such commodities range from oil, to silver and corn, from pork bellies to oranges or coffee beans. If you trade in commodities, you are buying or selling contracts for future delivery of the properties. You are also a gambler, for commodities are highly speculative. Their prices can fluctuate in minutes, since they are affected by everything from weather conditions to world crises. They are not for the inhibited. Trading in commodities requires intense attention. For a good laugh and a glimpse into the world of commodities trading, rent the Eddie Murphy movie *Trading Places*.

5. Precious metals and gemstones. You may have a fondness for gold or silver or diamonds. Jewelry isn't the only form in which you can invest in them. They are traded as commodities. But get good advice, for prices in these properties can rise and fall without warning or explanation. If you are buying a precious gem for yourself, connect with a reliable and trustworthy dealer. There is a considerable difference between the price at which a dealer will sell you a gemstone and the price at which a dealer will buy it from you at any given time.

6. Real estate. Over the long term, real estate has always been a good investment, usually appreciating in value, despite some ups and downs. If you are thinking of buying real estate, always bear in mind the old adage: "The three most important words in real estate are location, location, and location." One way to invest in real estate, without the headaches of property ownership, is to buy shares in a Real Estate Investment Trust (REIT). Most brokerage firms and financial institutions and some financial planners sell REITs. They are similar to mutual funds, because they pool the money of many investors.

There are three different types of REITs:

Equity REITs purchase commercial real estate, such as apartment buildings, nursing homes, office buildings, and hotels. They earn money by managing these properties. Later, they hope to sell the properties at a profit.

Mortgage REITs invest in the financing of properties, using the funds to make mortgage loans on commercial real estate. These REITs earn money by charging interest on the mortgages.

Hybrid REITs are a combination of equity and mortgage REITs. These REITs purchase some properties and make loans on others.

Shares of REITs are traded on the major stock exchanges, so you can buy and sell at any time. They are also required by law to pay out at least 95 percent of their income to shareholders. If you are looking for income, a REIT may be a good investment. Do not buy REITs that are not listed on an exchange or that do not sell regularly.

You can also invest directly in apartment houses, commercial rental properties, or land that is available for commercial development or likely to become available and thus more valuable.

The pluses: Investing in the real thing gives you a tax advantage, since the interest you pay on a first or second mortgage is deductible, as long as your mortgage loan is not greater than the amount you paid for the property plus any improvements you make. Taxes on your real estate are also deductible. Suppose you become a landlord by renting out property that you own. You can write off all maintenance, depreciation, and other expenses, including the interest you repay on your mortgage—up to $25,000 more than the income you get from the rent—as long as your own income is under $100,000 a year and you are handling the regular, daily management of the property yourself. If your income is between $100,000 and $150,000, you may deduct a part of such costs.

The minuses: The landlord's role is not always easy. You have to deal with contractors who don't show up for repairs. You have to placate demanding tenants. And you have to pay your mortgage, whether or not your tenant has paid the rent or you have space available.

When your money is in real estate, it is tied up. The risk is that the market may be down at a time when you want to sell, and selling—no matter where the market is standing—can always be slower than you expected. It usually takes time to negotiate a sale and for your buyer to get approval from lenders.

7. Collectibles. Many people collect things that increase in value, from antique automobiles to baseball cards, from stamps and coins to cut glass and first-edition books. Others inherit objects of value; just watch an episode of *Antiques Roadshow*, and you'll see the wide variety of objects, found in attics or passed down through the generations, that are worth four, five, and six figures. Collectibles bring you no income. But they can provide hours and even years of enjoy-

WHEN YOU WANT HELP WITH YOUR MONEY:
WHAT TO LOOK FOR IN A FINANCIAL ADVISER

-- PATRICIA SCHIFF ESTESS

You don't need to have more money than you know what to do with to be able to benefit from the services of a financial planner. A good financial adviser will listen to your hopes for the future, help you set goals, suggest strategies that will allow you to achieve those goals, and, acting on your instructions, implement those strategies for you. The best financial advisers help their clients make the most of the money they have so that they end up with more—or at least enough. Visit the Web site of the National Association of Personal Financial Advisers (www.napfa.org) to locate one near you. If you're thinking of hiring an adviser, seek out one who . . .

>> Has at least a two-hour initial meeting with you.

>> Meets with you face to face at least once a year—more often in the first year of your relationship or when you're going through one of life's difficult transitions.

>> Listens as well or better than he or she speaks.

>> Has an understanding of and sensitivity to your stated needs and dreams.

>> Has an ability to coalesce strategies around those needs and goals.

>> Works with people with similar incomes and net worth.

>> Has a program to keep you on the course you set for yourself and will help you revise plans when the need arises.

>> Will provide you with handouts, reading materials, checklists, and e-mail updates that are understandable and relevant to your situation.

>> Has a system to help you organize all your financial and legal paperwork.

>> Works with people with similar incomes and net worth.

>> Fully discloses what the fees or commissions are and what services are being provided.

>> Will work collaboratively with your other financial advisers, such as your accountant or insurance broker.

>> Has bona fide credentials, such as CFP (certified financial planner), though the letters don't ensure honesty or even knowledge. (They say merely that the person has had the interest and taken the time to learn more about money management.)

>> Has an appreciation of your uniqueness—for you are unique!

ment and, if you have collected something that becomes more and more rare over time, it can bring you a big payoff some day.

8. Annuities. An annuity is an investment contract that you buy from an insurance company. The idea is that the insurance company will provide you with payments at regular intervals over a fixed period, starting on some date in the future. When you buy an annuity, it accumulates interest that compounds, tax-deferred, until funds are withdrawn.

You can buy either of two types: a fixed annuity or a variable annuity. In a fixed annuity, often called a guaranteed income contract, or GIC, the insurance company guarantees the principal and a minimum rate of return. How can it do that? By investing your funds in fixed-income investments, such as bonds and mortgages. In a variable annuity, which is an equity investment, neither the principal nor the minimum payout is guaranteed. Your money is invested in stocks, bonds, and mutual funds. Some insurance companies allow you to split your investment between fixed and variable accounts.

Do you have to buy an annuity outright? No. You can buy it in installments, if the single-premium price is beyond reach. This is especially true with variable annuities. The insurance company will tell you its minimum dollar investment. It will also impose a penalty if you want to make early withdrawals—usually 6 or 7 percent in the first year, then decreasing by 1 percent each year, until there is no penalty. Because the money you invest in an annuity is tax-deferred, the government also discourages early withdrawal. It will take a 10 percent penalty on any amount you withdraw before

you reach 59½, and you must pay income tax on the dollars you withdraw. With that double hit for early withdrawal, this is definitely an investment you want to buy and hold until maturity. For more about annuities see Chapter Six.

FIXED-INCOME VERSUS EQUITY INVESTMENTS

When you buy stocks, you own something. When you buy fixed-income investments—Treasuries, CDs, guaranteed income contracts (GICs), and money-market accounts—you are lending money. Over time, owning has produced better results than lending. Here's why. Historically, the stock market has performed much better than other means of investing. Take the years from 1982 through 2002. All investments were up—$1.00 invested at the end of 1982 was worth $5.91 in real, after-inflation terms near the end of 2002. In the same period, $1.00 invested in corporate bonds was worth $4.44, while a Treasury bond was worth $1.62. Stocks have outperformed bonds and cash by a huge margin over the last 77 years.

Look at it this way: on average, if you had invested one dollar in Treasury bonds on the last day of 1925, you would have had $5.92 by the last day of 2002. If you had put one dollar in a corporate bond at the same time, it would have increased to $8.17. But if you had put your dollar in stocks at the same time, you would have had $172.92 by the end of 2002, in spite of the downward market of the last few years. Which would you prefer? Yet many people mistakenly feel safer with fixed-income investments; they forget that inflation is constantly eating away at the value of their holdings. Furthermore, the longer they hold them, the more value inflation consumes. Yes, you may say, but the stock market can decline suddenly, and it can stay down for a long time. Agreed. That is why you must start early and think long-term when you buy stocks. The longer you hold them, the lower the risk.

TRADING SECRETS

Rule No. 1: Be patient. See above.

Rule No. 2: Do your homework. Never buy a stock that you have not studied carefully.

You should know the goals of the company, who runs it, and what kind of earnings record it has, who its competitors are, and how economic trends might impact its future profitability. Many successful investors follow the rule of "buy what you use"—products that you are familiar with and see a continuing need for in the market-place—Home Depot or Slim-Fast, for instance. Health stocks are a profitable niche (as you might suspect from the price you pay for prescriptions). Others look for companies that are socially or environmentally responsible—and you wouldn't go wrong by looking for women in upper management and on the board of directors of the companies you invest in. As we mentioned in the last chapter, companies with the highest representation of women on their senior management teams had a 35 percent higher return on equity and a 34 percent higher total return to shareholders than companies with the lowest women's representation.

All that being said, while there are many ways to educate yourself through resources found online or in bookstores, or by joining an investment club, before you invest a lot of dough, you may find it valuable to consult with a securities analyst or other financial professional who specializes in securities trading.

Rule No. 3: Diversify for safety. You can make money in the stock market. You can lose money in the stock market. You always face risk. How much risk depends on the economy, on your particular investment goals, and on how you balance your portfolio to meet those goals. But you can reduce your risk by spreading your investments across different types of stocks.

There is no single investment that provides high current income, growth, and safety. No investment performs well all the time. Protect yourself against the effects of such uncertainty by owning various types of investments. Diversification is a way to balance risk and return. You diversify by owning both stocks and bonds, reducing your portfolio's exposure to any single part of the market. Diversify further by buying stocks of various companies in several different industries. If you decide you want to own drug stocks, then consider buying two or three different drug companies. That way, the performance is not dependent on one type of business or one company. When you buy bonds, "ladder" them by purchasing bonds with different maturity dates, so that you protect yourself from shifting interest rates. Note: Diversification can limit loses but not prevent them. (See Rule No. 6.) It does not guarantee that your portfolio won't suffer if the market takes a downturn. Care should be taken not to overdiversify.

Rule No. 4: Be an active investor. Review your portfolio regularly, and allocate your assets in response to market conditions or changes in your own goals. Asset allocation is a method of dividing your portfolio among stocks, bonds, and cash—a certain percentage allocated to each of the three categories. There are an endless number of asset-allocation strategies, but your allocation has to suit your particular situation, your feeling about risk, and your age.

Asset allocation may sound very much like diversification, but it goes beyond that—setting an aggressive, moderate, or a conservative investment course. You might start out with a conservative approach, for instance, then become more aggressive as you grow more comfortable in the market. You can change your allocation at any time, and you should shift your percentages as your life situation changes. A retired person, for instance, should aim for a more conservative balance than somebody 20 to 30 years younger, and therefore will have a lower percentage of stocks and a larger percentage of bonds and cash. The closer you are to retirement, the less time there is to make up for losses.

Appreciation of some of your securities over time might tilt your portfolio out of original balance. For instance, if your original allocation formula was 60 percent stocks, 30 percent bonds, and 10 percent cash, and your stocks have performed so well that they now make up 70 percent of your portfolio's value, you may want to sell off some of the stocks and reinvest the money in bonds to bring your portfolio back into balance.

Rule No. 5: Invest steadily. Dollar-cost averaging is a very effective strategy for keeping your average cost per share down. What's dollar-cost averaging? If you are putting money into a 401(k) plan through regular payroll deductions, you are already doing it. Your payroll deduction is always the same, but the number of shares that you can buy with that amount changes as the price changes; you buy more shares for each dollar when prices are down and fewer shares when prices are high. It all averages out in your favor, with your average cost per share lower than if you had purchased the same number of shares at one time. With dollar-cost averaging, you can be sure that you never buy all of your shares at the highest price.

You can use dollar-cost averaging outside of a 401(k) plan. Investing in mutual funds on your own? Just decide how much you can invest every month, and stick to it—regardless of market prices. Even better, ask the fund to arrange for your bank to make an automatic transfer every month into your mutual-fund account. The fund may set a minimum—probably between $50 and $250. Some funds will waive their investment minimums (usually $1,000 to $2,500) when you use an automatic investment plan. If you use a broker, place an automatic buy order once a month. Doing your own trading online? Discipline yourself to invest the same amount once a month.

Rule No. 6: There are no guarantees in the stock market. This can't be repeated enough. A company may or may not do well. Stock prices change every day. If you find yourself lying awake wondering whether the market price of your stock will go down tomorrow, you should be invested in more conservative stocks or bonds, or stick to CDs and GICs. But you do so at the risk of losing potential income for your retirement. Because this also can't be repeated enough: historically, the stock market has outperformed all other investments.

THE NITTY-GRITTY

Where do you buy stocks? They are bought and sold—or traded, to use the jargon of the business—on exchanges. The largest and probably best known in the United States is the New York Stock Exchange (NYSE), located on Wall Street. The New York Stock Exchange provides the facilities for stock trading and rules under which trading takes place. Stock trading on the NYSE occurs auction-style: In each transaction, stock is sold to the highest bidder and bought for the lowest offer. The companies traded on the NYSE must meet certain listing standards and are generally the oldest, largest, and best-known companies, known as "blue chips." The stocks of many smaller, less well-known companies are traded on the American Stock Exchange (AMEX), and regional exchanges are located in other major cities.

Other countries have their own exchanges. You may hear stock analysts quote results on the FTSE (pronounced "Footsie"); similar to the United States's Standard & Poor's 500 index, the Footsie is an index of the top 100 stocks traded on the London Stock Exchange—both can be used as a benchmarks against which to measure the performance of your stocks. The best way for a U.S. citizen to invest in foreign-owned firms is to buy shares in an international mutual fund.

Evening news shows regularly report the close-of-market results of two major trading sources, the NYSE and the NASDAQ—which stands for National Association of Securities Dealers Automated Quotations. On the NASDAQ, stocks are traded electronically, via computers and telephones, rather than through the interaction of brokers at a physical location, such as an exchange. This is called the over the counter (OTC) market. Brokers trade from their offices all over the country, using a sophisticated electronic network run by the National Association of Securities Dealers. Continuously updated prices are carried on their computer screens, while they buy and sell over the telephone. NASDAQ lists 3,300 companies—from small, emerging firms to corporate giants like Microsoft, Apple Computer, and Amazon.com. Many of the NASDAQ listings are in technology, telecommunications, banking, retail, and other growth sectors. Once considered the little kid on the block, NASDAQ has muscled up in recent years, wooing companies away from the NYSE, which once was considered the gold standard in exchanges; some companies now carry dual listings.

You can follow the ups and downs of your stocks through the business section of any good daily newspaper. The most comprehensive listings, of course, are in *The Wall Street Journal* and *The New York Times*. Stock tickers are now prevalent online, and many financial sites, such as Etrade.com and Internet service providers, such as AOL, will allow you to set up your own watch list of stocks, where you can track changes in price in 20 minute intervals. Before you begin trading, you might try setting up a watch list and tracking performance for a month or so, to get a feel for the action and measure your risk tolerance when stocks fluctuate.

When you're ready to buy stocks, you have three choices. First you can call a broker licensed to deal in securities. The broker will offer advice and handle all buy and sell orders, charging you a commission on every transaction—whether you are buying or selling. The rate of the broker's commission varies, depending on whether it is a full-service or discount brokerage.

If you are willing and able to do the research yourself, your second option is to choose your own stocks and bonds without the advice of a specialist. When you do this, you can either use a discount broker, whose commissions for executing trades are usually 40 to 70 percent less than those of a regular broker. Or you can place your orders yourself, using an on-line service, such as Etrade.com, Ameritrade,com, www.schwab.com, and others. You will be charged a fee for each transaction, generally in the $10 to $20 range, depending on the number of trades you make.

Should you put securities in your name or in a street name? There are advantages to each. If you register the security in your name, the certificate and all dividends will come directly to you. Every time you buy a stock or bond, you receive a certificate. This is your proof of ownership. Put it in a safe-deposit box, because it is a negotiable instrument. You'll have to pay a surety bond equal to two percent of the value of the certificate at the time the loss is reported, if you lose it. The downside is that you have to send the certificate to a stockbroker, if you want to sell it.

When you register stock or bond in a "street name," you are registering the security in the name of the brokerage house that holds it for you. You'll receive a confirmation slip, which is your proof of ownership. Dividends go into your account, instead of coming directly to you. You receive a monthly statement, listing all your stocks, all transactions, and all dividends received during the period. You can buy and sell with just a phone call to your broker, since the brokerage house has the stock certificate.

Your broker might ask you to agree to set up a discretionary account. If you do so, you are giving your broker the right to buy and sell without consulting you. An unscrupulous broker could churn your account—that is, buy and sell simply to make commissions. For your protection, most brokerage firms have millions of dollars of insurance covering each account against fraud, theft, or loss of securities. But you still don't want to give up control.

What about taxes? You pay income taxes on your salary, interest, dividends, and alimony, but you are taxed at a lower rate on profits from the sale of stocks, mutual funds, real estate, and other assets. This is called the capital-gains tax. (If you sell an asset at a higher price than you paid for it, you earn a capital gain. If you sell at a lower price than you paid, you take a capital loss.) Changes in the tax law in 2003 lowered the top capital-gains tax rate for individual taxpayers from 20 to 15 percent for investments held for more than 12 months plus one day (and down to 5 percent for low-income individuals). The rate on certain qualifying dividends (paid from a corporation that has already paid income tax on the earnings distributed) was also lowered to 15 and 5 percent, respectively.

You can use capital-gains losses, up to a maximum of $3,000 a year, to reduce your ordinary income, which in turn reduces the amount of income tax you pay. Say you have some stocks, bonds, or mutual-fund shares that have lost value; sell them and deduct the loss from your capital gains for the year. If losses outnumber gains, you can use your net loss to offset up to $3,000 of your income for the year, and if your capital losses exceed $3,000, you can carry them forward to future years. One caveat: If you change your mind and buy the security back at a lower price within 30 days, you can't deduct the original loss that year.

A good financial adviser can be a real asset for a beginner—or even a pro, as Patricia Schiff Estess, attests in the next section. He or she can keep you apprised of new opportunities and risks, carry out transactions for you, and advise you of the tax consequences of your investments, among other valuable services. Shop for one as you would for a lawyer or accountant. Look for an independent broker who doesn't stand to benefit from recommending one investment over another.

How much do they cost? Financial advisers are generally paid in one of three ways: Commissions, money-management fees, or flat fees. Commissions are the fees paid for executing securities trades. Money-management fees are different. You don't pay anything for individual trades; instead, you pay the adviser a percentage of the assets under management. For instance, you might pay an adviser 1.25 percent to manage a portfolio under one million dollars and 1 percent for one valued at more than a million. Other advisers negotiate a flat fee (say, $700 per year) to cover their services for a specified period of time. In any case, you should request that they disclose whether they receive commissions from financial companies for selling certain products or funds.

Next, Estess takes us along on her recent quest to find just such an adviser to help her invest the proceeds of the sale of her New York loft apartment.

My Money Manager—or Me?

COME ALONG AS A FINANCIAL EXPERT LOOKS FOR A FINANCIAL ADVISER TO HELP HER INVEST HER DOUGH

BY PATRICIA SCHIFF ESTESS

When people find out that I was the editor of a personal-finance magazine and that I write about money frequently, they'll usually start peppering me with investment questions. And if I'm with my husband when professional revelations are made, and they find out that he worked on Wall Street for 25 years before becoming an executive director of a social-service agency, then people swarm around both of us with questions. They expect us to have all the answers. But we don't know any more about what to invest in than any other person who reads the business section of a newspaper or watches *Lou Dobbs' Money Report* occasionally.

That's why, when we put our Manhattan loft on the market six months ago, we panicked. We figured we'd be getting a large sum of money, and we didn't know what to do with it.

The only thing our professional lives had taught us about financial advisers was to be cynical. I've listened to financial planners spout ridiculous generic advice, like: "If you're 40 years old, you should have 60 percent of your assets in stocks and 40 percent in bonds." (As though people haven't even heard of making money in real estate!) I've heard money managers assert their skills at outperforming the market. (Give me a break! How did you really do in the past few years?) And I've been bombarded with calls from stockbrokers touting some incredible offering. (I know, beyond a shadow of a doubt, that the only reason for the call is that business is slow, and they're trying to meet their mortgage payments.)

So my husband and I waffled. Despite how busy and interested in other things we are, we wondered, should we learn all we can about specific investments and make decisions ourselves? Or should we actually look for someone to help us?

We made some feeble attempts to find "the" right person. We called our broker, a long-time acquaintance, and asked her for suggestions on what we might do with the money, once we had it. Never got a call back. Her nonchalance made me rethink my skepticism. Maybe brokers really aren't interested in commissions . . . or maybe we were asking too much of her. We called to make an appointment with a fee-only financial planner, who told us that the initial consultation would cost us $300. (A turn-off if I ever heard one. Who pays someone before they're hired? It never happened to me.) On a recommendation from a friend, we spoke to a so-called financial planner (whose firm calls all of its associates financial planners), filled out a client profile, and received a printout of boilerplate information and recommendations on investments, diversity, and taxes. (Naturally, this truly unuseful tome was followed by umpteen calls at dinnertime, soliciting our account.)

Could She Be "The One"? Forget it, we decided. We're proceeding on our own, however feeble our attempt. Then, quite unexpectedly, a financial adviser I had met a couple of years before, when she and her mother were considering writing a book on the finances of divorce, called. I remembered our meeting well. They had asked me to come in to discuss the book with them. We had had a wonderful exchange of ideas, but nothing came of it. The book was never written. Now the daughter—let's call her Joan—wanted to talk to me about another writing project.

So I met her in her office, and we talked and talked—about money and life. About relationships, children, and aging parents. About how the brain takes a vacation when people go through an emotional transition, such as divorce, marriage, or the loss of a loved one. About how a good financial adviser is part psychologist, part financial guru. About people's (especially women's) general lack of knowledge in the area of finances and the good reasons why that's so. We talked a little about markets, economics, and investments—but very little.

"I don't know what the market is going to do tomorrow," she admitted. (Wow, that was refreshing.) And not once did she present the analyst's doubletalk of "on one hand" and "on the other hand." Best of all, she wasn't trying to sell me on herself. She didn't even know I was in a buying frame of mind.

I came home after our third "writing-idea" session and suggested to my husband that maybe he should meet Joan. Perhaps, just perhaps, she might be a good person to help us manage our money. Even more cynical than I, he railed at the idea. I suspect, though he would be loath to admit it, that part of his resistance had to do with her being a woman. Not that he's a chauvinist in any way, but I think the impression that was etched in his mind when he left Wall Street 18 years ago was "woman equals assistant."

So before I did anything rash, I spoke to a couple of people who were using Joan as their financial adviser. Both of them are men, and both are financially savvy (one had a background in investment banking).

"She really is my personal CFO," the investment banker said. "She is knowledgeable about the market, sees the big picture, and, best of all, she listens to my concerns and my goals and shapes a strategy around those."

"Never underestimate the importance of emotional understanding," the other said. "You can't talk about stocks and bonds outside the context of life."

Based on these testimonials, I set up a meeting with my

husband and Joan, so the three of us could talk about the possibility, and the possibility only, of her becoming our financial adviser. We'd both have to trust her if we were going to sign on. During that meeting, Joan asked lots of questions, talked a little (but in a rapid-fire manner, so you had to stay awake or you'd miss something), and listened intently. We spent at least an hour of the two we were there talking about life, our kids, our plans for the next year, and what we were hoping for in the future.

She had a few suggestions that had nothing to do with investing, such as the possibility of setting up a special-needs trust (one that provides money from your estate for a person with special needs without disqualifying that person—generally your child—from government support).

She also suggested we check out the stability of the company holding our long-term care insurance, since some companies were canceling this unprofitable (for them) coverage. She told us about funds she liked better than traditional mutual funds, called I-shares (index funds specializing in different segments of the market, and carrying lower fees than traditional mutual funds), something neither of us had ever heard about.

And we talked about ways to protect assets, while increasing the return on investments, such as writing covered calls and coupling that with a stop-limit order. (How that works is that for each 100 shares of stock you own, you can sell—write—a call option that allows someone else to buy your stock at a specific price—the striking price—over a specific period of time. The premium you receive from this option sale increases your income and gives you added protection should the stock drop. A stop-limit order is a standing order to sell a stock when it reaches a certain price.)

To be honest, very little of this technical stuff holds my interest. I understand it just enough to know it makes a degree of sense. But I'm not hot on active management of my stock portfolio. For the most part, I'm happy owning solid stocks of companies that make things that don't tax my technophobic brain, companies like Colgate or 3M, and holding them forever. I "get" the concepts of toothpaste and Scotch tape. I don't get metals futures or iPods. And I really turn off when someone talks about "technical indicators."

My husband, though, had his interest in the market piqued for the first time in years. He and Joan bandied terms and concepts around, while I focused on the pictures of her family on the credenza, wondering what her husband was like and how influential her mother must have been in getting her interested in this field.

She "Gets" Us . . . and Our Business. "What did you think?" I asked my husband, just steps after we left her office. "She seems knowledgeable enough," he agreed. "And I think she homed in on who we were and what is important to us. Okay," he conceded, "let's try it." Then his skepticism surfaced. "I just want to make certain she doesn't have free rein to do anything she'd like. And we'd better come out ahead, after she takes her annual fee."

That was three months ago. In the interim, Joan and I have exchanged umpteen e-mails, mainly dealing with developing a written statement, detailing our expectations of her—everything from outperforming the market to being able to get in touch with her when we need to talk. We had another two-hour meeting to solidify our goals and develop an investment plan for the year. She has called four or five times to talk about a specific investment and why she thinks it would fit nicely into our plan. But she's never pressured me. It's never: "We'd better do this now, or we'll lose out on a good thing." I spent one hour with Joan's incredibly organized and patient assistant, who walked me through all the benefits of our new account—free checking, a free safe-deposit box, and free ATM usage anywhere. While I love all the benefits I never had before, I wonder why people with significant accounts get perks (which they can afford to pony up for), while people with less money have to pay for these things. Doesn't seem quite fair to me.

My gut tells me this was a good move and that we're going to have a successful long-term relationship. But I'm reserving judgment. Three weeks after Joan made our first investment, the Dow fell 300-plus points and the NASDAQ dropped below 1950. Still, it's early in the game, and I don't have a year's worth of data from which to assess our money manager's skills. Though still cautious, I've become less cynical. Maybe, just maybe, we've lucked upon an honest, intelligent, sensitive financial adviser, who doesn't promise the world but delivers more financial savvy than two supposed experts are interested in having. I'll keep you posted.

Emotional IQ:
Telltale Signs that Your Financial Adviser Isn't for You

PATRICIA SCHIFF ESTESS

Dump your present adviser if you are made to feel . . .

>> **Stupid**, because something you suggested was dismissed out of hand.

>> **Pressured** into following his or her advice.

>> **Uncomfortable**, because you don't really understand the terms or strategies that are being suggested and you're afraid to keep asking for explanations.

>> **Unimportant**, because your adviser interrupts your meetings by taking phone calls.

>> **Unsure** about how much you're being charged in the way of fees or commission—even after you've asked.

>> **Disquieted**, because you only know your adviser from phone chats and e-mails.

>> **Angry**, because your adviser is making more money by giving advice than you are by receiving it.

Mutual Fund-amentals: One-Stop Stock Shopping. If you are putting money into a company 401(k) or profit-sharing plan, a 529 college savings plan or a Coverdell education IRA, chances are you already own stocks. Some 8,124 mutual funds are alive and well today in America, up from about 500 back in 1979, and 50 percent of all U.S. households have money invested on Wall Street through mutual funds. The mutual-fund industry, held up as the safest of investments, took a heavy blow to its reputation in 2003, when New York Attorney General Eliot Spitzer and the Securities and Exchange Com-mission charged a number of companies with excessive fee structures and improper trading activities that gave certain investors an advantage at the expense of others. The upshot: some firms were fined, their investors have been compensated for losses, and industry-wide corrective measures have been put into place.

Mutual funds still represent the easiest way for the average investor to enter the market. By their very nature (a mutual fund pools the funds of many participants and uses that money to purchase a large portfolio), they represent instant diversification at low cost. They are, in effect, one-stop stock shopping. When you purchase shares in a mutual fund, you also save yourself the time that you would otherwise spend researching individual stocks and bonds. Over the last 20 years, mutual funds have become a very popular, low-cost way for small investors to get diversification with the help of a professional money manager. (How widely diversified your investment is, of course, depends on how specialized the fund you select is).

Advantages of Mutual Funds. You get a number of other advantages beyond diversification, when you put retirement savings into mutual funds, including:

Low minimum investment. The required initial investment in many funds is as low as $250. Top minimum is seldom more than $1,000. In a word, getting started is within easy reach.

Professional management. This is one of the major attractions of mutual funds. You don't have to become a Wall Street expert. Professional managers study the market for you, analyze trends, keep reading up on financial information, and work hard to make smart decisions about the fund's portfolio.

Easy record-keeping. Mutual funds send year-to-date statements on your account frequently. Well ahead of tax time, they provide forms 1099-DIV and 1099-B, so you can easily report your income and capital gains to the IRS.

Automatic reinvestment. Setting up your fund so that dividends and capital gains are reinvested is easy and will maintain continual growth of your account.

Automatic withdrawal. You can request that your fund pay you regularly, even arrange for it to make direct deposits to your checking account. Retirees find this feature particularly practical.

Liquidity. Your mutual fund must buy back your shares any time you want to sell them. The best time to do so, of course, is when they are worth more than you paid for them.

Convenience and flexibility. Switching from fund to fund, as the market changes or your needs or objectives change, is easy within a family of funds. Usually all it takes is a phone call to switch funds or sell shares. This advantage is called "investment timing" in the jargon of the business.

How They Operate. Mutual funds buy securities and then receive dividends and interest from those investments. If your mutual fund sells a particular security at a profit, it usually gives you a capital-gains distribution that reflects the number of shares you own in the fund. If shares in the fund increase in value while you own them, you profit when you sell them. (Of course, if you have to sell them while the value of those shares is down, you end up taking a loss.)

When you purchase a mutual fund, the number of shares you receive depends on the net asset value (NAV) of the fund on the day you buy. To calculate the fund's net asset value, you divide the total value of all stocks and bonds it holds by the number of outstanding shares in the fund. The fund's net asset value is calculated daily, at the end of each trading day (4 PM, Eastern Standard Time), with its value moving up or down, depending on the market price of the number of securities it holds. If, for example, the net asset value is $12.23 on the day you invest $1,000 into a particular fund, you will receive 81.776 shares.

If you're purchasing mutual-fund shares with your 401(k) money, because you are in a tax-deferred plan, any capital gains or income that the fund generates will automatically be reinvested in the fund one or more times per year. If you are investing in mutual funds directly—in other words, not through a 401(k) plan—you have the option of reinvesting this income or taking a cash payout. When you reinvest the income, you are buying more shares in the fund.

What's on the Menu? Although most 401(k) plans only offer one or two fund choices, on the open market there is a smorgasbord of funds to choose from. They include:

>> Money-market funds, which invest in short-term, top-rated government and corporate securities and allow you easy access to your money.

>> Corporate bond funds or income funds, which aim for a high level of income by investing heavily in corporate bonds, as well as preferred stock and U.S. Treasury bonds.

>> High-yield bond funds, which purchase lower-rated corporate bonds (sometimes called "junk bonds") and offer more of a risk (although generally a higher return) than higher-rated bond funds.

>> Growth funds, which aim for long-range capital growth (as opposed to current dividends), by purchasing the common stocks of established companies.

>> Aggressive growth funds, which focus on capital growth by investing in smaller firms and developing industries and are slightly riskier investments than those sought out by growth-fund managers.

>> Balanced funds, which focus on conserving capital, promoting long-term growth, and providing you with current income by carefully balancing your portfolio between stocks and bonds.

>> Specialized funds or "sector" funds, which concentrate on a particular field, such as banking, health care, utilities, or high-tech, but hold a variety of stocks within that field in order to allow for diversification.

>> Tax-free or mutual-bond funds, which provide tax-free income to individuals in high-income tax brackets by investing in municipal (and, in some cases, state) bonds.

>> International funds, which invest in companies in other parts of the world (typically Europe and Asia).

>> U.S. government income funds, which buy such government securities as U.S. Treasuries, guaranteed mortgage-backed securities (GNMAs) backed by the federal government, and other notes.

>> Value funds, which buy stocks in undervalued companies, whose prices are lower than they seem to be worth, have dropped in value, or are currently out of favor.

>> Index funds, which purchase shares in all of the stocks held by a particular stock market index (for instance, the Standard & Poor's 500 Index) and which tend to outperform typical mutual-fund companies, because of their lower management fees.

Making Your Selection—or Re-evaluating the Fund You Have. Assess your financial situation (your age, how much time you have before retirement, your other assets, your tax situation) and decide which type of fund best suits your needs. Once you've zeroed in on a particular type, you can start tracking down the top-performing funds in that category. Check www.Morningstar.com for performance ratings on each fund.

Before you make a commitment to purchase a fund, however, take a good, hard look at its prospectus. Figure out what the fund's objectives are, how well it has met those objectives over the years, what fees it charges for maintaining your account and carrying out transactions on your behalf, and what procedures you must follow if you want to buy or sell shares.

Reading the Prospectus. Wading through the fund literature (you'll never find it on the best-seller list) can be a chore. Here are a few quick ways to decipher the fund-speak:

Be sure to look for a statement of investment objectives. This will reveal exactly what type of fund it is. If it's an aggressive growth fund, for example, you should expect to find the words "maximum capital appreciation" listed somewhere as a fund goal. If, on the other hand, it's a balanced fund, you should expect to see such words as "income," "capital growth," and "stability" woven into the fund description.

Check the per-share table; it will tell you how much each share of the fund has earned annually (both dividends and capital-gains distributions) since the fund's inception or over the past 10 years or so. The table will illustrate the fund's performance—erratic or steady—in both an up-market and a down-market, and it will likely include comparisons with the Standard & Poor's 500 or the Dow Jones index. Don't fall into the all-too-common trap of taking this record of past performance as some sort of "guarantee" of future success. Changes in the market or the fund's management style can quickly erase a golden track record.

Look up the policy on how to buy and redeem shares (it should establish the minimum purchase you have to make in order to open an account, as well as the minimum amount for additional purchases, and it should specify whether telephone transfers may be made). Check the breakpoints: Discounts are available for those who invest more than a certain amount. However, these discounts are often not passed on to the individual investor by the broker. Ask what the firm's policy is.

Best Investment Strategy. Dollar-cost averaging is an investor's best friend. By buying your mutual-fund shares on a monthly or quarterly basis, you can ensure that you never buy all your shares at the highest price and never sell them all at the lowest price.

Fees-Fi-Fo-Fum! Liability insurance and legal and administrative costs have already risen at all mutual funds as a result of the investigations of the last two years and the voluntary measures that have been taken to prevent further wrongdoing. Experts warn that the funds could try to pass those costs on to investors by raising already high existing administrative fees or charging them against fund assets.

Therefore, whether you are evaluating a new fund or re-evaluating your current fund, look carefully at the fee table in the fund's prospectus or any investor literature that is sent to you. The fee table should clearly indicate whether you must pay a sales commission on purchases (a so-called "load fee") or whether it is a "no-load" fund that does not charge you any upfront fees when you buy in.

Some other fees to watch out for when you're making your way through the fee table include:

>> A 12 (b)-1 fee: Charges of up to 1.25 percent per year to defray the costs of marketing and distributing funds.

>> Redemption fee: A fixed charge used to discourage fund holders from repeatedly buying and selling.

>> Contingent deferred sales charges (CDSCs): Hefty fees imposed to discourage you from holding shares for short periods.

>> Operating and management fees: An annual cost that is applied to both load and no-load funds and that has an impact on the return you receive on your investment. Check the turnover ratio—the amount of selling that is going on. The more trading that is done, the higher the operating expenses for the fund.

What about taxes? You will be taxed on any interest, dividends, or capital gains you receive from your mutual funds or the sale of your shares, whether you take those profits as cash or have the mutual fund reinvest them in additional shares. The tax on earnings is not deferred, as it is with mutual funds that are held within a retirement plan, such as a 401(k), nor is the money that you invest in mutual funds tax-exempt, as would be the case with money invested in a retirement plan. Watch out for double taxation. Make an accurate record of what you pay when you first buy any mutual fund. When the fund reinvests your interest, dividends, or capital gains, you are, in effect, buying more shares. Add the cost of those shares to your original purchase price. When you sell your shares (or any portion of them), that total cost is what you use to determine whether you have had a capital gain or loss.

Every January, your mutual fund will send you form 1099-DIV for the previous year for use in preparing your tax return. A copy will also go to the IRS. Some other key points: Whenever you sell shares, you must pay taxes—even if you are simply moving your money from one member of a family of funds to another. When you sell shares, it is assumed that those you bought first are the ones you are selling first. This is called the FIFO rule: First in, first out. Figure your gain or loss accordingly. If it works to your advantage, however, you can control your capital gain hit, by directing the fund to sell specific shares, purchased at a specific price.

SCAMS & SWINDLES

This chapter would not be complete without warning of investment scams. Widows, especially recent ones, are targets for scam artists, who read the obituaries and call when a woman is at her most vulnerable, promising security and investment rewards that will never be met. It is estimated that $10 to $40 billion is lost a year to investment fraud and deception. The exact figure isn't known, because many people are too ashamed to report it. No one likes to admit that they've been taken.

How do swindlers find their victims? Anyway they can. Here are some classic swindles:

By mail: As the number of financial investments has increased so has the number of newsletters covering them. The investment-letter scam offers several copies of a free newsletter, after which you only have to subscribe for a mere $250 a year. Each newsletter predicts how the market will go for the next month, in terms so general

that, much like a horoscope, you can read anything you want into the predictions. By the time you've paid the $250, the marketer of this letter has set up shop someplace else.

By e-mail: Watch out for spam e-mails and investment Web site bulletin-board messages touting "hot stock tips." Unscrupulous traders often post false information, designed to drive up the price of a stock. Then they make a killing by dumping their shares, while the price is still high. This is known as "pumping and dumping," and it is usually done using the stocks of smaller companies, called "small cap" stocks, which are known for their low valuations and potential to grow into "big-cap" stocks.

By telephone: On the phone, they are friendly, polite, and concerned. They quote the Bible and have even been known to join their victims in prayer. The investments they sell are generally very speculative or worthless, and they request that payments be made to a PO box. They make their killing and move to another location, before the victims catch on to the scam. Two men who set up a boiler-room operation in a Beverly Hills cellar made cold calls, selling nonexistent mutual funds and took in $1.3 million in investments—for themselves.

Through advertisements: A newspaper or magazine ad may promise returns that are far more attractive than conventional investments. Regulatory agencies monitor advertisements in major publications, but many swindlers manage to advertise once or twice and move on before they can be caught. Beware of advertisements that provide a 900-number telephone service for advice on stocks, bonds, and options. These recorded hotlines supposedly offer insider stock tips. For an added fee, you might be able to speak to the guru himself. You end up paying for the phone charge, plus a fee levied by the business on the other end. Legitimate investment houses offer 800 numbers.

Through referrals: In Ponzi schemes, the swindlers give large profits to their initial investors. Those investors then recommend the "investment" to their friends, who end up getting burned.

By masquerading as the real thing: Some swindlers will rent an office in a prestigious building, put out their shingle, and call themselves investment advisers, financial planners, or money managers. Some might even have legitimate credentials and are registered with the Securities and Exchange Commission. They present seminars, are guests or hosts on local TV and radio stations, and appear to be model citizens. It's business as usual with them, as long as they can convince their victims that profits are being reinvested to earn even larger profits or that the deal that turned sour will show a big profit within the next year. Meanwhile, they're pocketing your money.

A businessman named by his local Chamber of Commerce as Man of the Year lost nearly $2 million of his clients' money over a six-year period. He persuaded 14 clients, including his parents, to allow him to pool their money to meet the minimum dollar requirements accepted by a conservative growth fund. A year later, he started to secretly liquidate his clients' funds and moved the money into the commodities market. He sent out falsified account statements, forged clients' signatures to fool banks, and used one investor's money to pay another.

What's their line? They start by asking questions that have a yes answer—"Wouldn't you like to hear about a great investment?"—and continue with other questions that draw you in, giving you little chance to ask them questions. They will describe profits that are large enough to whet your appetite, but not so large as to make you suspicious. Of course, they will tell you that there is minimal risk. Finally, they will try to convince you that you must make a decision right away. Urgency is of the utmost importance; they don't want to give you time to investigate them or have second thoughts. "This is a once-in-a-lifetime deal, and you must take advantage of it before all the shares are sold."

How to Spot a Scam. Ask the following questions, whenever you are approached by someone trying to sell you an investment:

1. *Where did you get my name?* "An exclusive list of investors" could mean the telephone book or a purchased mailing list.

2. *Can you send me a prospectus?* They will, of course, say that there is no time. But any good investment will still be around tomorrow, no matter what sales tactics are used today. Insist on seeing a prospectus. A true prospectus includes financial data, a précis of the firm's business history, a list of its officers, a description of its operations, and mention of any pending litigation. The law requires a prospectus in most investments areas. The "Man of the Year" scammer sent out a sales brochure, instead of a prospectus. Failure to supply promised material is a red flag.

3. *What is the risk involved?* All investments have some risk, some greater than others. If the yield on the offered investment is unusually high, that should be a red flag that something isn't right.

4. *Can you provide me with references?* You want not only the names of happy clients (how do you know they're not just friends or co-swindlers?), but bank and broker/dealer references. Follow up that question with: "How long have you been in business and where are you located?" Be skeptical of newcomers who have no references.

5. *To whom do I make the check out?* If the swindler suggests that you make it out to him or her personally, forget it. The chances are the money will end up in their pocket and not in a legitimate investment. Even if you are told that it should be made out to a company, get the correct spelling and then do some checking. Ask if you can call them back. If they won't give a number, or if they do and you call and there's no answer, be very skeptical. The National Association of Securities Dealers (NASD) recommends that you don't buy investments over the phone, unless you have investigated both the person and the investment.

6. *Is the investment traded on one of the regulated exchanges?* Some bona fide investments are and some aren't. But fraudulent investments never are.

What can you do if you've been had? Be tough, demand your money back, and threaten to contact authorities. If you are lucky, you'll recover a small portion of your losses, though few victims do. The important thing is to report the swindle to the regulatory agencies. For registered stocks, contact the NASD (www.nasd.com). If you are dealing with unregistered stock or some other variety of scam, call your state's attorney general's office. The authorities might call for an investigation and begin legal action, impounding whatever funds the swindler still has left. Check to see if there is a class-action suit against the individual or firm. Chasing down swindlers takes perseverance. But they will not be found, if their victims don't report them. That's what they are betting on.

The bottom line is: always be skeptical. If somebody makes an offer that sounds too good to be true, it probably is.

ISN'T IT A WOMAN'S PREROGATIVE TO CHANGE HER MIND?

We end with another kind of cautionary tale. As we said when we started this chapter, investing is not for everyone all of the time. Your needs and your risk tolerance can change. Market conditions can shift, testing the mettle of the most stalwart investor. Particularly as you reach your retirement years, a bear market requires quick action to protect the value of your investments, or you'll run out of time to recoup losses. Below, in an article written for MAKING BREAD at the height of the Enron scandal, one writer describes the last straw that prompted her to cut and run like hell from Wall Street.

Even today, the lingering effects of the corporate shenanigans and outright fraud Secunda alludes to are felt on Wall Street. Securities regulations have changed as a result. But there will always be downturns and events that shake investors' confidence. That's when the smart investor will consult her heart and do what makes her feel comfortable.

Take-home lesson. If you could patent the ability to know, unerringly, when to hold them—and when to fold them—you could issue an IPO and become a zillionaire overnight.

Victoria Secunda is a breadwinner in the best tradition of MAKING BREAD, having worked hard and earned good money, doing something she loves doing, for many years. She managed her money carefully, bought and sold homes, got a divorce, raised a lovely, successful daughter, remarried, and invested for her retirement. Even today—after taking a hit in the stock market—she is living comfortably with her second husband, Shel, in a cozy Connecticut dream house—with garden.

ONE WOMAN'S OPINION: WHY I'M NO LONGER TRUSTING MY MONEY TO CEO'S WHO SPEND MORE ON LUNCH THAN I OWN

BY VICTORIA SECUNDA

LAST MONDAY, my husband and I lost our socks in the stock market. Not our shirts, but at least a third of our investments. After six nail-biting months watching Wall Street tank, we decided to cash in our remaining chips and call it a day, portfolio-wise. We are too old and too skittish to continue gambling our future, while CEOs and accounting execs spend more on lunch than we own and—the unkindest cut—are paid a king's ransom for failing.

It isn't that we've gotten cold feet, although, sockless, you could say that we feel a certain chill around the ankles. It's that, for us at least, the word "correction" has taken on new meaning. Once upon a time, a stock market dive was considered a fiscal reality check or "correction." Now I think it means the Department of Corrections, where the chieftains of Enron, WorldCom, yadda yadda (I haven't got all day; the list is that long) ought to cool their heels forever for losing other people's jobs and pensions.

In my view, the current market is not undergoing a "correction." I may be financially challenged, but I'm not stupid. This isn't 1987, the other time my husband and I bailed (and which we later regretted—okay, that one was stupid). The current market has unyielding "trouble" written all over it. First, the Republicans, and probably more than a few Democrats, are too cozy with well-heeled lobbyists and campaign contributors to institute the kind of change that would give average investors a shot at fiscal fair play. How's this for "fairness": Huge corporations can dodge taxes by incorporating in Bermuda and never set foot on the place; fat cats can profit from tax loopholes the size of Texas; and the rest of us get taxed to the max every time we sneeze, even as our investments tank. Why should we have a scintilla of "faith" in the economy or believe that a real "recovery" is on the way?

Plus I can't stomach the idea that some of these CEOs are all still zillionaires, notwithstanding the occasional sleep they might lose over the threat of a brief sojourn in a white-collar slammer or five-minute Katie Couric grilling. Add to this the possibility of more terrorist attacks and anthrax scares ,and people begin to feel at risk not just in their portfolios, but in their beds as well.

Bottom line: I don't believe that this country is going to be in the financial pink for a long, long time—long after my husband and I have repaired to that Great, No-load Mutual Fund in the sky. Heck, I hope I'm wrong. Call us crazy for folding when most folks are still holding. All I know is if I had in the bank today what we've lost in the last four years, I'd be sitting pretty. Wait a minute—I did have that much, at least on paper. Okay, so we're as guilty as the next guy for hanging on when the signs were all there that the stock-market deck was stacked.

Whatever. At least now we can sleep nights.

AFTERWORD:
THE BIGGEST SAVING SECRET OF ALL

In my introduction, I referred to MAKING BREAD as "the ultimate chick lit." To be true to that genre, this book should have a happy ending. In chick-lit novels, after all, the heroine—who's just spent 250 pages plotting and scheming to snag Prince Charming—gets her man, and everyone lives happily ever after. The reader doesn't see them when the honeymoon is over and they're hashing out who's going to pay the bills or pick up the dry cleaning after work, or arguing about what they have to give up so they can save money for their first house or their firstborn's college education.

MAKING BREAD's heroine doesn't need Prince Charming; she's independent and successful in her own right. She has a career that challenges and satisfies her, a savings account for emergencies, and a retirement account invested for her long-term security. She may already own her own castle. Sure, she's looking for love, but she knows that, even if Prince Charming never shows up, she'll always be able to take care of herself. She realizes that she is ultimately responsible for her own destiny. Her money gives her freedom of choice and freedom from worry. When she is introduced to the Prince at a business conference, he is attracted to her for her self-assurance. If they do marry, they never argue about money. And ten years later, if she catches him fooling around with her stepsister (go figure), she can afford to file for divorce. Money doesn't guarantee that you'll live happily ever after, but if you have it, you don't have to live unhappily ever after.

Much of this book has been devoted to dire statistics about women and money: On average, we live seven years longer than men, earn 76 cents for every dollar men make, and save half as much as men do for retirement. As a result of the wage gap and years spent away from the work force raising our children, we end up playing a million-dollar game of catch up.

"Those statistics don't apply to me," some of you may be thinking: "I'm making a good salary, and stashing away 6 percent in my 401(k) plan every pay period." Wonderful! But if you leave your job to raise your children, do you have a plan to compensate for the loss of wages and reduction in your Social Security and retirement benefits? And haven't you ever wondered how much your male co-workers, who have equal experience and education, are earning?

Of course, numbers don't tell the whole story; there are many exceptions—and happier statistics—to report: Women control 80 percent of the purchasing power in American households.

Fifteen percent of wives earn at least $5,000 more than their husbands. Women are starting businesses at twice the rate of men and pumping $3.6 trillion into the economy every year. According to a study by the market-research firm The Spectrem Group, a woman is the head of household and/or primary investment decision-maker in 2.3 million households with total assets exceeding $500,000.

We are a force to be reckoned with, and yet we are vulnerable. Divorce, widowhood, the responsibilities of motherhood, and caregiving all carry significant financial penalties for most of us, and there is an underlying issue of fairness that can't be ignored. With my tongue only partly in cheek, I am tempted to make a "modest proposal" to corporate America: How about paying reparations for the $200 billion in wages women lose every year as a result of the wage gap? Put it in a fund to help battered women or single moms.

The wage gap aside, why should a woman suffer financially for performing the most important role of all in society—that of mother, teacher, and muse to her children? Or caregiver to her parents, when they need her in their old age? Various political and economic solutions have been proposed over the years to help level the financial playing field for women—from paid family leave and onsite daycare facilities to pay-equity legislation and proposals to compensate stay-at-home moms for their forfeited Social Security benefits. We can't wait for these remedies. The best and quickest solution for each of us is to understand the risks we face and to take charge of our finances, NOW.

Money flows through our daily lives like a river; it's everywhere—in the dollar bills you handed the babysitter last night, the credit card you used to pay for gas this morning, the tip you left the waitress at lunch, the online bill payment you made from your computer at work, the dimes and quarters rattling around in the bottom of your purse. We handle it without thinking about it, and it slips through our fingers. A woman who earns $45,000 a year (and nine out of 10 women earn less than $50,000 annually) will make $2 million in her lifetime. If she invested $75 a week at 8 percent over her 40-year career, she would have $1,134,578 to draw upon for her retirement years, reports the Consumer Federation of America.

What are you going to do with your millions? We hope that this book will help you look at the big picture—the what if's and the why not's. *What if you are left alone in your old age? Why not follow your dreams to their happy conclusion?* Using the strategies we've outlined in MAKING BREAD, plan to make the most of your dough so that you can live the life you want.

There are many ways to save money—many things you'll find you can do without—once you decide to make your present and future security a priority. The best gift you can give yourself is money in the bank. But the biggest saving secret of all is realizing that life's most precious commodity is not for sale. You don't have to spend money to find your happy ending.

GRACIE'S GIFT: GENEROSITY OF SPIRIT.

We all know that money can't buy love, for instance. But in this consumerist society, we have been conditioned to show our love by spending money. The size of the rock your fiancé gives you is a measure of his love for you. The size of the box of chocolates you give your man on Valentine's Day shows him how much you love him. When a father foots the bill for a pricey Ivy League tuition or wedding reception for his daughter, he's showing her how much he loves her . . . and on and on.

Sure, it's great to be on the receiving end of extravagant presents, and spending money—if you have it—is one way to show how much you care. But some very special people in my life have taught me that there is a far more valuable gift. That is the gift of awareness, and it's a gift that we all can afford to give to everyone around us.

I first learned the lesson of generosity of spirit from a $10-an-hour receptionist at a magazine where I worked. The atmosphere at this small magazine, always on the verge of success and the edge of bankruptcy, was tense beyond words. The staff was small and the workload that each of us bore was enormous. Yet one day Gracie, who often had to borrow money at the end of the week to get by, noticed that my nerves were shot and that I hadn't had time to take an afternoon break, so she bought me a fruit drink. The $1.50 the drink cost was a fortune to her, but the fact that she took the time to notice that I needed a

pick-me-up made her gesture priceless . . . and no fruit drink ever tasted better. We began treating each other to drinks every afternoon, and somehow we both managed to survive that pressure cooker atmosphere.

Another friend who works in Philadelphia can't walk by a street person without handing out a dollar bill. By conservative estimate, I'd say he gives away $30 a week. Do those dollar bills make a big difference in the quality of the lives of the street people he talks to? On a material level, probably not, though you might be surprised to learn how much—a warm cup of coffee, a 99-cent Big Mac—a dollar still can buy. What's more important to them, I suspect, is the fact that he takes the time to notice them, to acknowledge their presence, to validate their humanity, to say a few words to them.

I *love* giving presents; in fact, I may be the worst offender when it comes to spending money extravagantly, foolishly, to show my affection. But what Gracie and other wonderful people in my life have taught me is this: The best present that those I love give me is their presence in my life. And it doesn't cost them a penny.

CONTRIBUTORS

MAKING BREAD wishes to thank the following contributors, whose work appears in this book, for generously sharing their money experiences and wisdom with our readers.

Allison Acken, PhD is a Los Angeles-based clinical psychologist whose specialty is helping women build their money-management skills. She is the author of *It's Only Money! A Primer for Women* and a contributing editor to MAKING BREAD. Visit her at www.womentalkmoney.com.

- For Better, For Worse, For Richer, For Poorer (Chapter Three)
- Take Our Marriage and Money Quiz (Chapter Three)
- Rent-Free At Last! (Chapter Three)
- Home Economics: No Downpayment? No Problem (Chapter Three)
- Been There, Done That, Smart Advice from a Third-Generation Single Mom (Chapter Four)
- It's Mind Over (Financial) Matters (Chapter Nine)
- It Started with a Cry for Hope— and Now, She's Finding Money Everywhere! (Chapter Nine)

Lisa Cohn is an award-winning freelance writer and co-author of *One Family, Two Family, New Family: Stories and Advice for Stepfamilies*.

- Stuff *The Brady Bunch* Never Mentioned (Chapter Five)

Marcia Eckerd, PhD is a licensed psychologist and partner in the Connecticut-based practice Associates for Children and Families. A contributing editor, she writes "The Working Mom's Shrink" column in MAKING BREAD.

- We Don't Hate You, Mom! (Chapter Four)
- Could Your Relationship Survive on One Salary… Yours? (Chapter Five)
- "Take My Desert Island Challenge" (Chapter Seven)

Patricia Schiff Estess is the former editor of *Sylvia Porter's Personal Finance* magazine, and the author of several books, including *Money Advice for Your Successful Remarriage, Kids, Money & Values* and *Work Concepts for the Future: Managing Alternative Work Arrangements*. She has written extensively on family and financial matters for many magazines, including *Reader's Digest's New Choices, Family Money*, and *Entrepreneur*. Estess currently runs a workshop series on reinventing retirement and is a contributing editor to MAKING BREAD.

- Would Job-Sharing Work for You? (Chapter Four)
- Know What You're Saying, "I Do" To (Chapter Five)
- Do 2 Part-Time Jobs = 1 Full-Time Job? (Chapter Seven)
- My Money Manager—or Me? (Chapter Ten)

Amber Fairweather, Lynnea Garrett, and Theresa Weems were Temple University students and interns at MAKING BREAD when they wrote for the magazine.
- The Buck Stops With Her (Chapter Seven)

JoAnn R. Hines is an award-winning author, career coach, and motivational speaker, as well as the founder of Women in Packaging, Inc. (www.womeninpackaging.org), an international association for professional businesswomen, and www.packagingcoach.com. She writes the "Success Guide" column in MAKING BREAD and is a contributing editor.
- The Office Politics of Pregnancy (Chapter Four)
- How to Raise Your Chances of Getting a Raise (Chapter Seven)
- It's Not Who You Know—But Who Knows You—That Counts (Chapter Seven)

Sharon Sorokin James is a Philadelphia-based attorney, children's author, and novelist. She is a contributing editor to MAKING BREAD.
- Vow to Tie the Knot Cheaply (Chapter Three)
- There's a Home-Sweet-Home Mortgage for Almost Everyone (Chapter Three)
- How Some Mothers Are Handing Down Smart Advice About Careers, Life, and the Value of a Dollar to the Next Generation (Chapter Four)
- Risky Business? Read This Before Starting One! (Chapter Eight)

- What Do You Do When You Want to Succeed in a Man's World? (Chapter Eight)

Elizabeth Kaminsky has extensive experience in personal finance and investor relations. She frequently writes about financial matters as they relate to women and is a contributing editor to MAKING BREAD.
- Woman to Woman: Putting Yourself Through College (Chapter One)
- Be a Calculating Woman (Chapter Two)
- Playing House: How to Protect Your Heart—and Your Wallet—When You Don't Have the Ring (Chapter Three)
- The Financial Rules of Living Together
- Feel Like a School Girl Again! (Chapter Five)
- Theirs is a Labor of Love . . . But Who Cares for the Caregivers? (Chapter Six)
- Where the Jobs Are Now (Chapter Seven)
- Let Them Eat Cake and Homemade Ice Cream (Chapter Seven)

Laurie M. Lesser works as a freelance editor and writer in Washington, D.C. She is at work on a novel about money and relationships.
- Charging into Trouble (Chapter Nine)

Linda Lindsey is a marketing professional who lives and works in Atlanta, Georgia. Visit her at www.facethefat.com
- My Cash Diet (Chapter Nine)

Gabrielle Madison is a pseudonym for a former MCI/WorldCom systems analyst.
- Report from the Trenches of Corporate America: A Survivor's Tale (Chapter Five)

Sabina Louise Pierce is a freelance photographer whose work has appeared in *The New York Times*, *Vanity Fair*, *People*, and many other publications. For more information, visit www.sabinalouisepierce.com

- Credit & the Self-Employed Single Woman (Chapter Two)

Rosemary Rys teaches public relations and communications at two universities. An accredited member of the Public Relations Society of America, she is the president of her own public- relations firm, and has spent 19 years as an award-winning practitioner in the field.

M.H. Flick is a public-relations expert living and working in the Philadelphia area.

They co-wrote:

- Network to Improve Your Net Worth (Chapter Seven)

Victoria Secunda is an award-winning author, whose work has appeared in *TV Guide*, *Harper's Bazaar*, *Redbook*, and *Glamour*, among other magazines. Her most recent book is *Losing Your Parents, Finding Your Self: The Defining Turning Point of Adult Life* (Hyperion). She is the executive editor of MAKING BREAD.

- To Buy or Not to Buy ... Oil Tank Insurance (Chapter Three)
- She Conducted a "Great Accounting"—And Saved 10 Grand (Chapter Six)
- My Five Biggest Money Mistakes (Chapter Nine)
- Why I'm No Longer Trusting My Money to CEOs Who Spend More on Lunch Than I Own (Chapter Ten)

Phyllis Staff, PhD is an experimental psychologist and the author of *How to Find Great Senior Housing: A Roadmap for Elders and Those Who Love Them*.

- "I Was At a Loss": A Caregiver Shares Eight Affordable Solutions to the Eldercare Dilemma (Chapter Six)

Jennifer Vishnevsky was a student at American University in Washington, D.C., and an intern at MAKING BREAD when she wrote for the magazine.

- What a Blast! (Chapter Seven)
- Wal-Mart ... Dollar Store ... Supermarket? (Chapter Nine)

Cheryl A. Young is a partner in the Family Law Practice Group of Wolf, Block, Schorr and Solis-Cohen LLP, concentrating in matrimonial law, including divorce, custody, support, property distribution, and abuse actions. For more information, visit www.wolfblock.com

- Something Old, Something New, Something Borrowed, Something Blue... and Don't Forget the Prenup (Chapter Three)

INDEX

I

J

K

L

M